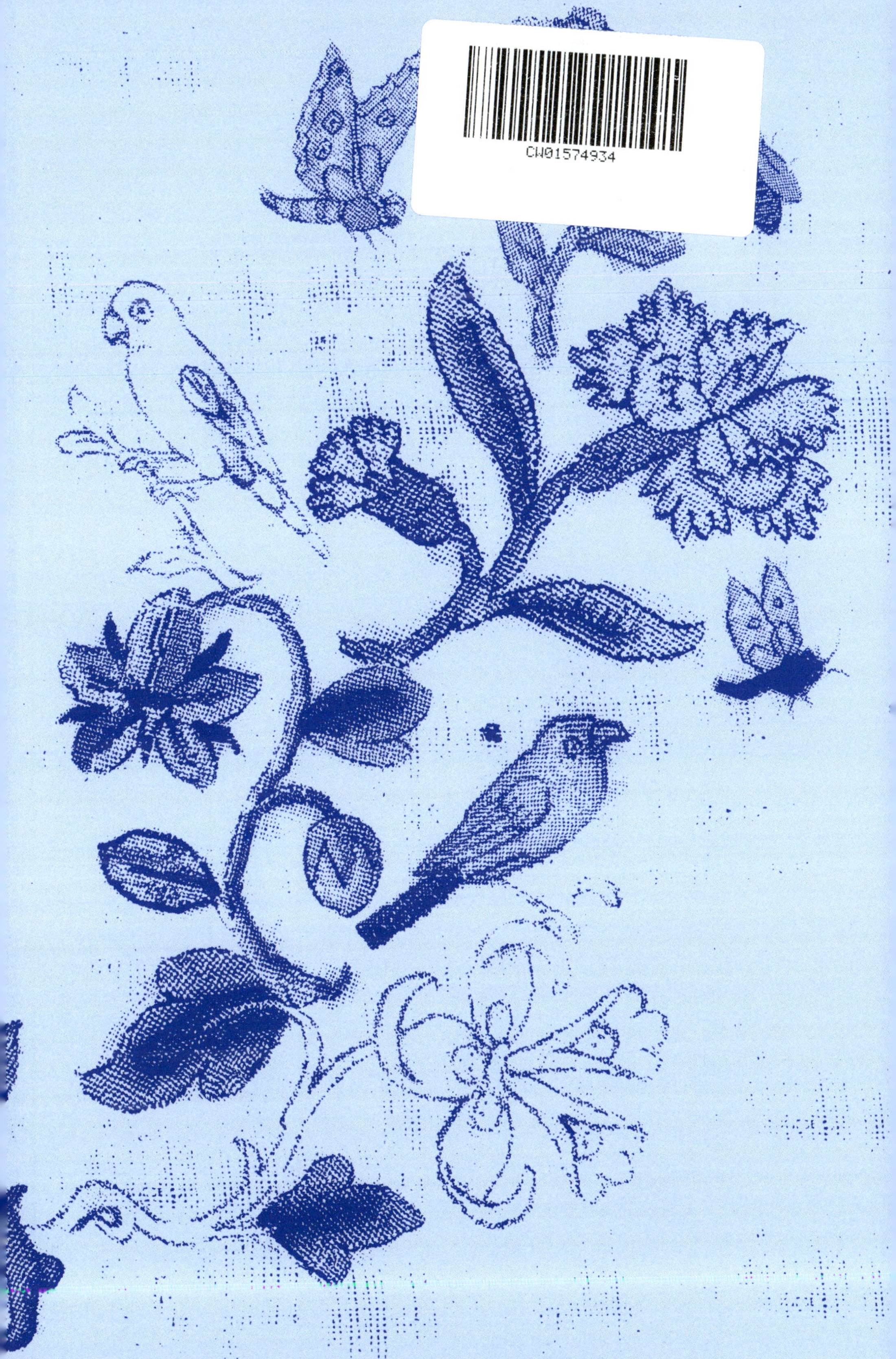

THE GRACES

THE GRACES

The Extraordinary Untold Lives of Women at the Restoration Court

BREEZE BARRINGTON

BLOOMSBURY CIRCUS
LONDON • OXFORD • NEW YORK • NEW DELHI • SYDNEY

BLOOMSBURY CIRCUS
Bloomsbury Publishing Plc
50 Bedford Square, London, WC1B 3DP, UK
Bloomsbury Publishing Ireland Limited,
29 Earlsfort Terrace, Dublin 2, D02 AY28, Ireland

BLOOMSBURY, BLOOMSBURY CIRCUS and the Circus logo are trademarks of Bloomsbury Publishing Plc

First published in Great Britain in 2025

A catalogue record for this book is available from the British Library

ISBN: HB: 978-1-5266-6378-8; EBOOK: 978-1-5266-6381-8; EPDF: 978-1-5266-6380-1

2 4 6 8 10 9 7 5 3 1

Typeset by Newgen KnowledgeWorks Pvt. Ltd., Chennai, India
Printed and bound in Great Britain by CPI Group (UK) Ltd, Croydon CR0 4YY

MIX
Paper | Supporting responsible forestry
FSC® C013604
www.fsc.org

To find out more about our authors and books visit www.bloomsbury.com and sign up for our newsletters

For product-safety-related questions contact productsafety@bloomsbury.com

To Rebecca

CONTENTS

	A Note on the Text	ix
	Prologue	1
1	Princess of Modena	11
2	Crossing the Water	29
3	Duchess of York	43
4	A Stepmother to Princesses	55
5	*The Masque of Calisto*	65
6	The Duchess of Mazarin	75
7	The Salon	91
8	A Tempestuous Courtship	97
9	The Prince of Orange	121
10	'The Popish Plot'	131
11	Going Home	153
12	'The Rye House Plot'	159
13	The Coterie	169
14	Courtships and Scandals	189

15 A New Era 201

16 Memento Mori 223

17 The Queen's Body 237

18 A Royal Prince 247

19 Farewell to England 259

Epilogue: The Final Exile 269

Dramatis Personae 283
Acknowledgements 295
Selected Bibliography 299
Image Credits 303
Abbreviations 307
Notes 309
Index 327

A NOTE ON THE TEXT

DATES

From 45 BC, Europe followed the calendar introduced by Julius Caesar, known as the Julian Calendar, but in February 1582 Pope Gregory XIII issued a papal bull which decreed firstly that the day after Thursday 4 October 1582 would change to become 15 October, not the 5th, and secondly that the New Year would no longer start on 25 March (Lady Day) but on 1 January. This is known as the Gregorian Calendar. When it was instigated, this calendar was used throughout Europe except for England, which continued to run ten days behind until the mid-eighteenth century.

To some extent this proves a complication for this book, which mostly takes place in England but involves exchanges with Italy, France and Holland. Where I refer to letters, I have retained the dates given by the writers. However, it is not always clear which calendar they are using: for example, when Maria writes to her brother in Italy from England do we assume she uses the calendar of the country she is in or that which she writes to? After much consideration I have not attempted to standardise any of the dates since such a task would involve too much speculation about the calendar used. In leaving the dates as the correspondents wrote them the material continues to exist within their world, within the dates and times as they experienced them, and to this end the information is presented as they left it.

NAMES

In the seventeenth century there were a handful of exceptionally popular names, particularly among women. Annes, Marys and Catherines fill the pages of this book, and where possible I have tried to simplify this by using surnames instead of first names. Though Maria of Modena became Mary in England, I refer to her as Maria throughout this book, in part to avoid confusion with her step-daughter Princess Mary and in part to retain her identity as an Italian princess, a fact which was certainly never forgotten in her lifetime. I have done the same with Caterina de Braganza, though she was known as Queen Catherine at court.

TRANSLATION AND SPELLING

Unless specified, the translations of letters and documents written in Italian and French are my own, and any mistakes are therefore mine also. In these translations I have used the modern spelling of words but in letters written in English I have retained original spellings so as to let the voice of the writer come through, and to try to immerse the reader in the world of the seventeenth century.

MONEY

When talking about money I refer to the original amount given in documents as well as an estimate of how much these sums would be worth now. To do so I used the National Archives Currency Converter, which uses historical documents to offer a guideline of exchange rates between the past and the present. They are, of course, open to debate, and are not intended to represent a completely accurate sum but to give a sense of scale.

Prologue

Though *Venus* we transcend in Form,
No wanton Flames our Bosomes warm!
If you ask where such Wights do dwell,
In what Bless't Clime, that so excel?
The Poets onely that can tell.

— Anne Killigrew, 'On a Picture Painted by herself, representing two Nymphs of Diana's, one in a posture to Hunt, the other Bathing'

In the privacy of a secluded glade, bathed in autumnal light, four young women commune together. The warm glow of the day's final rays falls on the russet leaves, casting a pink-orange glow on the clouds in the distance. Yet, for all the soft hues of this bucolic scene, the eye is drawn elsewhere. In the foreground of the canvas, seated by the fountain she has just bathed in, with her back turned to us, is a nude female form. The light of the painting emanates from her, illuminating the three women who accompany her. As the painting's title has it, she is Venus being 'attired by the Graces'. The other figures in the composition – the cupid swooping above, arrow in hand, and the satyr to the right carrying the fruits of the harvest – look away from their goddess. It is as though the light she exudes is too much for their eyes; they willingly blend into the muted auburns and greens of the background. By contrast, her three companions, her 'Graces', look upon her and each other with ease.

This is a scene of female friendship: of young women absorbed in conversation with one another. They might be the subject of our gaze – indeed, the painting directs our eye towards them – but they are not posing for a viewer. Nor does the painting invite us to take pleasure in spying on this vision of female intimacy, as so many other paintings do. Conventionally, the Graces are presented nude, as objects of the male gaze and of visual pleasure. Here they are clothed, and Venus is being 'attired', while the only male figures in the painting both look away. The painter does not want to make the subject a source of titillation; rather, they have applied their intricate knowledge of the classical tradition and subverted its conventions to assert a very different perspective: the female gaze.

I still remember the first time I laid eyes on this painting. On a blazingly hot day at the end of June 2019, I made my way to Lyon & Turnbull, a gallery just north of Hyde Park in London. Their exhibition, *Bright Souls*, brought together works by England's first three female painters: Joan Carlile, Mary Beale and Anne Killigrew.[1] As I wandered through the rooms dedicated to these three pioneering women, I kept being drawn back to this one panel: 'Venus Attired by the Graces', painted by the youngest, and least well known, of the three women, Anne Killigrew. I couldn't stop looking at it. There was something in the play between the brightness of the blue and red fabrics with the earthy palette of the landscape, the contrasts between light and dark; something in the way the women's gestures intersected with the lines of the trees in the background. Most of all, I was struck by a sense of friendship that shines through in a way that preserves rather than shatters the intimacy of the pose. But what made the painting especially compelling was its flaws: Venus's overlong, curved back and slightly too small head, idiosyncrasies which seemed at odds with the virtuosity of the rest of the composition. There was a blend of amateurism and brilliance that I'd never before seen in a single work. As I turned to the label beside it and saw the dates, I found that Anne Killigrew was at most twenty-four when she painted it. What really captured my imagination was the sense that I was looking at a highly gifted painter not yet in full possession of her gifts.

As I read on I learned that the figures were thought to represent real women: the painting was not just a depiction of female friendship, but a painting of real friends. 'Venus' was Maria of Modena, the Duchess of York and future Queen of England; and the 'Graces' were her maids of honour, young women who were indeed meant to 'grace' the court of Charles II. In classical mythology, the Graces were the three handmaidens of Aphrodite, the Roman Venus, who would bathe and dress the goddess of love, just as they do here, and would spend their time dancing or singing. They were also closely linked with the Muses and were reputed to inspire artists and poets to produce great works in praise of their beauty, their grace. Maids of honour, too, were expected to be ornamental, to sing and dance, to adorn the court, to be admired. But at the Restoration court (1660–85), the maids were considered fair game for the amorous pursuits – or, rather, the sexual predation – of the men around them. As a maid at this court, Anne Killigrew will have known this well, and in her painting she has taken this classical heritage and subverted it to her own ends. This is why it is such a powerful gesture that her Graces are clothed, and they are debating among themselves rather than dancing and displaying their bodies; they do not care about putting on a spectacle for the viewer. These Graces would produce their own art, rather than merely inspiring it. They are not objects for a male gaze, but, rather, a celebration of female agency and female intellect.

They may have been called 'maids' and depicted as 'Graces', but they were young women to be reckoned with. The central figure, Venus, Maria d'Este (known in England as Mary of Modena), was an Italian princess who had been forced to leave home almost ten years earlier, as a girl of barely fifteen, to marry the heir to the English throne, Charles II's brother, the future James II, a man old enough to be her father. She was a learned and devout girl, thrown suddenly into the world of dynastic politics, transported out of the convent in which she lived, and had hoped to become a nun, into the licentious court of Charles II. Yet, faced with these new surroundings, this new Duchess of York, and future Queen of England, would strive to create around her a community of brilliant young intellectual women, and to help unlock their genius. Maria was no more than twenty-seven when this panel was painted, and it is just one example of the talent that she helped bring into the world.

Who are the Graces who surround her? Crouching next to Maria/Venus and fastening her sandals is Anne Killigrew herself, not only the painter of this work, but also a prodigiously gifted poet. In the background, gossiping, with a look of irony on her face, is another young poet: Anne Kingsmill, the pioneering feminist thinker and writer who, under her married name of Anne Finch, would come to be considered one of the greatest poets of her lifetime. The identity of the third Grace is less clear. In the exhibition where I first encountered the painting, it was suggested that she was Sarah Churchill (née Jennings), one of Maria's first maids of honour in the 1670s who would go on to be the pre-eminent stateswoman of the eighteenth century, adviser to Queen Anne and later George I, builder of Blenheim Palace and founder of a dynasty which would later include Winston Churchill.

When I saw this painting, I realised that it presented a completely different account of the Restoration court from the one to which we are accustomed. It is not a story of the world of decadence under the 'merrie monarch', Charles II, where ten years of Republican rule under the Puritan Oliver Cromwell gave way to palaces of debauchery and licentiousness, where the poetry was erotic, the entertainments risqué and the lasciviousness underpinned by an all-pervasive misogyny, where the monarch could openly surround himself with his mistresses and illegitimate children living alongside his long-suffering wife, Caterina de Braganza. The women in Killigrew's painting are not like the portraits of Restoration women I had seen before, such as the Windsor Beauties that hang at Hampton Court Palace, a set of paintings in which the women of the Carolean court are all sexualised and painted in various states of seductive undress. Killigrew's painting offers a refreshingly different vision of the lives of women and the ways they could be seen.

Here, then, was the story of a group of brilliant women living as companions together at the court of one of Britain's least known queens, during a period of history that is often overlooked, yet crucial to the creation of modern Britain. But as I came to research their lives, I found that they were part of a much bigger story of women's artistic and intellectual activity – and friendship; they were just a few of the many women who lived extraordinary lives in and around the court of Maria of Modena. Some are well known, like the poet and playwright Aphra Behn, and Anne Finch and Sarah Churchill, but others are less so: the poet and playwright Anne Wharton, the writer Mary Evelyn and Maria's cousin Hortense Mancini, who founded what is often considered the first intellectual 'salon' in England. The unknown third Grace in Killigrew's painting became a symbol for all these untold stories. And if Maria of Modena is remembered today, it is for her part in the downfall of a dynasty: the rumour that was circulated when her son was born in 1688 – that she had substituted the 'deformed' girl she had given birth to for a baby boy and thus a male heir – has gone down in history as the myth of the 'baby in the bedpan'.

For a few short years these women lived and worked in close proximity. They refused to live by the social conventions of the day, which would have them be meek and aspire only to be wives and mothers. As Killigrew's painting tells us, they knew that they were capable of far more than this. Within Maria's rooms at St James's Palace, they shared not only the physical space but their thoughts and feelings, their hopes and dreams, uncertain of the mark they might make on history, or the legacy they might leave behind them.

As I explored the artistic and intellectual achievements of Maria of Modena's circle, I encountered not only the gender politics of the Restoration court, but one of the most controversial and little known periods of British history. When James succeeded his brother to the throne, his absolutist tendencies, combined with the instabilities of Charles's rule and the unresolved tensions between Catholics and Protestants, came to a head. The country hurtled towards a potential second civil war, resulting in the 'Glorious Revolution' of 1688. This can be depicted as the last time Britain was invaded by a foreign power; it can be depicted as a decisive step in the battle for supremacy between Holland and France in the late seventeenth century; it can be depicted as the final move in the religious wars that followed the Reformation, where a Catholic king was deposed and Catholics barred from political office; it can be depicted as the defeat of absolutist monarchy and the birth of British democracy and constitutional monarchy as we know it (the Bill of Rights of 1689 enshrined a new constitutional settlement); it can be depicted as the shift of power from the court towards parliament, from the aristocracy towards the rising merchant class and the emergence of a finance-driven capitalism that would fund, and profit from, the expansion of the British Empire and the Industrial Revolution in the following century.

But alongside these epochal changes is another story, which cannot be extricated from it: a story of love, friendship and betrayal; a story of a family tearing itself apart on the world's stage, of siblings, children, parents and friends forced to choose sides; of opportunists and adventurers, of stratagems and gambles that pay off, or go disastrously wrong; of public glories and private tragedies. And at the centre is a young woman, who was plucked out of a small convent in a minor Italian principality and thrown into the brutal dynastic and sexual politics of the Restoration court, who tried to navigate a politics she was ill equipped for, but who also sought to shape the world around her, by supporting female learning, literature and art. Her story is one of building and rebuilding her life and her relationships, only to have them continually fall apart around her.

❖

Writing women's history often means reading through absences. Even for these women, the archives are full of gaps: all were comparatively high-born, or even very high-born, yet much of their lives was never written down, and much that was recorded was never preserved. Unlike their male peers, their letters weren't routinely written in duplicate and archived, and for centuries that followed there were no scholars and publishers working to keep their writings in print, with historians of the past routinely favouring the stories of men over even some of the most remarkable women. How Anne Killigrew, for example, spent her first twenty or so years before arriving at Maria's court appears to be completely undocumented. One happy exception to this rule is found in the state archives of Modena, where letters from Maria to her family were meticulously preserved. Letters that she wrote to the nuns at the palace convent in Modena were kept for hundreds of years by the women there: women who saw the importance of keeping these precious documents. Their whereabouts are now unclear.

What does and does not survive through time is always a question of chance and in writing this book I kept coming up against these obstacles. But I also found that many of the people in this story had suffered something more deliberate; sources that ought to have been there had been purposely 'lost', even destroyed. James II kept detailed diaries throughout his life and thought consciously about his legacy. He wrote them to be developed into memoirs, so that he could tell his own story for future generations. He had these diaries with him in France when he died, and they were copied out and worked on, readied for posterity. But during the French Revolution these books became dangerous things to have. Their custodian attempted to smuggle them out of France, but he and his wife were stopped at the border. They were told that they were summoned to an interrogation in the morning. As the night went on, the fear of what would happen to them if the documents were discovered became too strong, and in a fit of panic they burned the memoirs in a bonfire. The next morning, they appeared as instructed but the interrogation turned out to be no more than a few routine questions. Ten minutes later, they were on their way. The memoirs, now reduced to ash, would have been entirely safe.

Sarah Churchill knew that she would be remembered and thought seriously about her legacy; she carefully curated her archive to reflect how she wanted to be known, and what she wanted to be forgotten. At several points over the course of her life she went through her letters and destroyed those she did not want to come to light. We find almost nothing there of the time she worked for Maria. After the Glorious Revolution, she did not want to be remembered as having been an intimate friend of the Jacobite king and queen. Likewise, in her memoirs she said almost nothing of these early years.

The household accounts of the Stuarts are mostly preserved, but for the fifteen years that Maria was in England, as Duchess of York and then as queen, we have almost no accounts at all. The two that remain are found in the Spencer family papers at the British Library, and the rest are missing. We cannot know for certain what happened to these records but the fact that they do not survive when the others do suggests they were deliberately removed. After the Glorious Revolution it was perhaps thought best to try to get rid of all traces of the deposed monarchs.

But the destruction of accounts and letters was not always a malign act. It might have been one of self-preservation. If after a political coup, with a king in exile and a new system of government being established, you found yourself with a cache of letters linking you to the past regime, what would you do? Often these were just people trying to protect themselves and their families.

It is a cliché that history is written by the victors, but it is not just a question of how history is written; it is also how it is preserved, discarded or suppressed. It is that which is left behind that decides what stories will be told. But the absence of evidence is not evidence of absence. We know that these women lived against the backdrop of one of the most important periods of British history. We know that they produced art, that they had friendships, that they thought and they loved. What follows here is not the story of victors and losers. It is the story of families, and particularly of one family, as it fractured beyond repair. It is the story of women who aspired to great things and to be remembered for their talents, but many of whose stories are only being discovered now.

The most illuminating evidence for how these women experienced the world around them is found in their own words: in the writing they left behind. Where possible, I use their own words to tell the story of how they navigated such a politically incendiary time, how they worked and how they used the limited opportunities they were given in a deeply patriarchal society to find ways to gain agency and forge lives of creative freedom.

Since the day I first saw Anne Killigrew's painting I have, in a sense, lived with these women. It is with gratitude to them that I offer their stories to you.

I

Princess of Modena

It is 1 December 1673. A young woman – barely fifteen, little more than a girl – stands on the shore at Calais, facing an icy sea. Two months ago she was an Italian princess, from a small duchy in northern Italy. Now she is the future Queen of England. Behind her is her childhood; before her is a life she cannot imagine, on an island one of her countrymen (the great painter Guercino, a favourite of her grandfather) described as 'cold, damp, and full of heretics'. But it is precisely because it is full of heretics that she is here: she has been tasked by the Pope with returning England to the true faith.

And so we find her, Maria Beatrice d'Este of Modena, waiting to board the ship that will take her to her new life. It was a vast warship, named the *Catherine* after the present Queen of England, her new sister-in-law, Caterina de Braganza, and it was a freezing, windy day. The crossing promised to be rough. This was the first time she had ever seen the sea: the beautiful city of Modena, where she grew up, is entirely landlocked, sitting deep in the plains south of the Po Valley, in the middle of the Emilia-Romagna region of northern Italy. In Maria's quiet life as an Este princess, she had never travelled further than the family's summer palace in the spa town of Sassuolo, a mere fifteen kilometres further south in that same plain. During her long journey through Italy and France, however, she had seen much: she had passed through the plains of Parma and Piacenza, the forests of Pavia, crossed the Alps at the Mont Cenis pass, travelled across and alongside the Rhône and Loire rivers, paraded through the manicured landscapes of Fontainebleau and Versailles. Only now did she reach the coast.

Picture the scene: the air thick with freezing mist, the sun just starting to rise, the waves crashing against the keels of the five ships sent by James, Duke of York, the husband Maria had never met. Modena can be cold in winter, when mist descends and renders the spire of the Duomo invisible, and which, in Maria's day, would have sat low around the buildings on the nine (now bricked-up) medieval Venetian-style canals which brought water from the Apennines. But these Italian winter months are short and soon forgotten when they give way to luxuriously warm springs and summers. The contrast of the damp and icy cold Maria met with in the crossing to England must have come as a shock.

Imagine, too, the noise: the crashing of the water broken by the shouts of the sailors loading cargo. They shouted in English, a language Maria didn't yet understand, but which was the language of the country she had now to call home: England, a place she had never even heard of three months before. It had already been two months since she'd begun this journey, on 5 October 1673, her fifteenth birthday; two months since she felt the warmth of Modena's autumn sun, breathed in the scent of grape vines in harvest, and heard the sounds of her convent sisters laughing, reading, praying together. And it was two months ago that she had looked into the eyes of her dear Mother Superior and prayed to God to give her the strength to bear her fate.

Standing there on the shore, imagine her reaching inside her pocket and drawing out two pieces of paper. They are from two of the most powerful men in Europe: James, Duke of York, heir to the English throne; and Pope Clement X. These two letters, short as they are, tell us her story thus far.

The larger is a grand, ornate document. It is written in Latin, though this is no obstacle to such an educated princess. It is dated 19 September 1673 and is from Pope Clement X. He addresses Maria as his 'dear daughter in Christ'.[1] He tells her of 'the anxiety which filled Us when We were informed of your repugnance for marriage'.[2] He exhorts her to 'place before your eyes the great profit which may accrue to the Catholic faith … through your marriage, and that inflamed zeal of good which may result'.[3] He assures her that she may open herself 'to a vaster field of merit than that of the virginal cloister'.[4] This letter changed her world: reading it, she will have realised that she would have to give up her wish to become a nun and leave her home forever. It had been decreed by God. James, the future king, was on the verge of publicly converting to Catholicism; if she bore him a son, then England would have a next generation of Catholic monarchs and the schism with Rome might finally be at an end.

When she read this letter for the first time, did she find comfort in knowing that the instruction came from the Pope? Did it make it feel sanctioned by God? Or did it feel like a man telling her what to do? This was, of course, the lot of most women in the seventeenth century, but it would have felt alien to her. For Maria had been brought up in an environment of powerful women and female learning.

Maria's father had died when she was just four, making her two-year-old brother, Francesco, the new Duke of Modena. Maria's mother, Duchess Laura Martinozzi, was named Regent until Francesco came of age. A woman of formidable intelligence and capability, Laura had been highly educated and was determined that both her children would be scholars in their turn. As such she took as much interest in Maria's education as in Francesco's. But Laura's personal attentions to the education of her children went beyond academic study: they needed to be strong and fearless. Maria was a timid child and her brother small and sickly, but Laura was anything but a soft touch. Piety, obedience and strength of character were of the utmost importance. When entreated by servants to be gentler to her son, Laura responded by saying 'better I should have no son than one without wit and merit'.[5] If Maria forgot the words of her prayers, she received a clip on the ear; she hated eating *soupe maigre* (a vegetable-based soup which was eaten during days of fast), but Laura would sit in silence and watch her until the bowl was empty;

Maria was afraid of the men who swept her nursery chimney, so Laura told them to stand closer to her. At all times she required the children to maintain what Maria would later call an 'awful distance' from her, and to observe a strict formality. This may sound like a kind of cruelty, but Maria and Francesco were not normal children: they were children of the House of Este.

The Estensi had been one of Italy's great ruling dynasties, but by the time Maria was born they were greatly in decline. Throughout the Renaissance, they held territories from Reggio Emilia to Ferrara: fertile lands and key strategic towns along the Po Valley. They had been great warriors, and they became great Renaissance patrons. But in 1598 the Pope banished them from the centre of their power in Ferrara, and they had to retreat to Modena with only a fraction of the territories they had once held. Ferrara had technically been a papal state since the twelfth century, and when Alfonso II d'Este died without a male heir, the Pope saw his opportunity to wrest back control of these valuable territories. Alfonso's cousin, Cesare d'Este, was widely recognised as the heir, but none would risk angering Rome to come to his aid, and he was forced to move the court to Modena.

It was Maria's grandfather, Francesco I, who, from 1629, began the process of rebuilding the dynasty. After his death, and that of his son shortly after him, Laura continued his work. Crucial to this was the children's education. They were the future of the Estes. They were initially taught by Laura's female confessor, Matilde Bentivoglio, and later by a governess whose name has been lost to us over time. Both women would leave the Este children to take the veil, and this left a profound trace on Maria. Bentivoglio founded a Carmelite convent in Modena, and the unnamed governess joined the Order of the Visitation of Holy Mary, in a convent which had been founded by Duchess Laura. This convent was attached to the palace by a Bridge of Sighs, and Maria's life was spent going back and forth between the two. It became her dearest wish to join her beloved governess there, once she was of age.

Maria, therefore, had lived entirely under female rule. Until August 1673 that is when, unbeknown to her, a group of men were setting in motion plans which would change the course of her life.

❖

Anne Hyde, the first wife of James, Duke of York, had died in 1671. No sooner was her body cold than talk turned to his remarriage. Anne's story was a sad one. She and James had met in exile, after the Civil War. The daughter of Lord Clarendon, chief adviser to James's older brother Charles, she was appointed maid of honour to his sister, Mary of Orange. James was instantly besotted, and they had a passionate affair. When Anne fell pregnant, James was quick to promise her marriage.

The announcement was met with amusement from Charles but horror from everyone else, particularly from his mother, Henrietta Maria, who had always hated Anne, considering her a 'loose woman' of few morals. It was 1660, and Charles's return to the English throne was now assured; both sons were expected to make dynastic matches with European royal families. Anne's father, Lord Clarendon, was a commoner, and he was suspected of engineering the match, though this couldn't have been further from the truth: he actually proposed that his own daughter be arrested for treason. Her name was dragged through the mud as, one after another, James's friends came forward to allege that they, too, had had affairs with Anne: the child, they said, could be anyone's. But James, and Charles, too, stood firm. It was his duty to marry her and marry her he did.

The child was a boy, and was christened Charles, Duke of Cambridge, but he died of smallpox seven months later. The passion of their affair soon dissipated, and the court always saw her as an upstart commoner. At her death she was little mourned and quickly forgotten, even by her two surviving daughters, Mary and Anne.

One question was soon on everyone's lips: who would be the next Duchess of York? Experience had shown that James was of a flighty, imprudent temperament. While Charles and his council drew up a list of eligible European princesses, James was already courting the seventeen-year-old Lady Susan Bellasyse, who had recently been widowed after an impetuous duel between her husband and his best friend resulted in the deaths of both men. Lady Bellasyse was described by one contemporary as 'a woman of much life and great vivacity, but of a very small proportion of beauty'; yet it was her intelligence and sparkling wit that James prized.[6] Anne Hyde had allegedly been the same, and throughout his life James's mistresses would be intellectual and witty, though not conventionally beautiful. The same contemporary who so derided Lady Bellasyse also quipped that James's mistresses were so plain that they must have been 'given him by his priests as a penance'.[7]

The marriage was not to be. The plan was betrayed to Charles, who told James in no uncertain terms that while he may have 'played the fool' once before, he would not be allowed to do so again. By this time it was becoming clear that Charles, after almost ten years of marriage to Caterina de Braganza, would not have a legitimate heir of his own; if James was the future king, then he must marry among the royal families of Europe. Charles also knew his brother's temperament: James was easily led, and the future Duchess was likely to be able to exert a great deal of power through him. Lady Bellasyse may have been disappointed to lose her chance to become the Queen of England, but she knew a good deal when she saw one and settled for being his mistress, along with the title of Baroness Bellasyse of Osgodby. She also made sure to keep James's letter of proposal, which she often brought out to exhibit when she was entertaining.

While Charles was fighting this fire at court, he sent James's Groom of the Stole, Henry Mordaunt, Lord Peterborough, as Ambassador Extraordinary to the Continent to begin negotiations for a foreign marriage. Peterborough was fiercely loyal to James, and the intimacy between them is testified by the way that James informally signed his letters to him, 'Your very affectionate friend'. The intended object of these negotiations was initially the beautiful Claudia Felicitas of Innsbruck. While James preferred his mistresses clever to beautiful, he nevertheless professed that 'good looks were an essential qualification' for his second bride. The various negotiations which followed are well documented. They were long, complicated and tortuous. But it is enough to say that Peterborough travelled through France and Germany, gradually crossing princesses from his list – some were spoken for, some were deemed too fat, some apparently had 'disagreeable' temperaments. Then one day, as Peterborough tells it, his travels took him to Paris, where he was invited to the Hôtel de Conti (which had been the house of Maria's aunt, Anne Marie Martinozzi, who had recently died), and there he saw a portrait of the young princess. He was instantly captivated. In this painting was 'such a light of beauty, such characters of ingenuity and goodness', he would later write in his memoirs, that he immediately sent a letter to England with the news that he had 'found his mistress and the Fortune of England'.[8]

The Estensi were a dynasty much in decline – in fact they couldn't even offer a dowry – but this did not put Peterborough off. The appeal of Maria's beauty should not be underestimated, and indeed Peterborough seems almost too devoted to this, but a chief attraction was her link to Louis XIV. Laura, Maria's mother, was the niece of Cardinal Mazarin, who had been Louis XIV's chief minister when he first became king, and she had grown up at the French court where she and her sisters were renowned beauties. In Maria's young face were unmistakable traces of her mother's family. A link between the Estes and the Stuarts would inevitably strengthen relations between England and France. Accordingly, Louis took a great interest in ensuring that the marriage would take place: he even paid the dowry himself.

Of course, there was one major obstacle: the fact that 'the Duchess her mother's, but more strongly her own, Inclinations did design her to a Religious life'.[9] In other words, Maria held no thoughts of marriage, to anyone. But this was little more than a momentary setback in the eyes of these powerful men. Letters passed back and forth between Charles II, James, Lord Peterborough and countless others, and it was decided that no other princess would do. Come hell or high water, Maria Beatrice d'Este of Modena would be the next Duchess of York.

Maria would have known nothing of this. We can imagine her walking through the white stone colonnades of the inner courtyard of the great Ducal Palace that was her home, crossing each morning over the Bridge of Sighs that once connected the palace to her beloved convent, but which no longer exists. It was a sheltered and happy life, of female companionship, education and devotion to God. She was blissfully unaware that the ground beneath her feet was shifting, that a man would soon arrive in Modena who would take her away from everything she held dear. But, by now, her mother was aware of this.

From a distance, Duchess Laura had been trying to delay the inevitable. Her agent in France, Abbé Gaspar Rizzini, had been approached by Peterborough, and it was he who had told Peterborough that Maria was to take the veil. He had then seen Peterborough's refusal to take no for an answer. Laura was well acquainted with the machinations of these men, and she decided to take matters into her own hands. Before Peterborough had even left France for Italy, she sent two messengers to intercept him, one of whom, Paolo Antonio Nardi, was brother of the Chancellor of Modena. Peterborough reported this visit to England, writing of his 'extreame amazement' when they arrived at his lodgings.[10] But this amazement can have been nothing compared to how he felt on receiving the message itself, whereby the duchess warned of the 'impossibility of her complyance in this affaire' and informed him that she had also written to Louis XIV with words to this effect.[11] But Peterborough was not deterred. Laura had to think again.

Nardi returned a few days later to say that the duchess would be delighted to consent if 'the honour [that] was supposed to be intended for the daughter might be transferred to any other Princess in that family'.[12] Indeed, there was another princess much closer to the duke in age, the thirty-year-old Leonora, though she also intended to take the veil. Laura wrote to Louis that she had been working on both princesses to agree to the marriage but, 'as to my own, all my efforts were in vain, but I have succeeded better with the Princess Leonora, my sister-in-law, and have at last induced her to conform to my wishes'.[13] It is difficult to know what game Laura was playing here. Clearly, she did not want to displease the French king, whose heart was so set on an Anglo-Este alliance – indeed, in this same letter she wrote that her attempts to persuade Maria had been 'in order to comply with your majesty's wishes' – but it is also clear that she worked more on Leonora and tried to spare her daughter.[14]

Laura was in an impossible position, caught between her duties as a mother and her duties as Regent. The decline of the Estensi over the previous century had meant that they had gone from a military to a soft power, and marriage was a key means of forging political alliances and furthering the dynasty. During this time, it was to be expected that daughters of ruling families would leave: sons stayed to rule, daughters were advantageously married off. Indeed, a diplomatic marriage for Maria had been discussed before, but it had come to nothing then and Maria's desire to become a nun had only grown. But Laura only had one daughter, and this was her sole chance to spread the Este dynasty abroad. To add to this, the Estensi well knew what it was like to be at the mercy of the Pope's power: it was a Pope who had banished them from Ferrara, and it was another Pope who now took an interest in Maria's potential marriage. The Pope's nephew, Cardinal Altieri, wrote to Laura's confessor that 'it is to be hoped that the piety of the Duchess may lead her to subordinate her own tender feelings to the service of God and of the faithful in that Kingdom … these considerations are so powerful that they should not only incline but compel the Duchess to conclude the marriage'.[15] If she helped bring Catholicism back to England, what glory this would bring to her family. Maria was not the only one being put under pressure.

James seems to have been happy enough to marry the elder Este princess, Leonora: Lord Arlington wrote to Peterborough that

'His Royal Highness having been informed he could not have the younger Princess for reasons not explained, he sent your Lordship despatches to address yourself to the elder'.[16] The motives for keeping James in the dark about Maria's desire to become a nun are not clear, though as a fellow Catholic it may be that this would have been enough to make him withdraw his addresses to her. He does not seem to have been aware of Leonora's desires either. But it was Peterborough primarily who put a stop to this match. He was determined that his master would have no one but the younger Este princess. He (and others at the English court) were convinced that at the grand age of thirty the Princess Leonora was past it, while Maria, not yet fifteen, had more than two decades of child-bearing ahead of her. Maria it would be. It clearly had not occurred to any of these men that Maria Beatrice d'Este might have a mind and a will of her own, and that she was prepared to fight for the right to choose her own destiny. This is perhaps with the exception of Laura's agent, Rizzini, who, though he held little power in the matter, continued to fight her corner to the best of his limited abilities.

When it was decided that the time had come for Peterborough to travel to Modena, the duchess was one step ahead of him again. As was their custom, the family had been spending the summer at their palace in Sassuolo, a place of remarkable beauty that had been built by Maria's grandfather, Francesco I. Even today, when the palace is open again after decades of restoration work, stepping inside its walls is like stepping into another world. The ceiling of every room, and often the walls, too, are covered with frescos by Jean Boulanger, each with a different theme, though all celebrating the brilliance of the Este family in their patronage and intellectual prowess. In Maria's day it would have been sumptuously furnished and the walls covered with masterpieces from the great Este collection: paintings by Veronese, Titian, Guercino. Maria always remembered the tranquil air of Sassuolo and considered the peaceful times she spent there as among the happiest days of her life.

But these quiet days were disrupted forever on 17 September when Laura learned that Lord Peterborough was on his way. She wasted no time in setting off for Modena and sent a carriage to intercept Peterborough a mile from the city to have him brought to the palace of Count Ugo Molza, where he was told he would stay, courtesy of the duchess. His apartments there were magnificent and luxurious, but they were also just next to the Ducal Palace. If he was to be in Modena, she was going to keep an eye on him.

The calculated impression made by Laura's treatment of Peterborough can only have increased later that evening when she called him to her presence under cover of darkness. Peterborough was taken through a back entrance to the palace, but, as he was walked through the sumptuous apartments which followed, he could not have helped but compare the sight with those found at home. The Este Palazzo Ducale, though not a large building, is one of the first masterpieces of Baroque architecture in Italy. The entire structure is looped around a colonnaded internal courtyard, with enormous white arches. This was quite an architectural feat: the arches were carved at the quarry in huge pieces, and then transported down the canals to be installed on site. The result is that the boundary between outer and inner space becomes fluid, as the upper and lower walkways in the colonnade take on the role of the main hallway. Inside, the state rooms are magnificently decorated. The ceilings and walls are covered with ornate carvings of putti, roses and Roman columns, and everywhere you see the Este eagle, all covered in gold leaf. In carved cornices in the ceilings were paintings by artists such as Tintoretto (which have since been taken out and are housed in the Galleria Estense in Modena). All was lit by candles from below, further illuminating the gold leaf above, so that it shimmered and shone.

The royal palaces of England, by comparison, were all in various states of disrepair and faded splendour. Once they had housed a great art collection – the works amassed by Charles I during his reign – but this, too, was a shadow of what it had once been. After Charles's execution in 1649, a large part of his collection was sold in the famous Commonwealth Sale to pay the country's debts after seven years of civil war. After his restoration, Charles II had sought both to restore his father's collection and to add to it, but many masterpieces remained abroad. The Estensi may have been a dynasty in decline, but compared to the English court their palace exuded an air of opulence and refinement.

When Peterborough found himself before Duchess Laura, in an upper room of the great palace, she stood at the window with her back to him. Even without seeing her face he felt the full imposing gravity of her presence. It is impossible to know exactly what happened in that room. The only surviving account of the meeting comes from Peterborough's own memoirs, written some twelve years after the event, and, unsurprisingly, he presents these negotiations rather in his own favour. But without any other record we must rely on his account, according to which the duchess received him with every courtesy as befitted his position as an ambassador to the King of England and ordered chairs to be set before them so that they might sit and converse. Peterborough got things underway. He confessed himself surprised 'to find difficulty in a thing the world judged to be so advantageous to all the parties'.[17] Laura calmly repeated to him facts that he was already acquainted with: that her daughter had a great aversion to marriage, that she wished to become a nun, that she was very young, and not of a strong constitution (the veracity of this last statement is not certain). She pointed out that Maria was very pious and the idea of marrying a prince not yet confirmed into the Catholic Church, whatever his private feelings may be, posed great difficulties. A papal dispensation would be needed, and there was no reason to think that this would be granted.

At this point in his narrative Peterborough saw fit to gloss over his replies to her doubts, reporting only that he 'answer'd what he thought proper' and that the duchess found these answers to her satisfaction.[18] He asked if he might be allowed to see the princess. Laura agreed that this should happen the following day. Peterborough's account leaves much to be desired, but if it is to be believed then it would seem that, by the end of their meeting, Laura was on the brink of agreeing to the marriage of her only daughter. She saw the advantage of having the heirs of the Estensi (and Laura's family, the Mazarins) on the throne of England. If it couldn't be Leonora, it would have to be Maria.

After his audience Lord Peterborough returned to his apartments at the Count's palace, satisfied that all was going according to plan, and eagerly looked forward to the long-awaited glimpse of the beautiful Este princess who, he was sure, would prove both charming and obedient. He should not have rested so easily. The following evening, when darkness fell, Nardi called on Peterborough and once again carried him forth to the palace in a small carriage, led him through the back entrance, through the apartments, out into the inner courtyard around which the palace sat, up a grand flight of painted stairs, past numerous doors and marble statues and into the same small room on the upper floor. The duchess was by the window as she had been the previous day and beside her stood a young woman. Peterborough claims to have addressed the princess with all proper compliments; he asked her pardon if he had 'discompose[d] her quiet' and 'cross[ed] her enclinations' and explained that as soon as he saw her picture in France, he knew that she was the only person that could make his master happy.[19] He said that he was even more convinced of this now that he saw her in person and assured her that when she got to know James, and saw his merits for herself, she would find that it would 'make amends for what she might now in some measure esteem a sufferance'.[20] Well said, thought Peterborough to himself, entirely satisfied that all that remained was her gentle compliance.

Maria listened with stoic attentiveness and, when he had finished, she made her reply 'with a little fierceness'. In the absence of Maria's own account to drawn on, here are Peterborough's words:

> She could not but wonder, why from so many Princes of more merit, who would esteem that honour and be ready to embrace

> it, they should persist in endeavouring to force the inclinations of another, for whom it was impossible to agree to a proposition of that nature; and that had vowed herself, as much as was in her power, to another sort of life, out of which she could never think she could be happy.[21]

At this point, with tears in her eyes, she begged him to 'divert any farther persecution of a maid who had an invincible aversion for marriage'.[22] In an extraordinary image, she told him she would rather throw herself into the fire than comply.

Peterborough's response to her entreaty shows how little he listened to her words. He was 'a little peek'd' at finding his wishes opposed and told her that, having seen her beauty, he could not obey. He 'could not believe ... that she was made for other end than to give Princes to the World'.[23] To this Maria had no answer but to leave the room, slamming the gilded door behind her. The duchess followed. Nardi urged him not to lose heart: 'the Ladies of Italy,' he said, 'when it came to be in earnest were to have no will, but that of their Friends.'[24] He felt that if Laura was satisfied that Maria should be married, then married she would be. If she had ever been so, Laura was by now no longer on her daughter's side. She sent for Peterborough the next day, said that she felt that a dispensation from the Pope was all that was required and began to speak of her daughter's dowry and maintenance.

Word from Rome followed three weeks later, not in the form of a dispensation – the terms of which were still being haggled over – but a letter, the letter we saw Maria with at Calais. How Maria spent these three weeks is not known. We can imagine interviews with her mother and her uncle, Prince Rinaldo (who himself would take holy orders, but have to give them up later in life in order to ascend to the dukedom), desperate attempts to persuade her, and forceful, adamant resolve on her part. But when Maria read the letter from the Pope, her determination broke down. She cried passionate tears, screamed and howled for two days straight, to the point that she had to be held down by force. Peterborough's account simply states that 'the princess then at last gave herself up to the will of her friends'.[25]

❖

On 20 September, at around eleven o'clock in the morning, Maria passed through the courtyard of the palace, which was lined with spectators come to wish their beloved princess well on her wedding day. She entered one of the large, gilded apartments in the palace and found herself before a makeshift altar. The room was filled with high-ranking members of the court as well as her mother, brother and uncle, but it was a relatively private ceremony and hardly what we might have expected for the wedding between the daughter of the House of Este and the heir to the throne of England. But this was a wedding by proxy, of the kind often practised for royal marriages when the bride and groom hailed from different nations. James's own parents had been married thus, with the infamous George Villiers, Duke of Buckingham, standing in for his friend, the future Charles I.

The marriage did not begin well. The Bishop of Modena refused to officiate as James had not officially declared himself a Catholic and, as yet, the Pope had not sent his dispensation. Without the Pope's express permission, the bishop feared excommunication. The humble clergyman who took his place was the court chaplain, Dom Andrea Roncagli, but at least he was a familiar face. For most of the long service, Maria remained at the altar alone. Peterborough stood in as proxy for the absent James, but since he was not a Catholic it was not deemed appropriate for him to take part in anything but the essentials. He waited in a chamber nearby. He later wrote that 'so much of the Service was done as seemed obnoxious to the Religion [he] did profess', though it could be added that Maria would likely have found his presence obnoxious, too, this man who had come and torn her life apart.[26] After the ceremony was over, she was publicly declared Duchess of York, and Peterborough took her by the hand

and led her to her apartments, where he left her until he was due to collect her for the wedding dinner.

Once the service was over, dancing, masquerades, comedies and music broke out in the cobbled streets of Modena and would continue all night. They must have been audible to Maria, who spent the next two hours waiting in her apartments, alone with her thoughts. When Peterborough collected her, he presented her with the jewels he had been carrying for all those months of negotiations, and which he had been charged to present to the new Duchess of York. The gift amounted to some £20,000 worth of diamonds, rubies, emeralds and other delights (worth over £3 million in today's money). But Maria had no interest in trinkets. Little did she know how much the duke would enjoy giving her expensive gifts, and how much she would have to pretend to like them. There would, however, be one piece of jewellery that Maria would prize all her life: the ruby ring James gave her at the confirmation of their marriage when she landed in Dover. Throughout her married life she kept it with her and would often say how precious it was to her.

While the street parties raged outside the palace walls, the court and bridal party retired early. The rather understated ceremony was only the warm-up act: the spectacles were still to come. Laura had grown up at the French court as a *fille de France*, and had lived as Princess, Duchess and then Regent in Modena for nearly twenty years. She knew how power worked, and the power of display. The following day, Sunday 1 October, saw a royal procession. The route from the Palazzo to the Duomo was a circuitous one, where adoring citizens could cheer and cry as the royal party passed in their grand coaches and finery. Maria's carriage led the way. She was accompanied by her mother, Princess Leonora (who must have been relieved that she was there as a guest, rather than the bride) and the 'Madama' (Lucrezia Barberini, the widow of Maria's grandfather, Francesco I). The first site the carriage passed, as it wound around the Arc de Triomphe, was the convent of the Order of the Visitation that Maria had so desperately wished to join, and which Leonora, who sat beside her, would be welcomed into soon after. We can imagine the surges of regret and relief which must have crossed over the hearts of each princess as they passed it.

The young Duke of Modena, Francesco II, rode beside them. His suit of rich brocade had been embroidered with delicate gold thread and pearls, while his sword and hat were decorated with diamonds: both must have shimmered in the bright Modenese sun. By his side was the comparatively dowdy Peterborough, who represented the Duke of York, wearing silks and lace, but no gold or jewels. Behind this pair a huge train of hundreds of knights bore banners depicting both the Este and Stuart coats of arms.

They arrived finally in front of the bright white marble façade of the Duomo, gleaming in the sun, and surrounded by luxurious tapestries which hung in front of (and hid) the churchyard. To the side stood an arch which had been specially built for the occasion, and which was decorated with images linking the house of Stuart and the House of Este: fleur-de-lis, leopards and a harp in the collar of the Garter for the former, and gold lilies with silver eagles for the latter. The marble lions which flank the Duomo's entrance had been given manes of sweet-smelling hyacinths (an impressive gesture considering it was October). The wedding procession was met by the Este courtiers, who stood together at the entrance, a considerable throng dressed head to toe in the most fashionable looks of the day: full skirts, stay-corseted bodices, highly piled wigs, long coats, all covered with gold and silver lace and sparkling jewels. Though dressed to the nines, all entered the Duomo with the gravity appropriate for the *Te Deum* which followed.

After the mass the court returned to the palace to celebrate the wedding feast. If the procession was designed to impress the power and splendour of the Este family on the Modenese citizens, the banquet was aimed at the representatives of foreign power. Though Modena is far from the sea, there was fish in abundance and so many kinds of game that Laura's private secretary (Guglielmo Codebò) wryly remarked that there must be no birds left in the forests.

Ornamenting the tables were *Trionfi* (Triumphs): sponges made of sugar, cake and rose marzipan, shaped to depict emblems celebrating the courts of Stuart and Este. There was Atlas resting on the globe, standing upon an eagle; Diana taming a wild leopard; a knight drawing his bow aimed towards a leopard with an eagle in its clutches; a gold coach, drawn also by leopards, carrying a noblewoman; an Arc de Triomphe supported by yet more leopards. In celebration of James, Lord High Admiral of the English fleet, we find Neptune driven in a chariot by resplendent seahorses, his trident bearing the phrase 'mihi soli obtemperat ut cequor' (he attends to me alone), the implication being that Neptune's favour was fixed on England in an early assertion of Britannia ruling the waves. The Estes, too, found their symbol there, an eagle placed in a starry sky. After the guests had feasted there was a ball, which went on into the early hours of the following morning.

Back in England James received the news of his marriage some days later. He was relaxing in his apartments with a small gathering of courtiers including Rachel, Lady Russell, a prolific letter writer and shrewd politician. That night she wrote to her husband:

> I will tell you the news came on Sunday night to the Duke of York that he was a married man. He was talking in the drawing room when the French ambassador brought the letters in and told the news, the Duke turned about and said, 'Then I am a married man.' It proved to be the Princess of Modena.[27]

James immediately sent word to his eldest daughter by Anne Hyde, the eleven-year-old Princess Mary, that 'he had found a play-fellow for her'.[28]

2

Crossing the Water

Let us return to Maria on the shore at Calais, and to that second, smaller letter in her pocket. It is written from London, in a delicate scrawl, the hand of her husband:

> London, 20 October 1673
>
> I am sending the bearer, Father Sheldon, whom I have appointed your first chaplain, to settle the affairs of your chapel with you; I have also charged him to inform you of what has happened here today, in order that you may not be alarmed thereat he will at the same time assure you that I have all imaginable impatience to have the happiness of seeing you, and to be able to assure you myself that so long as you live, I shall have all the love and true friendship for you that you can expect from me.
>
> James[1]

This letter is the only surviving correspondence between James and Maria. Though brief, it is a touching blend of tenderness and formality. 'All the love and true friendship', 'so long as you live': these words may have offered some hope or comfort for Maria's future life. The allusion to 'what has happened here' (the details of which, presumably, had been elaborated on by Sheldon) must, however, have given her pause. James was referring to the outrage of the English parliament when they discovered that the heir to the throne had married a Catholic princess. Letters that passed between Charles, James and Peterborough show that the initial hope had been that the new Duchess of York would have safely arrived in England before parliament returned from recess that October: in this case, the marriage would have been consummated and impossible to invalidate before parliament got wind of it. But, as we know, this did not happen. When parliament found out what was afoot, they begged Charles to reconsider, and to choose a princess or noblewoman 'of the English religion'. But Charles was firm. It was too late to go back. The proxy marriage had taken place, and Maria was on her way. But word had got out beyond the palace walls and rumours spread like wildfire: outlandish claims, such as that Maria was the Pope's bastard child, were rife. On Guy Fawkes Night the citizens of London expressed their horror by burning effigies of the Pope in the streets. A British envoy wrote that night that if Maria had arrived then, 'she would certainly have been martyred'.[2]

We cannot know how Maria reacted when faced with such a prospect. Up to this point, the only words we have of hers are from around a month earlier, during her time in France. The first is written from Lyon, dated 22 October 1673, and is addressed to her beloved Sister Mary, the Mother Superior at the Convent of the Order of the Visitation in Modena:

> I give you the news that we have arrived here in perfect health, God be praised. Mamma and I are not only well, but very well, and I am most impatient to have news of you, which will be so dear to me, and which, I hope to God, may be good. On Thursday we went to see the Sisters of the Visitation at Chambéry, and I cannot express the consolation it was to me to be there. I asked for your dear nieces, whom, to confess the truth, I caressed more than the others, and embraced more tenderly, for it seemed to me as if I were kissing your own hands, my most dear Mother. Those good Sisters willingly gave me their portrait, and I promised them mine, and told them I would have written to them, if I had known

their names. I must end by embracing your Reverence with all my heart.

Maria d'Este[3]

She adds a postscript: 'If I followed my inclination I would never cease writing to you, my dearest Mother, but as it is time to go to supper, I embrace you and all my sisters with all my heart.' In this affectionate letter we find that Maria still saw herself as the Este princess who had left Modena only a few weeks before, who is still utterly devoted to her 'dearest' Mother Superior, and who still signs herself 'Maria d'Este'. When Laura wrote to the convent at the same time saying she hoped 'that all may happen for the comfort of the Duchess, my daughter, for her comfort will ever be my own', we might read some concern for the shock Maria would have when she had to face her life as Duchess of York.[4]

Just a week later, on 29 October, when Maria writes her second letter, we find a shift in her attitude. Once again she assures her Mother Superior that she is well, and implores her to 'remember your daughter, although she is far away. I assure you my heart ever remains close to yours, and nothing will ever be able to separate them. Pray to God for me, and make your daughters, my dear Sisters, pray for me.'[5] Though in this letter we can feel her pain, she seems to be coming to terms with her fate: she signs herself Maria d'Este, Duchess of York.

❖

Over on the other side of the Channel, a small number of English courtiers awaited the Modenese arrival. The inclement weather meant that this was greatly delayed. Hours passed, each more tedious than the last, and boredom reached its peak when the court artist, Willem van de Velde the Elder, found himself sketching Lady Peterborough's carriage in a bid to pass the time. Van de Velde had been commissioned to document the journey of the new Duchess of York in a series of drawings, and they are the closest we can get to these moments. These intricate works are now dispersed across the collections of some of Britain's greatest museums: the British Museum, Cambridge's Fitzwilliam Museum and the National Maritime Museum in Greenwich. We don't know what these drawings were intended for – perhaps full-scale paintings which, if they were made, have since been lost to us – but they capture both the extraordinary grandeur of the event and the more banal moments.

The first image of the series is little more than a doodle. It shows the English ships on their way from Dover to Calais, to collect the Italian party. In the next, we find a rough but more detailed sketch of the embarkation at Calais. It presents a chaotic scene: wooden, rutted walls at all angles along and behind the shoreline, with steps leading up to small houses, around which people are busily moving to and fro. In the foreground are rowing boats, and in them we can just make out some seated figures; the Italian group are there ready to be cast off from the sands and rowed across to the great boats (they were called 'yachts', though these ships were used for war as well as leisure) that are waiting to the left of the image. Next, we find 'The Passage from Calais to Dover'. Great tall ships with the sails billowing in the winds, their vast shadows are traced in the water as they sail towards the white cliffs of Dover, which are just visible in the distance. It is an imposing scene, as befits the passage of the wife of a naval hero: James had until recently been Lord High Admiral of the English fleet – he had had to give up the post under the Test Act – and had acquitted himself heroically in both the French and Spanish fleets when still an exiled prince.

Had Maria been searching for clues about the world that awaited her, she'd have done well to note the names of the ships that had come to transport her across the Channel. She herself travelled in the *Catherine*, named after the queen. But alongside this ship (van de Velde presents it with the British flag flying proudly) was another great ship called the *Cleveland*, named after Charles II's most prominent mistress, Barbara Villiers, Duchess of Cleveland (Lady Castlemaine). What kind of world is this, one wonders, where warships are named not just after the queen but after the mistress, and where this is displayed openly in front of the new wife of the heir to the throne? The names of the other yachts displayed are also telling: the *Monck*, for instance, was named for the military and naval officer General George Monck, who, having been a prominent politician at the time of the Commonwealth, played an instrumental role in the restoration of the monarchy. Or two others, side by side: the *Mary*, which had been a gift from the Dutch in 1660, to mark the Restoration, and was named after the dear sister of Charles and James, who had married into the royal House of Orange; and the *Merlin*, a great warship which saw action in naval battles with the Dutch throughout the 1670s, when these two maritime trading powers became fierce military rivals. Indeed, the images we see are reminiscent of the naval battle paintings that van de Velde was commissioned to produce.

There are three sketches that each represent Maria's arrival at Dover. One is a rough sketch and the other two are far more developed. The first two are essentially the same scene, though from slightly different parts of the shoreline. A comparison between the two offers an insight into van de Velde's thought process: in the rougher work, he includes a very distant view of France, a small landmass in the far right of the drawing over which he has written 'kalis vrangrijk' (Calais, France) and then crossed it out. The view from this perspective is far more of the sea and the immediate coastline, but when he redrafted he chose to set the scene a little further into the coast. Here we lose the view of Calais, but gain the cliffs of Dover, which sit to the right of the drawing, and a glimpse of the town beyond the beach. The coastline is a hive of activity, full of people standing, waiting, walking. And we can see, very faintly sketched, the rowing boats just arriving on the shore.

The final sketch is by far the most detailed and gives the perspective of the east of the port of Dover. To the left we can see the white cliffs, and above them the castle and city walls, where James's parents – Charles I and Henrietta Maria – had first met some fifty years before. The shore is full of people rushing to greet Maria, who is seen on the sands, meeting her husband for the very first time. We can make out words, written in Dutch in brown ink, which translate as 'How the Duchess landed in the bay near the castle not far from the place where the king landed when he came to England in 1660'. The symbolism of the new Duchess of York, the wife of the heir to the throne, landing next to where Charles regained his crown, is clear: he restored the Stuart dynasty; she will guarantee its future.

When Maria stepped onto the sands of Dover, after a ten-hour crossing over stormy seas, to take her place as Duchess of York, the sun had just set. She was met on the beach by James and four of his closest attendants. There was little ceremony: James took her in his arms, confessed himself dazzled by the loveliness of her eyes, and Maria burst into tears. The accounts of Peterborough and Codebò focus on how she 'took possession of his heart as well as his arms' and 'captured the heart of the lord duke and the English nation'; but another observer wryly noted that she was visibly repulsed by his embraces.[6] This is perhaps not surprising: James was forty, and his once handsome features were scarred from smallpox and ravaged by his years at sea. His expression was described as hard and his mouth a little cruel, though he tried his best to show her kindness. She was a fifteen-year-old convent girl who had suddenly been grabbed by a strange man, even if he was technically her husband. Before this point, Maria will have met very few men, and they would never have presumed to touch her.

That same day the Bishop of Oxford read out the marriage contract between James and Maria in front of witnesses made up of the English nobility and the Este party. Beyond Maria's assent to this contract – spoken in French as the common language of the newlyweds – we have no record of her words, actions or feelings on this day. All that survives is a note scribbled in a diary, where he reported that she had been 'wedded and bedded that night'.[7] Later in life, however, when reflecting on these early days, Maria reported how she had cried every time she saw James, and how she struggled to adjust to her new role of wife and new life as an English duchess.

❖

Maria and James and their retinue stayed a few days in Dover before travelling to Canterbury and thence through Rochester – which Codebò disparagingly named a *città brutta* – to Gravesend. It was here that they again took to the water and were met by Charles II on the Thames. Once more we have recourse to van de Velde's visual accounts. We see a great ship in the centre, which carries the king, surrounded by a small fleet. On the right of the composition is Gravesend, where the British flag flies high from the shoreline. The meeting is detailed in another drawing, one of the most comprehensive of the series: here we see depictions of the people themselves. Every face is given individual features: some are rowing, some are looking about them, some are watching the scene unfold. In the centre of the piece there are two different representations of the encounter. The one on the right shows James and Maria making their way from their own vessel into the royal barge; the depiction on the left shows Charles and his (illegitimate) son, James Scott, Duke of Monmouth, moving from their barge into that of the Yorks. It was in fact James and Maria who decamped to Charles's barge, but perhaps van de Velde couldn't resist making a copy of the king in his fine clothes, extravagant wig and plumed hat, and so invented a second scene.

The handsome and charming 'merry monarch' was an instant hit with Maria. Unlike his brother, whose fair features came from their blonde and blue-eyed paternal grandmother, Anna of Denmark, Charles's face bore the unmistakable traces of the Medici blood that ran through his veins from their maternal grandmother, Maria de' Medici. This face was a comfort to the young Este princess, so far from home, and his manners were gentle and welcoming. Years later she remarked that he had been her first friend in England: 'always kind to me and was so truly amiable and good-natured that I loved him very much, even before I became attached to my Lord the Duke of York'.[8] He in turn remarked, somewhat enviously, that his brother was not deserving of such a beautiful and charming wife.

From Gravesend the royal party travelled together up the Thames to London, in the great long barges that we see in van de Velde's final sketch. As they approached the city from the water, they must have seen the blackened ruins of buildings still not rebuilt after the Great Fire of 1666, and then, as they got nearer to Whitehall, the grand houses of the aristocracy spread along the Strand. It is hard to imagine how different this stretch must have looked then in comparison to now. The Strand sat much closer to the riverbank, and at river level. The homes were almost the size of palaces, with extensive gardens leading down to the water's edge, each with their own landing bays to take their residents out onto the Thames. Travelling by river was the most convenient way for the nobility to get around; each of London's royal palaces sat on the banks of the Thames, and travelling by river one could avoid mixing with the hoi polloi, not to mention the stench of London's busy streets.

The boats took them all the way to the steps of Whitehall Palace, which must have seemed a peculiar place. Where now we see the Victorian neo-Gothic Houses of Parliament, the stately, wide road of Whitehall and the manicured gardens of St James's Park, in the 1670s this area was given over to an enormous, sprawling mass of buildings all bunched tightly together.[9] The only structure which still stands from this period is Inigo Jones's Banqueting House which, in its day, must have stood out as a small beacon of Baroque beauty amid the Tudor rabble. In all, Whitehall was more a small village than a royal residence and its outdated architecture and furnishings were reportedly uncomfortable. One French observer, the Marquis de Dangeau, called it 'one of the ugliest and dirtiest houses in the world'; Maria would later call it 'one of the largest and most uncomfortable'.[10] We can only imagine how it must have first appeared to her, Laura and Rinaldo after the quiet continental elegance of the Ducal Palace of Modena.

Throngs of people had gathered at the front of the palace, all hoping to catch a glimpse of the Modenese princess. But they were disappointed. The party made their way into the palace through a secret door around the back to avoid any potential disturbance: the mood in London was still unsettled by the prospect of yet another Catholic princess. Once through the door, Charles took his new sister-in-law by the hand and led her up a flight of stairs to his queen, who waited for them at the top. Caterina de Braganza had been Queen of England for eleven years of almost perfect misery. Her inability to conceive an heir while her husband sired one child after another with his many mistresses, combined with her shy manner and adherence to traditional Portuguese customs and dress, made her an object of general ridicule at court. But she had carved out her own life amid this torment and passed her days in devotion and prayer at Somerset House where, according to Codebò, the chapel singers were 'better than in Italy'.[11] We might have expected the queen to welcome the arrival of a fellow Catholic princess as a potential friend and ally, but it was not immediately so. The presence of such a young and beautiful girl, with all the promise of fulfilling her 'duty' and bearing England's future kings, filled her with coldness, which would later be played on by courtiers seeing fit to cause trouble for their own ends. The new sisters-in-law embraced when they first met, politely enough, but it would be some time before any real friendship blossomed. After some fifteen minutes of cordial conversation, Charles escorted Maria to St James's Palace, which was to be her new home.

When we look at St James's Palace now, we see little of the building Maria faced some 350 years ago. A fire in the early nineteenth century destroyed all but the North Gate and some adjoining rooms, as well as the Queen's Chapel and the Chapel Royal. The setting, too, is unrecognisable: when it was built by Henry VIII, the palace was outside London, surrounded by a vast parkland which would have reached all the way to what are now Kensington and Pimlico. The interiors were of dark wood panelling and low ceilings, with small, ill-fitting mullion windows and clunky furniture.

In an attempt to keep out the terrible draughts that swept through the corridors, heavy, thick hangings and tapestries covered the walls and windows, making the dim rooms even darker. After the bright, sun-kissed courtyards and loggias of the Este palaces, it must have been a depressing prospect. And probably no less so for James, who had been imprisoned there for a time during the Civil War and had said goodbye to his father forever in these same rooms.

One thing that the palace did offer Maria was a beautiful Catholic chapel, attached to its walls. It had been designed by Inigo Jones, who himself had spent time studying in Rome, and was a stunning architectural haven for a foreign princess. Building had begun in 1623 in preparation for the arrival of the Spanish Infanta, the prospective bride of Charles I. The marriage never took place, but Charles did marry a Catholic, the French princess Henrietta Maria, and the chapel was completed in 1627. In 1673 the chapel was notionally Caterina's, but she never used it, having another which was far more convenient at her home in Somerset House. Maria had been promised the chapel, as only made sense – she lived in the adjoining palace, after all. But the promise was a verbal agreement only, and when it came to it, she was denied the chapel. It was decided that to have her worship publicly as a Catholic, and to be able to appoint Catholic (potentially even Italian Catholic) priests to administer there, would be politically contentious. Maria had to content herself with a small oratory in her private apartments. She was furious. Laura was even more so. The one condition that had been insisted on was Maria's freedom to worship and she had been in England only a matter of days before this was taken from her. Laura wrote a strongly worded letter to Louis XIV, who voiced his support in his own strongly worded letter to James. James did not respond well. He sent a letter back to Louis claiming that Maria enjoyed the same 'free exercise' of her faith as the queen. This was a lie. Caterina enjoyed two chapels replete with choirs and full ceremonies, where Maria essentially prayed in a cupboard. It was not the most favourable start to her new life as Duchess of York.

Until Laura could be assured of her daughter's happiness, she determined to stay in London. The initial plan to leave after a week soon evaporated, and she was still there some three months later. Maria was happy to have her mother stay; indeed, she was her only real source of comfort, but life became increasingly strained for all under these conditions. The titles and hierarchies of the English aristocracy and those of Italy were not interchangeable, and snobbery was rife on both sides. Prince Rinaldo refused to address peers as 'Excellency', arguing that they were no such thing; the English ladies would not recognise the superiority of Duchess Laura, as to them she was 'only' a duchess. Laura audibly retorted that the English duchesses were 'subjects born' whereas she 'in her own territories raised money without any Parliament', in a reproach to both the English nobility and the king in one fell swoop: Laura was a powerful and independent ruler, while Charles relied on his ministers.[12] These troubles began immediately when, in Caterina's Presence Chamber, the king offered Laura a seat in her presence. Lord Conway repeated the incident to Lord Tyrconnell, saying:

> the King called for a chayre for her, upon which my Lady Suffolk, my Lady Falmouth and the rest of the Ladyes to the number of 20 that were of the Nobility, ran out of the Roome, as thinking themselves of equall quality to the Dutchesse of Modena.[13]

Soon Maria had to dine in private, as the English noblewomen objected so strongly to Laura being allowed to sit beside her when they had to stand. To add to all of this, parliament was soon to reconvene, and the continuing Italian presence was a source of consternation. It was time to leave.

After the New Year celebrations of 1674, Laura, Rinaldo and their train were on their way back to Modena, though matters had still not been settled regarding Maria's chapel. Maria was devastated and saw them off with eyes swollen from so many tears. Once their barge was out of sight, she retired to her room and refused to attend the evening's entertainments. She wrote a letter to her Mother Superior in Modena, full of heartbreak:

> I am in good health, dear Mother, thank God, but I cannot yet accustom myself to this state of life, to which, as you know, I have always been so averse, so I cry many times and grieve much, being unable to rid myself of melancholy – though, blessed be God, this is my cross.[14]

The days that followed must have felt especially lonely, though she had been able to keep two friends with her from home – the Contessa Lucrezia Vezzani Pratoneri was made a Lady of the Bedchamber, and Pelegrina Turini was made a Woman of the Bedchamber – along with some nine domestic servants, whose names are absent from the historical records. Added to this were several English noblewomen who were appointed by James: Lady Peterborough (now a Countess) was given the post of Groom of the Stole (or Mistress of the Robes as it is now called), in recognition of her husband's role in bringing the marriage about; Lady Bellasyse, still James's mistress, secured for herself the position of Lady of the Bedchamber. In this, James was doing no less than his brother, who had given the same position to Barbara Villiers, his mistress who bore him five illegitimate children, in Queen Caterina's household. There were five other Ladies of the Bedchamber: three of them (Catherine Elliott, who had been James's nurse, Margaret Dawson and Lady Apsley) had been Anne Hyde's ladies; the other two were Catherine Cornwallis and Elizabeth Bromley. In addition to this extensive retinue, Maria was given four maids of honour: Sarah Jennings (later Churchill), Isabella Boynton, Mary Kirk and Eleanor Needham. The so-called 'Mother' of the maids was a formidable harridan called Lucy Wise. A woman of fearsome temper indeed, on one occasion she attacked one of the girls, whom she believed transgressive, with a pair of galoshes.

Though she had been devastated to say goodbye to her mother when Laura and her train had left England, Maria's life at court gradually began to improve. By 13 February her spirits were high enough that she was found playing blind man's buff in her drawing room, with her maids and other young courtiers, and she found that she was already pregnant.[15] Records do not show how far along she was when she miscarried the child at the end of March, but she was pregnant again by the end of April.

She wrote to her brother in August. Her letters to Francesco were always full of the tenderest addresses, and she started this one 'caro caro il mio Fratello' ('my darling darling brother'),

> the other day I felt the creature that I have in my body, I do not know whether it will be a nephew or a niece, I know that you would have more taste perhaps in a nephew, and so I hope.[16]

With her family back in Italy, Maria set her mind to adjusting to her new life, and she never lost sight of why she was there: as the Pope had instructed her, she was to be the mother of princes.

3

Duchess of York

The English court must have seemed a strange and often hostile place to Maria in her first year. Though James was apparently devoted to her, she soon found out about his promiscuities. After they had been married five months, James's long-standing mistress, Arabella Churchill, gave birth to a fourth child by him, and it was clear that the relationship was ongoing. And while there were many courtiers and ambassadors who wrote of Maria's beauty and charm, there were several who were far less favourable. Those rumours which preceded her, that she was the Pope's illegitimate child, that she had come to force England back into Catholicism, to persecute English Protestants, remained strong. By simply being a Catholic princess she was seen by many as an enemy. That she was considered more of a threat than the Catholic queen, Caterina, was in part because it was by now an open secret that James had converted to Catholicism. If she were to have children, heirs to the throne, they would be born of two Catholic parents and might be Catholic themselves. England was that much closer to a return to Rome. And in this last sense they were not wrong; this was the point of her marriage. The Pope had instructed her that her duty was to produce Catholic heirs, to return England to the papal fold. How she was perceived, and the tensions between how she approached her duty to her faith and to her new country, would come to define Maria's life in England.

But Maria was determined to acclimatise to her new life. She worked hard, learned English quickly and her apartments at St James's were soon teeming with the most intellectual figures at court. From her first days she and the king got along splendidly, and he was often to be found at her levees, telling jokes, discussing the news of the day and even holding meetings with members of parliament on matters of state. When writing back to Modena, ambassador Montecuccoli reported that 'the Duke ... loves her tenderly, and does nothing without informing her. The King recognises her great spirit and esteems it highly ... there can be no doubt that she will be able to take a great part in affairs when she so chooses.'[1]

Charles could see that Maria had a formidable mind, and he knew his brother's nature. In these visits he was both testing and training her. He wrote to Laura that Maria's 'rare virtues and conversation engage me to give her greater and greater marks of affection and esteem, which I shall ever continue to her'.[2] Maria listened carefully and her letters to her brother show that she was acutely aware of the various political tightropes the king was balancing on. In the evenings laughter filled her rooms as dozens of courtiers descended. Card playing, dancing and gossiping were the main pursuits, but often the party would make music together. Maria was a gifted harpist and James in turn was a skilled guitarist. Gradually the English palaces were hosts to opera and other musical delights. John Evelyn recorded such an event in a diary entry dated 5 January 1674: 'I saw an Italian opera in music, the first that had been in England of this kind.'[3] This opera was probably *Ariane, Or the Marriage of Bacchus*, which had been adapted from a French opera, which itself had been adapted from Monteverdi's *L'Arianna*. And there were several offerings made to the new duchess: February 1674 saw a ballet performed; Shadwell and Locke's semi-operas, *The Tempest* and *Psyche*, were put on several times between 1674 and 1675. This last opera was printed, and the dedication to the Duke of Monmouth suggests that the entertainment was his idea, in homage to his beautiful new aunt-in-law (who was nearly a decade younger than him).

James Scott, Duke of Monmouth, was the eldest illegitimate child of Charles II. He had been born James Crofts, in exile in 1649, to Charles and a woman called Lucy Walter, who died when she was just twenty-eight of a venereal disease. Throughout Monmouth's life there were rumours that Charles had secretly married Lucy, and that Monmouth was his legitimate heir; rumours that Charles refused to verify. But as the eldest, and most loved, child of the king, he was married at the age of fourteen to the eye-wateringly wealthy Anna Scott, Countess of Buccleuch. She was twelve at the time. He took her surname on marriage, and her title, which was raised from Countess to Duke and Duchess. But despite her youth, Anna was no wilting flower; in March 1673 she was described as 'one of the wisest and craftiest of her sex', with 'much wit'.[4]

It is unsurprising that Maria got on well with Monmouth and Anna, and in August 1674 they collaborated on a staging of the Siege of Maastricht, which Monmouth had fought in the previous year. John Evelyn reported the scene:

> In one of the meadows at the foot of the long Terrace below the Castle [Windsor], works were thrown up to show the King a representation of the city of Maestricht, newly taken by the French. Bastians, bulwarks, ramparts, palisadoes, graffs, horn-works, counter-scarps, etc., were constructed. It was attacked by the Duke of Monmouth (newly come from the real siege) and the Duke of York, with a little army, to show their skill in tactics. On Saturday night they made their approaches, opened trenches, raised batteries, took the counter-scarp and ravelin, after a stout defense; great guns fired on both sides, grenadoes shot, mines sprung, parties sent out, attempts of raising the siege, prisoners taken, parleys; and, in short, all the circumstances of a formal siege, to appearance, and, what is most strange all without disorder, or ill accident, to the great satisfaction of a thousand spectators. Being night, it made a formidable show. The siege being over, I went with Mr. Pepys back to London, where we arrived about three in the morning.[5]

Maria may have been young, and was in many ways very innocent, but she was no fool. She knew that all eyes were on her and that many were set against her, hoping she would fail. She also knew that in order to succeed she would have to be faultless: the most charming, the most delightful, the most demure, the most elegant princess that they had ever seen. As Maria spent day after day walking through the palaces of Whitehall and St James's, hardly speaking the language of those around her, seeing so few friendly faces, she must have felt terribly lost. But amid her suffering, she found courage. On every wall of each of the palaces she would have seen the remnants of the great, if now depleted, art collection of Charles I.

Charles I's mania for collecting great masterpieces had led him to purchase the extraordinary collection of the Gonzaga court in Mantua when they had needed to raise money quickly to defend themselves against invasion. This Gonzaga collection had been one of the greatest that has ever been known, and it was predominantly assembled by Maria's relative Isabella d'Este, who had been Marchioness of Mantua in the early sixteenth century, and had been a patron of Leonardo, Titian, Mantegna and Raphael.

Maria knew, as she walked past these same works, that this glory of England was the glory of her female ancestor. And here she would have found strength. She was young, but she understood her duty. She was an English duchess, but she was also an Este princess, and, like the great Isabella, she would use her position as duchess to emulate her forebears, wielding soft power as a patron of the arts.

Court poets and painters saw this opportunity to gain her patronage, and Maria's arrival heralded artistic activities, though she received fewer offerings than Caterina de Braganza had when she came to England in 1662 (Caterina was offered twenty-two poems, Maria just five). When Caterina had arrived only two years after the Restoration, as Queen of England, an atmosphere of celebration reigned throughout the court. And though she was a Catholic, Charles was not (at least in public), and there was little worry about their children being raised outside the English Church. Maria arrived in quite a different climate; thirteen years of rule had not made Charles unpopular exactly, but reality is never as good as the idea, and his relationship with France and Louis XIV was a source of concern for many in parliament. Combined with this, the arrival of Maria amid unsettled mutterings at court around Catholic heirs and papal interference kept many voices that would otherwise have celebrated low.

Her arrival was even met with some cruel and scurrilous pamphlets, which hoped for her to 'be envenom'd with the pox' and to 'Die before twenty, rot before sixteen'.[6] We do not know if Maria knew of these, but they were far from anything she would have encountered before. One satirical poem, perhaps written by John Wilmot, Earl of Rochester (who she certainly would come to know), was called 'Signor Dildo'. It offered a slur on many of the women at Charles II's court and the bawdy decadence attached to it, but Maria's arrival seems to have been the impetus for it.

> You Ladies all of merry England
> Who have been to kiss the Dutchess's Hand,
> Pray, did you lately observe in the Show
> A Noble Italian call'd Signior Dildo?
> This Signior was one of her Highness's Train,
> And helpt to conduct her over the Main;
> But now she cries out, to the Duke I will go,
> I have no more need of Signior Dildo.[7]

If Maria read this, she may well have been shocked. She was a young woman, tenderly educated in a convent, and here she has been transformed into a lusty debauchee. What is striking, too, is that she had only just arrived in England, but her body was already an object of comment and public interest. Though here her body is spoken about in terms of her sexual appetite, it would not be long before she was objectified in terms of her fertility.

But there were several for whom the arrival of a real Este princess was a cause for great excitement. The reputation of the Estes as patrons had preceded her in the form of the great poet Torquato Tasso, who had spent many years patronised by the Este family at the court in Ferrara in the 1560s. Several of his works had been translated into English in the previous century and continued to be a source of inspiration to poets and painters alike. And now, a scion of the dynasty who enabled his work was with them in England. In Maria, they could not have chosen a more willing recipient of artistic offerings. One of the first came from the poet Edmund Waller, who presented Maria with a book of his verses containing a dedication praising her beauty, her wit and her artistic judgement.

Waller was known for his 'occasional poems', his panegyrics, and we can see his brilliance in this genre in his dedication to Maria:

> Madam! I here present you with the rage,
> And with the beauties, of a former age;
> Wishing you may with as great pleasure view
> This, as we take in gazing upon you.

He writes that it is her presence that gives him the ability to write – 'your brighter eyes inspire / A nobler flame, and raise our genius higher' – though at the same time attests that her great mind is a source of awe:

> While we your wit and early knowledge fear,
> To our productions we become severe.
> Your matchless beauty gives our fancy wing,
> Your judgment makes us careful how we sing.

But all of this serves only to make the poets try all the more to write their best works, and to produce only the best for their Este princess, for the inheritor of Tasso's glory:

Lines not composed, as heretofore, in haste,
Polished like marble, shall like marble last,
And make you through as many ages shine,
As Tasso has the heroes of your line.[8]

But even more than this, while Waller spoke of her as an Este, he also claimed her as 'the subject of the British muse'. Maria was delighted with his offering, and she decided to give Waller a task. She handed him her own copy of Tasso, inviting him to write another composition in it, to prove his worthiness to be a Tasso to her. Waller accepted the task and approached it with due gravity, taking the whole summer to pen the following lines:

Tasso knew how the fairer sex to grace;
But in no one durst all perfection place:
In her alone that owns this book, is seen
Clorinda's spirit, and her lofty mien,
Sophronia's piety, *Ermina's* truth,
Armida's charms, her beauty and her youth.

All of these characters – Clorinda, Sophronia, Ermina, Armida – feature in Tasso's *Jerusalem Delivered* and they each possess abundant virtues: strength, piety, faithfulness, beauty, courage, intelligence. But Waller claims Maria is the only person in existence who combines all of these in one. He goes on to praise her mind as well as her beauty: 'Our princess here, as in a glass, does dress / Her well-taught mind, and every grace express', and he ends his poem with another allusion to her lineage, and to her role as the muse and patron of poets: 'More to our wonder than *Rinaldo* fought, / The hero's race excels the poet's thought.'[9] Rinaldo is the hero of Tasso's *Jerusalem Delivered*, and here Waller makes the claim that however wondrous Rinaldo might have been, Maria is even more so. The fact that Rinaldo is an Este family name is also played on, as it was played on by Tasso. Waller suggests that Maria as an Este heir even surpasses her family.

Another hopeful poet was a friend of Waller, John Dryden, who was the poet laureate (and the first to hold this title).[10] His offering was epic in both scale and subject. He visited the exiled John Milton and asked for permission to write a court masque based on *Paradise Lost* and, rather extraordinarily, permission was granted.[11] Why Milton, a man of outspoken Republican sympathies, who had written against Charles I and his policies, who had not only supported Cromwell but worked for him, who upon the Restoration had been allowed to live but in political exile, should decide now that he was happy for his great epic to be turned into a decadent court entertainment is hard to explain. But Milton, too, had read his Tasso: when writing his masterpiece he had drawn heavily from *Jerusalem Delivered*. Both the council of the devils in Book II of *Paradise Lost* and the opening of *Paradise Regained* borrow extensively from Canto IV of Tasso's epic. Perhaps Milton also appreciated the allure of an Este princess, and the fittingness that his work be adapted to celebrate the legacy of Tasso's verse. While Milton was in exile, *Paradise Lost* continued to be popular and had recently been reprinted when Dryden made his request.

Dryden called his work *State of Innocence* and made a start on what would surely have been the most ambitious court masque ever to have existed. But this turned out to be its downfall. The work was never performed and indeed the music was never even written, so enormous was the undertaking. How could the battle be staged, how could 'darkness' be made 'visible'.[12] When Dryden finally gave up on the project some years later (1677), he had the script published, with a lengthy dedication to Maria, praising her many virtues – her wit, her beauty, her taste, her learning – and paying tribute to her legacy. He writes that 'they whom in all ages poets have endeavour'd most to please, have been the beautiful and the great' and that 'both these are so eminently joyn'd in the person of Your Royal Highness, that it were not easie for any, but a poet, to determine which of them outshines the other'. He goes on to say 'I can easily resign to others the Praise of your Illustrious Family', while at the same time referencing their greatness 'both in peace and war' and speaking of the 'so many Generals and Heroes' which Maria, as the mother of princes, will emulate with 'those which you are to produce for the English Chronicle'. After writing of their glory as a powerful ruling family, Dryden goes on to speak of the Estes as that 'to which Ariosto and Tasso have ow'd their Patronage; and to which the World has ow'd their Poems'. But he says that even considering all these things, it is Maria's beauty that he 'could not without extream reluctance resign … to another hand'. There is no danger of anyone accusing the poet of being negligent with his praise in this respect, as the next two pages of very small type are dedicated to this theme. But he leaves the final page to speak of her virtue and the qualities of her mind. There seem to have been no bounds to his flattery, as he writes 'your Person is a Paradise, and your Soul a Cherubin within to guard it'. This may all seem rather extreme, but it is a perfectly crafted address which falls well within the standards of dedication of the time, which seeks to raise the dedicatee to the heights almost of God himself. Dryden sought her patronage, and in this dedication he is reminding Maria of her duties when he talks of 'this new Honour of being Your Poet'.

As traditional as the patronage of poets was the patronage of artists, and almost immediately upon her arrival Maria had her portrait done by the court painter, Sir Peter Lely. To have a portrait painted by the principal court artist was almost a rite of passage, but a closer look at the resultant painting suggests that, for Lely, this was no ordinary commission. While he would always paint certain details himself, by this time Lely had an extensive studio at work to produce his many commissions. It was not at all unusual for paintings to be executed by multiple hands, and the sitters no doubt expected that this would be the case. But in this painting of Maria we find that Lely didn't leave any of the work to his studio: the brushwork is entirely by his own hand. The painting is as thoughtful as it is fashionable. Maria's clothes are in vogue in a style of loose 'undress', though Lely already knew enough about his sitter to paint her with a little more propriety than other court women exhibited. Her hair falls in gentle ringlets around her face and down her shoulder. As she stands in three-quarter profile, looking out at the viewer, she reaches out with her right hand to pick a delicate orange blossom. These flowers were often depicted as symbols of innocence and purity in images of young brides, and here the blossom is used to celebrate her marriage. The pearl that hangs on her dress just in front of her heart speaks of her virtue.

And it wasn't just the established artists at court who benefited from her patronage. Soon artists began to travel to London, seeking her out. In 1674, Benedetto Gennari arrived from Bologna, and she immediately commissioned him to produce devotional works. This was in direct emulation of her forefathers: Gennari had been a student of Guercino, who had been patronised by the Este family in Ferrara. Guercino had refused the invitation of Charles I to join his court in London, but Gennari had actively sought out the patronage of Charles's son and daughter-in-law.

Gradually Maria began to find her feet. Though she had started her life in England with many enemies, even those who had most strongly opposed her had to admit that she possessed abundant good qualities. She became popular at court and enjoyed taking part in the many entertainments that it provided. The court of Charles II was one full of merrymaking, as Maria will quickly have discovered. In the first months after her arrival she will have attended plays, balls and French ballets. One ball, recorded by Evelyn, took place in her rooms: 'I saw the great ball danced by all the gallants and ladies at the Duchess of York's.'[13] And she had brought with her a troupe of actors of the *commedia dell'arte*, the likes of which London's stage had never seen. They would be frequent visitors to the court over the next decade. Both Charles and James were particularly supportive of the theatre, and Charles had spent some £730 (around £75,000 in today's money) transforming the Great Hall at Whitehall Palace into a permanent theatre, for 'Masking, Plays, and Dancing'.[14] Each also acted as patrons to theatres: Charles's was named the King's Theatre and James's the Duke of York's Theatre. At the King's, symphonies were played before the curtain rose, and the Duke of York's was famous for its dancers, who performed in 'the English style'.

The managers of the theatres were also playwrights and courtiers: Thomas Killigrew was the manager of the King's Theatre, while the Duke of York's was run by William Davenant until his death in 1668, when it was taken over by Thomas Betterton. These theatres had a monopoly on the city, in part because of their royal patronage. They performed the old classics, Shakespeare, Fletcher, Beaumont, but also the plays of their managers and other contemporary writers, including Aphra Behn. Behn was the first woman to make a living as a playwright and was one of the most celebrated of her day. Maria became an ardent theatregoer, and regularly attended plays with her maids throughout her life in England. As such they will have been among the earliest audiences of this trailblazing figure, and Maria must have liked what she saw: Behn would go on to compose poetry for her once she became queen.

One of the earliest entertainments Maria will have seen was a performance of *Mustapha* by Robert Boyle, Earl of Orrery. It starred the famous actress Elizabeth Barry as Isabella, the Queen of Hungary, and Maria was so taken by her performance that she reportedly 'made her a present of her wedding suit and employed Barry as her English tutor'.[15] Perhaps this extraordinary act of generosity was an impetuous gesture of youthful enthusiasm, or maybe it is an insight into how she viewed her role as Duchess of York, future queen mother of monarchs. In 1685, when she was Queen of England, she replicated this gesture and lent her actual coronation robes to Barry to perform the role of Queen Elizabeth, in a performance of *The Unhappy Favourite* by John Banks.

The symbolism of the beloved Queen Elizabeth, the chaste Virgin Queen, married to her country, wearing Maria's own coronation robes, would have been powerful. But in these early days, by taking lessons with Barry, Maria showed her intention to 'become' English, and in giving her wedding clothes Maria was sending a clear message: as the wife to the heir to the throne she would be a generous patron to worthy talent, especially to talented women.

4

A Stepmother to Princesses

Maria's role as a patron was not limited to artists, writers and actresses: she took an active interest in the women around her, in her maids of honour and particularly in her new stepdaughters. The princesses Mary and Anne were born in 1662 and 1665 respectively and were the only surviving children from the marriage of James, Duke of York, and Anne Hyde. They had lost their mother when they were young, and neither remembered her well, but they had enjoyed a closer relationship with their parents than was usual for royal children. They lived together at St James's Palace, frequently dined together as a family, and James in particular showed an affection for them which was often commented on. He especially favoured Mary, who increasingly resembled him with her heavy curls and bright eyes. Where Mary was pretty, lively and clever, Anne was a quiet child who lived in her sister's shadow.

Both children were plagued with poor eyesight but in Anne it caused a squint which often gave her an expression of mistrust, whether she felt it or not. Anne's eyes became such a problem for her that she was sent to her grandmother in France to see a specialist, though she was never cured. This time away, combined with her natural reticence, meant that Anne grew up more emotionally distant from her parents than Mary, who was a favourite of all at court. Though they were second and third in line to the throne, it was never considered for a moment that they would become Queens of England, and they were treated as any royal or aristocratic daughters would be – that is to say that they received very little education but were raised to be delightful ornaments. As such they learned to speak French, to sing, to play instruments and to dance, but they learned hardly anything about geography or history, or even about the constitution (which would prove problematic for the princesses when they each subsequently became Queens of England). The classics made no appearance at all.

In the nursery they will have had playmates from some of the court's leading families. Their governess, Frances Villiers, had six daughters, all of whom were raised alongside the princesses in the nursery, and they became firm friends. Sarah Jennings was often found among them when she visited her sister, Frances, at court. Frances, nicknamed 'la belle Jennings' on account of her great beauty, was a maid of honour to Anne Hyde. When Sarah took up the same post with Maria, she had already learned much of the working of the court from her older sister. Another of their playmates was Anne Lee, the niece of John Wilmot, Earl of Rochester. Lee was a little older than the princesses, and arrived at court in 1665, when she was just six years old, under the care of her grandmother, Anne Wilmot, Countess of Rochester, who was a lady in Anne Hyde's household and a close friend of her mistress and of James, too. When 1673 came, Anne Lee, like Maria, was just fifteen, and like Maria, she, too, was married much against her will. Her husband was Thomas Wharton, a feckless fortune-hunter who treated her abominably.

When Anne Hyde died in 1671, the princesses were moved to the more traditional setting of Richmond Palace. Richmond had been built by Henry VII in 1501 and had housed the heirs to England's throne ever since. The change in the princesses' circumstances perhaps reflected the fact that they now had to be seen as potential future monarchs in a way that had not been deemed necessary before. Charles II's ten-year marriage to Caterina de Braganza had produced no children, and now that Anne Hyde was dead, with no male heirs, James's daughters were his successors. Mary and Anne formally became children of the state: all decisions regarding their education, their marriages, their lives, were to be made by the king and parliament. It must have been a considerable blow for James, though not a surprise. Anne Hyde had converted to Catholicism early on in their marriage and though James did not officially follow suit for some years, his preference for Rome was widely known. It was imperative that Mary and Anne would be raised as good English Protestants and their removal from St James's would keep them safe from the perceived dangers of their father's popery. Their religious education was taken seriously, and it had a profound effect on both of the princesses, but especially on Anne. Anne was of an impressionable temperament and was easily guided by those she admired. She was told as a child that Catholicism was sinful and wicked, and for the rest of her life she believed this with all her heart.

In the nursery the princesses and the other children will have been educated together, though this consisted of very little academic study. When, in 1664, Margaret Cavendish wrote *Sociable Letters* (a series of fictional letters from a woman to a female friend) of the deplorable state of women's education, she was referring to just the kind of education these daughters would have received in the royal nursery. She wrote that 'their Education is onely to Dance, Sing, and Fiddle, to write Complemental Letters, to read Romances, to speak some Language that is not their Native'. She lamented that this was 'an Education of the Body, and not of the Mind, and shews that their Parents take more care of their Feet than their Head, more of their Words than their Reason, more of their Musick than their Virtue, more of their Beauty than their Honesty'. Indeed, reason, virtue and honesty were not qualities which were highly prized at the court of Charles II, and Cavendish's assertion that this education would make 'the Body a Courtier, and the Mind a Clown, and oftentimes it makes their Body a Baud, and their Mind a Courtesan' would have described most of the most prominent courtiers.[1]

This is also an accurate account of the education that the princesses and their playmates received. They spoke flawless French, and they had a full-time dancing master, Monsieur Gohory, who was employed to teach not only the princesses, but also Maria. When Maria arrived at court she will have been expected to take part in balls, and perhaps even in masques, though there are no records of her participating in any theatrical entertainments. Being an Italian convent girl she will have been completely unfamiliar with English dances, so a tutor will have been a necessity. But his name features in her account books up to 1682 (indeed, he may well have continued with her after this point, but no other account books survive for the ducal household), which suggests that she had some partiality for dancing.

The princesses received drawing lessons from the renowned miniaturist Richard Gibson, who also served Charles II as his court dwarf, a role he had previously held for both Charles I and Oliver Cromwell. Gibson's associations with both the monarchy and the republic remarkably do not seem to have been held against him by either faction, and he clearly had an aptitude for survival. He became especially close to Princess Mary, and when she left England to be married he went with her, only returning to England in her royal train in 1689. Letters from Mary to her great friend Frances Apsley often refer to Gibson's imminent arrival, and suggest that he acted as a go-between with their letters.

Though their English reading and writing skills remained appalling throughout their lives, the princesses were both prolific letter writers and used this medium to carry out their passionate friendship with Frances Apsley (who was lady-in-waiting first to their mother and then to Maria). Many of these letters survive, as first Mary, and then in later years Anne, took up the pen. Looking at the letters we can see some hints of a literary education: Mary and Frances address each other as Clorin (Mary) and Aurelia (Frances); and Anne was Ziphares to Frances's Semandra. Perhaps they had read the pastoral poetry which had been so popular for the previous century, or perhaps they were emulating the great Katherine Philips – 'the matchless Orinda' – who had only died in 1664, and whose Society of Friendship was made up of friends and poets all of whom had pseudonyms taken from French pastoral romances. Or maybe they had more direct sources in plays by Dryden (*An Evening's Love*) and Massinger (*The Maid of Honour*), both of which have characters called Clorin and Aurelia and which the princesses very likely would have seen. The Dryden play is certainly a strong contender for their inspiration. It was first performed for Charles II in 1668 – which Pepys saw and reported that he did 'not like it, it being very smutty' – and was often played at court.[2] Mary was only a child, but no plays, however 'smutty', were off limits to the children of the court, and both she and Frances will certainly have attended these performances.

Likewise, Ziphares and Semandra were taken from a play by Nathaniel Lee, called *Mithridates* (written in 1678), which the young princesses and Apsley acted in (in these roles) at court in London, and Anne would perform in it on several other occasions. It is a play of forbidden love in which Ziphares falls in love with the daughter of his master, Semandra. Anne had specifically charged her elocution teacher (and famous actress), Mary Betterton, to help them with their roles. One performance may have taken place at the home of Henry Bennet, Earl of Arlington, where one of the viewers, potentially even one of the participants, will have been his ten-year-old daughter Isabella, who the princesses will have known well since she was married to their cousin, Henry Fitzroy, an illegitimate son of Charles II.[3]

What makes the letters between Mary and Frances, and then Anne and Frances, particularly interesting is that they set up a private world in which Mary (as Clorin) or Anne (as Ziphares) is the husband of Frances (as Aurelia and then Semandra). The letters are full of their daily lives and gossip, and they often scold each other for not showing due affection to their wife or husband, speaking of their 'marriage' as though they were a long-suffering couple. Frances was older than both princesses; when these letters began Mary was nine and Frances nineteen, and Anne was around fifteen to Frances's twenty-eight. We might wonder about Frances's reasons for indulging these childhood infatuations, but they offer a fascinating insight into the inner lives and minds of these figures as children and young women. Mary's friendship with Apsley gradually shifted away from this romantic discourse, but for Anne this was more formative. The pastoral play allowed her to have a friendship of equals, where she was not a princess to be treated differently. It was the first of four significant and passionate friendships for Anne. Next was her Lady of the Bedchamber, Mary Cornwallis, who would be supplanted by Sarah Jennings, the beautiful, streetwise girl whom Anne looked up to from their days in the nursery. Sarah was her great passion, and in Anne's transition to queen the relationship was preserved by the nicknames of Mrs Freeman and Mrs Morley. But Sarah, too, would be supplanted, by her cousin, Abigail Masham.[4]

❖

From her earliest days in England, Maria put much time and energy into establishing a relationship with her stepdaughters; reports show that she was often with them and that she delighted in their company. The Contessa Lucrezia Vezzani Pratoneri wrote that she observed 'the most cordial mutual affection between the Princesses and the Duchess – they are always together' and that 'the Duchess amuses herself with the Princesses, whose conversation is very pleasing to her'.[5] But her interest in them went beyond friendship. She took her role as stepmother seriously. Their mother having died when they were so young, Maria was determined to fill the gap left behind as best she could.

It was far too late to rectify their virtually non-existent educations – even if she had been allowed to play any part in them – but Maria quickly observed the talents they did possess. Where the princesses excelled was in all things musical. Anne in particular had a wonderful singing, and also speaking, voice, and Charles employed Mary Betterton, who also taught Maria, to 'instruct [them] in elocution', which she did from 1674.[6] Both princesses were beautiful dancers, and many hours were spent with dancing tutors developing their talents. A great deal of attention was also paid to Anne's guitar and harpsichord practice, which she developed under the stern discipline of her music master. Maria became a great supporter of those talents, and a court masque, in which they would take the leading roles, was the perfect environment to show them off. She set about commissioning one. This was also the perfect moment to cement her position at court, and she did so using its own particular language.

Though it had its roots in Italy and in France, the court masque became a peculiarly English genre of entertainment, in which members of the nobility and royal family, often alongside professional singers, dancers and musicians, would present a musical spectacle to the rest of the court. The theme was always based around the glory of the monarch and the greatness of their reign, usually involving the crown triumphing over evil and bringing peace and plenty to the realm. The masque reached its peak during the reign of Charles I, when the entertainments became increasingly lavish, opulent, dramatic and excessive in praise of his virtues, not to mention expensive: the equivalent of millions of pounds in today's money could be spent on a single evening. The masque became a symbol for the decadence of Charles I's court, and his increasingly problematic remove from his parliament and people. It is perhaps unsurprising that Charles II was tentative about continuing this tradition after his restoration.

In commissioning a masque Maria was reinvigorating English court traditions, traditions which foregrounded the kind of splendour and soft power with which she had been so familiar at the Modenese court, and this English masque would have some Italian flair. Its form closely resembled entertainments performed at the weddings and festivities of the Italian nobility, which would present five spoken plays, each of which was punctuated with musical *intermedii* (interludes). In Maria's masque, too, there were five acts (all performed by members of the court), each of which was rounded off with a singing and dancing number performed by professional singers alongside courtiers.

The first thing Maria had to do was select a writer. The obvious choice was John Dryden; as poet laureate, his duties would have included producing court entertainments, but one member of the court had other ideas. John Wilmot, Earl of Rochester, was involved in a feud with Dryden and saw this as a good opportunity to humiliate him. He suggested the writer John Crowne. Crowne was an unlikely choice: he had written some comedies, but he had never tried his hand at anything of this scale. But Rochester had no difficulty in persuading the Duchess of York that Crowne was her man. Crowne reports in his preface to the masque that he 'was invaded, on the sudden by a Powerful Command, to prepare an Entertainment for the Court'.[7] Perhaps Maria liked the idea of giving a slightly obscure writer the opportunity to show what he could do.

The next question was the subject of the masque, but Maria had little hand in this. Crowne wrote that he was given 'but some few hours' to choose it and Charles II, no doubt with a mischievous twinkle in his eye, suggested the story of Callisto, taken from Book II of Ovid's *Metamorphoses*. Crowne had recently had some success with his *Andromache* at the Dorset Garden Theatre; another classical tale shouldn't be a problem. The Royal Collection was full of visual representations of this myth. Perhaps Charles looked around him and saw a tapestry, based on the 'Diana and Callisto' from Titian's *Poesie*, that his father (having seen the original in Spain in the 1620s and had Rubens make copies) had commissioned from Francis Cleyn at the royal tapestry workshop at Mortlake.[8] Or maybe the conversation took place in his closet at Whitehall, where he had hung a representation of the myth by Johann Rottenhammer.

Ovid's story is representative of the kinds of tales found in his *Metamorphoses*, in telling of mortals who get mixed up with the gods and the terrible consequences. Jupiter sees Callisto, one of Diana's nymphs, and is overwhelmed by her beauty. One day, seeing her alone, he takes the form of Diana and lures her to a quiet part of the wood where he rapes her. She is cast out from Diana's huntresses and gives birth to a son, incurring the wrath of Juno, who then transforms her into a bear. Some years later Callisto's grown-up son is out hunting, and she becomes his target. Jupiter saves her by turning both mother and child into stars, the constellations of the Great and Little Bears.

It would be difficult to think of a less appropriate story for a court masque in which two of the leading roles were to be taken by the eleven-year-old Princess Mary and the eight-year-old Princess Anne. Charles must have been greatly amused. Seeing his problem, Crowne rewrote Ovid and made the story more appropriate for the setting and cast. Jupiter's seduction is unsuccessful, and the masque becomes concerned with virginity and purity overcoming all. But he wrote of his difficulties in the published work: in his dedication 'To the Reader' he compared the writing process to 'the invention of the Philosopher's Stone' but claimed that his task had been 'a difficulty greater' than even that.[9] The irony of his 'purifying' the story was that it was performed in an environment which was anything but pure and virginal, and used a cast full of mistresses and illegitimate children. A closer look at the cast and the narrative gives us an insight into the court at this time: we see sexual licentiousness, female friendships, the unstable return to a majesty from the past, and evidence of England's economy becoming increasingly fuelled by colonialism and slavery.

Calisto was an extravagant production on a scale big enough to rival the masques of any of the previous Stuart monarchs, and it entirely dominated the court for a full six months. Rehearsals were at least three times a week – 'on saterday nights tusedy nights and Thursday nights and ... at other tymes' – and more than a hundred courtiers were involved in the production, each of whom had individually made costumes, some run up at their own expense, some at the expense of the crown.[10] Dancing masters were employed to help with the choreography, including one Monsieur St André, a famous Parisian ballet choreographer employed by Charles II. Chapel singers were taken from their other duties to be part of the production, actors were brought in from the theatres and a fifty-three-man orchestra was put together – in part from the King's own musicians – made up of violins, guitars, trumpets and harpsichords.

Christopher Wren was employed to add extra galleries to the theatre for seating, and to extend the stage into the pit to allow for more players to appear together. The pit was further reduced by the placement of the musicians there, much as we have in theatres today.[11] The painter Robert Streeter was employed to design the set, a representation of Somerset House and the Thames, which could transform into a pastoral woodland, and which was the most spectacular that had yet been attempted at Charles II's court. Maria was making a bold statement about the kind of role she intended to play as Duchess of York.

5

The Masque of Calisto

22 FEBRUARY 1675
THE HALL THEATRE, WHITEHALL PALACE, LONDON

The evening has just drawn in. The backstage of the Hall Theatre at Whitehall Palace is bustling with excitement and activity. Everywhere courtiers and actors are in various states of dress and undress as they don their elaborate costumes and adorn their hair and faces with powders and jewels. It is tightly packed as some 170 people crowd together in the small room. Excited chatter merges with the sound of the musicians tuning their instruments. The two princesses, Mary and Anne, are merrily pulled and prodded by their eight dressers, giggling with nervous excitement; Sarah Jennings (maid of honour to Maria, Duchess of York) stands elegantly while two ladies place the finishing touches of jewels and ribbons on her shimmering silk and taffeta garments, transforming her into the god Mercury; in the corner sits the chaste Margaret Blagge (maid of honour to the queen, fittingly playing the virgin goddess Diana), a picture of piety, reading a book of devotions; James Scott, Duke of Monmouth, his hair full of elaborate plumage, practises his moves; the famous singer Arabella Hunt begins her vocal warm-ups.

In the auditorium Maria sits beside James, the queen and the king, who has a spaniel on each knee. She has a prime view of the stage before her. The broad proscenium arch is lit from below with flickering candles, catching the shadows of the curtain which softly billows as the players scurry around behind it. She looks around the room, which is gradually filling with chattering courtiers, all looking forward to the evening's entertainment. Among the faces in the crowd may even have been a young Anne Killigrew, attending one of her first court entertainments. Maria shares the nervousness of the players waiting in the wings. After all, this evening's entertainment is her idea. For the last six months the cast have been frantically rehearsing their parts. And then, suddenly, a whispered hush fills the room. The curtain rises. The scene is set. The play begins.

The curtain draws back to reveal Moll Davis, a famous actress and former mistress of Charles II, leaning against an urn. She is the River Thames. Six figures surround her: two of the queen's ladies-in-waiting, playing her attendant nymphs (Peace and Plenty), and four professional singers, representing the four parts of the world (Asia, America, Europe, Africa). They stand in perfect stillness within an impressive recreation of Somerset House. Then they come to life to perform the prologue in which the greatness of London, and of England, is celebrated. Those courtiers who were alive to see the heyday of the court masque under Henrietta Maria and Charles I must have felt transported back in time as they watched the thinly veiled celebration of the glory of monarchy: problems arise but are quickly solved by the greatness of England and its king. But though it harks back to earlier days, this masque is decidedly of its time, and in it we can see much of the contemporary Stuart court.

The four continents of the world each in turn offer the Thames their greatest gifts: Europe offers their 'noblest Arts', Asia gives exclusive access to their 'jewels', America gives their gold and Africa, troublingly, promises 'Thou for thy Slaves, shalt have these Scorched Sons of mine'.[1] Each of these gifts were already key parts of England's identity: Europe's 'noble Arts' had been actively collected by the royal family and the court for generations, and its treasures adorned the walls of the great houses and palaces, but the other three continents need a little more scrutiny.

When Charles married Caterina de Braganza, she brought with her the territories of Goa and Bombay. Charles soon gifted Bombay to the East India Company and extended their power through a series of charters granting them the right to mint money, take part in wars and to 'acquire' new territories. One of the consequences was increased trade with China and other Eastern countries. The reference to jewels in *Calisto* may be an allusion to the increase in precious stones being sent to England by the East India Company. The Royal Society – of which both Charles and James were such avid supporters – were keen to acquire gems in order to study their mineral properties.

As well as Bombay and Goa, Caterina's dowry gifted several African colonies. They added to England's already widespread colonial expansions, particularly on the West African coast and the Americas, where they ran numerous sugar plantations. When in *Calisto* Africa offers its people as slaves, it is in reference to the active part that England – and Charles and James specifically – were playing in the expansion of the slave trade at this time. On his restoration, Charles had set up the Royal Africa Company with merchants in the City of London, and made his brother, James, the governor. When James became king, he appointed Edward Colston as his deputy governor. Initially the company aimed to exploit the gold mines found along the coast, particularly around Guinea, but this soon changed, and the company became one of the most brutal, and certainly the most prolific, traders of slaves. The Royal African Company was responsible for sending more African slaves to America than any other company over the entire course of the transatlantic slave trade. By the 1680s, the company was so established that they were sending 5,000 slaves a year to England's extensive Caribbean and American colonies. James was so much a part of this that many of the slaves were branded with the letters 'DoY' to avoid any doubt about who they 'belonged' to. The profits were enormous, the price irreparable.

As well as references to empire and trade, we find those directed closer to home. In the attempted seduction of Callisto by Jupiter disguised as Diana we see a reference to a recent scandal at the court. The *Memoirs of Grammont*, an account of the life of Count Grammont at the court of Charles II, written by his brother-in-law, Anthony Hamilton (a relative by marriage, too, of Sarah Jennings), tells us how Mrs Hobart had recently fled the court under a cloud, having attempted to seduce one of the maids of honour in Maria's household. Mrs Hobart observed that the maid was susceptible to flattery and, as she prepared a bath for her, told her how much more beautiful, charming and graceful she was than her fellow maid, 'that silly creature Jennings'. But the same Sarah Jennings was just next door, had heard all and was seething with fury. The memoirs tell us that 'it was not long before the report … spread through the whole court'; Sarah got her own back. In the masque the character of Jupiter was played by Lady Henrietta Wentworth, newly at court, and the cross-dressing scene becomes one of female seduction. The titillation of this scene for the court is complicated by the fact that Henrietta, as the seductor, Jupiter, was only thirteen, and Princess Mary, as the preyed-upon nymph, only eleven. But there was little time for childhood at the court of Charles II; several of the girls they grew up with were already married by their ages (such as Isabella Bennet), and others were being groomed as mistresses.

The Hobart affair was one of several scandals of the time, and just a few months after this performance one of the queen's maids of honour had to go to France in disgrace, having had a miscarriage while dancing at a court ball; the father of the child was most likely James. In fact, there were so many scandals in the 1670s that Mrs Jennings, mother of Maria's maid of honour, Sarah, tried to remove her from the court saying that 'two of the maids had had great bellies att Court, and she would not leave her child to have a third'.[2]

The masque is concerned with the triumph of chastity over sexual licentiousness, and there are many jokes at the expense of the latter. Any audience member who heard Mercury cry, 'Oh! no one can resist a King' would have tittered, and when Jupiter is accused of neglecting his duties in favour of pursuing women, they might have cast a glance towards their merry monarch.[3] When Juno is forced to tolerate her husband's latest conquest in her train, it would have been hard not to look over at Caterina, who lost a lengthy battle to have Charles's infamous mistress, Barbara Villiers, Duchess of Cleveland, removed from her household. Maria was in a similar predicament to Caterina in there being daily proof of her husband's infidelities among her own ladies-in-waiting. Juno cries to the audience in a soliloquy:

> My Blood grows hot! and must I then be us'd
> For ever thus? for ever thus abus'd?
> Must every trifling Nymph, that looks but fair,
> Entice from my Embrace my *Jupiter*?
> . . .
> But we poor Wives endure the greatest shame.[4]

We do not know what role Maria played in the casting of the production, but it was Anne Fitzroy, Barbara Villiers's daughter by Charles II, who was made to stand and deliver this monologue, which was so clearly aimed at her mother. A point was scored for wronged royal women.[5]

But it wasn't just the mistresses and the king who were the target of the masque's jokes: the so-called 'court wits' were implicated, too. The 'wits' were, on the whole, rakish libertines who were close to the king, and who were playwrights and poets. In 1671 two notorious wits, Charles Sedley and Charles Sackville, had printed a compilation of poems by their cronies, called *The New Academy of Compliments*, which detailed how to court and seduce beautiful young women. The collection was so popular it was already in its third print run by the time *Calisto* was performed. Dissemblance, flattery and disguise were the favoured strategies. These tactics are used in Crowne's masque, too, though they do not work, and the figures who attempt them are subjected to scornful derision. In counselling against libertinism, the whole masque exposes the corruption of the groups of men closest to Charles. Unsurprisingly, Crowne lost the recently gained support of Rochester – one of the seediest of the wits – after this public display.

The masque was a great success, and through it we can see Maria starting to acclimatise to her life in England. On 19 August we read of a picnic she attended at the Duchess of Monmouth's house, with the princesses: 'they din'd in fresco abroad in ye fields under trees, & spent the afternoon in gentle recreations, as cards, walking & ye like, but after supper her R[oyal] H[ighness] and ye company diverted ymselves with dancing & made it pretty late before they came home.'[6] And in an image painted by Simon Verelst from 1675, we see her every bit the confident Duchess of York, as she stands tall and proud in her riding gear. But this is not just any outfit: Maria wears men's clothes. And they are not just any man's clothes, but the suit James wore on the day he first met her at Dover, which is now preserved at the Victoria and Albert Museum in London. Considering that James was a tall man, and powerfully built, and Maria comparatively diminutive, it seems likely that she had her own version of the coat made to match him. James adored this painting of Maria, and had it hung in his private bedchamber.

Throughout the process of staging *Calisto*, Maria had attended rehearsals and helped with its development, right up until she gave birth to her first child – the 'creature' she had written to her brother about in August. The production was delayed so that she could attend after her recovery. Maria was always closely watched and reported on, especially regarding her pregnancies, and we have the following account of the birth. On the evening of 9 January, Maria played ombre (an immensely popular, fast-paced, gambling card game) until midnight, with the Duchess of Monmouth and she 'supped and slept well'. On the morning of the 10th, she heard two masses, dined with the princesses, 'and after dinner gave birth to a fine Princess'.[7] Her labour was fast, and the baby was born after three hours. Among the witnesses were the king and queen, who gave his brother a warm embrace. It was not the hoped-for boy – as

James wrote to his nephew, William of Orange, 'it is but a daughter, but God be praised, they are both very well' – but the birth of a healthy child meant that Maria could have children, and that was enough for now.[8] They named her Catherine Laura – Catherine after the queen, and Laura after Maria's mother.

Being a devout young woman, Maria called for one of her priests and had the child baptised in her room as a Catholic. When Charles came to visit her to give her his good wishes, she told him what she had done. He smiled and patted her hand. That was all very well, he said, but the child would be raised in the English Church. She would be baptised again, as a Protestant. This christening took place – very publicly – soon after in the Chapel Royal. Princesses Mary and Anne, and the Duke and Duchess of Monmouth were godparents.

What would have become clear to Maria at this moment was that her children were not just her children, they were the children of the crown. She might give birth to them, but she had no say in their upbringing, especially in matters of religion. The children were allowed to live at St James's Palace with their parents so long as there was no attempt to interfere with their schooling, especially in matters of religion.

Even though the Anglican christening had been made a public affair, and the child had been a girl and therefore only fourth in line to the throne (after James, Mary and Anne), anti-Catholic hatred was never far away. In the winter a man who called himself Lucanzy came forward declaring that he had been subjected to a violent attack from Maria's own confessor, a French Jesuit named Père St Germain. He claimed he had been threatened into publicly recanting his religion and returning to Catholicism. A reward of £200 was offered for Father St Germain 'dead or alive'. This was the precursor to a far greater and more sinister plot, which would come to change Maria and James's lives for the worse.

But for now, life continued as before, with Maria throwing herself into the life of the court, and into her role as stepmother and now mother. Maria wrote to her brother at the beginning of May that she had no time to write more than to say she was well as 'today the Princesses are performing a Comedy with other young ladies with dancing and music, and so I am very busy'.[9] The reference to 'other young ladies' tells us, too, that she was already surrounding herself with the young women of the court – perhaps these ladies were some of her maids, like Sarah Jennings.

She was also straight back into her role as breeder of heirs; she may have just given birth to a healthy child but it was only a girl, and she would need a son before she could say she had truly done her duty. She wrote to her brother again in June telling him that the rumours he had heard of her being pregnant again were no longer true; after six or seven weeks, she had lost the child, she had '*disperdere*', 'dispersed'.[10] She wrote that she was almost recovered, but rather tired. And no wonder; her body was so much a topic of public speculation that at not even two months pregnant they were writing of her hopes. That he wrote to her again of rumours is clear from a letter she sent to Francesco dated 15 August, saying that she had gone to Windsor for the summer since she had 'no suspicions' of being pregnant.[11]

By October, she was pregnant again, but tragedy struck. Maria wrote to Francesco apologising for not having written to him recently. She explains:

> for a long time I have been very much afflicted by the death of my dear daughter, and then for having miscarried three days after her death. Everyone says, and I believe it, that the affliction I had from this [the death of her daughter] was the cause of my miscarriage, but praise be to God, one must conform in all things to his holy will, one cannot live in this world without suffering.[12]

Catherine Laura had died, and the grief had caused a miscarriage. This had all happened just a week after Maria's seventeenth birthday. At this young age she had already had four pregnancies and had lost her only child.

The extent to which life was expected to go on is borne out in another letter, from December, which tells of a recent ball she had been to in celebration of Queen Caterina's birthday – which was 'really very beautiful' – and that she had been going often to the 'comedia', and playing cards, though this latter activity was rather in the absence of anything else to do since the weather had turned so cold that they were housebound.[13]

But a diversion was on the way. In the same letter Maria wrote: 'I have no news to give you except that it is said here that Duchess Mazarini is to come, whether it is true, I do not know.'[14] The Duchess of Mazarin was the scandalous Hortense Mancini, Maria's mother's cousin, who had travelled through Europe to escape her brutal husband. Maria's lack of certainty of her cousin's movements would not last long: Hortense arrived the following day.

6

THE DUCHESS OF MAZARIN

Ortensia Mancini was born on 6 June 1646 in Rome, to Girolama Mazzarini (sister of Cardinal Mazarin) and Lorenzo Mancini (a Roman baron). She and her sisters were raised with some education, partly from intermittent periods spent in convents (a habit several of them would continue throughout their lives, though not always by choice) and partly from exploring the delights of their father's extensive library. Lorenzo was well educated, if a little unusual in his intellectual tastes. Along with the more traditional works of Tasso and Ariosto, among his collection were books on astrology and necromancy, and the children were given free rein to sample whatever they chose. Ortensia would inherit her father's interest in the dark arts and would later shock a dear friend by speaking of Fontenelle's *Entretiens sur la pluralité des mondes* (*Conversations on the Plurality of Worlds*) over the card table, and uttering phrases of magic and the occult. But as a child her favourite books were epic Italian romances. Little is known about her childhood, though it seems to have been a relatively happy one. But when her father died in 1650, she, with her sisters Marie, Olympe and Marianne, and their Martinozzi cousins, Laura (Maria's mother) and Anna-Maria, left Rome for Paris to join their uncle and to be raised alongside the Dauphins, the Dauphines and the high aristocracy of the French court. They were six of the *Mazarinettes*, the seven famously beautiful nieces of Cardinal Mazarin, and he had decided the time had come for them to fulfil their destinies. They were his legacy, and his aim was to arrange advantageous marriages, which would raise the Mazarin name and join it with the great ruling families of Europe.

The ship that met them in Rome must have been an extraordinary sight. It was custom-built in Genoa according to the specifications of Mazarin, who was determined that his family should travel in style. Not only was this fitting for the relations of the first minister of France, but he needed them to get used to the luxury of their new lives as quickly as possible. The living quarters of the ship were furnished with expensive furniture, chairs richly upholstered with embroideries, and all around were curtains and cushions of exquisite crimson fabrics. Ortensia would later reflect on the sight in her memoirs, describing the ship as a 'moveable house'.[1] She wrote that 'it would take too much time to portray all its beauty, its order, its riches, and its magnificence. Suffice it to say that we were treated like queens … throughout our voyage … the tables of sovereigns are not served with more pomp and brilliance than was ours four times a day.'[2] Such comforts even extended to the speed of their travel: the galley slaves, who were at all times hidden away from view at the bottom of the ship, were ordered to row particularly slowly to allow for a smooth and stately journey. On the decks above, the family began to shed their Italian customs and to become French; Ortensia became Hortense.

When they arrived at Marseille one week later, their destination was not the court in Paris. They would have another eight months of education before they were ready to be presented to the Sun King. Their teacher would be the seventh *Mazarinette*, Laure-Victoire Mancini, Hortense's sister, who was now the Duchess of Mercœur. She had made exactly the kind of marriage that Mazarin desired for all his nieces: her husband was Louis de Bourbon, the grandson of Henri IV.[3] Laure and Louis's grand estate was in Auvergne, conveniently halfway between Marseille and Paris, though nearly 300 miles away from either. There the Italian family learned how to be French: how to dress, how to speak, how to greet guests (alarmingly for them, this was to be done with a kiss), and the various rituals involved in day-to-day life at the court.[4] Their arrival in France was acknowledged with sumptuous gifts of silver candlesticks and decadent sugared treats. Over the course of these many months, it started to dawn on the young Martinozzis and Mancinis just how important their uncle must be.

When they finally arrived in Paris in February 1654, their first stop was the Mazarin Palace, which would be their new home. Though the Cardinal had tried to get them ready for their new lives, nothing could have prepared them for the splendour they found there. The building was enormous and inside the walls were covered in frescos and masterpieces painted by some of the greatest artists of the Renaissance and Baroque: works by Raphael, Titian, Caravaggio, Mantegna, Leonardo, Giorgione and Carracci were part of a collection of nearly 900 paintings, and the halls and gardens were full of antique Roman statues (some of which had been bought in the Commonwealth Sale after the execution of Charles I). Every room was full of expensive furniture and the walls were covered in large mirrors and ornate tapestries. They can hardly have had time to take in their new surroundings before they were whisked off in a carriage to the only slightly more opulent Louvre Palace to be presented to the King and Queen Regent, Louis XIV, and his mother, Anna of Austria. Within weeks of their arrival Mazarin's mission had begun: Anne-Marie Martinozzi was married to Armand de Conti, a Bourbon relative of the king. The other nieces must have wondered who would be in store for them, and while Hortense still had some years before it was her turn, Laura was married to Alfonso d'Este of Modena the following year.

Hortense's early years at court were formative ones in terms of her character and tastes. At the French court she spent her days moving in and out of the various salons, listening to witty and intellectual conversations, and attending concerts, plays and ballets. This life was briefly interrupted by a period of more formal education when she was sent to accompany her sister Marie to the Convent of the Visitation in Faubourg Saint-Jacques, as their French needed a little more work. They were away for eighteen months of reflection and learning. The convent in France was somewhere between a finishing school and a correction centre for wayward daughters. At the convent, the sisters were subjected to a more rigorous education than they had perhaps been used to, and their days were spent studying literature, the Bible, philosophy and art. The education the Mancini sisters received there may not have been unlike the one Maria enjoyed in the convent of the same order in Modena. But unlike Maria, Hortense does not at this point seem to have been seriously intellectually inclined, though she was still just a child. When her younger sister, Marianne, joined them she wrote to their uncle that Hortense 'thinks only of her pleasure' in contrast to their sister Marie, who spent hours 'reading … Plutarch, Seneca, and philosophy'.[5]

Those eighteen months must have felt long to Hortense, who loved nothing more than lively company, but the sisters were finally able to leave the convent and her life at the French court resumed in its routines of singing and dancing and playing instruments (she was particularly adept at the guitar). Hortense was popular at court, though all knew the ambitions her uncle had for her. She took part in festivities and entertainments; one ballet she danced at was Molière's *Alcidiae*, which was written for the king to show off his balletic abilities.[6] It may have been at some such event that, in 1659, Hortense caught the eye of the exiled Charles II of England. He was instantly captivated with her and asked for her hand in marriage, but of all his nieces Mazarin had highest hopes for his favourite, Hortense. She was, after all, only thirteen years old, and she could, he felt, do better than an impoverished king without a crown, or even a country. Though the Restoration was only months away, Charles's prospects did not at this point seem promising. Mazarin wrote that 'The King of England has offered to marry my niece Hortense … but I replied that he was paying me too great an honour.'[7] When Charles reclaimed his throne in May 1660, the Cardinal regretted passing up this chance for Mazarins to become heirs to the English crown, but it was too late. Charles needed to make a diplomatic match among the royal families of Europe and even the offer of 5 million livres (around £17,000,000 in today's money) was not enough to tempt him; Hortense was, after all, from an 'upstart', power-grabbing family, who were aristocratic, but not royal, and Charles understood his new responsibilities as monarch. When Charles did marry, he was unlikely to have regretted the loss of the Cardinal's money: Caterina de Braganza's dowry was £500,000 (around £56,000,000 in today's money) as well as the profitable lands of Bombay and Tangiers, and the promise of free trade with all of Portugal's many colonies.

In 1661 Cardinal Mazarin was on his deathbed, and he was determined to arrange a marriage for Hortense before he died. He had made her heir to his great fortune and art collection, as well as to his dukedom, and it was imperative that it fell into the right hands. His choice was Armand Charles de La Porte de La Meilleraye, the son of Cardinal Richelieu's cousin, Charles de la Porte, who had been a great man. Richelieu had written that Charles was 'un des hommes du plus grand mérite ... de son temps' ('one of the men of the greatest merit ... of his time'). His military career and advantageous marriages had made him a wealthy and respected man, but his son, Armand, showed far less promise. Like Maria, Hortense was just fourteen, and, like Maria, she had no say over her future.

Armand was seventeen years older than Hortense and had been desperately in love with her since she was just nine and he was twenty-four. He had watched her dancing at court balls, and seen her glitter among the French nobility, and was determined to have her. Mazarin may have been fooled into thinking that Armand took after his father more than he did, and the joining of great wealth with great wealth may have made sense to a dying man who cared more about legacy than happiness, but anyone who had met the betrothed couple would have instantly seen how disastrous a marriage it would be.

Armand was a possessive, puritanical, reclusive, jealous man. Hortense was open, fun-loving, vivacious, witty, spirited, and loved nothing more than to be in company. Initially the couple lived at the great Mazarin Palace, and Hortense began her married life there full of hope. She opened the house up for parties, concerts, plays and banquets – in an early version of her later salons – and she began to support other women with literary ambitions, acting as a patron to Marie-Catherine de Villedieu. The poet's gratitude is borne out in her dedication of her first collection, *Recueil de poésies de Mademoiselle Desjardins* (1662), to the Duchess of Mazarin, who she says was responsible for 'the first productions of [her] genius'.[8] Hortense settled into her new role and prepared herself for a happy life.

But Armand was not of the same mind. He hated being in company, and perhaps even more than this he hated the sight of his beautiful, vivacious wife happy in company. The marriage deteriorated quickly. She later wrote that 'as soon as he knew I was happy in some place he would make me leave it'.[9] Fiercely jealous, Armand took her away to their various country estates. His obsession with purity led him to deface some of the most remarkable pieces in Cardinal Mazarin's great art collection: paintings and sculptures of nude gods and goddesses deemed lewd and irreligious were all but destroyed. It was said that he forbade the female servants from milking cows in case the act incited them to lustful thoughts, and that he made sure of their never finding suitors by maiming them, knocking out their front teeth. To Hortense his cruelty was hardly less severe: he isolated her from her friends, he sacked any servant she appeared to favour, he prevented her from using the carriage and laughed in her face when she asked to use it. Hortense's *Memoirs* tell of his 'implacable hatred for anyone who loved me, and whom I loved'.[10] Every evening before bed he made her hand over her jewels for fear that she would take them in the night and use them in order to leave him. All the while he was mismanaging the Cardinal's legacy and estates; the once great fortune was gradually dwindling.

Hortense lived in this way for seven long years and bore four healthy children during this time. But finally, on 13 June 1668, she ran away from her tyrannical husband and her young children, who she would not see again for at least a decade, and fled, with her brother, Philippe, to her sister Marie in Colonna. Marie's marriage to the Prince of Colonna was scarcely happier than Hortense's, and she, too, would leave her husband, in fear of her life, with Hortense in 1672. Though Louis XIV declared himself Hortense's protector, this meant little in practice. He did not want to get too far on the wrong side of the wealthy and powerful Armand. Hortense travelled from place to place, virtually penniless, and often in disguise for fear of being kidnapped: her husband would stop at nothing to get her back, and she relied on the kindness of old friends and strangers for protection.

The closest Hortense came to security was during the short years she spent in Chambéry at the Savoy court, where the Duke, Charles Emmanuel II (another former suitor for her hand), took her into his protection. As his mistress, she lived well and soon began to live the life she had wanted in Paris. She began a salon, which was frequented by the greatest intellectuals, writers, thinkers and musicians, of Savoy. At last she had found her place in the world, safe from her husband's clutches. It was during these years that she again met the daughter of her dear childhood companion and cousin, Laura Martinozzi. When she had last seen Maria she had been a mere baby, and Hortense was impressed by the young woman she saw before her. Maria was travelling across Europe to take her place as Duchess of York at the English court, and she stopped at Chambéry on her way.

When the Duke of Savoy died on 12 June 1675, Hortense was once again plunged into precarity. The long-suffering Duchess of Savoy wasted no time in ridding the court of her rival, and even wrote to Armand to tell him that he could come and claim his wife whenever he chose – she would not protect her. Hortense had to get out, but there was nowhere to go, and she had no money. Yet fortune smiled upon her once more, this time in the form of an English courtier called Ralph Montagu. Montagu was acting as the ambassador to France at the time, and as soon as he heard of her change of circumstances he went to Chambéry with an offer: an invitation to the court in London.

❖

For the past four years Louise de Kéroualle, Duchess of Portsmouth, had been the *maîtresse en titre* of Charles II. She had been maid of honour to his most beloved sister, Henriette – known affectionately as Minette – and had come to England after her mistress's tragic death in 1670. Minette was twenty-six when she died, and Charles never recovered from the loss of his sister. Louise was a source of comfort to him in his grief. But she had the interests of France at heart and the ear of the king at her disposal and was deeply unpopular at the English court. One particular faction – led by George Villiers, Duke of Buckingham, and Henry Bennet, Lord Arlington – wanted nothing more than to see her fall from favour, and greedily sought the toppling of her influence. In their eyes, the answer was simple: Charles needed a new mistress, one who was anti-French and who would represent their own interests. It seemed to them that providence had smiled on their cause when the Duke of Savoy died. It gave them Hortense Mancini. It made perfect sense: Charles had loved her enough to want to marry her when they had last met, and though that was fifteen years ago, time had not diminished her beauty or her charm. Plus, Louis XIV's lack of support might easily turn Hortense against him and, by extension, France. Unlike Louise de Kéroualle, she was not French by blood, but Italian, and proud of it; she never lost her Roman accent. For Hortense, becoming Charles II's mistress was less of a priority, but London's great appeal was its distance from France and surely, she thought, she would find a welcome reception at the English court with her young relative, Maria. It was agreed, though Montagu felt it prudent to make the trip seem like her idea. She was to go under the guise of a burning desire to see the daughter of her much beloved cousin, and to make her own way there.

Hortense left Chambéry 'on horseback and wearing a plumed hat, and a peruke' and was accompanied by twenty horsemen, a groom, four valets, two maids (one of which was her loyal companion, Nanon) and a black boy, a slave the Duke of Savoy had given her as a gift.[11] Opinion is divided but it is possible that this boy was Mustapha. Hortense owned several slaves who she kept with her as companions – as was fashionable among the wealthy aristocracy of the courts of Europe – but she became particularly close to Mustapha. Reports of him dining at the table with her later shocked the English court, who would never have allowed such an intimacy with one of their servants, let alone one of their slaves.

Their journey was not an easy one. At all costs, Hortense had to avoid entering France, which made for a circuitous route. If she were to enter French territory, she would be in danger of arrest and of being forcibly returned to her husband. But in avoiding France Hortense risked other perils: she had to travel through countries which were being torn apart by wars, and where she had no friends to help her on her way. She went through Germany and Alsace – which were deep in the Franco-Dutch wars that consumed much of Northern Europe – before arriving in Switzerland. Her days were long, but she was an excellent rider and made good progress on horseback. When she looked for rest and sleep, she made do with the shelter of forests. She once again became the 'vrai héroïne de roman' that Madame de Grignon had called her in Marseille some years before, when she was first on the run from her husband, with plenty of spirit but 'point de linge blanc' (no clean clothes).[12]

Far from being worn down by struggle and hardship, Hortense seems to have thrived during this time, though some of her old friends disapproved of her attitude: in November 1675 Sidonia Marquise de Courcelles wrote to her lover that 'what is most strange is that this woman triumphs over all her misfortunes by an excess of folly which has no parallel … she thinks only of enjoying herself'. She wrote that when Hortense arrived to rest in a German village 'she was on horseback, befeathered and bewigged, escorted by twenty men' but that 'she talked of nothing but violins and of hunting parties and everything else that gives pleasure'.[13] Hortense's fortitude in such circumstances is extraordinary, and what becomes clear from such accounts is that nothing could sustain her spirits more than having her liberty.

Sidonia seems to have followed Hortense's progress keenly, for she wrote again that her old friend – who she titled 'The Mazarin' – had 'left Augsburg on her way to Munich in Bavaria'. Her intended destination was Brill, where she would take a boat to England. She knew that one of her husband's cronies awaited her there, ready to kidnap her and take her back to France, but this was her best chance. She boldly carried on and, dressed as a man in her peruke, successfully boarded a ship without being discovered. How she managed this we can only imagine; from the descriptions we have seen she does not seem to have blended easily into the background. She joked in her memoirs of how little anyone was ever taken in by her disguises.

Hortense arrived in England on 18 December – a little off course – at Sole Bay, Harwich, after a choppy crossing. An eyewitness wrote of the landing of 'a lady with six or seven attendants, who, they say, was related to the Duchess of York'.[14] We can assume then that she arrived with her groom, her valets, her maids and Mustapha. Once she had disembarked, she again took to horseback. Ralph Montagu met her shortly before she entered London and escorted her to the home of his sister, Lady Elizabeth Harvey, in Covent Garden, where Hortense was initially to stay. She declared that she wished to remain incognito, as she was exhausted from her trip, but the sight of the beautiful duchess and her entourage, bedraggled and filthy from their long journey, was too extraordinary a sight to allow her arrival to remain a secret for long. After a matter of hours, the courtyard outside the house was thronging with people, all desperate to catch a glimpse of the famous Duchess of Mazarin. For famous she was. After publishing her candid memoirs earlier that year in France, Hortense had become a celebrity, and her infamous reputation preceded her physical arrival. An English translation of her work appeared in 1676, shortly after her arrival, and throughout Europe it went through many reprints. It is easy to see why the memoir was so popular: it reads like a romance novel as much as a memoir. Indeed, her good friend Marie-Catherine de Villedieu, wrote a novel in 1672 called *Memoirs of the Life of Henriette-Sylvie de Molière*, which has much in common with the life of our heroine in its twists and turns of fate, disguises and near misses. Even the initials of the protagonist are the same. Hortense had always enjoyed writing, and she wrote in her memoir that even as a child in France she would 'shut [herself] up alone and write down everything that came into [her] head'.[15] Here she could use her skill to her advantage. These memoirs were primarily written and published to try and garner sympathy for her cause.

Though immediately discovered in England, Hortense's location was not known in France, though speculation was rife. Madame de Sévigné wrote to her daughter on Christmas Day that 'Madam de Mazarin for her part is rambling around the world. It is thought that she is in England.'[16] Hortense had arrived safely and was far from the reaches of her husband. As she allowed herself to breathe a sigh of relief, she must also have wondered what her new life in London would be, and how she would be accepted at court.

❖

From a letter written by Lucrezia Vezzani Pratoneri, we can surmise that the arrival of Maria's cousin was not welcome: Pratoneri wrote,

> I think we shall soon see the Duchess Mazarin in England, which greatly displeases Her Royal Highness, and the Duke also, I believe, but it is not to be prevented; some efforts have been made to hinder her, but she will come.[17]

What these 'efforts' were is not clear, but Pratoneri's next letter suggests that the arrival was not met with quite so much resistance as might have been supposed: 'The Duchess Mazarin has arrived, and now nothing is talked of in the Queen's and Duchess's apartments but the beauty of that lady.'

Whatever reservations they may have had before her arrival, Hortense initially found a home in the apartments of James and Maria, at St James's Palace, and it was not long before she was given her own lodgings. Lady Chaworth writing to Lord Roos said that 'The Duke of York hath bought a new-build house of Lord Windsor in St. James Park and given it to Madame Mazarin to live in as long as she continues there.'[18] To say that it was in St James's Park does not quite signify how close Hortense remained to the York household: the house was in fact attached to the palace.

Maria was right to be wary of the effects of her cousin's arrival. She soon became embroiled in the kinds of court politics that she had assiduously avoided for the last two years. It was well known at court that Hortense had been brought to England by Montagu in the hope that she would displace Louise de Kéroualle as the King's mistress. It was also therefore well known to Louise de Kéroualle. Maria had never liked Louise and ensured that she never spent more time with her than was absolutely necessary; she certainly never called on her. But when Hortense arrived, and familial courtesy demanded that Maria visit her in her rooms, Kéroualle was furious. She complained to Charles that she was not being shown equal respect by his brother's wife and demanded to be satisfied. Charles spoke to James and, knowing the hold Louise had over his brother, James carefully broached the subject with Maria. We can only imagine her response in private, but in public she did her duty, and the next time James went to Kéroualle's apartments, Maria accompanied him. The king was delighted. As far as Maria was concerned this was the end of it, and she attended a ball at court that evening in reasonable spirits.

But word of Maria's visit had got around, and there was one member of the court who was most displeased to hear of it. When Queen Caterina arrived at the ball, Maria made a low curtsey to her, according to social convention, but rather than be acknowledged as she would have expected, she was coldly ignored as the queen turned her back on her. Maria was humiliated. All her efforts to stay out of these kinds of games, to stay on the right side of everyone, were ruined in one fell swoop by the presence of her notorious relation.

But despite this, Hortense became something of a companion to Maria, and was reported to have been every day in her rooms. The Marquis of Ruvigny (the French ambassador in London) wrote to Louis that 'The Duchess of York has affection for her. She is always with her.'[19] Her presence must have been a comfort to Maria when she found in January 1676 that she was pregnant again. Maria found it difficult to be excited. She wrote to her brother on 5 February to thank him for his good wishes on the news, and assured him 'that I have taken care, not leaving home yet'.[20] Later that month she wrote again: 'The fear that I have of miscarrying is so great that it is a month that I have not left home.'[21] From her letters we find that she actually didn't leave St James's for three or four months, so great was her terror of miscarrying her child. The pressure of having a healthy heir, combined with the fears of a woman who had suffered miscarriages and the death of a child before, must have made this pregnancy excruciating.

Another frequent visitor to Maria's bedroom was Charles, and he and Hortense had plenty of time to get to know each other when they met there on a daily basis. Charles, too, had had previous interactions with the current Duke of Mazarin, who had had the nerve to write to him requesting he pay back money given by Cardinal Mazarin when Charles was in exile, and he offered a compassionate ear to her troubles over her money.[22] Both he and James wrote to Louis asking him to support her. Her uncle had made her his heir, but she could not access the money without her husband's authorisation, and James and Charles reminded the king of Mazarin's intentions that both Hortense and her husband have equal share in the fortune. They asked him to make Armand send her the money that was rightfully hers. Louis was not impressed by this interference and refused to help, though it risked Hortense's anger against him, anger she relayed to Charles. Charles gave her an enormous pension of £4,000 a year (around £450,000 in today's money), and it seems likely that the pair were soon lovers. By August 1676, along with the pension, Hortense was granted splendid apartments at Whitehall. Louise de Kéroualle certainly had reason to be worried. Another of Charles's mistresses, the actress Nell Gwyn, whose wit was unrivalled, and who had never liked Kéroualle but got on well with Mancini, elaborately went into public mourning for the death of the hopes of the Duchess of Portsmouth, stalking the court dressed head to toe in black and loudly lamenting Kéroualle's fate.

As her relationship with the king progressed, Hortense began to spend increasing amounts of time with Charles's daughter by Barbara Villiers, Anne Fitzroy, Countess of Sussex, and they often met in her apartments. Anne was fourteen and had recently been married to a man she had little in common with. He preferred to be in the country, she in London, and their paths rarely crossed. Anne and Hortense were soon inseparable: they went hunting together, took fencing lessons and walked for hours in St James's Park. One record tells of the pair swordfighting in the park in the middle of the night, wearing nothing but almost see-through nightdresses; they drew quite the crowd. It is almost certain that the two were lovers; Saint-Évremond casually wrote at this time that Hortense 'has claimed lovers of both sexes'. But this was not a scandal. For women, beauty being attracted to beauty was not thought odd, and Hortense and Anne were social equals. Where same-sex attraction (between women) was not acceptable was when it crossed class boundaries, as may have been the case with Mrs Hobart, Maria's Mother of the Maids. Charles was not concerned in the least by the relationship, though Anne's husband's patience wore thin when his wife refused to go to him in the country when summoned. Transgression from the marital bed could only go so far, and in the end he sent armed guards to Hortense's rooms to forcibly escort his wife to a convent in France until she had learned to be more compliant. Neither of Anne's parents stood up for her.

Around this time, the affection between Hortense and Maria finally exposed Maria to the scrutiny of the court wits. A poem called

'Rochester's Farewell' – which is somewhat reminiscent of 'Signor Dildo' – began to circulate. It was a scurrilous piece of work, based on the debaucheries of court, and of Hortense Mancini in particular. Some of it was certainly penned by the Earl of Rochester, but more than one author seems likely. Maria was implicated by association when Rochester and his accomplices suggested that the reason Maria had not taken male lovers was that she had her three favoured ladies to satisfy her: Mrs Bromley and Mrs Hyde (who were two of her Women of the Bedchamber), and of course her cousin, Hortense. Where in 'Signor Dildo' Maria was said to have given up her sex toy in favour of James, here she is said to be taking female lovers to supplement her appetite:

> Let now the Dutchess take no further care,
> Of humorous Stallions let her not despair,
> Since her indulgent Stars so kind have been,
> To send her Bromley Hyde and Mazarine.[23]

The poem goes on to say that Mancini has supplanted the Duke of Monmouth in Maria's inner circle, and in so doing has replaced what was wit and fine conversation with lechery and debauchery, and that the transition was not a difficult one for Maria to make.

> This last doth banish'd Monmouth's place supply,
> And Wit supplanted is by Letchery.
> For Monmouth's he had Parts, and Wit, and Sense,
> To all which Mazrine had no pretence.[24]

Perhaps the author had not spent much time with the Duke of Monmouth who, though devastatingly handsome and charming, was not overburdened with intellect. In a short amount of time, all that Maria had worked for appeared to be hanging by a thread. Fortunately, this seems to have been the last time Maria was exposed by the reputation of her cousin.

If Charles did not mind Hortense's affair with his daughter, he began to grow concerned by her affair with the dashing Prince of Monaco, who seemed to have a stronger hold on her affections than the king. Charles was open-minded, but he needed to come out on top. In Hortense's new relationship, he became the butt of jokes at court, and he found he was not able to laugh along. Almost as soon as it had begun, the affair between Hortense and King Charles was over. After initially withdrawing her pension and considering sending her back to France, he forgave her for her misdemeanours. Her pension was restored, and they remained friends for the rest of his life.

What becomes clear is that Hortense was never interested in gaining the kinds of political power that people like Bennet and Montagu had in mind for her. She simply wanted freedom. In many ways, being freed from the position of royal mistress, and the pressures that such a position would entail, she could live exactly as she wanted. She resurrected what she had lost in Chambéry: her salon.

7

The Salon

In the 1670s London saw an explosion in the number of coffee houses. The coffee house had its roots in the Ottoman Empire where, since the fourteenth century, they were places where men could go to discuss the news of the day, to play board games and to meet friends. By the seventeenth century, coffee houses could also be found throughout Persia and in Europe, initially in Italy – in Venice and Livorno – and then Austria – primarily in Vienna – before two were opened in quick succession in England, both in Oxford. It is perhaps unsurprising that the city that was home to one of England's two universities at that time would be the first to embrace this new culture of debate and freedom of speech, though in 1674 the historian Anthony à Wood would write that they were responsible for 'the decay of study, and consequently of learning'.

It was not long before London followed the new trend, and the first coffee house in the capital was set up in 1652 by a man called Pasqua Rosée and his master, Daniel Edwards, a merchant of the Levant Company. They had been living in Smyrna (modern-day İzmir) in the Ottoman Empire, and they applied what they saw there to the City of London. Their shop was perfectly situated by the Royal Exchange, and it was not long before others opened their doors to London's inhabitants. In 1660, Pepys wrote of his first experience attending one, saying, 'I find much pleasure in it through the diversity of company – and discourse.'[1] Between 1663 and 1675 the number of coffee houses in England grew from around eighty to over 3,000.

As in the Ottoman Empire, Persia, Italy and Austria, the coffee houses in London were places where men went to discuss, among other things, the political affairs of the day, and they were often considered hotbeds of political intrigue. As time went on, they each took on different personalities. One might be frequented by a particular branch of exiles, another by a faction of the court, for example. They were places of intellectual freedom for all walks of life, the likes of which had never been seen before in London. But, as with the coffee houses all over the world, they were exclusively for men.

A more elite place of learning and intellectual explorations in London was the Royal Society, which was founded in 1660 and was patronised by King Charles and James, Duke of York. The society – having been called 'the philosophical college' or at times 'the invisible college' – became 'the Royal Society' in 1663, after the king formally bestowed his patronage. Its aims were to explore the unexplored and to try to understand all aspects of how the world and nature worked. The results were thrilling, but they, too, were for men alone. In 1667 one woman was invited to attend, though it was only once, and she was certainly never allowed to become a member. She was Margaret Cavendish, a fiercely brilliant poet, critic and philosopher, whose groundbreaking work would be influential for many years after her death in 1673.

Using the models of the salons of Italy and France – such as those hosted by Isabella d'Este and Catherine de Vivonne (Marquise de Rambouillet) – Hortense Mancini's salon worked in opposition to the burgeoning coffee houses of London, and the more elite Royal Society. It was equally open to women as well as to men. There was some precedent in England for salons hosted by women, such as those of Mary Sidney and Lucy Russell, who lived in the Elizabethan and Jacobean periods. They were great patrons of (usually male) writers and were also writers themselves. But Hortense's salon operated in a different way. At her salon, women could play an equal part to men in discussing literature, science and the affairs of the day. Some pursuits were more like those readily available at the court: singing, dancing, playing musical instruments and especially gambling. But even in this women were allowed more liberty than might initially meet the eye.

Broadly speaking, women in the seventeenth century had no legal status. They were the property of their fathers until they married, when they duly became the property of their husbands. If independence was what they sought, then the most they could hope for would be a childless widowhood. There were occasions where women might inherit a father's property, but they were few and far between. They therefore had little to no control over money, being almost entirely unable to own any. But, at basset – which was the favourite game at Hortense's salon and at the Carolean court more broadly – they could spend as much as they wished, asserting a kind of liberty and independence they could only dream of in their day-to-day lives. Basset was a gambling card game, which bore some resemblances to both snap and blackjack, but with a far more complicated set of rules. It originated in the fifteenth century in Italy but was introduced into Paris by Cardinal Mazarin, and perhaps Hortense herself brought it to London, ombre (the rules of which are similar to hearts) having been the gambling game of choice at court before this. Basset was a game of complete and utter chance, with players dealt thirteen cards each, on which they could place blind bets, and which were then winners or losers depending on whether or not the cards matched in rank to the next ones dealt. The stakes were high: Nell Gwyn was reported to have lost £1,400 in a single sitting (around £200,000 in today's money).

Hortense's salon was one of a kind. People came and went at all times of the day and evening – she operated a complete open-door policy – and through its doors came some of the greatest minds of the era, such as Aphra Behn, Peter Lely, Edmund Waller, the scholars Isaac Vossius and Henri Justel and the writer Gregorio Leti; some of the most powerful courtiers, Louise de Kéroualle (once she was safe in her role as mistress again), Nell Gwyn, Moll Davies, Barbara

Villiers, Henry Jermyn, the Duke of Monmouth and the Duke of Buckingham, to name but a few. The king himself was a frequent guest, as was James. And Maria may have been one of the illustrious guests who attended. No first-hand accounts place her there, but the absence of evidence is not evidence of absence. Considering how close she became to Hortense, and how appealing she would have found a place where women would sit alongside men as intellectual equals, discussing literature, art and politics, her attendance seems very likely. Sarah Jennings was certainly one of the salon's guests; perhaps Maria took her favoured maids to take part in the conversations on offer. What made the salon particularly unusual was that people of all different religious faiths were welcome and could debate topics of politics and religion side by side. Together they read Montaigne, Plutarch, Cervantes, Racine, Patri and La Fontaine.

Hortense was a collector of exotic animals, in particular monkeys and birds, and her menagerie was part of the salon's attraction. We can picture the scene from letters and reports from people who were there: Hortense dancing and playing the guitar, 'English ladies danc[ing] too, and kick[ing] up their heels to show off their pretty legs clad in green silk stockings', Hortense's servant, Dery, singing 'in his golden soprano voice', and other guests scattered around reading quietly in 'a large chair by the fireside with one of the books ... from the library'.[2] French food was served, and it was also here that champagne was first introduced to England as a fashionable drink; it caught on. Hortense's great friend Saint-Évremond claimed that no other wine was worth drinking. He wrote to a fellow exile 'spare no cost to get Champagne ... there is no Province that affords excellent wines for all seasons but Champagne'.[3] Though the wine flowed in abundance, it was not a place of drunkenness or debauchery, and Hortense had Mustapha to shield her from any male suitors who became too amorous after a few too many glasses. On one occasion Saint-Évremond remembers Mustapha quoting the *commedia dell'arte* to him, saying, 'Non beve vino.'[4] Indeed, many reported how well Hortense managed her household and her events:

> There is no private Gentleman's house more orderly, and regular than hers … All people converse in her house with a familiarity full of zeal and respect … She alone of all women, can play with her servants, without lessening herself: her presence doth banish their presumption, without taking away their freedom.[5]

Saint-Évremond playfully teased Hortense, telling her that she should be more involved in the salon discussions, and complained that she cared more for cards than conversation, but at the same time reported that all who attended 'marvel at her ability to create an atmosphere of joy, openness, equality, freedom, relaxation, animation, and informality, that is somehow at the same time suffused with order, respect, and discretion, and guided by some inner harmony'. He pronounced that 'the greatest freedom in the world is to be seen there, and an equal discretion: everyone is more commodiously us'd there than at home; and more respectfully than at court … There is certainly nothing so well regulated as this family.' And he was certain that the credit lay entirely with 'Madame MAZARIN', who 'diffuses thro'out the whole I do not know what sort of easy air; something free and natural that conceals the regulation of it'.[6]

Hortense also partook in the kinds of artistic patronage expected of a high-ranking courtier. She had her portrait painted by the leading artists, including Peter Lely, Godfrey Kneller, Benedetto Gennari and perhaps even Mary Beale: a beautiful sketch of Hortense in Beale's hand is preserved at the British Museum in London. As was fashionable at the time, they painted her as Cleopatra, Diana, Aphrodite and other classical and biblical heroines.

The salon was a great success, though some – like Montagu – were piqued that she did not secure her role as Charles II's mistress, or even seem to desire to do so. But Hortense remained, always and at all costs, entirely herself. Freedom was what she craved, and freedom was what she had gained.

8

A Tempestuous Courtship

The year 1676 saw a summer of easy pleasure. Maria had just given birth to a daughter, who they named Isabella after Maria's great Este ancestor. And though she was visibly disappointed to be told it was a girl, this seemed to matter little to James, who gave her a beautiful silver filigree set of fruit dishes as a gift.

The usual summer residence of Windsor was being extensively renovated, but the court found other ways to entertain themselves. On 24 September Honoré Courtin wrote of a party he was giving. It was to be on a boat, sailing on the Thames, and was one of many such entertainments during the summer of that year. Picture the scene: the warm autumn breeze, the laughter of courtiers looking forward to hours of merriment as they swarmed to parties on the water, in London's great parks and at sumptuous country estates.

But this party, as recorded by Courtin, is of particular interest because of those who attended. He writes that he has invited 'Madame Mazarin, Madame de Sussex, Madame Hamilton's sister, and Mademoiselle Trevor'.[1] This is a relatively early record of 'Madame Mazarin' at court entertainments, and as 'Madame de Sussex' is also present, we can see that their friendship had not yet become the object of scandal. 'Mademoiselle Trevor' was Maria's new maid of honour, Mary Trevor. Trevor had replaced the disgraced Mary Kirk, who had left the court after giving birth to a baby boy in June 1675 in the maids' lodgings at St James's Palace, the father of whom was not certain. The Earl of Musgrave was one possible contender, the Duke of Monmouth another; the Duke of York was also a likely candidate.

But who was 'Madame Hamilton's sister'? 'Madame Hamilton' was Lady Frances Hamilton ('la belle Jennings'), who had been maid of honour to Anne Hyde before her marriage to George Hamilton, soldier, courtier and close friend of Charles II. The sister referenced here, therefore, is Maria's maid of honour, Sarah Jennings. That she was referred to as the sister of 'Madame Hamilton' rather than as Mademoiselle Jennings suggests that she was not well known to Courtin, though she had lived at court for three years or more by this point. We can glean from this something of the early court life of Sarah Jennings; she had lived perhaps a little more under the radar than many of the women around her. And though she was considered very beautiful – described even by her severest critic, Delarivier Manley, in the satirical *New Atalantis* as 'everything that's splendid and ravishing', with 'sweetness in her eyes, invitation in her looks' – her sister was a famous beauty.[2] Perhaps she lived a little in her shadow. Sarah was never vain about her beauty. She remarked later in life that while she had been fortunate in her looks, and beauty was highly valued at court, there were more important things. Her hair, however, of a reddish honey hue, she admitted being pleased with, calling it 'the best thing I had'.[3] 'Madame Hamilton' herself is notably absent from the party; her husband had died in June that year.

Courtin's was one of many letters which flew between the palaces and noble houses of England and mainland Europe during these early years of Sarah's life at court. All were full of gossip and reports of every minute detail of court life. In some of them we find other references to the young 'Mistress Jennings' and can gradually gain a picture of who Sarah was, how she lived, her relationship with Maria, with her fellow maids and with the young princesses, as well as with those who courted her. Using her own words and the words of those who were there, we can try to reconstruct her world, starting here, in September 1676, on the River Thames.

Courtin's report suggests that Sarah Jennings was included – or was at least beginning to be included – in the social circle of Hortense Mancini, and she probably began to attend the Mancini salon around this time. Sarah would have been sixteen years old, and the salon must have appealed to her quick and curious mind. Though we don't know when she undertook the work, Sarah translated some English fables and a work by La Fontaine which were read and discussed at the salon. Today these translations are found in her collected papers, which form part of the Blenheim catalogue housed at the British Library.[4]

Hortense and Sarah seem well matched for friendship: they were both intelligent, independent, sharp-witted and, while in this scene set by Courtin she is with Mary Trevor, Sarah did not initially find friends among her fellow maids. Sarah had, however, been instantly noticed by Maria, who constantly sought her company. Over the years, Maria suffered from insomnia, and letters tell of how she would call for Sarah to walk with her in the night and sit with her when she could not sleep. But Sarah also had friends at court from her intermittent periods in the royal nursery as a child, like the Villiers daughters. She would become particularly close to Barbara Villiers (not to be confused with the mistress of Charles II), and this friendship would continue throughout their lives. Though few records have remained to tell us about this friendship, in later life Sarah reflected, ''tis certain I had more fondness and inclination for her then any body I ever knew in my life, except such as is not necessary to name'.[5] Another friend she found early at court was a woman called Mary Fortrey. When Sarah later wrote of this friendship, she said that 'Mary had a great deal of sense' and that during her early days at court 'she gave me the best advice I ever had, when I was so young and ignorant, that it was of great use to me'. With friends such as this, combined with her own moral compass, Sarah was more protected than many of the young women at court.

Little is known of Mary Fortrey, and if she had not corresponded with Sarah, or if Sarah had not left behind her memories of their friendship, we might not have known she existed at all. But hers is one of the first friendships of Sarah's which is documented, with several letters surviving between them from a period in 1674, when Fortrey was staying with family in France. Sarah was just fourteen. The friendship that emerges from this correspondence is one of warmth and youthful intimacy. She begs Sarah to write soon: 'I find I love you so well I cannot help wishing for a letter from you every week.'[6] Mary is clearly bored, and she begs for news, writing that there must be some, for 'in a desert you could not want intrigues, and in a court 'tis impossible'.[7]

In another letter, Mary begins with a playful rebuke at Sarah for not sending her more interesting content: 'Though I can receive nothing from you without joy, yet let me tell you your letters are very insignificant.'[8] As with the other letter, she is desperate for interesting news from the court and is disappointed in her friend who seems to be so unwilling to gossip. In the absence of real stories, Mary turns to invention, writing, 'I'll make you judge if tis possible after such an adventure to have you ever out of my thoughts', and what follows is an elaborate story worthy of a Spenserian romance.

Mary writes of a visit to a magnificent 'house of the kings' in Blois, where she wends her way through tiny passages and maze-like staircases to find 'an old man sitting with a huge perspective [a telescope], which he rested on the wall'.[9] Here the story really takes its mythic turn: she describes him as 'in a strange wild habit, with a mightily long beard almost to his feet, and I begun to fancy him one of the Ancient druids I had read of in romances'. He tells her that the 'perspective' he looks out of 'was left him by an enchantress and which had formerly belonged to one of the sybils' and that through it he could see what was happening in any part of the world. He begins to tell her of all the things he can see, but she 'had no patience' to hear of these places once she realises what the telescope can do. She knows what she wants to see. The story turns to full comedy as she, 'shoving him almost off his seat … turned it … towards England' and finds herself 'so lucky it seems as just to hit upon St Jeameses

Park'.[10] But he can shove as well as she, and he reclaims the telescope, describing to her what he finds in the park. He sees hundreds of women, who may be angels, and says he thinks it must be 'paradise that he saw for of all he had seen in this world he never found anything so beautiful as what he saw there'. From these hundreds of women, he zooms in and, by some miracle, 'made an exact description of ten I believe of my acquaintance'. But of all these ten there is one who catches his eye, and Mary's description of this moment deserves a longer quotation:

> but at last giving a great cry out of a sudden, 'I see' said he 'a young beauty coming down the great walk which has rays about her head like a sun, but 'tis impossible for me to distinguish at this distance whether 'tis the lustre of her complexion or of her eyes that produces them, she is in a crowd that follows her wherever she goes, but there is nine people that never quits her one minute, she has without doubt a wit and goodness as extraordinary as her beauty for of these nine adorers there's not one that reproaches her of any kindness to one more then another but she carries herself with such an equality that she obliges all, all admires her & there's not one of them that is either jealous or envies the happiness of one another, a thing unheard of before amongst rivals.'

What he sees is the force of personality that Sarah undoubtedly had, even at this young age. She is the one who draws his eye, the one with 'nine adorers' following behind. After this Mary wryly remarks that 'he would have run on an hour after this', and when she realises that the description must be of Sarah she exclaims: 'I had not patience to live a minute longer without seeing you.' What follows is the height of delightful farce:

> I shoved him something rudely off his seat, and taking his place I saw you standing, as he had described you. You can't imagine the joy I had in that sight, I was like a thing transported, I shouted

> and hollowed after you, called you by your name a hundred times as loud as I cold hollow, 'Mrs Ginings, Mrs Ginings', but Mrs Ginings was cruel to nothing but me, you never as much as turned your head that way and I was only answered by the Echoes, who all found a pleasure in repeating your name after me, I however never ceased calling to you 'til at last I saw you turn in to St Jeameses House.

With Sarah indoors, and the light from her being gone with her 'it grew so dark 'twas impossible for me to see any longer' so Mary 'came down to my company' and 'told them what had happened to me'. But, she confesses, she 'was so hoarse with hollowing after you I could hardly speak' so the relaying of information was rather tricky. She signs off the letter with the playful wit she began it, posing herself as a travel writer telling of strange adventures:

> If I have writ too long a letter 'tis your own fault who are always desiring one, and as for the story, they say 'tis allowed to all travellers to tell things a little extravagant, I thought I might take the same liberty as well as others and I am sure my adventure is as surprising maybe as anything that has been met with in this age.

What Mary writes in her letter is amusing, arch, wry, and it is easy to see the friendship which existed between the two. But it also tells us much more: the old druid finds ten women 'of my acquaintance' and says he can tell that they are always together, without jealousy or any sort of unkindness between them. It is a utopian vision of female friendship and companionship, such as Maria always sought to foster in the maids and ladies of her household at 'St Jeameses' Palace.

❖

When Sarah attended the party on the Thames in September 1676 described by Honoré Courtin, she was in the midst of a tumultuous romance. Courtin wrote that 'the young ladies' admirers will be there too', and Sarah's suitor was very likely one of the guests. His name was John Churchill. He was young and handsome, and was a protégé of James.

Churchill came from a family of a similar rank to that of Sarah, though perhaps a little higher. And, like the Jenningses, they had little money to put to their name, perhaps even a little less. Both families hoped their children would increase their fortunes through marriage. The Churchills had lost their wealth (as many families did) fighting on the losing side in the Civil War. John's father, Sir Winston, was charged the great sum of £4,500 (over £450,000 in today's money) by the Cromwellian regime, as a fine for his role as captain in the Royalist cavalry. This event scarred Winston, who chose as his family motto *Fiel Pero Desdichado* (Faithful but Unfortunate). This motto has been carried through to the present-day Dukes of Marlborough, and John must have felt it keenly, particularly when, in his mid-to-late twenties, he had to give up his inheritance so that his father could sell their lands and pay his debts. These experiences must have influenced the heart and mind of the young John Churchill, and when it came to choosing sides again, some forty years after his father, he would be wiser than his family had been. He kept his options open, and joined with the victors when he knew they couldn't lose.

When John's elder sister, Arabella, was sent to court in 1663 to be maid of honour to Anne Hyde, the family had few hopes for her success there: she was described by a contemporary as 'a tall creature, pale-faced and nothing but skin and bone'.[11] They underestimated her: she was clever and had a sharp wit. It was therefore inevitable that she soon caught the eye of James. The story goes that the court was out hunting, and Arabella was thrown by her horse. As she lay on the ground, concussed and bruised, James rushed to her side, and, with her skirts in disarray, revealing her legs, Cupid released his arrow on the heart of the prince. One bystander reported their shock that 'limbs of such exquisite beauty could belong to Miss Churchill's face'.[12] Arabella was his mistress for more than ten years, and she bore him several children. Rather than regret the loss of their daughter's virtue, the Churchills expressed a 'joyful surprise that so plain a girl had attained such high preferment'.[13]

This preferment was certainly useful to the family: John was sixteen when he became page to James and was quickly taken under the duke's wing. On his brother's accession to the throne, James had been made Lord High Admiral, and he took an interest in all things military. Churchill accompanied him to military parades and drills, and the young man was captivated by the rhythm of the soldiers marching and the deep beat of the drums, watching them deftly fall in and out of formation. At that moment he knew he wanted to be a soldier, and James was keen to foster his ambitions. On 14 September 1667, not long after John's seventeenth birthday, James gave him a commission as an ensign in the King's 1st Guards. After several years away at war, he returned to the court in 1671 a military hero.

He also began an affair with Barbara Villiers, the King's longstanding mistress. Barbara was generous with John who was, after all, the son of an impoverished family, and who found that he could do with rather more money than he had. Over the course of their affair Barbara reportedly gave him around £5,000 (almost £600,000 in today's money) to help him get ahead at court, though she wryly observed that it was a lot of money 'for very little service'.[14]

James had tried several times to gain higher positions for his favourite, but the affair with Barbara held him back from high preferment. One night, when Charles arrived at his mistress's door, he was met by sounds of scuffling. When he entered the chamber, he walked over to the wardrobe and threw open the door: there he found John Churchill. Both Barbara and John fell to their knees, begging forgiveness. Charles curled his lip and said that he forgave John, 'since you must do it to earn your bread'. But forgiveness was only to a point: it would be a little time before he would countenance Churchill rising at court. By the 1680s, however, Charles had taken Churchill deep into his confidence, and often used him for delicate diplomatic missions. They were also frequently to be seen playing tennis together.

When in 1673 Sarah Jennings had won one of the four much-coveted posts of maid of honour to the new Duchess of York, John Churchill also took his place in the royal household at St James's Palace, as Gentleman of the Bedchamber to James. By this point, Barbara's star was on the wane, and she resigned her hard-won post as the queen's Lady of the Bedchamber. She had increasingly got into trouble for refusing – as a Catholic – to attend Anglican services (something which had been overlooked before) and then, in 1675, came the final insult: Louise de Kéroualle's son was given a dukedom, an honour not bestowed on any of Barbara's many children by the king. Though when she returned in 1682 they were able to retain a deep friendship, when she left the court in 1675, Charles's final cutting words to her were apparently: 'Madam, all that I ask of you … is live so for the future as to make the least noise you can, and I care not who you love.' Her reign was over, and Louise's had well and truly begun. John, by this point displaying a ruthless streak, felt he had got out of her all he could. She was discarded and left for France, and his pursuit of Sarah Jennings began.

When Sarah joined the court, she held the advice of her sister close to her heart: 'in so dangerous a situation' as the court, she needed to ensure 'not to dispose of her heart until she gave her hand'. This proved easier in theory than in practice when she met the dashing John Churchill. Sarah herself described him as being 'as handsome as an angel' with 'uncommonly large' eyes, a 'beautifully formed' mouth, with a figure 'as fine a one as you could see' and a 'red and white complexion' that 'could put the fair sex to shame'. It was observed by others that 'his manner was irresistible to either man or woman'.[15] John was also already famous for his great military heroism: 'no one in this world … could possibly have done better than Mr Churchill has done', wrote the nephew of the French General Marshal Turenne, who John had served under.[16] And the Duke of Monmouth loudly asserted that he was only alive because John had so heroically saved his life on the battlefield at Maastricht. But his reputation as the lover of Barbara Villiers had preceded him, too, and Sarah knew she would need to be on her guard.

Maids of honour were sent to court by their parents in the hope of their securing advantageous marriages, and sometimes they did – Isabella Boynton (Sarah's fellow maid of honour) married Maria's Master of Horse, Wentworth Dillon, 4th Earl of Roscommon – but they were also the primary prey of the men of the court: the wits, the Gentlemen of the Bedchamber, the king and the Duke of York. Sarah will have known about this from her sister, Frances, who had been maid of honour to Anne Hyde, and she soon experienced it first-hand when James began to make unwelcome advances towards her. At the end of 1675 Maria's secretary, Edward Coleman, wrote that 'Her Royal Highness has very ill luck with her maids of honour', due to the percentage of the girls who had already found themselves in disgrace.[17] By 1676, of the four women who had initially been appointed maid of honour to Maria, only two remained untouched by scandal: Isabella Boynton, now respectably married, and Sarah Jennings. The first to fall was Mary Kirk who, as we saw, was a mistress of the Duke of Monmouth. Monmouth, however, did not long mourn the loss of his mistress; he moved swiftly on to another of Maria's maids, Eleanor Needham. And it would not be long before her replacement, Mary Trevor, would fall into scandal and ruin, though hers is a more tragic story.

Eleanor Needham was not the only woman Monmouth, 'ever in some amour', was seducing. At *The Masque of Calisto*, he had seen the beautiful Henrietta Wentworth play Jupiter, and his heart was lost. Theirs was to be a lifelong romance, though neither would live more than ten years longer. The affair was discovered by the unlucky Mary Trevor, and letters between Princess Mary and her friend Frances Apsley detail the whole story. Mary tells Frances how, when Trevor found the lovers, they 'both beged very hartely' that she would keep the affair a secret.[18] They particularly begged her to 'tel no body of it but espetialy Mrs. Jennings'; in other words, the worst person Mary Trevor could tell would be Sarah.[19] Was Sarah such an object of fear? Or did they assume the first thing that Sarah would do would be to go to Maria?

The maid of Mary Trevor was not at all happy about the secrecy; she said, 'the divel take her if she did not tel Mrs. Jenings the first time she see her'. In the end, Maria was written to by 'Mrs Worsley', and she straight away asked Sarah to go and see what was going on. Upon her arrival 'Mrs trevors maid was as good as her word'; she told her all that had taken place. Princess Mary, in the spirit of gossip, wrote that 'the duches hering of it was mighty angry', as was Eleanor Needham, who left court with the promise that 'nobody shal never her of her more'.[20]

What is also interesting about this is that, when Maria first heard about the scandal, she sent Sarah to find out what it was all about. This suggests both an intimacy and a like-mindedness; she knew that she could trust Sarah to view the matter as she did and to report back honestly. Eleanor Needham attempted to redeem herself in Maria's eyes: Princess Mary wrote to Frances Apsley that 'it is very trew that Mrs. Needham did wright a letter to the Duches but what it was I can not tell for nobody did see it but herself but this I can tel the duches said that if it ware trew that was in the letter she wold be found very inosent'.[21] However, Maria 'wold not believe it to be trew', and Eleanor Needham left the court in disgrace, though she continued her affair with the Duke of Monmouth.[22]

This might have been the end of it, but the vengeful heart of the Duke of Monmouth was piqued. He blamed Mary Trevor and came up with a plan to ruin her. He called on his friend Thomas Thynne to seduce and abandon her. Thynne saw the fun he might have in such a plan and began to court her, promising her marriage and love. He was a wealthy man – he was nicknamed 'Tom of Ten Thousand' – and was heir to the sumptuous estates at Longleat, so the prospects he offered a penniless girl like Mary Trevor were great indeed. To ensure his success, Thynne enlisted the help of Mary's mother, telling her that he wished to marry Mary, but would not do so unless he could be made certain that she could produce an heir for him. Mary's mother, tempted beyond reason by the thought of her daughter becoming Lady Thynne, told her daughter to give him what he wanted. Mary submitted, fell pregnant and was abandoned.

Thomas Thynne received his own punishment. When he came to marry, his choice was the wealthy widow Elizabeth Percy, Countess of Ogle, but he had a rival in a dashing visitor from Sweden, Count Karl Johann Königsmark of Sweden, who was not happy to have been gazumped, and he ordered Thynne's assassination. Thomas Thynne was killed when riding in his coach, on 12 February 1681, and a mocking ballad of the time reads:

Here lies Tom Thynne of Longleat Hall
Who ne'er would have miscarried;
Had he married the woman he slept withal
Or slept with the woman he married.[23]

With all this considered, it is perhaps unsurprising that when Sarah started to receive attention from John, her mother became uneasy for her honour.[24] She knew the dangers facing her beautiful daughter, and it must have seemed very unlikely that Churchill's attentions were serious. Sarah was, after all, of no great rank and with no fortune to speak of. What could there be to attract the serious intentions of a handsome and ambitious man such as Churchill, who had no clear reason to settle for less than an heiress? But she underestimated her daughter. When Mrs Jennings tried to remove her daughter from court, Sarah utterly refused.[25]

Mrs Jennings was also living at St James's Palace at the time, under the protection of the Duke and Duchess of York. She was still trying to extricate herself from the terrible debts left by her estranged husband after he died, and living at court kept her safe from her creditors. Maria was happy to help her friend's mother by offering a safe haven, but this was the extent of her support for Mrs Jennings, and she would not part with Sarah on her mother's whim. As we can see from gossiping letters from the time, there was no question of Maria siding with anyone but Sarah. Lady Chaworth wrote on 23 November 1676,

> Mrs. Jennings and her daughter, Maid of Honour to the Duchess have had so great a falling out that they fought: the young one complained to the Duchess that if her mother was not put out of St. James's, where she had lodgings to sanctuary from debt, she would run away, so Sir Allen Apsley was sent to bid the mother remove, who answered with all her heart she would never dispute the Duke and Duchesses commands, but with the grace of God she would take her daughter away with her, for two of the maids had had great bellies att Court, and she would not leave her child to have a third. So rather than part with her, the mother must stay.[26]

Maria knew Sarah well enough to know that she would have a clear head, and she probably already knew the details of the attachment with John. She would take responsibility for her friend's happiness.

For some time at least there was a kind of peace between mother and daughter, and Sarah and Maria's lives at court could carry on. The winter of 1676 was so cold that the Thames froze, and the solid river became a place of merrymaking. The Duke of Monmouth fashioned a horse-drawn sledge, which Maria had 'much pleasure in ... and is pulled up and down the ponds in them every day'.[27] The king, too, enjoyed being pulled around on the ice by his son. It is a happy scene of a family playing together. And in the gardens of the palace, we read that,

> The duchess is much delighted with the making and throwing of snowballs and pelted the duke soundly with one the other day and ran away quick into her closet and he after her, but she durst not open the door.[28]

The frozen Thames became the centre of festivities and fun, and Maria and Sarah were often to be found there.

The peace in the Jennings family, however, was not to last. A month later – on Christmas Day – Lady Chaworth reported:

> Mrs Sarah Jennings hath got the better of her mother, who is commanded to leave the Court and her daughter in itt, notwithstanding the mother's petition that she might have the girl with her: the girle saying she is a mad woman.[29]

Sarah had won the battle, and Maria and James sent her mother packing. She may only have been sixteen, but Sarah was already smarter than her mother had given her credit for, and she knew how to navigate this world of 'dangerous and modish gallantries'.[30] She had seen Mary Kirk and Eleanor Needham – and would later see Mary Trevor – in their disgraces, and she was not going to let that be her. Sarah never forgot Mary Trevor's fate and wrote of it later in life.

> Her I did know when I was a Maid of Honour at Court, who persuaded her daughter to trust Mr Thynne and to go to bed with him, because he said he wou'd not marry any body, till he knew whither he could have a child. This design succeeded, but he did not keep his word. And I saw my self this woman go out of the Gallery where the Maids liv'd with Infamy, wringing her hands and saying, her mother had undone her by her advice.[31]

At this time there were few boundaries at court, and they were easily crossed; it was not at all unusual for young ladies to entertain their lovers in their bedrooms. John was often found in the bedchamber of the maids, and he reportedly delighted in untying and tying Sarah's garter ribbons. This was not considered particularly unusual or scandalous, but this kind of liberty, or intimacy, could easily develop into far more. But what becomes clear from reading the letters between Sarah and John is that Sarah set her own boundaries, and she stuck to them. Though the letters are undated we can try to reconstruct their context from what they say. In doing so, however, we may fall into Sarah's trap. Later in life she thought a good deal about what she wanted her legacy to look like, and she actively edited her papers. This means that we have very few letters written by her, and those written by John are only the ones she allowed to be kept in the Marlborough papers. She revisited these papers several times in later life, and records that she destroyed many of them. Those that remain were ones that she says she 'read over in 1743, hoping to destroy them, but I could not do it'. We can assume then that these letters are ones which were of a strong sentimental attachment.

They tell us much about their courtship, about their lives at court and about their characters. John was always known for being calm and rational, unflappable in almost any situation, but on the face of it the letters present a young man who is struggling with a great passion. Is this evidence of the great hero overcome by his tumultuous feelings? Perhaps. But though his words are of passion, his hand, while not neat, is deliberate. He never makes a mistake; not a single word is ever crossed out, and the lines and characters are all completely uniform. Perhaps the gentleman protested too much, perhaps even these desperately romantic letters are to some degree exaggerated for effect. Sarah's letters are calm by comparison, though she was known throughout her life to have had a wild temper. But her refusal to accept his explanations, her general intransigence and unwillingness to forgive, these are qualities we can recognise in her, both in this courtship and in her later life. In contrast to John's, her writing is almost illegible at times, and it remained so throughout her life. She would often joke about her 'rediculous hand'.[32]

If we are to believe John, Sarah was rarely kind to him, always professing that he could not love her and that she would not see him, tactics perhaps that she initially used to protect herself and her heart. His letters are full of sentiment, and display little of the hero who was reportedly so full of poise. He writes that he has 'no thoughts of any joy but that of seeing you' and worries about what she might be hearing about him, pleading 'do not be so ill-natured as to believe any lies that may be told you of me'.[33] He begs to see her, saying that he is 'never truly pleased than when I am with you'.[34] He cries with love for her 'for my soul there is no pain so great to me as that when I fear you do not love me' and with frustration at what he sees as her obstinacy in refusing to believe his declarations: 'had it not been for shame I could have cried.'[35]

We cannot know exactly when John started to court her – perhaps he saw her in *The Masque of Calisto* and was swept away by her beauty, or danced with her in the rooms of Maria one evening, as one historian has posed – but the courtship was certainly well under way in 1676, when he joined Honoré Courtin's party on the Thames. Courtin seems to have taken a great interest in the passion and reported that that summer John had refused a post as lieutenant colonel in the French (at that time allied) army because he 'prefers to serve the very pretty sister of Lady Hamilton'.[36] Some months later he wrote, 'there was a small ball last Friday at the Duchess of York's where Lady Hamilton's sister who is uncommonly good-looking had far more reason to wish to cry than to dance'.[37] He goes on to explain why: John's 'father urges him to marry one of his relations who is very rich and very ugly'.

The 'very rich and very ugly' woman described by Courtin as the Churchills' choice was a young woman called Catherine Sedley. She came from a family which was deeply embedded in the court. Her father, Charles Sedley, was a writer and dramatist, and one of the most notorious of the court wits.[38] Catherine's mother was not much more promising: by this time she had been sent to a convent in Ghent on grounds of violent insanity. Catherine was described as being 'as mad as her mother, and as vicious as her father'. Certainly, she inherited her father's wit, and she arrived at the court a street-wise and savvy young woman, though her independent spirit may well have been interpreted as a kind of madness for a woman in the seventeenth century.

Catherine may not have been beautiful, but she was highly intelligent – John Evelyn recorded meeting her in 1673, reflecting that she was 'none of the most virtuous, but a wit' – and it is perhaps not surprising that, when she was made maid of honour to Maria in 1677, she soon became another of James's mistresses.[39] Catherine reportedly remarked that she never understood what James saw in her, as she had no beauty and he did not have enough wit or intelligence to comprehend just how witty and intelligent she was. To Maria's agony Catherine would retain a hold over James that none of his other mistresses, and arguably not even Maria, could ever compete with. Later in life Maria would enlist her priests to try to convince James to send her away, and she endured many long years of suffering on account of the affair.

Catherine must have seemed a worrying contender for John's hand, if not his heart. Though not beautiful, like Sarah, she, too, was exceptionally clever and, more importantly, she was exceptionally rich, the sole heir to a great fortune. For Sarah there was a very real fear that John would give way to his parents' wishes. She may have thought there was some truth in Courtin's claim that 'Churchill himself is also said to be not a little avaricious'.[40] Both will have heard the gossip 'from the various ladies at court that he has pillaged the Duchess of Cleveland, and that she has given him more than the value of 100,000 livres'.[41] She will also have heard of the ruthless way he behaved towards her: 'they make out that it is he who has quitted her and that she has taken herself off in chagrin to France to rearrange her affairs'.[42] The main things Sarah learned from this story were that not only was John ambitious and that he wanted to make his fortune, but that he was also not opposed to taking a mistress, and not afraid to cut his losses on an unpromising prospect. However, John's intentions do seem to have been honourable from an early point in his courtship of Sarah: Courtin wrote that John's father 'will not consent to his marriage with Miss Jennings', so we know that he asked.[43] But once this blessing was refused, John may have seriously thought of marrying for a better price. The Churchills were in dire need of funds, and John knew this.

But Sarah held firm: she was not going to become his mistress, and if he wanted her in his bed, it would be as his wife. She wrote to him 'if it were true that you have that passion for me which you say you have you would find out some way to make your self happy, it is in your power, therefore press me no more to see you since 'tis what I cannot with honour allow of'.[44] Later in life Sarah wrote: 'Since I can remember … though I can give no account how it came to be so, I never feared anything so much as to do the least things, I imagined, could possibly bring any shame upon me.'[45] She was proud of having preserved her reputation at 'a court where Vice and folly had all those marks of honour and approbation as might dazell the eyes of young persones'.[46] John was not going to have his cake and eat it.

In their correspondence, tensions ran high. Sarah wrote to him with hardened resolve:

> As for seeing you I am resolved I never will in private nor in public if I could help it, and as for the last I fear it will be some time before I can order it so as to be out of your way of seeing me, but surely you must confess that you have been the falsest creature upon earth to me, I never own that I believe I shall suffer a great deal of trouble but I will bear it, and give god thanks though too late I see my error.[47]

Sarah was genuinely worried that John would marry Catherine, and this is a rare letter in their correspondence in which she admits to caring deeply for him. She is mostly contained and aloof, but here we see her heart on the line. But always with Sarah we need to be careful, as she curated her archive to ensure that we can only see what she wanted us to see. This letter even has a helpful note, written from her to us many years later: 'This letter was writ when I was angry at something, his father and mother had made a disagreeable noise in the town about when they did intend to have him marry a strange creature for money.'

In the correspondence as she has curated it, John does not come out well. He wrote to Sarah's maid that her mistress's 'usidge to me is so barbarous that sure she must be the worst woman in the world or else she would not be so ill-natured'.[48] He continues, dramatically, that he encloses a letter for Sarah and that 'it is very reasonable for her to take it because it will be then in her own power never to be troubled with me more if she pleases'.[49] He sums up with a true tug at the heartstrings: 'I do love her with all my soul but I will not trouble her, for if I can not have her love I shall despise her pity, for the sake of what she has already done let her read my letter and answer it, and not use me thus like a footman.'

After many letters back and forth in which each accuses the other of not loving them sufficiently and of being false, we see a profound change in their relationship. They agreed to meet, and we can assume that during this meeting John made up his mind that it was Sarah he would marry, and we can also assume that she believed him. We cannot know precisely what was said, except that they decided their best chances of marriage were to be found in the sympathy of Maria. With their families against them, and no money of their own, they needed a strong and compassionate ally. But Sarah was still tentative: 'I have made my reflections upon what you said to me last night and I am of the opinion that could the dutchess obtain what you ask her you might be more unhappy then if it can not be had.'[50] Sarah seems sure that marriage with her, even on the terms that Maria may be able to offer them, would not ultimately make him happy. Is she testing him one last time? Is she reminding him that in marrying Catherine he would be rich in a way that she could never offer? She asks him 'to say nothing of it to the duchess on my account'.[51]

He responds to her cool-headedness with his usual ostentatiousness: 'my heart is ready to break, I wish 'twere over, for since you are grown so indifferent death is the only thing can ease me.'[52] But he gives her the reassurances she needs: 'if that the duchess could not have effected this I was resolved to have made another proposal to her which I am confident she might have effected, but it would not have brought so much money as this.'[53] He turns the tables on Sarah, accusing her of wanting greater riches: 'I wish with all my soul that my fortune had been so considerable as that it might have made you happier.'[54] He laments that she would rather go to France with her sister than be with him, that Frances is turning her against him, before promising her that 'if you command me death I will die'.[55] Frances was visiting Sarah on her way to France, and though she may well have offered her the chance of a holiday to escape the potential heartbreak of John choosing to marry Catherine Sedley, there is no indication beyond this letter that Sarah ever had any intention of going.

As throughout their correspondence, Sarah's reply is measured and unemotional and makes clear that all is settled between them: 'If your intentions are honourable and what I have reason to expect you need not fear my sisters coming can make any change in me or that it is the power of anybody to alter me but yourself.'[56]

All was reconciled, and though his letters are still full of morose longing to see her, there do not appear to have been any more quarrels. In a sign of reconciliation, he sent her two puppies, writing: 'pray see which of those two puppies you like best, and that keep.'[57] In a rare portrait of Sarah from this time, we see her holding a King Charles Spaniel. It is tempting to think that it might be this very puppy that she holds so tenderly in the painting. Indeed, that the dog is of particular sentimental value is likely since throughout her life she was rarely painted with any kind of accessory. She rests the dog on a ledge in front of her, and one of its paws droops over her arm. Following the line of the paw, we can see a gold ring, framed by her sleeve and the curve of the dog's body. Is this a marriage band? Perhaps in this one instance she decided to commemorate that precious gift, given at the true beginning of their life together. Both of the Churchills were King-Charles-Spaniel enthusiasts and kept the dogs at their home at Blenheim Palace, for hunting as well as for companionship. Sarah particularly favoured the red and white strain, and they are named 'Blenheim' in homage to her.

The letters between Sarah and John tell us about the life of the court as well as of their budding romance. We see the daily evening gatherings in Maria's drawing room (which seems to have been the main place in which they met), card-playing and gossiping; we see the movement of the courts between St James's Palace and Whitehall; we see that they spent time at the homes of Mrs Berkley and Mrs Brownley; we see that John even sometimes waited for her in the bedchamber of the maids, at one point staying 'above an hour'.[58] Their letters were passed through Sarah's maid, Mrs Mowdie, by 'the duke's back stairs', where John often described himself lurking hoping to hear from her.[59] We get a glimpse into the day-to-day life of Maria: 'the Duchess goes to a new play today and afterwards to the Duchess of Monmouth's there to dance', and we see Maria's frequent bouts of insomnia.[60] John writes, 'I hope you was so wise as to value your own health before your duty to the Duchess, so that you did not walk with her at 5 this morning', and at another time, 'I hope your getting up has done you no harm.'[61]

The other thing that becomes apparent is that while James and Maria had taken them into their hearts, neither John nor Sarah enjoyed working for the Yorks. They complain about the long hours of waiting around, of asking permission for everything, and the tedium of sitting about, playing cards and gossiping in the drawing rooms. Their time was not their own: John writes things like 'the Duchess has sent me word that the duke will see me this afternoon, so that at night I … hope to see you in the drawing rooms', and 'if the Duchess sees company I hope you will be there, but if she does not I beg you will then let me see you in your chamber.'[62] At the heart of these friendships was an imbalance of power; John and Sarah relied on James and Maria for their employment, they were subjects, and were expected to be available when they were wanted, to go where they were instructed. The affection the masters felt may not have been as reciprocated as they imagined.

John Evelyn wrote of court life as one of 'extreame slavery and subjection', which he was grateful to not be part of.[63] Considering that actual slavery was approaching its peak under the particular patronage of James and Charles in England at this point, this is clearly a gross overstatement. Though it does tell us about the way that this life was experienced by those who were part of it. Sarah and John were temperamentally unsuited for this kind of service, and it seems that some resentment grew over these years, resentment which would grow into something far more dangerous ten years later. When Sarah became 'the favourite' of Princess – and later Queen – Anne, it was under very different, and far less deferential terms.

The next year, 1677, brought an unexpected change in Sarah's circumstances: her brother Ralph died and overnight she became, with her sister, a joint heir to her family's land and money. It was not much, but it was something. With this new prospect, Maria, too, gave them some help, though it is not certain what form this help took. Shortly before this, John had bought the position of Master of the Robes to James, and though rumours were rife about how he achieved this (gossip had it that Barbara Villiers had 'earned' the money by spending a night with an old, and very rich, philanderer, and had given the money to her amour), perhaps it was Maria who gave John the funds to buy the post, and who spoke to James to ensure the appointment.[64] The post gave John £100 a year, on top of the £200 he had as Groom of the Bedchamber.[65] The combination of this position and Sarah's inheritance meant that the pair could finally afford to marry, which they did in Maria's rooms sometime in the autumn of 1677. In the ducal accounts book we can see this change take place, as two notes were added at the end of the record: 'An order to pay Mrs Churchill 200 per annum from Christmas 78', and 'A pension of three hundred pounds per annum granted to Mrs Sara Churchill to commence from our Ladys day 80'.[66] The numbers 78 and 80 reflect the dates they are to begin – 1678 and 1680 – though why the amount should change after two years is unclear.

Maria will have known that John's family wanted him to marry Catherine Sedley, and she will also have known of her husband's affair with her, but when John and Sarah went to her, asking for her help, she gave it. She could have ridded the court of her rival but instead she chose to help her friend. Maria had not been able to choose her own path, but she gave her 'favourite' the chance to do so. Alongside the financial help Maria gave them, she also sent Sarah some beautiful pendants as a wedding gift. John saw them before Maria had them sent, and he wrote to Sarah, 'I believe you will like them, for they are to my mind very fine.'[67] When he wrote this, John was awaiting his instructions from Charles to go to Holland, either to wage war or to broker peace with William of Orange. By this point he had gained a secure position in the inner sanctum of Charles, James and Maria, and all three of them would trust him with secret letters, missions and delicate diplomatic embassies in the years to come.

Though convention dictated that maids of honour should resign their posts when married, Sarah's marriage was a secret: initially no one but the couple and Maria knew. However, this probably did not last long: in a customs record from the end of October 1677 we read of a 'scrutore' which had arrived 'from Italy for the Duchess of York' which was to be delivered 'at Madam Churchill's house', in 'St Martin Fields' along with other trunks from France containing the latest fashions.[68] If the marriage of John and Sarah was a secret then we would not see 'Madam Churchill' listed openly at the end of October, not long after their marriage. In reality the marriage was probably something of an open secret, and Sarah will have divided her time between John's Jermyn Street house and Maria's court at St James's. But she officially continued in post until the summer of 1678, when Sarah moved in with her in-laws in Minton. This new arrangement must have been a peculiar one considering that the Churchills had been so opposed to the marriage. And Maria will probably have said goodbye with a mixture of sadness for herself and joy for her friend.

9

The Prince of Orange

Hortense Mancini's salon had been growing from strength to strength, and its creative outputs were remarkable. Saint-Évremond frequently composed music for events held there, and for Charles II's birthday in 1677, a ballet, called *Rare-en-Tout*, was commissioned by the king and was performed for the court on 29 May. This operatic comic ballet was written by a new member of the salon: a Huguenot refugee called Anne de La Roche-Guilhen. La Roche had arrived in London at the beginning of 1677 having fled religious persecution in France, where she had been active as a novelist and translator of French, English and Spanish texts. The salon was a place of double refuge for La Roche: she found safety in London and an intellectual haven in Hortense's home. The ballet was a work of collaboration with other members of the salon, including the French Catholic Jacques Paisible, who had been in London since 1673 and had worked as an oboist for the King's Musick since that time. Paisible wrote the music and Saint-Évremond was the ballet's director.

This opera ballet showcased the talents of the salon to the king, but it may also have had another purpose. It was commissioned by Henry Bennet, Earl of Arlington (or he was at least very involved with it), and was dedicated to his ten-year-old daughter, Isabella. Indeed, the main female character is called Isabelle. The dedication praises her virtue, her wit and her beauty, and she probably performed the role of her namesake. La Roche had been acting as her governess (which will have aided Isabella's mastery of the French language). We know, too, that she had been taking singing lessons from Marie Anne Mancini (Hortense's sister who was in London at this time), and her talents were greatly praised. In this light the opera takes on the role of a kind of homage to the young girl, much as *Calisto* did with the Princess Mary. *Rare-en-Tout* was the first court production to be attempted after *Calisto*, which had been so successful in displaying the talents of the young ladies of the court.

Isabella had already been married 'advantageously' to the King's (illegitimate) son by Barbara Villiers, Henry Fitzroy, in 1672. Since she was just five and he nine, the ceremony was more of a betrothal, with the intention for a confirmation ceremony to take place once the children were older. When *Rare-en-Tout* was performed the marriage had not yet been reaffirmed, and it was by no means certain that it would be. Arlington was clearly keen for his daughter to be educated and cultivated and was equally keen to show this to the court. John Evelyn reported in his diary of her beauty and sweetness, and La Roche wrote of her wit. *Rare-en-Tout* was perhaps then always in part conceived as a means through which to showcase the talents of this child. Charles requested an entertainment, and the salon obliged. Hortense's star shone brightly with the king, and when he opened parliament that year, he had her sit directly behind him.

The opera, however, was not a success and was the last of its kind at court. Evidence says nothing of the reception of Isabella, though there is no reason to think that it was not favourable: it was the French performers who were criticised, as the court asserted the superiority of their English players. One can't help wondering if the outcome was decided before the performance began. At the performance the whole court would have been present, including Maria, since it was intended to celebrate Charles II's birthday. Did she already know this brilliant young girl? Or was this the first time she had seen her? And what did she think when she saw her? A young, talented, beautiful girl, who had had no chance even to dream of a life different from what had been decided by the men around her. At ten years old, she was being put on display, as a pawn in the political game her father was playing.

Though there was merrymaking at court, England had (in league with France) been embroiled in a costly war with the Dutch, and in November 1677 William of Orange arrived at court to discuss with Charles a peace settlement between their two warring countries. Maria wrote to her brother: 'The Prince of Orange arrived two days ago to treat of some affair with the King. I have not seen him yet, as he went directly to His Majesty who is at Newmarket.'[1]

When Maria did finally see William for the first time, her impression was unlikely to have been favourable. A contemporary account described him thus:

> His nose aquiline, his cheeks hollow, the mouth large with irregular and extraordinarily long teeth, and a pointed chin … the length of his face is disproportionate to his stature … the most complete physiognomy of an eagle that it is possible to see. The hands are … long, dry and bony, always dirty, crooked and with alarmingly long nails, more like talons than hands … Weak and unsteady on his legs, he walks ill and with his head low. A hump on the right shoulder … and his hollow and asthmatical stomach make him look more hunch-backed than he really is.[2]

While the description may be an exaggerated one, William clearly did not cut a romantic figure. This was a shame, since the peace made between Holland and England would come at a price for James's eldest daughter. After all, what better way to make peace than to throw a princess into the bargain? Princess Mary was just fifteen, the same age Maria had been when she too had been forced to depart for a new life.

The marriage negotiations were so quick, and so secretive, that not even James was consulted. He was incensed: he hated his nephew William and couldn't believe that he should have so little say over the marriage of his favourite daughter. Charles had always promised he would be consulted, and when confronted he admitted that this was true, though he retorted 'but odd's fish, he must consent'.[3] Mary was a Stuart princess: her marriage was political, not personal; the Netherlands was a maritime rival and Charles needed William onside. It goes without saying that Mary was not consulted either. In fact, she was the last to know.

Since Charles did not have any legitimate children (though he had many illegitimate), James and his children were the heirs to the throne. As it stood in 1677, Mary, as the eldest child, was poised to be Queen of England unless James and Maria had a male heir. She was a great prize for William, whose role as head of state in Holland was only held by appointment. But William had quibbled – he demanded to see Mary before he made any commitments; he also wanted assurances that she would be docile and compliant – he did not want any 'trouble at home'.[4] To ask to see the bride was a great insult, but while James was seething, Charles, hiding his irritation, outwardly put on a show of amusement.

For William, this insult was payback for the last time he had visited his uncles in London. He had only been nineteen, but was already austere and humourless, and the older men had delighted in mocking the serious young man. They, along with the court wits, had got him blind drunk and he had disgraced himself trying to break into the rooms of the maids of honour in the middle of the night, and had to be forcibly restrained. In the intervening eight years he had changed very little, and he still held a grudge.

Upon seeing Mary, William declared that he was satisfied. But James insisted that the terms of the peace be arranged before any marriage took place: he did not trust his nephew and he wasn't about to give his favourite daughter away for nothing. William prevaricated and complained at his ill-treatment. He threateningly alluded to the many friends he had in the country. He had them over a barrel and was enjoying it. In the end, all was agreed. Charles pointedly remarked to William, 'Nephew ... remember ... love and war do not go together.'[5] Only now did Mary learn her fate. That evening, still reeling with sadness and anger, James took Mary into her closet and told her that she was to marry her cousin. As Maria had been, Mary was devastated. And, like Maria, she wept and cried. Her tutor, Dr Edward Lake, wrote in his diary, 'her highness wept all that afternoon and the following day'.[6] When Maria took her in her arms and tried to comfort her, reminding her that she, too, had felt the same, but she had got used to her new life, Mary could only reply between sobs, 'Yes, but you came to England, I must leave it.' Mary may have underestimated how unpleasant leaving Italy for England as winter approached would have been. Maria remembered all too well the pain she had felt when she had been forced to make a political marriage. She had been lucky that, though he had many faults, James had turned out to be kind to her, even someone she could love. She must have recognised the difficulty that Mary would have in trying to find happiness with William, who was reportedly an unpleasant man and showed little interest in his new bride. Mary was a lively young woman, hardly more than a child, who adored dancing and games; the Dutch court was reportedly deadly dull.

Maria went to Charles. Was it truly necessary that this marriage should go ahead? Could he not spare Mary? He answered that it was, and that he could not. Behind his calm demeanour lay constant strain. Holland was a naval power, and he had to ensure peace with the Dutch. On top of this, parliament was afraid of how close England was becoming with France (though they did not know about the secret treaty Charles had signed with Louis, in which he would be paid for announcing himself a Catholic). Their fear of a Catholic succession was never far away and, by marrying Mary to a staunch Protestant ally, Charles was buying some more time. Later Maria wrote to her brother: 'I am very sorry to lose her because I love her so much.'[7]

When the marriage was announced to parliament, James was made to give a speech, saying, 'he did herin, and would in all his actions, aime at the security and peace of the kingdom, and would never hinder but that his children should be educated in the religeon of the Church of England'. The response was one of 'generall joy', but it cost James a great deal to have to say those words.[8]

The tension at the court was palpable. Maria was heavily pregnant, and the child might be a boy. William was marrying Mary on dynastic grounds – if James had no male children, it was a safe bet that through his marriage he could become king. The wedding took place on William's birthday, 4 November. It was a small, private affair, held in Mary's bedroom, at nine in the evening, and was officiated by Henry Compton, Bishop of London (with whom James shared a personal and mutual dislike). Anne could not be there as she had taken ill a few days before. John Churchill was one of the few guests, which says much about his intimacy with the family by this time. Charles spent the day behaving badly: at one point during the ceremony he started loudly chivvying Compton along: 'Come Bishop, make haste lest my sister be delivered of a boy and so disappoint the marriage!' When asked, 'Who giveth this woman?' he cried out, 'I do!' at the top of his lungs. Then, when William placed some coins down saying, 'With all my worldly goods I thee endow', Charles heckled Mary with 'gather them all up and put them in your pocket, for all tis clear gain!'[9] William looked straight ahead of him, never deigning to look at his bride, who wept quietly throughout the service.

When it was over there was a reception in which various state officials came to formally congratulate the couple. William began to get twitchy; he had a strict bedtime schedule of 10 p.m. At 11 p.m., Maria and Caterina took the young bride to her closet to undress her for her wedding night. Alone together, these three women worked in silence and probably in private pain. Each of these royal women had been taken from their homes and their lives; they all served as pawns in the political games of the men around them. In the streets there was much rejoicing, with church bells ringing and bonfires lit throughout London.

While the women performed their tasks the men of the court did the same with William, though no doubt with much obnoxious jollity at the young man's expense. When Mary got into bed, and William next to her, the king drew the curtains of the marriage bed in front of selected members of the court with gusto, shouting, 'Now Nephew, to your work! Hey! St. George for England!'[10] Mary must have been mortified, but William, too, felt that he again had endured a great deal at the hands of his English uncles. He would not forget it.

Three days later, Maria went into labour. As with her other children, the labour was fast. James recorded the birth in his pocketbook: 'Charles, Duke of Cambridge, our first-born son, born Nov 7th 1677, just after a quarter before ten at night.' According to Edward Lake, the birth was met with joy throughout the court, with the exception of 'the Clarendon party', by whom he meant the faction that supported the Princess Mary and William of Orange as the heirs to the throne.[11] William was visibly annoyed to have lost his chance for the English throne. Lake wrote that 'the court began to whisper of the prince's sullenesse'.[12]

The baby's christening took place the following day with William, Mary and Maria's little daughter Isabella as godparents. The governess of the royal children, Frances Villiers, stood in for Isabella, who was far too young to carry her brother to the font. He was named Charles, after the king, and given the title of the Duke of Cambridge.

But the court the prince was born into was gradually being overcome with cases of smallpox. It was by now certain that Princess Anne had come down with the disease. And many soon became ill and died, including the princesses' governess, Frances Villiers. William had already been itching to get home and became even more keen to leave the court as soon as possible for fear of infection. Both his parents had died of smallpox – his father shortly before he was born and his mother when he was just a boy – making an already terrifying disease even more so to him. The first days of marriage had not gone well. William had tried to command Mary to move to Whitehall, most likely with concerns over her safety as St James's was rife with smallpox, but his manner was so bad that she felt he was trying to separate her from those she loved and could not understand why. A row ensued, and the couple hardly saw each other after this.

When they finally left for Holland, it was reported that both Mary and Maria cried inconsolably. Mary left England without being able to say goodbye to her sister, and with fear in her heart that she would never see her again. It was thought that Anne should not know that her sister was gone, for fear of worsening her illness, so James arranged for forged notes to be sent to Anne, purporting to be from Mary, for some time after she had already gone. When Anne recovered, she took the news with quiet resignation and consoled herself with moving immediately into Mary's far more luxurious apartments at St James's Palace.

When Anne began to feel stronger, she went to visit her stepmother and her new baby brother. She leaned over his cot and gave him a sisterly kiss. He died of smallpox a few days later. Maria wrote to her brother, Francesco, in Modena:

> with tears in my eyes I write to you of the terrible news of the loss of my dear son whom it pleased God to take to Himself in the middle of yesterday. You can imagine how distressed I am. How great was the joy that I had when he was born, and even greater is the grief that I have for the loss of him. But one must have patience, God knows what he does, may his holy will always be done. He knows that I would have been too happy if my son had been spared.[13]

Edmund Waller took the opportunity to pen a poem of grief and consolation to his patroness. He writes that though 'heaven, as a first fruit, claimed that lovely boy', there is hope ahead: 'The next shall live to be the Nation's joy'. He likens the loss of this young prince to a plant that flowers little in its first bloom, but which will later yield great flowers: 'the failing blossoms which a young plant bears / Engage our hopes for the succeeding years'. And he goes on to say how many things in the world and nature took time to flourish. Even in this darkest of times, Waller throws in a little flattery, saying that Maria is the greatest example of all as to how long the world has had to wait for the perfect princess: 'How long in vain had Nature strived to frame / A perfect princess ere her Highness came?' He speaks of the need for patience 'for joys so great' as the birth of a prince but implores her to be comforted with hope for the future.[14] William of Orange, on the other hand, was notably pleased to have the throne back in his sights so quickly.

Sarah, meanwhile, though still a maid of honour to Maria, saw an opportunity after Mary left to get closer to Anne, and their friendship began to grow. Maria was naive. Her sheltered upbringing at the Este court and convent had left her ill-equipped for a court of backstabbing and intrigue, where everyone was out for themselves and all were playing double hands. It never occurred to her that those to whom she showed friendship would do anything but reciprocate. But Sarah was a true creature of the court and, though young, was already a political operator. James and Maria were next in line to the throne, but who would succeed them? James had long been a Catholic, and Maria had been persuaded to marry him by the Pope for this very reason. For the last ten years, he had mostly kept his religious worship private, but now he was being increasingly open about it, and this was causing problems. And without a male heir, the princesses were still the next in line to the throne, and Maria's son had just died.

Anne was always intellectually limited, and deeply impressionable. She was thus an easy target for the powerful personality of Sarah Churchill, who began to poison Anne against her stepmother and father. This was not difficult. Religion had already planted a seed of contention at the root of the family. Sarah needed to make sure she had options and decided to play both hands at once: she remained in Maria's court and continued their friendship, but also ensured she was close to Anne, and that meant going behind Maria's back.

10

'The Popish Plot'

13 AUGUST 1678
ST JAMES'S PARK, LONDON

It was common in St James's Park to see King Charles II walking unattended but for a troupe of spaniels. He believed his subjects should have easy access to their king, and he always claimed he had little to fear. Once, when his brother urged him not to go out alone, he replied, 'depend upon it James, no one will kill me to make you king.'[1] On Easter Sunday 1676, James had walked with his brother to church, stopped at the door and publicly declared his resolve to no longer attend Anglican church services, and tension had been mounting ever since. There were many in parliament and the court who wanted to see him removed from the line of succession altogether and have Charles's illegitimate son, the Duke of Monmouth, made heir to the throne, claiming that Charles had secretly married Monmouth's mother, Lucy Walters. Others pressured Charles to divorce Queen Caterina and marry again, ideally to a Protestant princess who would give him a Protestant heir. Charles was in a difficult position: if he came out too strongly in favour of James, he risked angering the parliamentry faction that demanded James be barred from the succession. If he agreed to change the line of succession he would be setting a precedent that a monarch could be chosen, and thereby undermine the entire principle of hereditary monarchy. His tactic was to refuse to say that his son was legitimate, and also to refuse to throw over his loyal wife. But he always gave the impression that he might change his mind.

As Charles sauntered along the manicured paths of St James's Park on 13 August 1678, he was approached by a familiar face: Christopher Kirkby, a chemist and member of the Royal Society with whom Charles had carried out scientific experiments. But this was not Royal Society business. Kirkby told Charles of a grave Catholic plot which he claimed had penetrated the core of Charles's own court. He told Charles that he had seen a document with over 100 names of Jesuit conspirators, that a group of assassins was planning to shoot him, and that if that plan failed the queen's own physician, Sir George Wakeman, was poised to poison him.

Charles did not believe a word of it. He asked Kirkby for his proof, and Kirkby offered to bring to him the individual who had told him of the plot, a man called Israel Tongue, a fervent hater of Catholics who was widely considered to be mad. It is unlikely that the king had ever heard of him, or of his co-conspirator, Titus Oates. Charles agreed to give them an audience with Thomas Osborne, Earl of Danby, who was the Lord High Treasurer. He did not believe the story but considered it best to follow the correct procedure: let the man speak before the charges were dismissed, let him be found to be a fraud. It was a gesture that he, James, Maria and many of their friends would pay for dearly.

What Danby thought of Tongue and Oates when he met them is not clear. Perhaps he believed what they told him, or he did not see that the document they claimed to have found, with details of the conspiracy and conspirators, was forged, or perhaps he – as one of James's enemies – saw an opportunity. He advised Charles to take the plot seriously and began an investigation, of which Monmouth was put in charge. This investigation would contribute to Danby's downfall when it took on a life beyond anything he could have imagined. Though trusted by Charles, Danby had made few friends while in power, but had many enemies who were looking for any opportunity to bring him down. The court was a nest of vipers. Though Danby had been the one who had brought the traitorous plot to light, he would ultimately be accused of concealing it. By 1679 he was impeached and forced to resign his position as Treasurer.

As the months went on, the infamous pair were questioned before Danby, before the king and before parliament, and the tales they spun became more and more outrageous. Soon they were claiming that Catholic families were planning to rise up against Protestants, to murder them in their beds, to take to the streets with guns and knives, pillaging and torching the City of London as they went. They were playing into existing conspiracy theories, claiming that Catholics had started the Great Fire of London in 1666. Tongue was clearly insane, and his testimony was not taken seriously, but Titus Oates was a different matter altogether. Dryden described him as having sunken eyes and a loud, harsh voice, but also as having great self-possession. He had a powerful and compelling presence, and he used this to his advantage.

If anyone had cared to investigate Oates's past, they would have found that prior to this moment in the spotlight he had left Cambridge – where he was known as a 'canting fanatic' – after a year, but then lied and said he had his degree to gain a licence as a preacher.[2] He had then accused a local schoolmaster of sodomy with his students to try to gain his post, had later fled London on charges of perjury, was dismissed from the clergy for drunkenness and blasphemy, and sacked as chaplain to a royal navy ship, again for blasphemy (and for sodomy). By the end of the decade, he had been received into the Catholic Church and was living a double life: one part within a Catholic community, the other writing incendiary anti-Catholic propaganda with Tongue. He used his time at a Jesuit college in Saint-Omer – from which he was expelled for blasphemy, not understanding Latin (in which he had professed fluency), and for his shockingly violent verbal attacks on his monarchy and fellow students – to gain a deeper knowledge of what he called 'Jesuit secrets'. He claimed to have gained his information about the plot from his time posing as one of them.

The things that Oates said were clearly ridiculous. He claimed to have been to Whitehall Palace and to have been shown the passages through which members of the plot would carry out their devious tasks, but when asked to show the investigators it quickly became clear that he had never entered the building before that day; he claimed to have met the Regent of Spain, Don John of Austria, but gave a wildly inaccurate description of his appearance. Titus Oates was a fantasist peddling a wild conspiracy theory, that not even the highest members of government (least of all Charles) believed. The claims he was making were utterly implausible, but in the febrile anti-Catholic atmosphere of the court, to many he was a godsend. Though Danby began to openly express his doubts, Oates's tale appealed to many in parliament and the court who wished to see James removed from the line of succession, and who wanted to ensure that Catholics were kept down. The fact that he was clearly lying and discreditable did not matter. And, of course, some *did* believe him, partly because they wanted to: what he said played on their deepest prejudices.

For the next three years London and the court were thrown into turmoil: Catholics were hounded, attacked, imprisoned, abused and even executed as traitors, when they had done nothing wrong.

❖

In the autumn of 1678, though the conspiracy was gaining flight, Maria said nothing of it when she wrote to her brother that she, Princess Anne and the Duchess of Monmouth were to visit Princess Mary in Holland. Mary was four months pregnant but was very ill and it seemed likely that she had lost the child. Maria writes: 'she is anxious to see me and her sister. We too have a great desire to see her, for truly, I love her as if she were my own daughter.'[3] Around this time Maria started to address Mary affectionately as her little Lemon, as she had married the Prince of Orange. Anne must have been pleased to see her sister again, and also her friends from the nursery, Elizabeth, Katherine and Anne Villiers, who had gone with Mary as maids of honour. Their sister, Barbara, was no doubt part of the contingent who visited from the English court. She had stayed in

London to join the household of Princess Anne and became increasingly close to Sarah Churchill.

Anne and Maria were not able to stay in Holland for long, and we have little record of their time there, beyond James's letters to William thanking him for his gracious hospitality. But the court they returned to in London was in chaos. Maria wrote to her brother in November that 'there are so many hoaxes, so many supposed conspiracies and so many accusations here that it is impossible to write a hundredth part of them'.[4] She was probably referring here to the impeachment of five Catholic lords: William Herbert, William Petre, Henry Arundel, John Bellasyse (the husband of Maria's dear friend, and erstwhile mistress of James, Susan Bellasyse) and William Howard, who was a close friend of James. These accusations were clearly fabricated. Charles himself pointed out that Bellasyse was so gouty he could barely stand, and that Arundel and Howard (though related) hated each other so much that they had not said a word to each other in a quarter of a century. Was it to be believed that these ancient men, from ancient loyal families, were now to be feared as potential assassins? Anthony Ashley Cooper, Earl of Shaftesbury (James's greatest enemy at the court), claimed they were, and had them sent to the Tower of London, where they remained for many years; Petre died there in 1684, and Howard was executed as a traitor in 1680. James tried to intervene for his friend, but to no avail, and when Maria reported the news of his death to her brother, she wrote that he 'died with great resolution as a good Catholic, declaring himself, above his soul, innocent of all that they had accused him of, and he made a beautiful speech before he died'.[5]

By December 1678, things had only got worse. Maria wrote:

> [Since] my return I have had little joy, since there is nothing here but lies and hoaxes, and of such a kind that I have never heard of, those who have accused the Queen herself, but I hope in God that these men will be discovered and that they will be learned.[6]

Not even Queen Caterina, surely the most loyal woman to Charles in the entire country, was safe from the conspiracy. But Charles was furious, and Oates soon realised he had gone too far; he revoked his accusation. Others were not so lucky. Maria wrote again just a week later to report that her friend and secretary, Edward Coleman, had been executed for his alleged part in this made-up plot. Unfortunately for Coleman, he had been writing to the French court about the possibilities of England returning to Catholicism, but these were old letters and certainly said nothing of a great and bloody Catholic uprising. But they were taken as proof, and he was condemned to a traitor's death. When he went to the scaffold, to his gruesome fate of being hanged, drawn and quartered, it was reported that he went bravely, and that 'he died a Catholic'.[7] The loss of Coleman to the conspiracy was painful to Maria, and the future looked bleak. Hortense Mancini was accused of being a conspirator, and Maria feared deeply for this woman who had become a close companion. It was not surprising that she was targeted: she was a heady mix of Catholic, French and Italian. The French ambassador, Barillon, wrote to Louis, 'I think your majesty will learn with some surprise that Madame Mazarin was named today by Oates as an accomplice in the schemes formed against the state and religion. The King of England mocked this accusation and spoke to me of it as something that was utterly ridiculous. But he says the same of the Lords who are in the Tower and have been tried by the courts.'[8] With Coleman's fate fresh in her mind, Hortense began to think that she should leave England and go into a convent while she still had the chance. Her sister Marie was living in one in Madrid, and she thought seriously about joining her there. She decided to stay, perhaps at the beseeching pleas of her dear friend, Saint-Évremond, who feared that, if she left, she would never come back. 'You will find yourselves locked in a convent', he maintained. But though she stayed, her exile- and émigrée-attended salon was under threat when parliament ordered all Catholics (excepting traders, travellers and homeowners) to leave England.

Maria wrote to Francesco that 'the state of all Catholics in this country moves one to pity' and she expresses her compassion for the 'many poor wretches [who] are forced by necessity to abandon our holy faith' for fear of their lives. The Italian theatre troupe that had newly arrived – upon her request – from Francesco's court in Modena were afraid to play their comedies before the court, and even when they did no one wanted to be seen to attend. Maria tells how 'to my great disgust I have been forced to send away all my English servants who are Catholics, all being forbidden by parliament to come to court'.[9] Hortense Mancini was forced to send her two French servants back to France.

The beginning of the new year in 1679 brought little change. Maria told her brother:

> We have undoubtedly had the most melancholic carnival I have seen in my life, there has been neither a ball, nor a comedy, except for the occasional Italian, but not often, the poor people [the acting company] have nothing to show for it, because here we have so much skulduggery, even though there is no Parliament, that no one wants to laugh.[10]

Charles thought things might die down if Maria and James left court for a while. James refused to go unless given a direct order from the king which soon followed. But when it came to it, Charles lamented having to part with his brother and sister-in-law, and Maria later recalled that when he went to see them off on their sea voyage, he attempted to delay them, saying with tears in his eyes, 'the wind is contrary, you cannot go on board'. She regretted her sharp response: 'How sire? You are grieved? You who send us into exile! Of course we must go, since you have ordered it.'[11] They took with them very few members of their household; Maria was allowed Lady Roscommon, Margaret Dawson, Contessa Lucrezia Vezzani Pratoneri and Pelegrina Turini. Their children, Anne and little Isabella, were ordered to remain in London.

The voyage to Rotterdam in March 1679 took eight days, and the sea was indeed rather rough. There they were met in great state by twenty coaches and royally escorted to Brussels. Though they were supposed to stay at the Hôtel de Bassigny (where Charles II had for a time lived during his exile), their rooms were not ready in time, so they were taken to the palace of the Prince of Ligne. Maria soon decided to make the most of the opportunity to visit Mary again in The Hague. She wrote from Brussels to her brother:

> Tomorrow, I go to Holland to see the Princess who is poorly with a fever and pains, but no further hope of a child, since she has passed the nine months since her pregnancy in great loneliness … I shall stay a few days until she is better, since she wishes to see me as much as I wish to see her.[12]

Their stay in The Hague was a miserable one, though they were pleased to see Mary and to be able to comfort her. Maria wrote to Lady Bellasyse who, despite having been James's mistress, had become one of Maria's closest friends.

> You cannot imagine the pleasure I have to hear any news from dear England, let 'em be what kind they will. Them as you sent me were very pleasant ones and made me laugh which few things do at this time, being as sad and melancholy as it is possible for anyone to be, and I think I have great reason to be so. Pray don't fail, if you love me, to tell me all the silly news you know, and of all kinds.[13]

James, too, wrote home often, though with a more political bent. He wanted vengeance for what was being done to him, and to his fellow Catholics in England, and believed that Charles must make a stand and show who was in charge, saying that parliament – and indeed any who opposed the monarch – were not to be trusted. He wrote to his brother of betrayed kings of the past: 'remember Edward II,

Richard II, and the king our father.'[14] When James wrote this letter, he had no doubt heard of the machinations of parliament. The conspiracy had given them increased leverage to oust Catholics from the court, and they began to draw up the exclusion bill, which they would present for debate before parliament in April 1679, and which would (if successful) see James barred from the line of succession unless he renounced his Catholic faith. This was the first of three times that the bill was to be brought before parliament and was the beginning of what became known as the Exclusion Crisis.[15] At the head of this was Shaftesbury, who could not escape suspicion for his own role in the origins of this 'Popish Plot'. This bill would have seen Catholics banned from becoming monarch, and it had a lot of popularity among the emerging Whig faction of parliament.

There were multiple views of who should take James's place; many favoured Princess Mary, but many, too, favoured the Duke of Monmouth. During his investigations of the Popish Plot, Monmouth had begun to be influenced by the Protestant fear of Catholicism, having previously asserted that he believed in freedom of worship for all. He was also having his head turned by those who would make him king.

When James wrote in warning to his brother, he knew that the bill had already had two hearings, had received widespread support (207 votes to 128) and that it had only been prevented from passing by Charles swiftly dissolving parliament to prevent a third reading. Charles did not respond to James's pleas but found them worrying amid the political crisis. He told Barillon, 'When I am dead and gone, I know not what my brother will do; I am very much afraid that when he comes to the crown, he will be obliged to travel again … to leave his native soil.'[16]

❖

When the Yorks returned to Brussels, they were housed at the Hôtel des Hornes (which today is the Collège Jan Berchmans), and in August 1679 were joined by friends: Sarah and John Churchill,

Sarah's sister Frances, the princesses Anne and Isabella, Lord and Lady Peterborough and Lady Bellasyse (whose husband had just been arrested for his apparent role in the Popish Plot). They, too, travelled via The Hague and saw Mary, and it was there reported that Anne and Sarah were virtually inseparable.

Another addition to the party in Brussels was Maria's mother, Laura. She was in the midst of a quarrel with her son, who had taken on his role as ruler, and her removal from Modena was not entirely of her own choice, but she took the opportunity to see her daughter again after five and a half years. Laura wrote to Rinaldo that she found Maria quite grown and 'full of goodness and grace ... My lord duke adores her and thanked me again for having given her to him. Certainly, he is a most excellent and amiable gentleman.'[17] It is difficult to say who Maria was happiest to see again, but the arrival of so many beloved friends and family must have eased the suffering of her exile.

But the party were not all together for long, for at the end of August 1679 Charles II fell gravely ill. The Duke of Monmouth, who was at William and Mary's court, decided to return to England. Hearing of this, several loyal courtiers, including Louise de Kéroualle, thought it wise to call James back from exile. James's summoning was as much about being on site if the worst should happen and Monmouth be declared king as it was about seeing his brother before he died. James left Brussels on 29 August, disguised as a common man – wearing 'a blacke peruque only, and a plaine stuffe suit, without his starre and Garter' – and set out by post for England with Lord Peterborough, and John and Sarah Churchill.[18] Sarah was expecting a child and took the opportunity to return to London for the birth. When they arrived at Dover from Calais, John donned a French scarf and took the lead as the head of the party. They were recognised, but their disguises were respected, and the postmaster did not give them away. When they arrived in London they headed for the home of Allen Apsley, James's Treasurer and the father of Anne and Mary's great friend Frances, and they spent the night there.

This must have been a nerve-racking time for everyone. If Charles died, James would be king. Would parliament accept a Catholic monarch? Who would remain loyal? Who would change sides to the next heir? And who would that next heir be: James's daughter Mary, or the illegitimate Duke of Monmouth? Charles recovered from his illness, but the questions asked then were a dress rehearsal for the events that would be played out again almost a decade later.

When James arrived at the palace, he fell to his knees and begged forgiveness for arriving without royal permission. Though he had been summoned he was instructed to pretend it was his idea. He found his brother recovered and exceedingly happy to see him. But his stay was not to be long; he still had many enemies at court, and the political situation was little changed. He was to return directly to Brussels, with John Churchill and Lord Peterborough accompanying him. James protested that if he had to go back into exile, so too should Monmouth. He no longer trusted his nephew and was worried that he was becoming too much of a figurehead. And he was worried, too, about the favouritism that Charles showed him. Monmouth was furious, but he did as he was told and left England for Holland. The frictions developing between nephew and uncle would never heal, and the family which had once been close began to splinter.

Maria was beyond happy to see James, having suffered 'a thousand fears and apprehensions' while he was away, due to his 'many enemies in England'.[19] And he brought positive tidings. They were ordered to move their exile closer to home, to Scotland, where James was given the role of the King's Lord High Commissioner. Maria was pleased to leave Brussels, recognising that while they were not going back to London this was a step in the right direction.

They initially went back via The Hague and dined with Mary and William. When they parted the following day, Maria could hardly have imagined that she would never see them again. Here Maria also said goodbye to Laura, and the parting was a tearful one. Maria's sadness can hardly have been tempered by her journey, for a rougher crossing cannot be imagined. The high winds pushed them to the Norfolk coast, where they docked, and John Churchill was sent ashore with a letter for Charles, pleading the case of Maria, who was so ill that she had been vomiting blood. Charles, of course, took pity on his beloved sister-in-law, and the royal party arrived at St James's Palace on 14 October.

Though they knew in their hearts that they would not be allowed to stay, they were happy to be back in their home for even a short time. But they soon realised that they were not met with joy by most courtiers, who preferred to hedge their bets than show outward support for the couple. That is, except for the Duchess of Monmouth, who went to call on them promptly. She, too, had just returned to court after a period spent in France. James and Maria enjoyed but a week in London before the plot again reared its ugly head, resulting in Lord Peterborough, Lord Castlemaine and Lady Powis being sent to the Tower.

Charles implored Maria to stay behind in London, to let James go into exile without her, and she must have been tempted. Once again, her daughter, Isabella, and Princess Anne were to stay behind, and the idea of parting from them again must have been terrible, especially as Isabella was increasingly frail. But Maria's sense of duty was stronger than anything else: she would be with her husband. James knew that his wife was intelligent and strong, but he was still overwhelmed by her loyalty to him at this moment. Years later he recorded in his memoirs how, even when she had nearly died on the voyage and probably faced just as arduous a journey again, she was determined to be companion to him during his 'misfortunes and hardships', calling it 'a kind of martyrdom'.[20] After the terrible journey by sea, Charles agreed that they should travel to Scotland overland.

Their time in England coincided with another event: the unexpected confirmation of the marriage between Isabella Bennet and Henry Fitzroy. Isabella had just turned twelve and was now considered old enough to become a wife to the sixteen-year-old. John Evelyn was in attendance and wrote of the great wrong he felt had been done in giving so exceptional a young woman as Isabella to such a rogue as Henry.

When the marriage had been first performed in 1672, Evelyn had written that he 'took no great joy at the thing', and it seems that his views had not changed. Fitzroy had been sent away to sea, but was still found to be very wild, and Evelyn wrote at the marriage in 1679 that:

> This sweetest, most hopeful, most beautiful, child, and most virtuous, too, was sacrificed to a boy that had been rudely bred, without anything to encourage them but his Majesty's pleasure. I pray God the sweet child find it to her advantage, who, if my augury deceive me not, will in a few years be such a paragon as were fit to make the wife of the greatest Prince in Europe! ... My love to my Lord Arlington's family, and the sweet child made me behold all this with regret.[21]

We have no record as to who was in attendance, though we know that the marriage took place in her father's apartments at Whitehall, that the Bishop of Rochester officiated, and that the king was present. Perhaps her friend Mary Evelyn was there with her father, and maybe Maria and James were also present, to witness yet another young girl given in marriage without any say in the matter. John Evelyn finished his diary entry with a note of sceptical optimism:

> the Duke of Grafton affects the sea, to which I find his father intends to use him, he may emerge a plain, useful and robust officer: and were he polished, a tolerable person; for he is exceedingly handsome, by far surpassing any of the King's other natural issue.[22]

Whether or not he was to be confirmed in his hopes of the improvement of Henry's character, at least Isabella was able to enjoy the beginning of her married life without her husband.

❖

Upon arrival in Edinburgh, James and Maria were received by cheering crowds. Though the temperature was freezing (it was 22 November) Maria rode into the city in an open carriage. Thousands rushed forward to kiss her hand, and in a rare humble gesture James condescended to rise and take off his hat to them. They entered the grounds at Holyrood Palace, their home during their stay, to the pealing of bells and the sounds of pipes playing 'The King enjoys his own again', a Cavalier anthem written by Martin Parker in 1643. This tune would take on added significance just a decade later, when it became a stalwart song of the Jacobite cause.

Part of the reason they were so welcomed was that Scotland had been rather neglected by the Stuart monarchs. When James I had left Edinburgh some eighty years before, promising to return every three years, he went back just once, in 1617, and Charles I had hardly shown more willing (indeed, the Civil War which saw him deposed began in Scotland). Charles II hated Scotland, and reportedly said after 1650 that he would rather be hanged than ever go back there.[23] James, who also held the Scottish title of Duke of Albany, was seen as a true Scottish Stuart, come to take a position of government. During his time in Edinburgh, the Scottish parliament passed an act of succession which promised that James would be the next King of Scotland. While back in England parliament were about to present another exclusion bill, Scotland promised their loyalty. And they also promised to entertain their future king to the best of their abilities. As Christmas approached, they held an enormous banquet with splendidly dressed and decorated food: gilded salmon, turkey with the royal arms emblazoned on the skin, sumptuous venison pastries and other delights all surrounded with golden fringing.

The palace at Holyrood was far more appealing than those in London. Architecturally it was closer to the Este palaces, built in the classical tradition around a beautiful internal courtyard. The ceilings in the large rooms were high and all was comparatively modern, ornate marble and plaster, thick new tapestries and hearthrugs. The windows looked out onto the dramatic mountains beyond. But while the palace was more comfortable, Edinburgh did not immediately agree with Maria, as she found the bitter cold and winds unremitting.

Soon, however, she found ways of brightening up their time in exile and wrote to Lady Bellasyse that she was 'as well pleased as I can be out of England', and that she had plans to dance that night 'which I have not yet done since Christmas'. Considering this was only written on 16 January, we must assume that in London she was used to dancing very frequently. She also reports that 'my maids are going to act another play, tis to be Aurenzeb'.[24] *Aurengzebe* was a play by Dryden which had been written and first performed at the King's Theatre in 1675. That Maria uses the word 'another' is suggestive of other, unrecorded, entertainments in exile. Churchill, too, wrote back to Sarah of the coming performance, 'most of the Duke's and Duchess's servants have parts given in "Aurenzebe", which is to be acted by them before the Duke and Duchess'.

Sarah gave birth soon after the York party returned to Scotland, a girl, whom they called Harriot. In a letter dating soon after, John wrote to Sarah: 'Pray let Harriot know by some very intelligible sign that I am very well pleased with her hair and that I long to see her, hoping that since she has her mother's coloured hair that she may also be like her.' And it seemed his wish was soon to be granted: just as the Yorks were starting to settle into their lives in exile, they were recalled to England in May. John wrote to Sarah when he was waiting for the boat: 'I hope all the red spots of the child will be gone against I see her, and her nose straight, so that I may fancy it to be like the mother, for as she has your coloured hair, so I would have her be like you in all things else.' When John arrived home to Jermyn Street, he found that Harriot had died. The red spots had been a sign of the dreaded smallpox. He never got his wish to see her honey-coloured hair.

When Maria had arrived back in London, she wrote to her brother that after eight long days of travel, 'I have at last by the grace of God arrived safe and sound in this place where I hope to stay for a great while if it pleases God.'[25] In London they were greeted by cheering crowds: though the Popish Plot was far from over and had stoked up considerable bad feeling, they still had many loyal supporters. But James's days in England were spent under constant pressure, as his brother and friends attempted to convince him to change his religion. Even Maria was called on to help, though she laughed at the idea.

Their days were often spent at Newmarket, in revelry and horse riding, but the atmosphere was tense. Perhaps sensing that he didn't have much time, James took the opportunity to petition Charles for John's advancement: a governorship, or an admiralty, maybe an ambassadorship to Paris, considering how proficient John's French was. Charles suggested The Hague. Indeed, it seems that William requested him: 'the English Colonel is a man of no experience in public affairs, but that the Prince of Orange wishes to have him, and wants no other man as English Minister,' wrote Barillon to Louis. But all this came to nought. When the increasingly fraught political situation meant that James and Maria were returned to exile in Scotland, they again took John with them, and Sarah stayed behind. Since he was going back into exile, James wrote that as long as he was not in England 'I would not willingly have Churchill from me'. He found that John – who was described at this time as James's 'only favourite' – was too important to him.[26]

Back in exile, James began to take a more serious role in government. His arrival did not begin well. When the royal party rode up to Edinburgh Castle, to the sound of a royal salute, the cannon burst. It had been an object of some importance to the nation: Mons Meg had reportedly been given to the Scottish King James II by the

Duke of Burgundy, as a sign of his support, in 1457. To this day it is one of the largest cannons ever made and, in its day, when fired its thunderous boom could be heard from two miles away. By this point it had been out of military service for over a century, but still played an important ceremonial function – it had saluted the marriage of Mary Queen of Scots to the Dauphin of France in 1542. When the cannon was fired for James, and the barrel burst, there were mutterings among the Scots that the English had done it on purpose, out of jealousy that their cannons were so inferior; it was an Englishman who had loaded the cannon, after all. For James, the accident was a terrible omen.

Reports of James's tenure differ enormously. Some say that he used his position to rout out Nonconformists, who he witnessed being tortured 'with an unmoved indifference and with an attention, as if he had been to look on some curious experiment'.[27] Though it is unlikely that James really witnessed any interrogations, he certainly gave his consent for torture to be used, and during his time in Scotland James reportedly showed signs of his preference for absolutist rule. However, such accounts should be viewed with caution. The above quote comes from his great enemy Gilbert Burnet, who would have delighted in exaggerating the horrors of James's actions. The Scottish bishops wrote in praise of James in Scotland saying how well he ruled there, that he was 'highly complimented by all, and seemed to have overcome all difficulties'.[28] As ever, the records passed down to us are full of factional politics, and the truth remains somewhere murkily in between.

Maria, at least, was by consensus a triumph, and during this longer period away she began to host tea parties and other entertainments in her rooms. Caterina de Braganza had famously brought tea drinking to England when she arrived in 1662, and it was Maria who now introduced it into Scotland. There are a few surviving letters from James to his favourite niece, Charlotte Lee, Countess of Lichfield (another of Charles's children with Barbara Villiers), which tell us something of how the ducal court passed their time in Scotland.[29]

Many of his reports suggest that the stay was often tedious: he wrote, 'we have here very long days and no hot weather and this toune begins to be very empty of company'.

In Edinburgh, on 28 January 1681, Maria wrote to her brother telling him there was no good news. The Commons were still trying to vote for James's exclusion from the throne, this time in favour of his daughter Mary. Charles had again prorogued parliament to prevent the bill from being heard. James, she says, had sent a man to his brother to ask him if they might return, but she had little hope of success. In the meantime, they were all trying to carry on as though all was well. She wrote, 'this evening I must dance, I have great difficulty in enjoying myself, and I often have melancholy, to tell the truth I have many reasons for having it, but I want, however, to try to overcome it'.[30] She would have to bear her exile for more than a year longer.

And soon she had to bear another source of melancholy: on 2 March, Maria wrote to one of the nuns in Modena of the death of her five-year-old daughter Isabella back in London:

> It has pleased God to send me a great grief in taking from me one of the dearest things I had in the world, and which I hoped He would have left me, of His goodness, to be a comfort in my afflictions; but the Lord gave, the Lord hath taken away, blessed be the name of the Lord. It comforts me to think that I have more angels to pray for me, and I ought to feel honoured that whereas other women bear children for this world, I have borne all mine for God.

James wrote to Charles asking for Anne to be able to join them in their grief, and Maria wrote to Sarah Churchill. Sarah was in the final months of pregnancy with her second child. Another girl, Henrietta, was born in July, and by September Sarah was on her way to Scotland to comfort Maria. She left her baby in the care of friends in the country. John wrote to her from Berwick, where he went to meet her en route, to remind her to bring coffee, since they had no such comforts in Scotland. Sarah would remain in Scotland for the next eight months.

Though they continued to mourn the loss of their child, James's letters during the summer suggest that life began to pick up a little, as the weather improved and family and friends joined their ranks. He wrote that 'the Dutchesse and my Daughter ride abroad almost every day', and tells throughout the summer of the ways they all entertain themselves: 'bassett [sic] is much in fashion, and some tyms we go to the plays ... I am a going to see them this afternone, so that I have not tyme to say more.' The play he speaks of here was performed by 'players come out of Ireland', but he also reports that the court put on performances, as they were wont to do in London: this from 26 November, 'my daughter acted on Thursday last, for the thurd time and last time her play, there were five of them that did their parts very well, and they were very well drest, so that they made a very fine show, and such a one as had not been seen in this country before.'[31] The play that James refers to here was almost certainly Nathaniel Lee's *Mithridates*, which we know had a profound effect on Anne.

This play, then, was performed in exile, but it was not the first time Anne had played in it; James says that it was the third time he had seen her act it. The play was most likely first seen at court, perhaps to honour Queen Caterina. Nathaniel Lee wrote in the dedication to the printed copy that the queen 'had been pleased to grace him with her Presence, and promised it again with such particular praises'.[32] It was a few months before this performance in exile that we have the first record of Anne addressing Frances Apsley as 'Semandra' in a letter from 18 June that year.

Considering this performance in exile, it is likely that Sarah Churchill – who had joined the party in September – was one of 'the five of them that did their parts very well'. Indeed, a copy of the play text was recorded in her personal inventory of books in the 1690s, and she had a history of acting in court performances.[33]

Which role might she have taken? Records suggest that Anne played Semandra in this production, and that she was coached in this role by a man named Joseph Ashbury, who was the leader of an acting troupe in Scotland called the Smock Alley Players. Perhaps it was thought more seemly for her to take on the female role, or she may have chosen to change her part. Did Sarah Churchill play her Ziphares? It was certainly during these months in exile that Sarah and Anne became even closer than before, and Anne did not like to be without her.

For the other cast members, we should look to Maria's maids: another account says that the play was performed by 'Lady Anne, the duke's daughter, and the Ladies of Honour'. Records for Maria's household accounts are scarce, and for these years in Edinburgh there is very little to go on. The best attempts to reconstruct her household involve looking at who were recorded as her maids by Chamberlayne (though he is often unreliable) and from seeing if there are crossovers between the 1677 book and the 1682 book, which are housed at the British Library. For the years of 1680 and 1681, there are no records at all, but for 1679 Chamberlayne recorded Miss Brooke, Mary Clarke, Katherine Fortrey and Catherine Sedley. We know that Catherine Sedley did not go to Scotland with them; her affair with James caused Maria pain for many years, and one of the few advantages of exile was not having to live in close proximity to her. Maria's Ladies of the Bedchamber were her previous maid of honour, Isabella Boynton, and Susan Bellasyse, the latter of whom was back in England sending her news. So perhaps we should look to Miss Brooke, Mary Clarke, Katherine Fortrey and Isabella Boynton to make up the numbers.

As her maids were involved, Maria may well have had a hand in this production. Having complained to her brother in December of 1680 that 'here we have no comedies', she could have taken matters into her own hands, and we know it was not the only performance the court in exile organised. In Brussels she had arranged for a performance of a comedy, *The Man of Mode*, which had been written in

1676 by George Etherege and dedicated to Maria, and earlier that year her maids had performed Dryden's *Aurengzebe*. These performances, however, did not ingratiate the court with their hosts. Such entertainments were not usual in Edinburgh, and in particular one so risqué as *Mithridates* was shocking indeed.

The royal court in Scotland heard much of the machinations of parliament. In December 1680, Maria wrote to her brother that the House of Commons had passed the exclusion bill, but that it was rejected in the Lords, and that they were planning to try to limit James's powers if he were to become king making him a 'Rè di carte'. She adds 'we do not yet know what they will resolve, only that it will not be good for us.'[34]

The plays were one way to distract them from their worries, as James had done in exile in Paris in the 1650s. Another (for Maria and her ladies at least) was embroidery, and a sampler found in the Burrell Collection in Glasgow may date from this time in Scotland. We do not know whether she made it herself or if it was a gift from one of her maids, but it is a precious example of the kinds of ways that women of the court passed their days. It was precious, too, to Maria, who kept it in her possession until her death. The work is curious: the style of dress appears older than would have been fashionable in the 1680s, and the piece is unfinished.

By this time James was getting used to his exile, even writing that 'we here do not passe our tyme so ill as you in England thinke we do, for we have plays, ride abroad, when tis good weather, play at Bassett and have a greate deele of good company.' Maria, on the other hand, was finding it rather harder to be contented, and the loss of her daughter Isabella was a grief she could not forget. She wrote to her friend Elizabeth Clifford, 'I cannot send you a word of news from this dismal place'.[35]

Maria lost herself in prayer and a great deal of horse riding. She became thin and ill, and though she was an accomplished horsewoman she had a near-fatal fall in October. She was riding fast, the horse stumbled, she was thrown, but her skirts got caught in the stirrups and she was dragged and kicked as the horse continued running. She must have been a terrifying sight for James, who caught up with her; she was unconscious and covered in blood. The fears for her life were increased by the fact that she was very recently pregnant again. James wrote to Charlotte that,

> You will by the last post have heard what a terrible fall … the Dutchesse had and really 'twas a miracle she was not spoyled, and 'tis a great mercy she had no more harme, she is now God be thanked as well as can be expected after such an accident, and her legs mend apace but yett tyde to ly on hir bed, or sitt in a chaire, and it must be yet some days before she must walk.

In January there was dancing at the court in Holyrood, but Maria was not yet ready to join in. James wrote: 'we have now downe right winter weather … so that there is no sturing abroad … the Dutchesse plays often at Bassett, and my daughter dances country dances as offten, which the Dutchesse cannot yet do, her leg not being quite well enough for that tho she walks about.' Though her injuries were considerable, miraculously she did not miscarry. She was probably pleased to have an excuse not to dance; in all her pregnancies she suffered with terrible sickness.

11

Going Home

In England, the Exclusion Crisis was coming to a head. The exclusion bill was to have its third reading, and it was very likely to pass. If that were to happen, the result would be that James (and any future Catholic heirs) would be banned from the line of succession, and there was a strong chance that the Duke of Monmouth would become the heir. The two readings of the bill thus far had only been prevented from passing by Charles dissolving parliament, but he knew this could not go on indefinitely. Tensions between the Whig and Tory factions had spilled over into the London populace, and the city had become an unruly hotbed, in which bonfires raged, and increasing numbers of the population were walking around armed with daggers and knives. It felt as if it was only a matter of time before chaos ensued, and the different parliamentary factions were each stoking their side of the feud. Charles moved the parliament to Oxford, in part to escape the violence of the city and in the hope that things would settle down in their absence, and also because he knew that he had more power there than in London, for Oxford had always been a Royalist stronghold. Charles will have remembered being garrisoned in these collegiate walls as a child with his parents during the Civil War of the 1640s.

The house had sat for a week, and it was only going to go one way. The majority were in favour of removing James from the line of succession. Charles could not take any risks. The 28th of March 1681 began in the same way as every other day in the final week of March 1681. Charles II had left his apartments at Balliol in a sedan chair, with another following behind, and made his way to where parliament sat at Christ Church. But unlike previous days, the second chair did not carry one of his Gentlemen of the Bedchamber: it held the royal crown and robes of state. When the king arrived in the Lords Chamber, he put on these trappings of monarchy. He placed his robes over his shoulders, and the weighty jewelled crown – which had been made for his coronation twenty years before – on his head. He sat on his throne, looking every inch the king.

Parliament had been sitting and debating a point of constitutional law when Black Rod (whose role is still to this day to control who enters the parliamentary chambers, and who summons MPs to hear the King's Speech at the opening of parliament), at this time a man named Sir Edward Carteret, had entered and told them their king required their presence. They quickly rose and made their way to the Lords Chamber, where they found their monarch seated in state. When all were present, Charles addressed them.

> My Lords and gentlemen. That all the world may see to what a point we have come, that we are not like to have a good end when divisions at the beginning are such, therefore, my Lord Chancellor, do as I have commanded you.[1]

His chancellor, Heneage Finch, Earl of Nottingham, obeyed, saying: 'His Majesty has commanded me to say that it is his Majesty's royal pleasure and will that this Parliament be dissolved, and this Parliament is dissolved.'[2] Once these words were spoken, Charles stood, walked out of the room and made his way straight back to London. Shaftesbury and others refused to move; they insisted that parliament still sat. For an hour a core group of Whigs stayed, but the King's army was stationed just outside Oxford, and gradually the number of those willing to try to make a stand dwindled.

Shaftesbury was the last to accept defeat, but finally he, too, left the chamber, never to return. It was the last time parliament would sit under Charles II: he never called them again.

When all was over, an Oxford scholar named Zaccheus Isham wrote to a friend that 'we have not been so much an University here of late, as a stage; upon which very suddain turns, and changes of state affairs have been acted. What denomination the Drama must have, cannot appear till the event; for the Last Act is not yet come, & we must expect other revolutions.'[3]

Parliament was increasingly becoming divided into two factions: the Whigs (who supported the bill, wanted greater tolerance for Protestant Nonconformists and wanted more checks on royal power) and the Tories (who supported the established Church, the king and the hereditary principle). This crisis was essentially the beginning of the two-party system in British government, but at this stage the rumbling undertones spoke of a potential second civil war. The Whigs were the stronger party, but they did not have the status quo on their side. In this third attempt to bring the bill before the Commons, Lord Shaftesbury proposed that Monmouth be declared legitimate and, more radically, insisted that parliament legislate to pass both this and the exclusion bill without the consent of the king. Shaftesbury had overplayed his hand, and this was the beginning of his swift fall from power. He was arrested for high treason, and fled into exile in Holland, where he died in 1683. But the divisions which had been formed continued to bubble away, and Isham would be right when he predicted that there would be 'other revolutions'.

By the time the Exclusion Crisis was over, at least twenty-two people had been executed as traitors in the Popish Plot, many were still awaiting trial and countless more lost their livelihoods and suffered immeasurable abuses. The anti-Catholic hysteria that always simmered beneath the surface had been stoked up and released. Effigies of the Pope had been burned on huge bonfires; Catholics were chased from their homes, threatened, beaten. Anti-Catholic propaganda filled London, some of which came in the form of playing cards, which depicted scenes from four perceived Catholic plots, some from the previous century: the Spanish Armada, the plot of William Parry to assassinate Elizabeth I (known as 'Dr Parry's Plot'), the Gunpowder Plot and the Popish Plot.

By 1681 the appetite for punishment and bloodshed had begun to wane. Several of the priests who had been executed had been pillars of their communities, and Protestants and Catholics alike were disgusted by their gruesome fates. The hysteria was over almost as quickly as it had begun, and Oates's fall from grace was equally swift. He was ordered to leave the apartments he had been given in Whitehall at the end of August. He did not go quietly, shouting abuse at the king and denouncing James as a traitor. He was arrested and fined £100,000 (the equivalent of around £11,500,000 in today's money), which seems a small price in comparison to the suffering he had caused. James would be less lenient. When he became king, he ordered that Oates be retried. His new sentence was life imprisonment, with the additional humiliation of being paraded through the streets of London and whipped for five days of every year of the rest of his life. The sentence began immediately. The next day Oates was pilloried. After two more days he was stripped, tied to a cart and taken from Aldgate to Newgate while constantly being whipped. The following day he was whipped from Newgate to Tyburn, the scene of the executions of the victims of his plot. James did not forgive or forget. He had lost close friends in Oates's seditious conspiracy, friends who had died painfully, though they were innocent. It would be many years before Catholics were allowed to stand in parliament, in the Commons or the Lords. London and the court were irrevocably altered by the events of 1678–81. It would not be the last time that James and Maria would have to suffer at the hands of an anti-Catholic conspiracy.

Meanwhile, James was called back to London where Charles agreed that he and Maria could end their exile and come home. By 1682, Maria had been in exile for three years. Her days had been punctuated with playing cards, a pursuit she described a few months before as one she had been 'reduced to'.[4] But in April, finally, the end was in sight. She took up her pen and wrote to her brother in Modena, 'Caro fratello',

> My Lord Duke is still in England, and he receives a thousand favours and graces from the King. They have gone from Newmarket to London where his Majesty wants me to join them, and in two or three weeks the Lord Duke will come and take me in a *gran vascello* that is safer and has less movement than the *Saltiti* boats, I hope that God will accompany me and that I will arrive safe and sound at home.[5]

This *gran vascello* (large ship), which was considered so preferable to the *saltiti* (or jumping boats), was called the *Gloucester*. It was a great warship, beautifully decorated with carvings by Grinling Gibbons, and was designed to undergo voyages to the West Indies. It had taken part in several military battles and campaigns: the invasion of Jamaica (1655), the Battle of Lowestoft (1665) and the Battle of Sole Bay (1672) – in which the *Gloucester* was commanded by James, as head of the Royal Navy, against the Dutch – to name but a few. But since these battles it had been extensively refurbished, and was due to sail to Tangier, to continue England's colonial conquests. The ship's captain, Sir John Berry, was ordered to first escort the Duke of York to Edinburgh, and to return with Maria and her remaining household in tow, before setting off for Morocco. They boarded the ship at the beginning of May, and among the passengers were John Churchill, James's brother-in-law James Hyde and James's favourite hound, Mumper.

They set out on 3 May but soon ran into trouble. On the morning of the 6th, the ship ran aground on the Norfolk coast by Great Yarmouth. This treacherous spot was well known, and there had been heated debates over the course of the night before, particularly between James, a seasoned sailor, and the captain, concerning the best way to navigate the dangerous sandbanks. The captain of the *Gloucester* was also an experienced sailor and did not take kindly to criticism, even from the heir to the throne. We do not know who favoured which course or who won the battle of wills, but in the early hours of the morning the ship crashed violently onto the sandbanks and water quickly began to flood the vessel. Within an hour the *Gloucester* had sunk to the bottom of the sea. It is estimated that up to 250 of the 330 on board drowned. Competing accounts tell very different stories about the decisions made on board the *Gloucester*, and blame was apportioned according to existing loyalties. It perhaps goes without saying that there was a faction that blamed James; they said that he prioritised saving his dogs over the men on board – though if this were true then James's favourite hound, Mumper, would not have been listed among the casualties. And though neither dog nor priest, James's brother-in-law, James Hyde, who he was close to, was also among the dead. We will never know what really happened, though perhaps inevitably it was the captain who was given the official blame, arrested and charged.

On the night of 7 May, in Edinburgh, Maria was getting ready for bed when James's equerry, Colonel Griffin, was announced in her chambers. As soon as she saw his haggard face she feared the worst. The last time he had arrived like this it was with a message from Charles II to tell her that her daughter Isabella had died. She asked him where James was and was told he was in her antechamber. When she saw James, he told her what had happened, of all the men who had been lost. He told her that they would have to tell Lady Peterborough – who was in exile with them – that her nineteen-year-old nephew, Lord O'Brien, was among the dead. For the rest of her life Maria said that she trembled every time she thought of the sinking of the *Gloucester*.

The ship that was to take them back to England was called, ironically, the *Happy Return* and had been part of the *Gloucester*'s convoy. Maria was heavily pregnant, and she was levered onto the ship in a chair with pulleys. She did not travel with Lady Peterborough, who was worried that she would upset Maria with her weeping, so much did she grieve for her nephew.

12

'THE RYE HOUSE PLOT'

James and Maria returned to cheering crowds welcoming them back to England. Celebratory bonfires lit up the streets of London, and Dryden wrote a poem for Maria, to welcome her home. It was called 'Prologue to the Duchess on her return from Scotland' and heralded a new age of patronage from the beautiful duchess. He wrote that without her the nation had been a cultural desert:

When factious rage to cruel exile drove
The Queen of beauty and the court of love,
The Muses drooped with their forsaken arts,
And the sad Cupids broke their useless darts.
Our fruitful plains to wilds and deserts turned,
Like Eden's face when banished man it mourned.[1]

Maria is described as 'a Venus', who 'brings every grace triumphant in her train'.[2] Her grace and beauty alone, Dryden proclaims, will be enough to overcome the 'Faction, Strife and Pride' that had led to her exile.[3] Of course, as a poem it might claim to be a prophecy, but it is really rather desperately trying to imagine this harmonious future into existence. And what ultimately stands out in Dryden's poem is not the reconciliation that Maria might bring to the nation, but, rather, the struggle she faces:

Distempered Zeal, Sedition, cankered Hate
No more shall vex the church and tear the state;
No more shall Faction civil discords move.[4]

And as it was, Dryden's vision of an end to factionalism and civil discord was hopelessly over-optimistic, as the coming years would show. The letters flying to and from the court as Maria's pregnancy progressed present a court irrevocably divided. And Maria became increasingly fretful; the pressure of producing an heir was so strong, and despite her many pregnancies she still had no living children. James was worried about his wife and wrote to Maria's mother, Laura, asking her to come and be with her daughter for the birth of the child. Laura dutifully came, but her arrival only produced rumours that she had smuggled a baby boy with her, to secretly replace the royal child if it proved to be a girl. Rizzini wrote back to Modena that she was 'afraid of becoming the victim of some insane action by the disturbed populace'.[5] A few weeks later, Maria did indeed give birth to a daughter, who they called Charlotte.

Where the Tuscan ambassador wrote that 'the friends of the court had counted upon a prince, and are the more disappointed', Barillon wrote to Louis XIV that 'the Duke's enemies rejoice that he has not got a son.'[6] He reported that 'the King greatly hoped the Duke of York would have a son, that it would have helped to dissipate the factions of the malcontents.'[7] The events of six years later would show that this hope was misplaced. Revealing also is his suggestion that, had the baby been a boy, 'the hope of the Prince of Orange would have been deferred'.[8] Deferred, but not altered. Barillon did not think that William would consider the birth of a son to be the end of his ambitions to be King of England, even in 1682.

But as these diplomats mused on the significance of the birth and the sex of the baby, the child was weakening. Princess Charlotte lived for little more than six weeks. The French ambassador wrote to Louis XIV, 'The Duke is in deep affliction, for it leaves him with no hope of living children.'[9] We can only imagine how Maria must have felt at having lost yet another child. She was now twenty-four and she had suffered two miscarriages, borne three babies and had no living children. This was not unusual for the time: child mortality rates were horrifying, with around 40 per cent of children born not surviving past infancy. But this can have been of little comfort to Maria as she watched her children die, particularly since James's mistresses appeared to have more luck than she did.[10] Queen Caterina was the only person in her circle who could come close to sympathising: she had not been able to conceive at all, while Charles's many mistresses bore him many healthy children.

Laura did not stay long at court after the child died. Perhaps she took to heart Rizzini's concerns when he said 'it is to be hoped that one day she will realise the bad effect caused by her visits to this capital in such difficult times.'[11] For these difficult times were far from over. In June 1683, a genuine plot was discovered, one that aimed to assassinate both Charles and James, and would have seen the Duke of Monmouth crowned as King of England. Maria wrote an account of it immediately to Francesco:

> I have great news to send you, which is about a conspiracy, not false but true, hatched by the Presbyterians against the people of the King and Lord Duke, which was discovered by one of that party and others who confess the same thing, saying that when the King and Lord Duke returned from Newmarket, they were to have many men on horseback ready in such a place and to kill them all, they say, and at the same time they were to solicit many men in London and in other cities of the Kingdom, which would certainly have happened if the fire that followed Newmarket had not brought forward the return of the King to London by a few days so that they were not in order. Some are in prison and their confessions agree, one says that Milord Shaftesbury (who is dead) knew all of this but it is believed that many living people of great quality are also aware of it and it is hoped that they will be named.[12]

This became known as 'the Rye House Plot', and many 'men of quality' were involved, including the Duke of Monmouth. This plot had been some time in the making – indeed 'Milord Shaftesbury' had died in January 1683 – but the different factions involved meant that the planning had been chaotic. Some aimed for a republic, others to make Monmouth king. Some said they did not want the death of the king at all, simply to make him reconsider his position over the succession, and to bring him to heel with parliament. The plan had been for some hundred men to lie in wait in a building on their route – Rye House – which was owned by the Republican Richard Rumbold. When Charles and James returned from Newmarket, the gang would ambush their carriage and kill those inside. But they suffered a setback; a fire at Newmarket meant that the royal party returned to London earlier than expected. As the plotters regrouped and planned their next move one of their number, a man named Josiah Keeling, changed his mind. He went to the king.

By July, many of those involved in the plot were known and Maria wrote to tell the Mother Superior in Modena that thirty-six people were already in prison and had confessed all. A commemorative medal minted in 1683 says something of how the plot was viewed. On one side, Charles II is depicted naked as Hercules, with the Hydra rearing its many heads towards him. The heads depict the devil, as well as the leading courtiers involved in the plot: Monmouth, Lord William Russell, Hampden, the Earl of Essex and Algernon Sidney. The inscription at the top – PERIBVNT FVLMINIS ICTV (They will perish by a lightning strike) – is borne out by the hand of God reaching through the clouds, like Zeus, holding lightning bolts. On the other side, before a panorama of London, two wolves hang from a gibbet. They represent Algernon Sidney and William Russell, who had already been executed when this coin was minted. The inscription reads DEVS NOBIS HÆC OTIA FECIT (God has given us freedom), above the dove of peace holding an olive branch.

On the heads of those who had not been rounded up Charles had put a bounty of £100 (around £12,000 in today's money). But on his son, Monmouth, he set the price at £500 (around £60,000 today) 'desiring to have him dead or alive'.[13] There were many who thought that it had been Monmouth's rebellion, and that he had aimed to make himself

Protector, or even king. But Charles was not of this mind. When he was told of Monmouth's involvement, he tried desperately to keep his composure, but soon left the council chamber. He went shakily to the rooms of Anna Scott, and there he wept his heart out with his son's wife.

Monmouth had sought refuge at Toddington, where Henrietta Wentworth lived with her mother, Philadelphia Carey Wentworth. The romance which had begun after *The Masque of Calisto* had developed into a deep love. Initially, the passion was unconsummated, and Philadelphia did all she could to protect her daughter's honour from such a known womaniser. But when she began to arrange a marriage between Henrietta and the Earl of Thanet, Monmouth intervened. He was already married but he begged for her hand himself and threw himself and his love on their mercy. Somehow, Philadelphia was convinced, and despite being unable to marry, they lived together at the family home as if the ceremony had taken place. Though he was wanted for treason, Monmouth found happiness at Toddington. During this time in hiding there he wrote poetry reflecting on his sense of peace:

From plots this place is free
Heer w'ill ever bee
W'ill sit and bless our stars
That from the noises of wars
Did this glorious place give
That thus we happy live.[14]

Monmouth became a different man with Henrietta; his affairs were over, and they spent much of their time praying in the family chapel. His love for her was reciprocated and it seemed that they had both found a peace and happiness.

While publicly there was the bounty on Monmouth's head, Charles actually knew exactly where he was. At the same time as Charles suggested they set up watch over Eleanor Needham's house – knowing full well that that amour was over – he began a secret correspondence with his son. Monmouth promised his father that he had never been part of a plot to kill him, that he had only wanted to bring him to his senses with regard to parliament and to James. Charles believed him and they began to plan how best to proceed in getting Monmouth publicly forgiven and back at court. They knew that the person they would really need to convince was James.

After much toing and froing, James, Duke of Monmouth, arrived at Whitehall Palace on 25 November 1683 and requested an audience with his father and uncle. He said he had come to beg for pardon. When he was brought before his father and his uncle, he fell on his knees weeping and begged forgiveness. To everyone's amazement, forgiveness was granted. The shock of the King's magnanimity was played on later in the year at the Duke of York's theatre, when Aphra Behn staged and published her *Romulus and Hersilia*, complete with a loosely veiled Epilogue referencing Monmouth's great transgression:

> And of all Treasons, mine was most accurst;
> Rebelling 'gainst a King and Father first.
> A Sin, which Heav'n nor Man can e're forgive
> Nor could I Act it with the face to live.

Treason and sin it may have been, but Monmouth initially returned to court life as though nothing had happened. Maria wrote in amazement to Francesco in November, 'yesterday he came to court and now he is here just as he was (except that he does not have his riches) and just as if he had not done a bad thing in the world.' She writes that James, too, 'has forgiven him' and 'will forget everything if he can, but it is a very difficult thing. Everyone is surprised, but no one dares to speak seeing that the King is so inclined to favour this.'[15] For a time it seemed that they might all move forward as a family again, but it soon became clear that the plot could not be put behind them so easily. With his fellow conspirators awaiting trial, and some still being captured, Monmouth began to fear that having confessed to his role in the plot he would have to give evidence against his friends. This he could not honourably do. As things came to a head at court, with a heavy heart Charles sent a servant to tell Monmouth that he was banished once more. Anna watched her husband go, but returned to the royal fold and her intimacy with the York family was in no way diminished. On Christmas Day she was seen taking communion with Princess Anne at St James's Palace, and she continued to spend her time with Charles, James, Maria and Anne. But her marriage was over.

The Duke of Monmouth went to Holland, to stay with William and Mary, and Henrietta Wentworth, with her mother, Philadelphia, went with him. He may have disgraced himself in England, but Mary was delighted to have her childhood friend with her and welcomed the arrival of a friendly face. It is difficult to know what had happened to Mary in Holland in these early years of marriage. Records from the time are deeply partisan: some are in favour of William, and say that they fell in love and all was well; some have a English bent and say that the marriage was on rocky ground from the beginning. Some contemporary reports say that William could not wait to be away from her when he went to oversee his army, but early letters from Mary to Frances Apsley tell of how she missed William when he was away, and how she longed to be reunited with him. She found more in him than she had expected when they married. It is true that he and his court were rather more reserved than that which she had left behind, but she grew to think highly of both William and the court. She observed how clean and well-ordered everything was and found their composed manners unexpectedly to her liking. She was popular with the court, who found her open temperament a vast improvement on her aunt, who had been Princess of Orange before her, and who had hated Holland and never bothered to try and hide it. At this new court, Mary began to think differently about the pastimes she had enjoyed up to this point and saw that there was another way to live. When she wrote her memoirs in 1689, she said that in Holland she had 'led a life so suitable to my humour'.[16]

But trouble had been brewing for a little while. The British ambassador at The Hague, Henry Sidney, had written in 1680 that Mary's chaplain, Dr Ken, had spoken to him, saying that he was 'horribly unsatisfied with the Prince of Orange. He thinks he is not kind to his wife.' The chaplain went so far as to speak to William about his conduct, and was nearly thrown out of the court for his interference. And, by 1683, it indeed seems that Mary was being subjected to cruel treatment from William. The French ambassador, D'Avaux, gave details:

> Until now, the existence of the Princess of Orange had been regulated thus: from the time she rises in the morning till eight in the evening, she never leaves her chamber, except in summer when she is permitted to walk about once in seven or eight days. No one has the liberty to enter her room, not even her lady of honour, nor her maids of honour, of which she has four, but she has a troop of Dutch chambermaids, a detachment of whom mount guard over her every day and have orders never to leave her.[17]

Mary did not speak Dutch, and these chambermaids did not speak English, and much of her English household had been dismissed. William was systematically breaking her spirit by isolating her from her past life as an English princess. And it was working. To add insult to injury, William was having an open affair with Mary's maid of honour and childhood friend, Elizabeth Villiers.

But Monmouth's arrival brought a lightness to Mary's days, and she was allowed out of her exile to go walking and ice skating with him. They became inseparable. James was stunned that his daughter and son-in-law would harbour what he perceived to be a dangerous fugitive in their court, and he wrote telling them so. Perhaps William wanted to keep an eye on his illegitimate cousin for, if Charles were to die, Monmouth might set himself up as a rival candidate to Mary for the throne. Or perhaps he, too, welcomed Monmouth as a friend. They had fought side by side in battle (after other battles fighting on

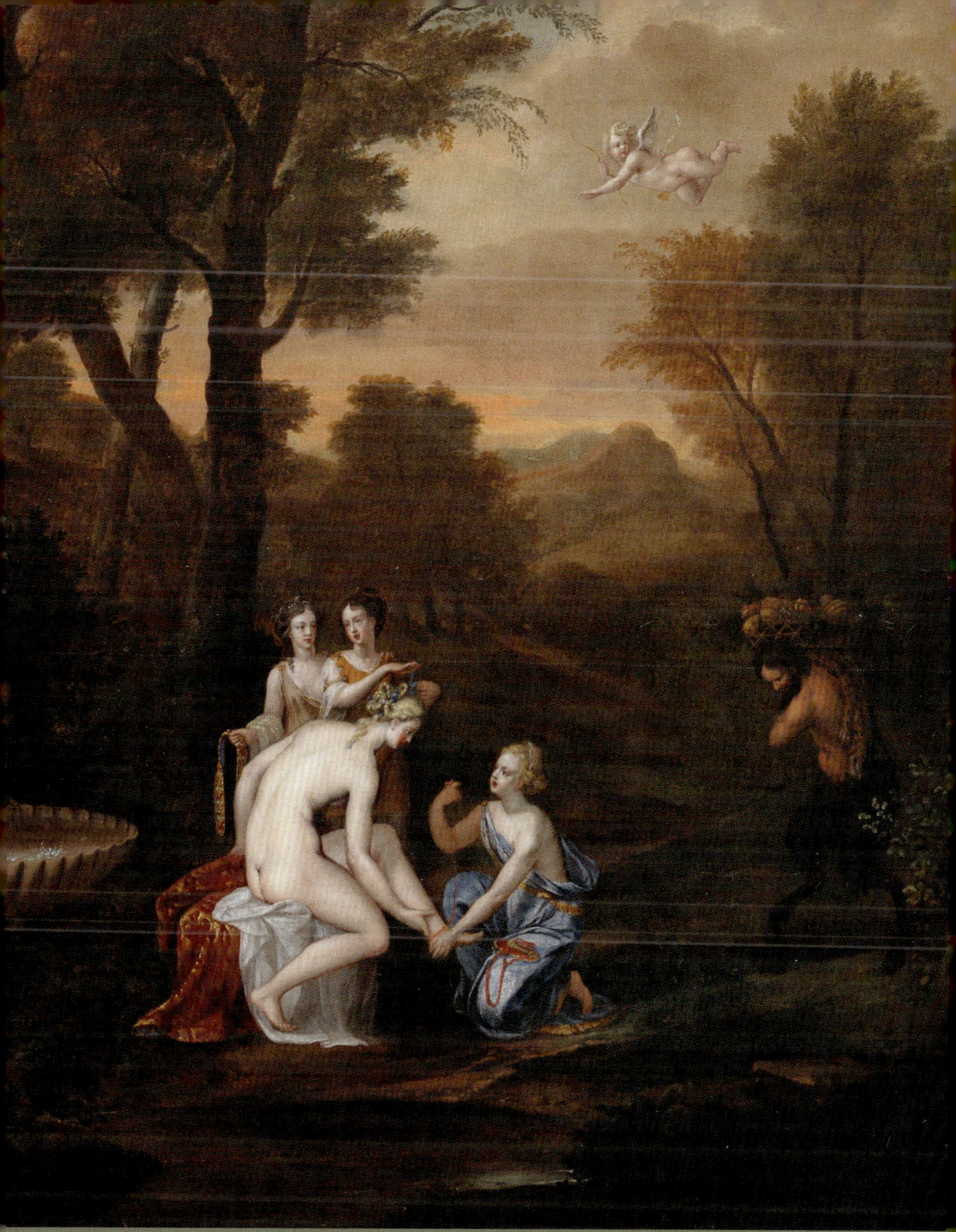

This painting is thought to be an allegory: Maria of Modena is Venus and the Graces her maids of honour. Killigrew positioned herself in pride of place, crouched before her mistress, deep in conversation. And the painting contains another personal touch: the robe that Venus sits on is the same as that worn by James II in his coronation portrait by Killigrew.

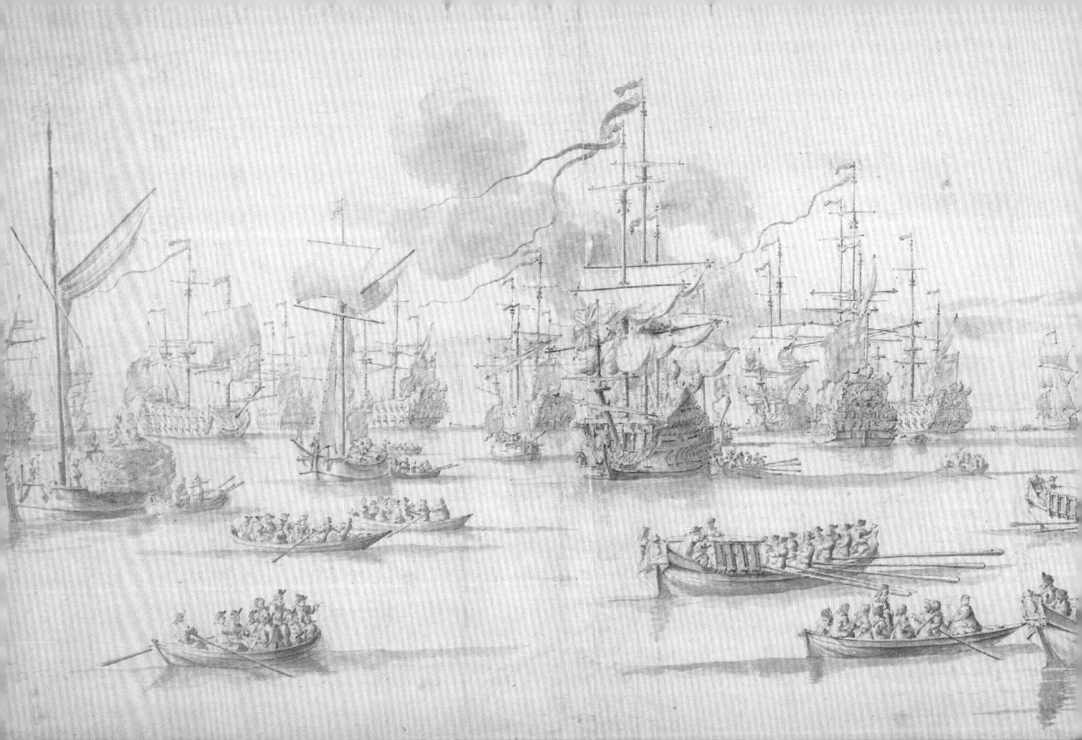

Willem Van de Velde the Elder was commissioned to make a series of sketches depicting the journey of Maria from Calais to London. In this sketch we see the small fleet ready to sail for London from Gravesend. To the right of the picture, the English flag is raised, and swarms of people stand at the dock as the royal party start to embark, ready to begin the final stage of their journey.

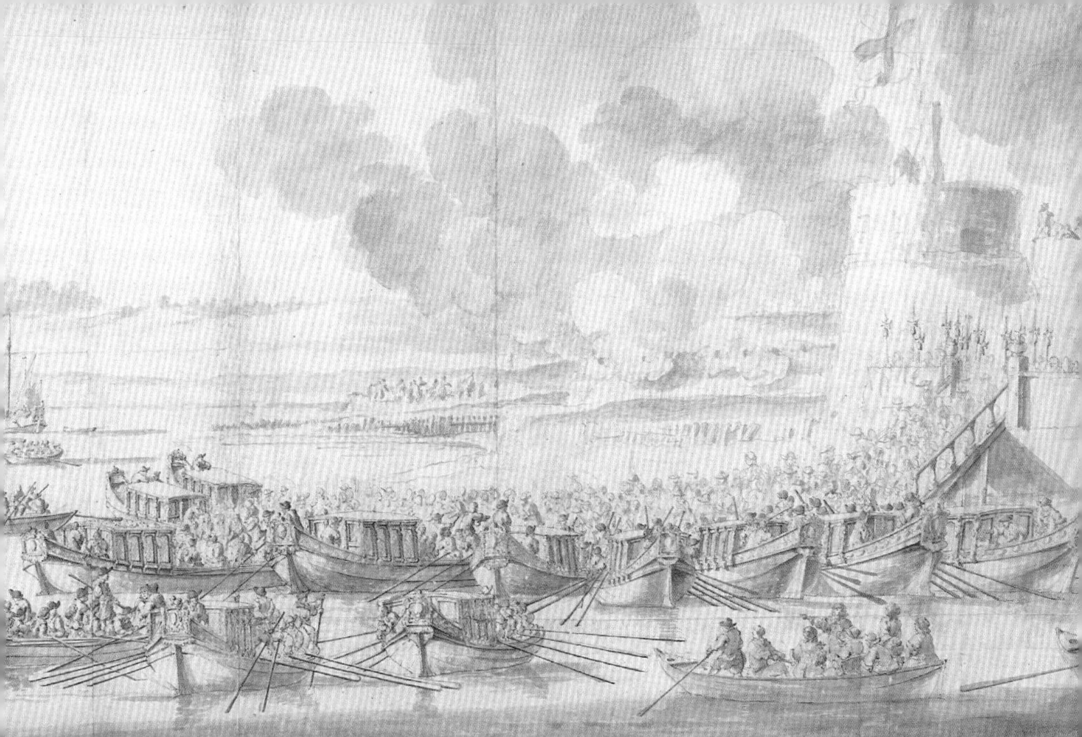

But in the crush of people, we cannot differentiate between regular citizens and the royal family. The scene tells us something of the informality of the court under Charles II, who was always available to be seen by his subjects. It must have been a shock for Maria, who was unlikely to have been in such close proximity to the citizens of Modena.

Mary is painted as Diana, the virgin Goddess of the Hunt: in motion, holding her bow and arrow and with her loyal greyhound following closely behind. The portrait seems to foretell her role as Callisto – a nymph in Diana's train in *The Masque of Callisto* – a few years later.

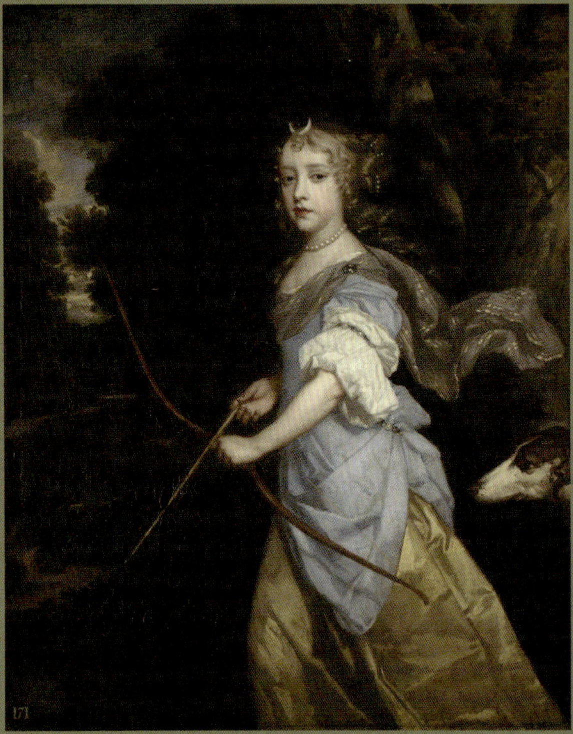

When Maria arrived at the court the princesses Mary and Anne were just eleven and nine years old, respectively. These portraits give a sense of them as the children she would have met.

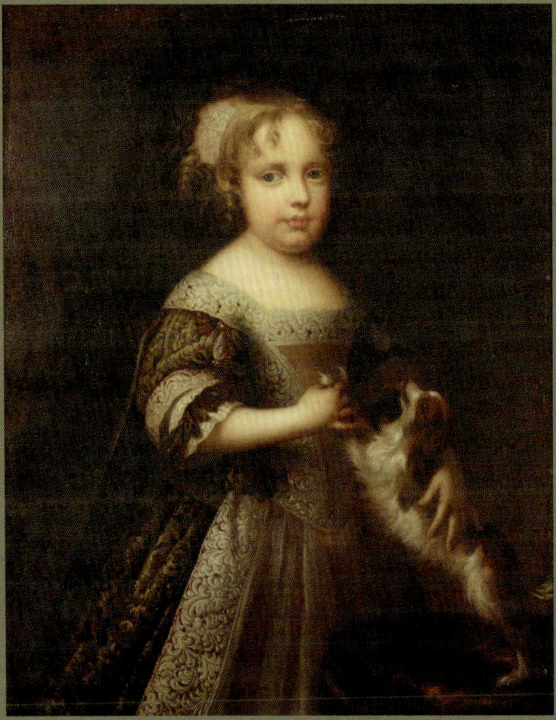

This touching portrait of Anne and her doting spaniel was probably made in Paris when the princess was consulting doctors at the French court (she suffered throughout her life with terrible eyesight).

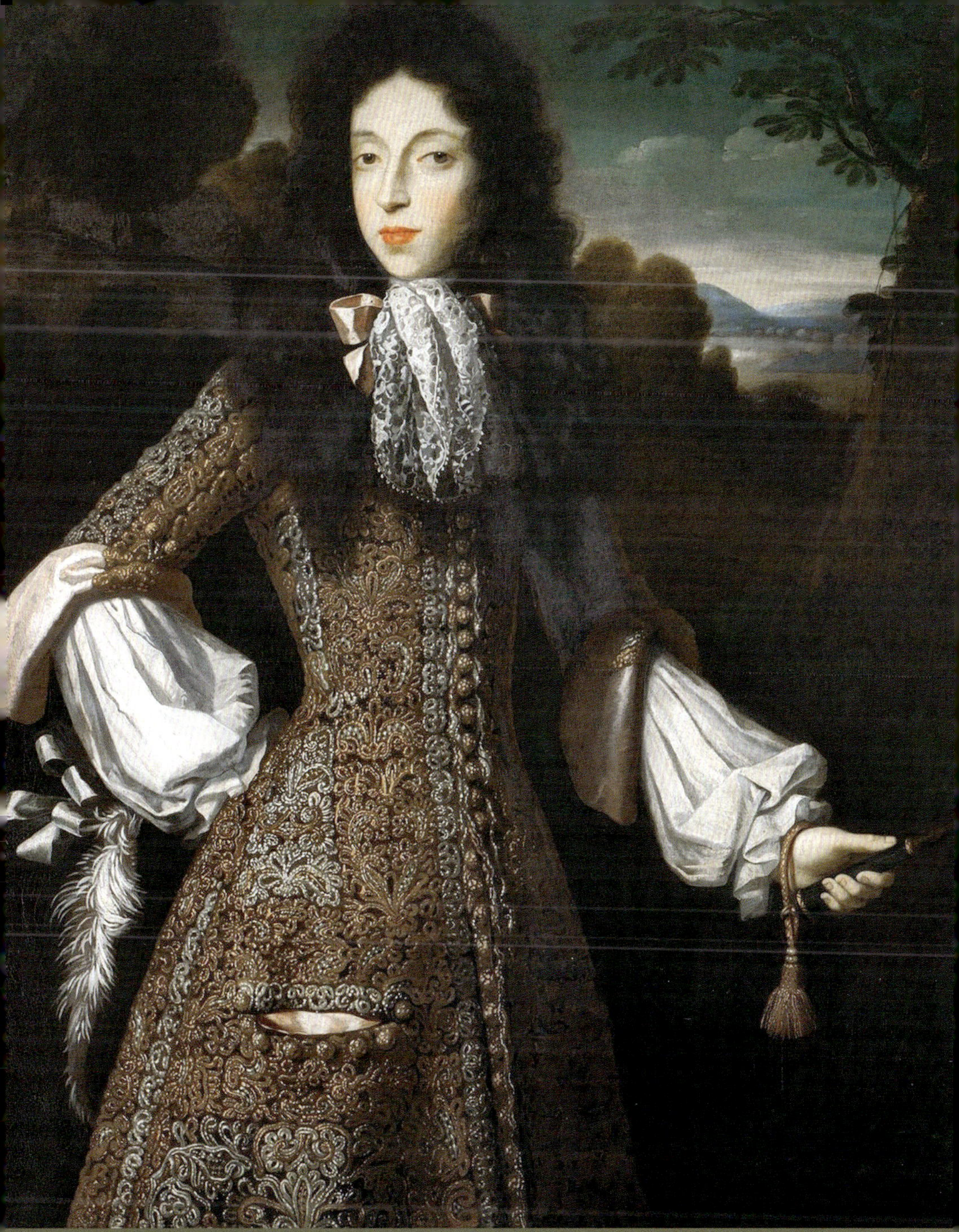

This is an early portrait of Maria at the English court, painted around 1675. In it we can see her passion for horse-riding (something she and James shared), as she stands holding her riding crop. Her clothes are perhaps unexpected: they are men's clothes, a replica of the outfit that James wore to greet her on the shores at Dover two years before.

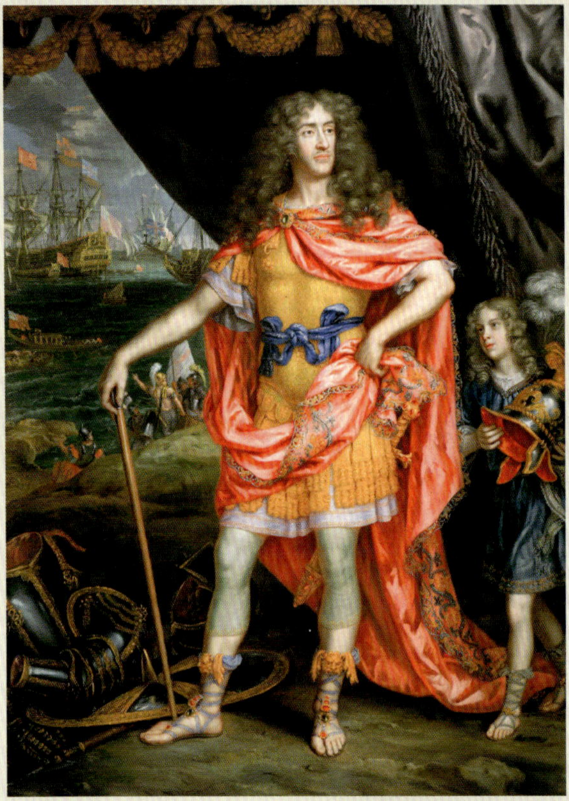

James is here depicted as Mars, the God of War, surrounded by the armour of his father, Charles I, which was housed in the Tower of London. The ships in the background are a nod to his role as Lord High Admiral of the Fleet, a role he would soon have to relinquish when the Test Act barred all Catholics from holding public office. The boy who stands beside him is thought to be his protegee, John Churchill. It is reminiscent of the reports of James taking John to survey the troops.

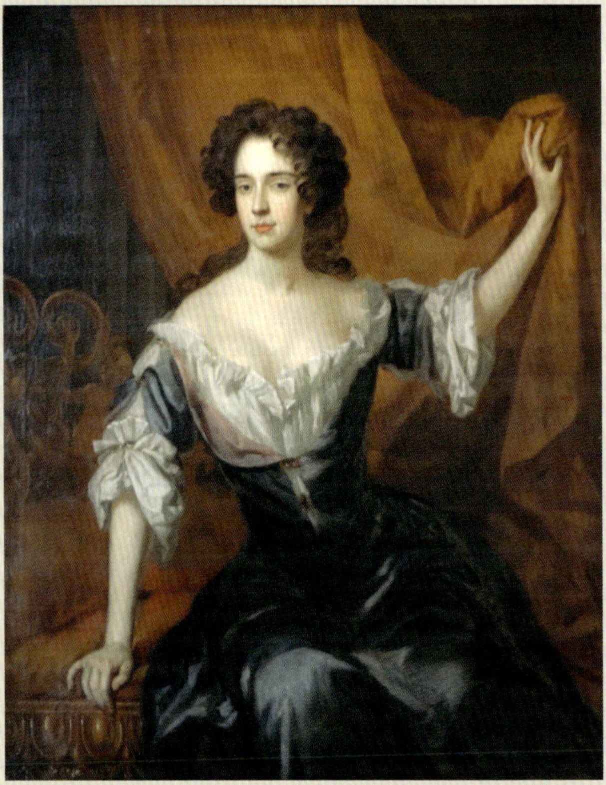

When this portrait was made, Catherine Sedley was firmly ensconced as James's mistress. She would hold a power over him that perhaps no other women that James ever met could match. She was witty, intelligent and often outrageous, and here she is presented with all the confidence that she was famous for.

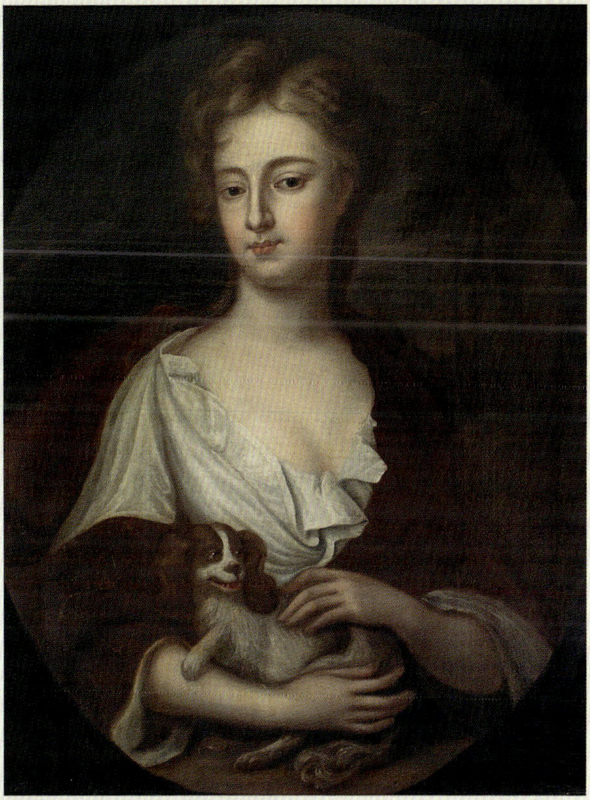

This is a rare portrait of Sarah Churchill from her early years at court, in Maria's household. The spaniel she holds in her arms is perhaps the same that John Churchill gave her as a gift when they became officially engaged; its resting paw points down to a wedding ring just beside her arm. Sarah favoured the red-and-white variety of King Charles spaniel, which has been named Blenheim in her honour.

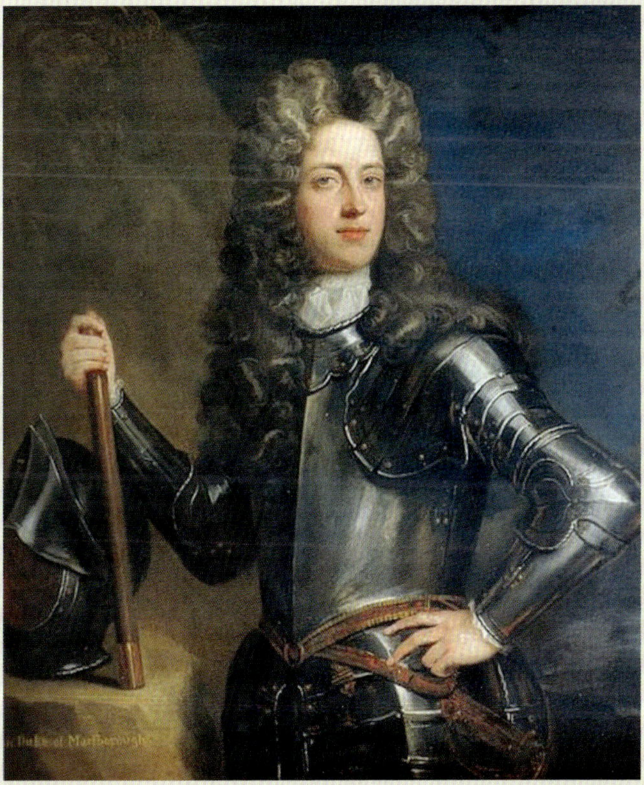

John Churchill arrived back at the English court a military hero following the Siege of Maastricht. Here he is painted in full armour as though newly returned from battle.

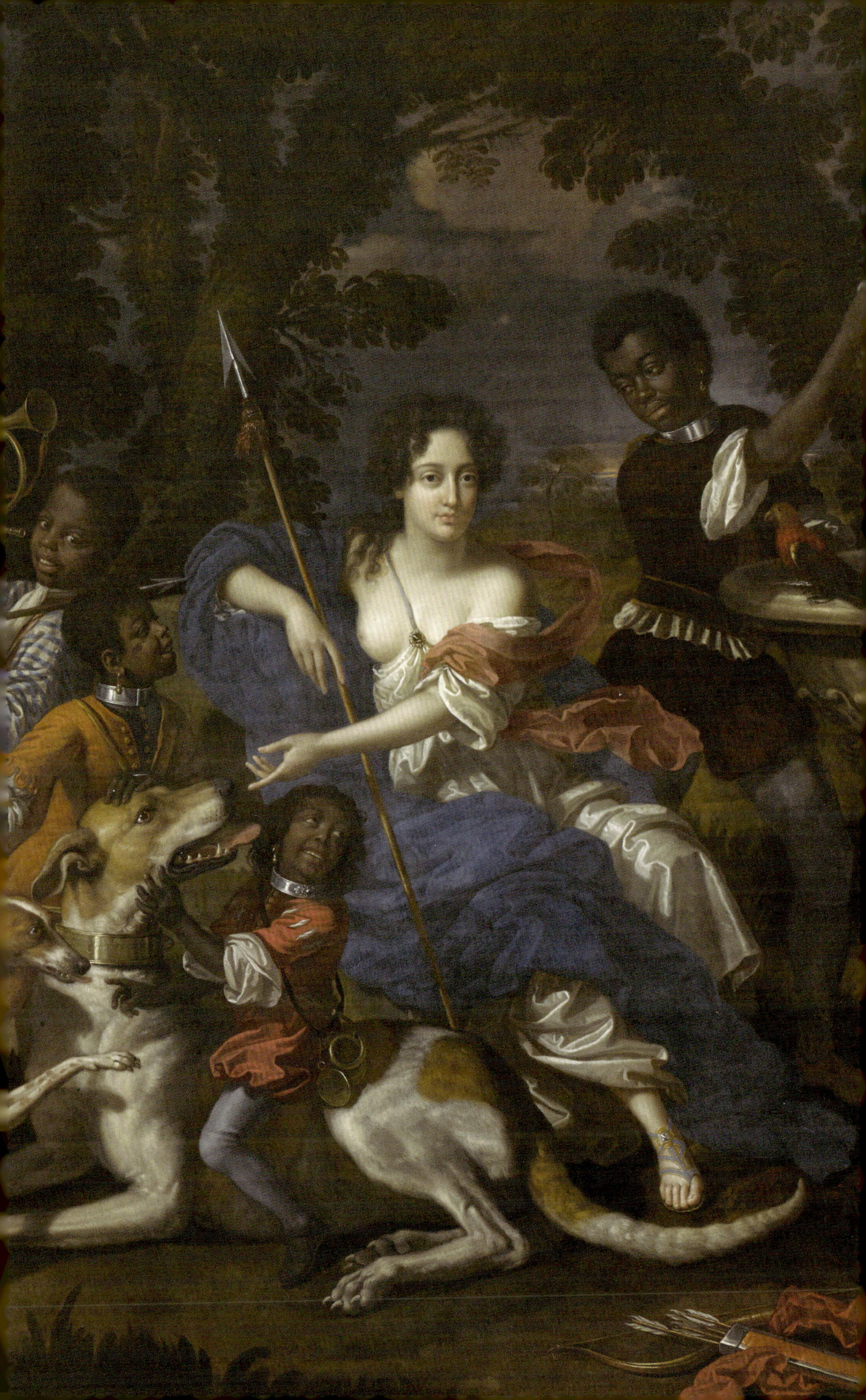

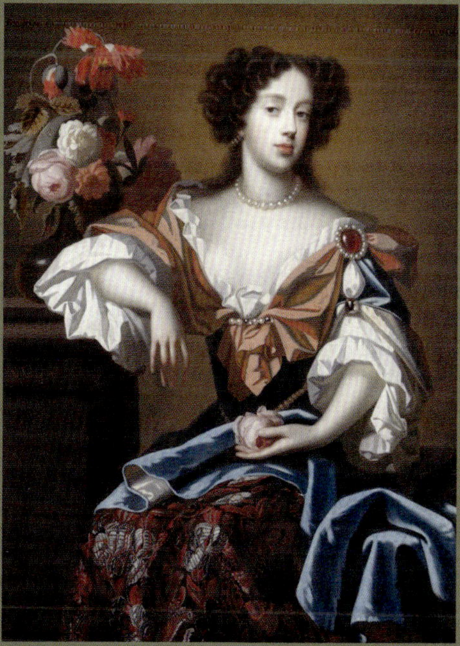

This portrait of Maria by Simon Verelst is one of many that the artist made of his patron. Vereslt was a particularly gifted painter of flowers and here we can see him using that skill both in the bouquet on the table behind Maria and the rosebud she holds in her lap – as well as in the velvet patterning of her skirt.

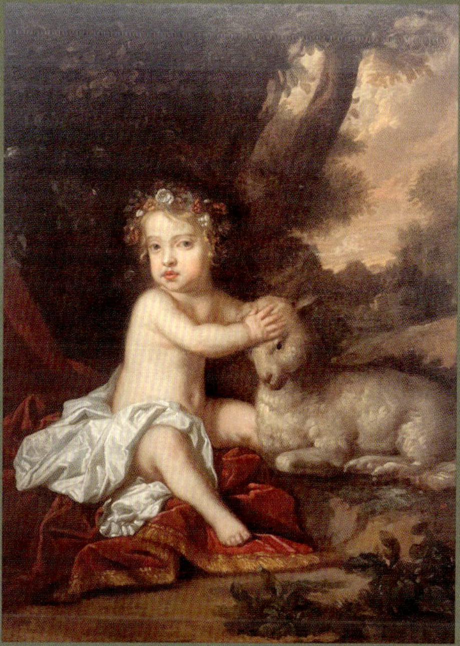

Here Isabella is shown at just about one year old. Her innocence and youth are highlighted by the lamb whose head she caresses, in a posture which seems to reference John the Baptist. Isabella died in London in 1681, when Maria was in exile, around the time that the adjacent portrait of Maria was made.

Left: Hortense Mancini is depicted as the goddess Diana, from the story of Diana and Actaeon found in Ovid's *Metamorphoses*.

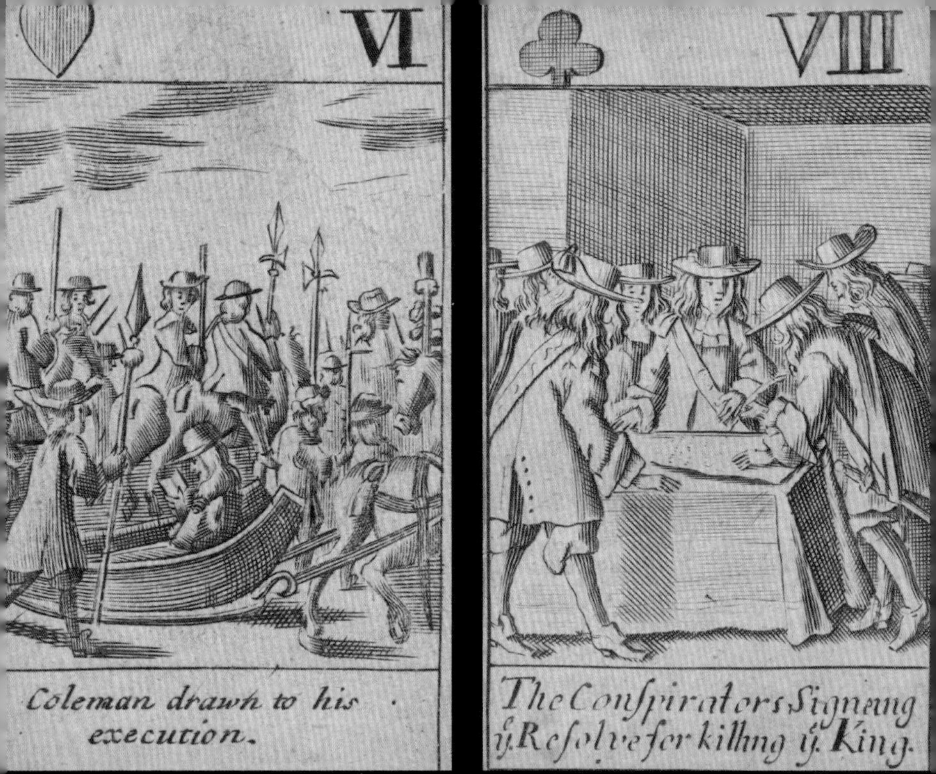

Playing cards were often made to commemorate political events, and the two seen here depict scenes from the Popish Plot. The first, the 6 of Hearts, shows Maria's ill-fated secretary Edward Coleman being taken to his place of execution for treason. The second, the 8 of Clubs, shows the supposed conspirators standing together and plotting the death of King Charles II.

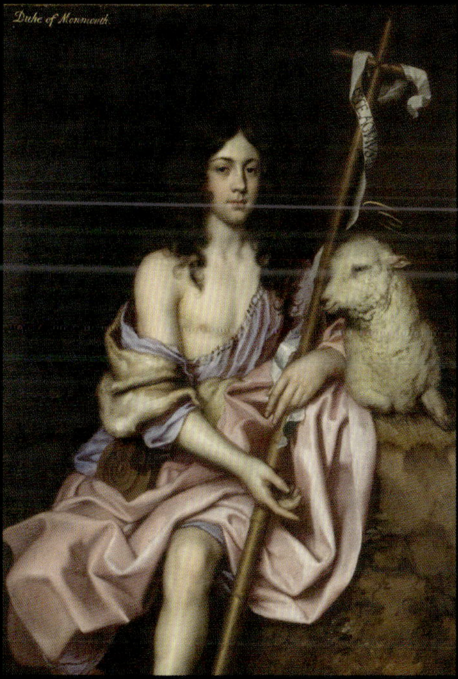

It was often fashionable at the Restoration court to have your portrait painted in the guise of a biblical or classical figure. Here we see a playful image of James, Duke of Monmouth, as John the Baptist. He would have been little more than thirteen years old in this image, but at the court of Charles II this was old enough to have lost much innocence, as the image suggests: we see his sensual posture, legs a little apart and his clothes barely staying on his body. It is a pose reminiscent of one of Caravaggio's boys.

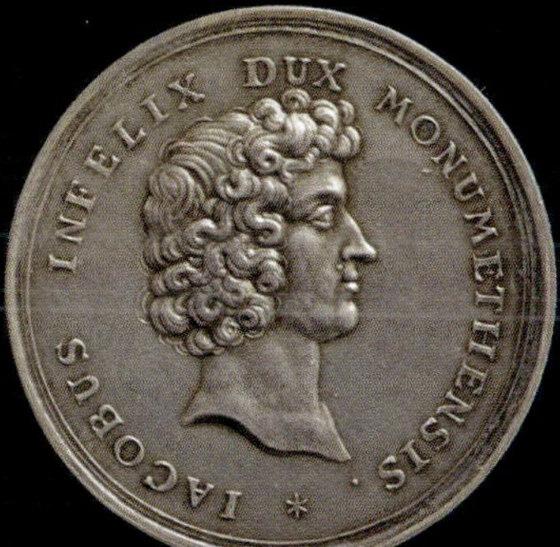

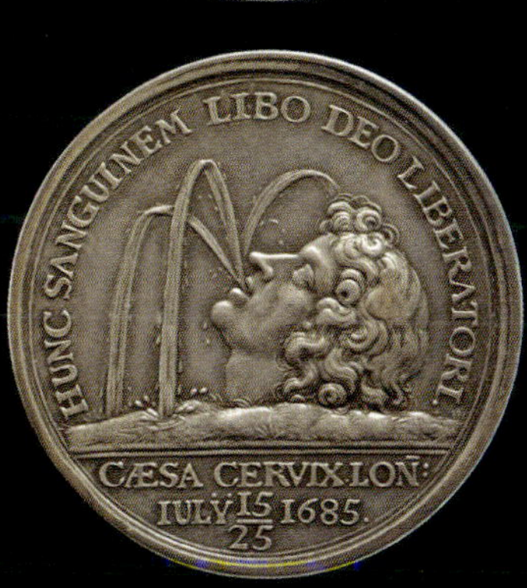

Medals and coins were often minted to commemorate political and historic events. This medal was made after the execution of the Duke of Monmouth, and aspects of that gory event are captured in the image, as blood spurts out of the mouth of his decapitated head. The caption reads, 'hunc sanguinem libo deo liberatori' ('I offer this blood to God the Liberator').

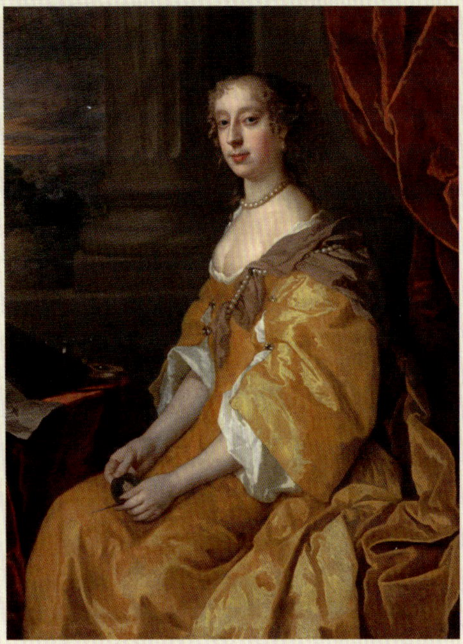

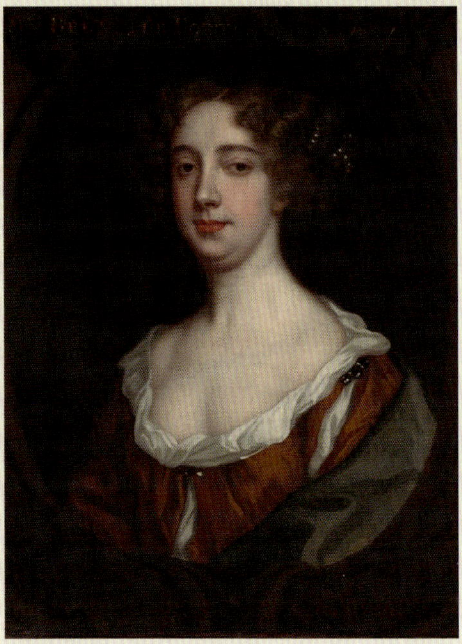

This Peter Lely portrait is thought to depict Anne Killigrew. It is both traditional and subversive: a woman in fashionable clothes painted before a classical column, but before her is a sketch of her own making. She is both courtier and artist.

This image, painted by the Studio of Peter Lely, is the only known surviving portrait of Aphra Behn. It was made circa 1675, which is perhaps around the time that Maria would first have encountered Behn and seen her plays on the London stage.

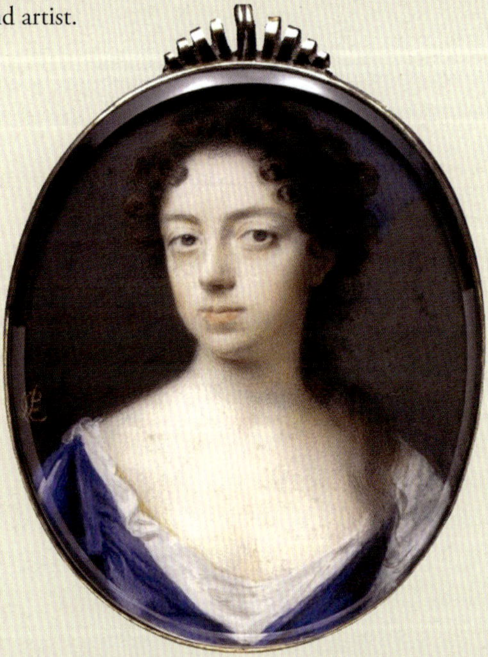

As with the above image of Aphra Behn, this is the only known portrait of Anne Finch. It is a miniature by Peter Cross, perhaps designed to be worn as a pendant, and was probably painted after the Glorious Revolution of 1688, when she was living in exile at Eastwell Park in Kent.

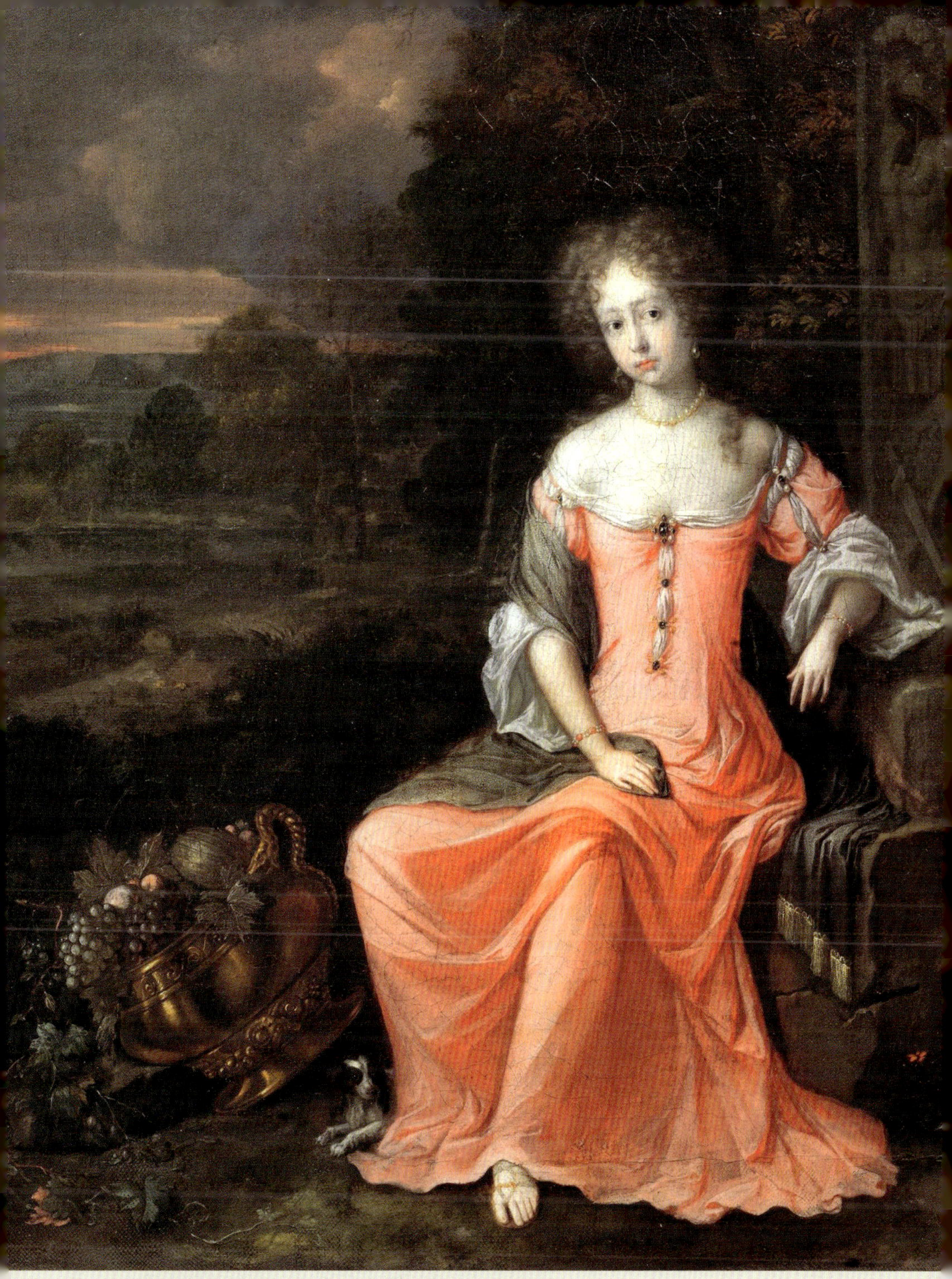

This painting by Anne Killigrew, of Venus mourning Adonis, is thought to be a self-portrait and is one of the few extant works by the artist. On the surface it looks like a portrait of a woman of the Restoration court wearing fashionable attire in a landscape scene. But closer inspection finds that she sits at the base of a tomb and at her feet are red anemones, which, according to myth, began to grow from Adonis's blood as it spilled onto the ground.

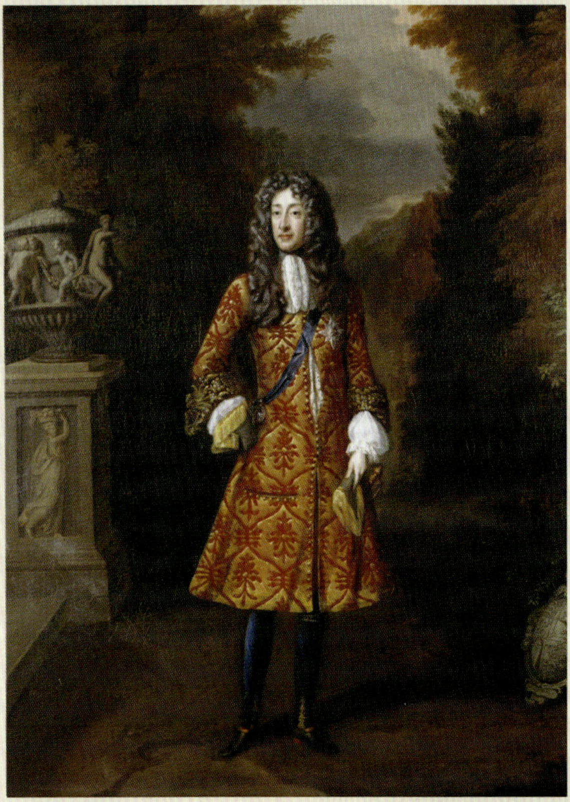

This portrait of James II by Anne Killigrew was commissioned to celebrate his coronation and is the first recorded instance of a female artist in England painting their monarch from life. In a further testament to the intimacy Killigrew found at James and Maria's court we notice that the beautiful, embroidered coat that James wears here is found in another of Killigrew's paintings; in *Venus Attired by The Graces*, Venus sits on this very coat, waiting to be dressed in it. The fact that they wear the same clothes here acts as a playful allusion to that portrait of Maria by Verelst from 1675, in which she wears James's clothes.

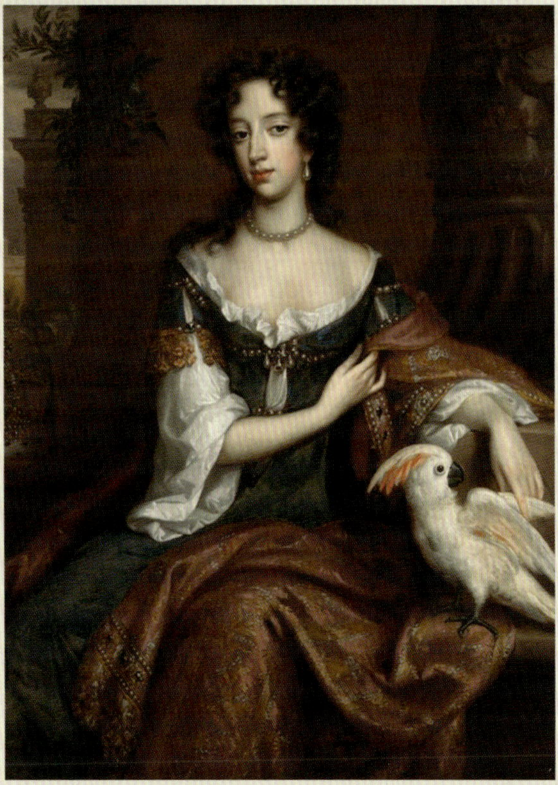

In William Wissing's portrait we glean something of Maria's colonial interests, as she sits caressing the wing of her much-loved salmon-crested cockatoo. This bird came from Moluccas (now part of Indonesia) and its inclusion by Wissing speaks to Maria's involvement in the East India Company. Perhaps the bird was brought back to her on the *Modena*, a vast ship named in her honour and which first sailed (as part of the East India Company) in 1685.

These two images shows the different kinds of propaganda that circulated in 1688 after the birth of James Francis Edward Stuart.

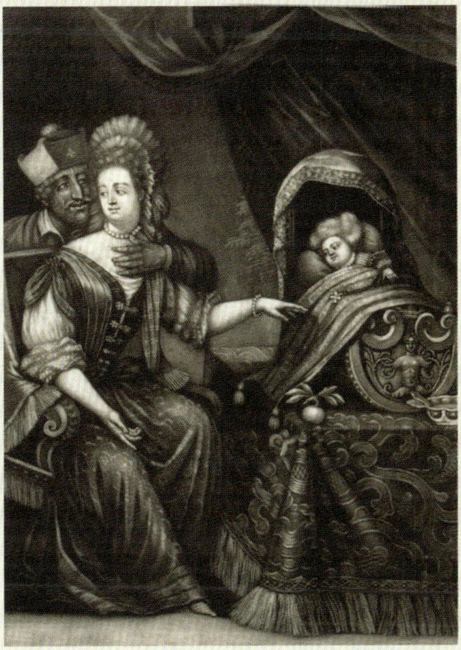

In the first we see Maria sitting by her child's cot, gently rocking him to sleep. Behind her, lasciviously embracing her, is Father Petre, the hated Jesuit confidante of James. The implication is that James has been cuckolded, and that Petre is the father of the child. But the image implies a second conspiracy: we see a windmill, a reference to the rumour that the child was not born of Maria at all but had been snuck into the birthing chamber in a bedpan, and that he was actually the child of a miller. This was printed in Holland and widely disseminated.

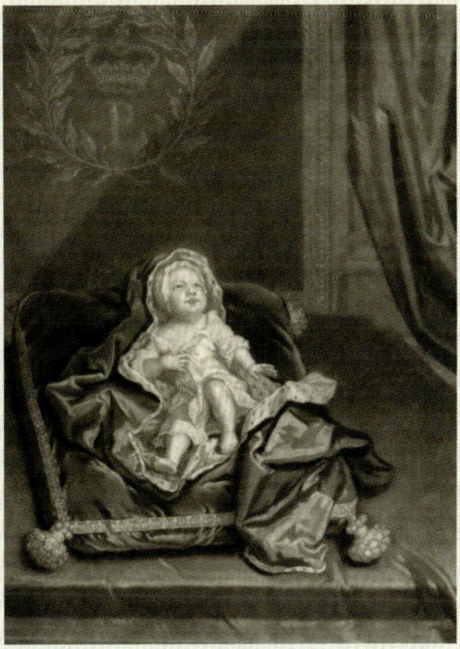

The portrait of James Francis as a baby lying on a velvet cushion was made by the court artist Godfrey Kneller. Kneller painted the royal family frequently and when he heard the rumours surrounding the birth of James Francis, he reportedly scoffed, replying that he knew the faces of both James and Maria so well that he was certain the child, who resembled them both, was the true prince. Both this image and the one adjacent to it were printed and extensively circulated in England and in Holland.

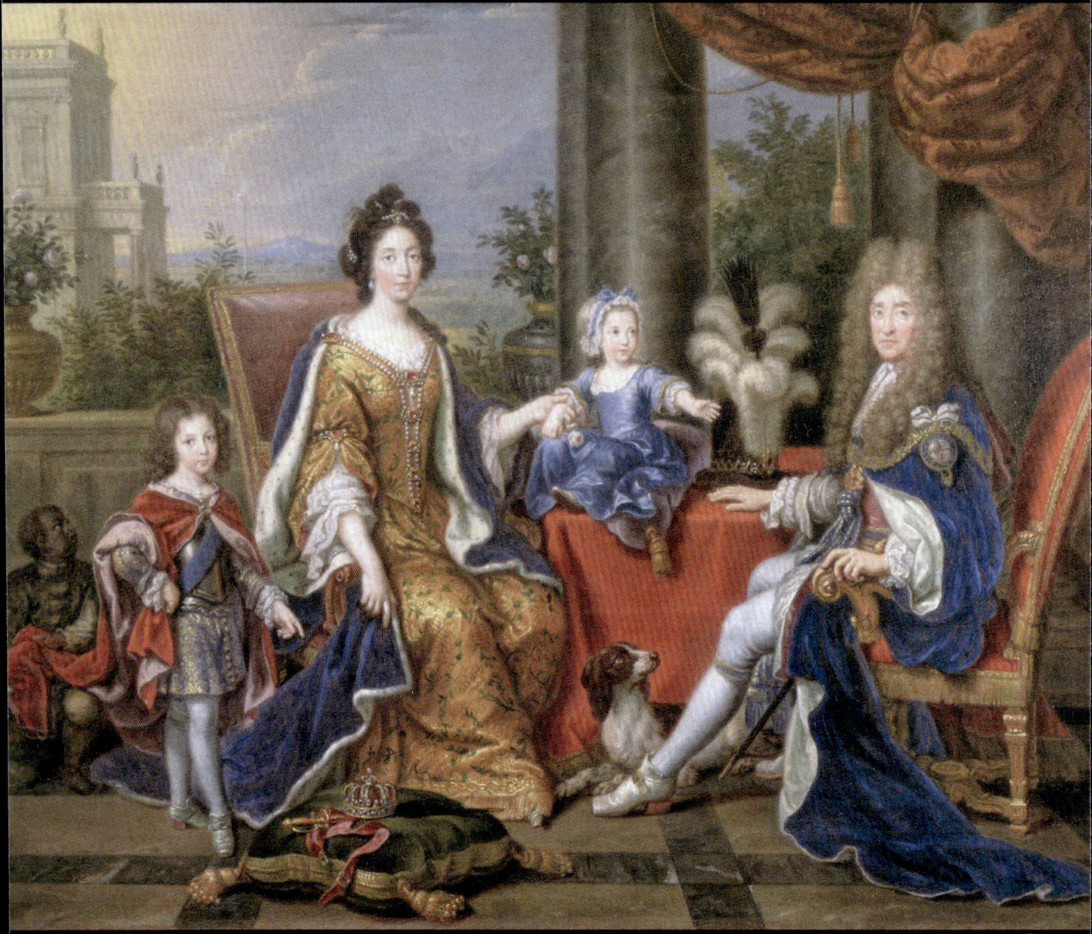

Maria and James continued to use visual propaganda while in exile, and this family portrait by Pierre Mignard was sent to Maria's family in Modena. It was probably a *modello* for a larger work, which remained in James II's possession until his death. In it we see the royal family in full regalia, but the crown sits on the floor, the foot of James points towards it and the hands of both Maria and the child, James Francis, gesture towards it as well. The image clearly states that James is the king, and James Francis is his heir.

opposing sides), and they had become close over the years. Accounts from this time tell of a warm friendship between the three cousins which it may be unjust to presume was not genuine. Unlike the court in England, William and Mary were happy to receive Monmouth's mistress, Henrietta Wentworth, at the court as well. Mary will have known Henrietta from childhood, and these days they spent together in Holland were happy ones.

The routing of the Rye House Plot, and the imprisonments, executions and exiling of the conspirators diffused much of the power that the exclusionists in parliament had gained over the previous years. These tensions continued to bubble away under the surface, but Maria had several comparatively peaceful years ahead of her. And in these years she was able to focus on her role as a patron.

After ten years as Duchess of York, Maria still craved that lost world of the convent, the hallowed environment of learning and friendship where she had been surrounded by like-minded women. Though she had adapted to her life as an English duchess, it must have been hard to get used to an environment in which so few around her had anything like her education. But fortune had finally smiled on Maria in the form of two new maids of honour who joined her court in 1682 – Anne Kingsmill and Anne Killigrew, who would both make extraordinary contributions to the history of English poetry and art. They were intelligent, educated, talented and creatively ambitious. They embodied Maria's hopes of fostering the kind of intellectual community of women in which she had grown up as a girl in Modena.

13

The Coterie

Alas! a Woman that attempts the pen,
Such an intruder on the rights of Men,
Such a presumptuous Creature, is esteem'd,
The fault, can by no vertue be redeem'd.

— Anne Finch, 'The Introduction', *Miscellany Poems with Two Plays by Ardelia*

Anne Kingsmill and Anne Killigrew were true children of the Restoration: Killigrew was born some time in 1660, when England was welcoming its monarch back from exile, and Kingsmill in April 1661, as the country prepared for his coronation. Neither of these women knew anything other than life under a Stuart monarchy, though their Royalist families would have remembered the Protectorate all too well. But when they arrived at the court it was with very different experiences of the world. Anne Kingsmill had lived a secluded life in the country, with her uncle, brother and sister. Her father, Sir William Kingsmill, had been something of an amateur poet and when he died had left ample provision in his will for all three children to receive a good education – the girls no less than the boy. They spent much of the following years with a neighbouring family, the Ishams, whose children were a similar age to the Kingsmill children. The head of that family, Justinian Isham, had been the student of Francis Bacon and was one of the earliest members of the Royal Society. Other members of the Society, such as the scientist Robert Boyle, as well as the polymath Thomas Browne, were part of his circle. At the dinner table, Anne Kingsmill will have encountered not only discussions about the political and military currents of the day, but also debates about natural philosophy and the new empiricism. And she was encouraged to take part in these conversations and was always made to feel that her opinion was valid. These London visitors also brought with them gossip from the court and the young Anne no doubt heard all about the arrival in 1673 of a beautiful Italian princess, barely eighteen months older than she was.

The Kingsmill and Isham children were brought up reading the classics in their original languages; they studied the Bible, French, literature, history, geography and even a smattering of Italian and Spanish (which would come in useful to Anne when she was sent to court). On top of a classical education, she also had an inheritance from her father of £1,500 (around £160,000 in today's money) which she would inherit upon turning twenty-one. Unlike many women of the time, she would inherit whether she married or not. She therefore had all the advantages a young woman in the seventeenth century could hope to have, and even more.

But having grown up like this, in the countryside, Anne Kingsmill was probably rather more innocent of the ways of the world than Anne Killigrew, who from a very early age will have seen up close the ways the court operated. Anne Killigrew had always lived in and around the court. Her uncle, Thomas Killigrew, was a renowned playwright, a friend of Charles II and manager of the King's Theatre, and was one of the key figures in licensing women actors. Her father, Henry, was the almoner of James, Duke of York. Her aunt, Elizabeth, had been one of Charles II's mistresses in exile and mother of one of his many illegitimate children. They were restoration courtiers in the truest sense of the phrase.

Their origins, by contrast, were rather murky. The Killigrews were an ancient Cornish family, who had ruled the south-western shores of Falmouth as pirates for two centuries. They had a free hand in Falmouth, which had been a small place, and it was in no small part down to the Killigrews that it was built up into a prosperous town. Even today you will find streets named after them. But they were also wealthy, corrupt, notorious, ruthless, and all with the sanction of the crown which turned a blind eye to such plunderings when it was mostly Spanish ships that suffered. When James I became King of England, one branch of the family decided to head to court. It was these courtly Killigrews that Anne was descended from, though the wild pirate genes lived on in her uncle Thomas and his son Harry.

What Anne Killigrew's education consisted of is not entirely clear. Her father, Henry, was a learned man, with an extensive library, and though we don't have evidence of Anne's education, the work she produced – poems and paintings – suggests that it must have been extensive. Her first biographer, Anthony à Wood, wrote that she had been 'tenderly educated', a phrase which leaves much to be interpreted, though he uses it in the context of her artistic career, saying that 'she became most admirable in the Arts of Poetry and Painting'.[1]

Her poetry certainly tells us something of the kind of learning she had obtained, even if not how she obtained it. She uses many different poetic genres and registers, and her work is full of allusions to ancient Greek and Roman literature, though it is hard to be sure if she was able to read either of them in the original. Her father was a gifted Latinist, and his own writings demonstrate his penchant for translation; it is perhaps not a leap to suggest that he taught and encouraged her to follow in his footsteps, ensuring that she had the skills to do so. And though we know very little of her mother, Judith, two significant facts have come down to us through the ages: she was an exceptionally gifted lutenist, and she owned a second folio of Shakespeare that is now housed at the Folger Library in Washington, DC. Anne's verse tells us that she was conversant with the poetic trends of the previous century; perhaps as a child she would sit and read this mighty tome.

Given the closeness of her father to James, and her uncle to the king, Anne Killigrew probably knew Maria before she joined her household: they would frequently have been found in the same circles given her father's close (if complicated) position to James, and the court was a small place. We may even speculate that it was James who suggested Anne as one of her maids, or Maria who requested it. Anne will have grown up knowing the other daughters of noble families, like Isabella Bennet and Sarah Churchill, and will perhaps have felt more confident than Anne Kingsmill when she arrived in Maria's household.

Between 1682 and 1685, these women will have been much together at the court: Isabella Bennet Fitzroy lived in St James's and had grown up nearby in the part of St James's Fields which had been built to house the aristocracy by Henry Jermyn and, in part, her father Henry Bennet. Sarah Churchill divided her time between Princess Anne's court and Maria's and moved into her own apartments near to the princess's in 1684.[2]

The two Annes came from families who valued women's education and who championed their abilities, and they grew up with no reason to think that being a woman should, or would, prevent them from pursuing their ambitions as poets and painters. But they were quickly to discover that society would say otherwise. As young and ambitious poets, they would find that they were simply not afforded the same opportunities as men, and that the men around them would consider them a joke, a threat or a combination of the two.

The world of the court was a cruel place, as Anne Killigrew found when she circulated one of her poems. The problem was not that the poem was ridiculed: in fact, the opposite was the case. The poem was praised, but a rumour clearly started going around the court that she, a young woman, could not have written it. Angry and humiliated, Killigrew wrote a poetic rebuttal to the slander. She told of how

> Embolden'd thus, to Fame I did commit,
> (By some few hands) my most Unlucky Wit.

But, ah, the sad effects that from it came!
What ought t'have brought me Honour, brought me shame![3]

Having received early encouragement from some 'judicious' readers, she had felt 'embolden'd' to send a poem out to a broader group. She does not tell us who these first readers were, but we can guess that they were the other women in her coterie[4]; maybe Anne Kingsmill and Maria. But having circulated the work, she did not get the response she was expecting. The imagery which follows is devastating in its violence, as she likens herself to the victim of one of Aesop's fables:

Like *Esops* Painted Jay I seem'd to all,
Adorn'd in Plumes, I not my own could call:
Rifl 'd like her, each one my Feathers tore,
And, as they thought, unto the Owner bore.[5]

She stands in a crowd alone, people ripping her feathers from her body that they claim do not belong to her. They strip her naked, leaving her vulnerable. She can only watch as 'My Laurels thus an Others Brow adorn'd'.[6]

As this line indicates, it was not simply that people were saying that Killigrew could not possibly have written these verses; they clearly had someone specific in mind as the real poet, someone already celebrated who 'had so rich a store / Of Sacred Wreaths that circled it before'.[7] Killigrew does not name them or give any hints as to who they might be. They are, however, most likely a man. We know this because Killigrew claims that this would never have happened to Katherine Philips: when it came to Philips's 'Orinda', her sex did not 'at all obstruct her fame': if anything, it made her more celebrated.[8] The Republic under which Katherine Philips lived was not a utopia for women, but it does seem to have occasionally fostered environments in which women were able to obtain recognition as artists. And under the Restoration also, women like Aphra Behn were able to work successfully. But what was occasionally permissible for a woman outside the court was not tolerated in the vicious atmosphere within it, dominated as it was by the male wits.

Katherine Philips, the great example of female poetic talent of previous decades, was a figure of inspiration for aspiring female poets of Killigrew's generation. Killigrew protests that if Katherine Philips could do it, she could, too. But Killigrew's parallels with Philips go beyond this: Philips, too, lost control of her work during coterie circulation, when an unauthorised volume of her work was printed. But unlike Killigrew, Philips was met with praise, and no one said the works were not her own. Killigrew finds that while 'my Numbers they Admir'd ... Me they scorn'd'.[9]

The poem is a beautiful demonstration of Killigrew's skill. It employs the very tropes that her critics said she was not capable of. It is a challenge: if you think I didn't write that, how about this? Take, for example, this image of the branch: she calls 'each verdant tree' a possible Daphne, the nymph who was transformed into a laurel tree to escape the unwanted sexual advances of Apollo. It was the leaves of the laurel tree that were made into wreaths to adorn the brows of garlanded poets.[10] As the branches on Killigrew's trees grow, so do her ambitions, and her work blossoms. The sprouting of her poetry turns into laurel crowns from Daphne's tree, 'as Garlands to empale my Brow'.[11] But these garlands do not sit gently on her head, they 'empale' her, taking on a symbol of martyrdom; they are less the poet's crown than Christ's crown of thorns. By the end of her poem, she has given the laurel crown to the great poetess of an earlier generation, Orinda (Katherine Philips), who had been made immortal through her fame, and to whom all other poets must show deference, as 'ev'ry Laurel, to her Laurel, bow'd'.[12]

Killigrew refuses to be put off by the men who claim she cannot write and defiantly cries that she will keep writing her 'Deathless Numbers from my Tuneful Lyre'. She likens herself to another abused woman from classical mythology: Cassandra.[13] Cassandra was the daughter of Priam, who was cursed to see the future but not to be believed, who saw the fall of Troy but could not stop it. Killigrew likens her plight to '*Cassandras* Fate', the heroine who was 'believ'd too late'. Both Cassandra and Killigrew are women whose language was beyond the understanding of those around them.[14]

It is not clear which was the poem that Killigrew circulated among 'some few hands', only to have her authorship denied, but I would suggest that the poem in question could well have been *Alexandreis*, an unfinished epic which details the life of Alexander the Great.[15] It is the first to appear in the collection published after her death and is followed by a line from her father: '*This was the first Essay of this young Lady in Poetry, but finding the Task she had undertaken hard, she laid it by till Practice and more time should make her equal to so great a Work.*' After she received such a response it is no surprise she might choose to wait before proceeding. If this is the case, this might give another hint as to why the court wits were so quick to disparage her: either they thought it was inconceivable that a young woman might attempt to write about this masculine hero, or they simply wanted to punish her for her hubris in writing on a supposedly 'male' theme: the epic genre was considered the domain of men, even more than other poetic forms.

Killigrew's *Alexandreis*, however, though it claims to be about the 'Man that never equal knew', actually spends most of its time talking about the Queen of the Amazons and her army of 'warlike virgins'.[16] Killigrew turns the story into a celebration of female power. Indeed, we can see her writing herself into this masculine epic tradition as she opens with a direct reference to Virgil's *Aeneid*. Killigrew writes, 'I Sing the Man that never Equal knew' and then goes on to detail the exploits of the hero, just like in Virgil, who began 'Arms and the man I sing' before introducing his hero.[17] As in Virgil, after a few lines Killigrew places her invocation to the muse: 'Ah that some pitying *Muse* would now inspire / My frozen style with a Poetique fire'.[18]

But this image also implies that she is working with a more recent feminine tradition of updating or adopting epic narratives. For in 1679, another female poet, Lucy Hutchinson, published an epic entitled *Order and Disorder*, based on the book of Genesis, the same topic that had inspired Milton's *Paradise Lost* a decade earlier. Where Hutchinson asks her muse to 'quicken' what is 'dull' with 'celestial fire', Killigrew asks her muse to 'inspire' what is 'frozen' with a 'Poetique fire'. Both are women poets, calling on a female muse to give them inspiration to tell a narrative normally reserved for male poets. Hutchinson's poem had only recently been published, but the fact that Killigrew references her alongside Virgil suggests a deep engagement with both classical and contemporary literature, as well as respect for her work. Killigrew's work is an example of extraordinary poetic skill in one so young, and one of real erudition.

Having seen the fate of her friend when she circulated her work at court, Anne Kingsmill was more reluctant to display her talents. She later reflected,

> itt is still a great satisfaction to me, that I was not so far abandon'd by my prudence, as out of a mistaken vanity, to lett any attempts of mine in Poetry, Shew them selves whilst I liv'd in such a publick place as the Court, where every one wou'd have made their remarks upon a Versifying Maid of Honour; and far the greater number with prejudice, if not contempt.[19]

Maria's court offered a haven for these women, a place where they were free from the scrutiny of the wits. The friendships they found there were sources of safety and freedom, away from the oppressive worlds they lived in. Indeed, Anne Kingsmill would look back on this time spent under Maria's guidance in years to come, writing of her 'superior sense' and her 'endearing sweetness to her happy friends', and of how 'Bless't were the hours when thro' attendance due / Her numerous charms were present to my view'.[20] This court, these rooms, were a central point for these women to learn, write, dream together.

In Maria's rooms they read Tasso, and translated Italian, French, Latin and Greek. They painted and played instruments. In this environment they flourished. And they also developed friendships, with each other, with Maria, and with other women who lived in and around the court, women like Isabella Bennet.

In Killigrew's coterie poems, Bennet went by the name of 'Alinda': there is a poem explicitly making this link – 'A Song On The Duchess of Grafton Under the Name *Alinda*' – but Alinda also appears as a character in one of Killigrew's three 'Pastoral Dialogues'. By giving her friend this literary alter ego, Killigrew was emulating Katherine Philips's Society of Friendship, a group made up solely of women each of whom had alter egos taken from pastoral poems: Philips was Orinda, and fellow members Anne Owen and Mary Aubrey were Lucasia and Rosania respectively. So integral did these names become to Philips's poetic universe that, when her poems were published in a volume after her death, the title included her epithet, 'The Matchless Orinda'. So when, in the 'Pastoral Dialogue', we come across the phrase 'Matchless *Alinda*' (l. 88), we can have little doubt of the echo that Killigrew was creating.

Isabella's pastoral name of 'Alinda' was probably inspired by a character from John Fletcher's *The Pilgrim*, a play first performed in 1621 and revived for the Restoration stage. In Fletcher's comedy, Alinda is a strong female character who refuses to marry as she is told to, determined that she will choose her own husband (a dashing young man called Pedro). She absconds from her father's house and the majority of the play consists of the men looking for her and her outwitting them in various disguises. She gets her happy ending. So, too, in Killigrew's 'Pastoral Dialogue' Alinda successfully outmanoeuvres an attempted seduction by a swain. She outwits him, she defends herself and her rights and he is left baffled and stupid. This was not Isabella's fate, betrothed as she was when little more than an infant to a brutish husband (Henry Fitzroy), but by borrowing the alter ego from Fletcher's comedy, Killigrew is able to imagine a world in which Isabella could choose her own destiny and dispose of her heart as she saw fit; in Killigrew's poetry she is allowed a different story.

It is difficult to know for certain who else was part of this coterie, but there is evidence to suggest that two other young women may well have been sharing work and inspiring each other; among Evelyn's papers at the British Library are found poems by Killigrew and also the poet Anne Wharton – who had grown up in the royal nursery – as well as the poems and diaries of John Evelyn's daughter, Mary.

We do not know when Anne Killigrew began to write poetry, or when this coterie may have begun. Killigrew's poem 'The Discontent' suggests that she had started to write before she had met such like-minded people. She writes of friendship as a 'rich cordial' which she does not yet possess in any quantity.[21] But Anne Killigrew soon found her like-minded friends, in Maria's rooms at St James's, and it was not long before she and Anne Kingsmill began to collaborate on a project close to their heart: a masque in honour of their duchess, the facilitator of this coterie and of their creativity. The story was Venus and Adonis. As Dryden had predicted when he wrote of her return from Scotland, this 'Venus' (Maria), had indeed brought 'graces triumphant in her train'. It came to fruition in early 1684, when its two authors, the 'Graces' in Maria's train, were twenty-two and twenty-three respectively.

Records of performances at the court are unreliable, and there is no record of the staging of this masque at court, but it was probably intended as a Shrove Tuesday entertainment. Shrovetide festivals were often held as decadent celebrations before Lent began. In Italy and France, it would follow a period known as Carnival, which ran from Epiphany to Lent. While in England this was less structured, a Carnival of sorts still took place, and Shrovetide was an honoured tradition. While Maria and James had been away in exile, the Shrove Tuesday festivities seem to have been put on hold, as indeed had most court entertainments. But when they returned, things got back on track. They had returned to a court forever altered, though they may not have realised the extent of it then, nor imagined what the consequences would be. But on the surface, things were to carry on as though nothing had happened. And what better way to celebrate their return and Charles's apparent 'victory' over parliament than to show a new work as a Shrove Tuesday entertainment? And what could be better for Maria than that the work should be undertaken by her new, precociously talented maids of honour. This was the kind of patronage Maria had been trying to enact since she arrived in England a decade earlier. And so, in the absence of records, we can imagine the scene.

❖

SHROVE TUESDAY, 1684
MARIA'S DRAWING ROOM, ST JAMES'S PALACE

A general hush falls over the small court assembled in Maria's rooms. A stage has been set; an orchestra begins to play. The opening chords are bright and regal, in the style of a French overture. A procession begins to enter, a mixture of courtiers and professional musicians dressed as shepherds and shepherdesses. In the centre is Cupid. It is a soprano role, played by a young woman, or perhaps a castrato. He begins to sing. He berates his companions for their inconstancies in love, joking that 'At court I find constant and true / Only an aged lord or two'. For though they are in the countryside and appear to be humble peasants, the scene he describes is a court. He addresses them as 'Courtiers' and protests, 'there is no faith in you, / You change as often as you can'. But the reprimand is a playful one, and it is not long before he calls on them to join with him in pastoral pleasures:

> Behold my arrows and my bow
> And I desire my art to show:
> No one bosom shall be found
> Ere I have done, without a wound,
> But it would be the greatest art
> To shoot myself into your heart;

Thither with both my wings I move,
Pray entertain the God of Love.

And the prologue ends with a call for 'Lovers to the close shades retire, / Do what your kindest thoughts inspire'. The curtain closes, and opens again on a blissful bower, where Venus and Adonis lie in a loving embrace. The scene begins as one of seduction, as Adonis asks:

Venus, when shall I taste soft delights
And on thy bosom lie?
Let's seek the shadiest covert of this grove
And never, never disappoint expecting love.

Venus's reply is forthcoming. She calls him a 'delightful youth ... full of beauty and of truth' and promises that he will find her 'Always tender, ever kind'. But they are interrupted by the sounds of bugles and hunting horns: 'Hark, hark the hunters, hark, hark the hounds! / They summon to the chase, haste haste away!' Adonis says he cares not to hunt, having 'already caught the noblest prey'. But, of course, Adonis goes, and Venus is left with Cupid and a group of putti. She wiles away the time until Adonis's return teaching them about the art of love. She tells them that she keeps Adonis's love through a policy of *treat him mean and keep him keen*. It is a policy she regrets in the final act, when Adonis is brought onto the stage injured and dying.

In other versions of the Venus and Adonis story, which tend to focus on the beautiful young hunter who attracts the goddess of love, only to be mauled to death by the animals he hunted, Venus is a figure of mockery: an older woman making a fool of herself with a younger man. In Shakespeare's poem, Venus is reduced to a desperate figure chasing a beautiful youth who has no interest in her and who wants only to get back to the hunt. But in Kingsmill's version it is Venus who is given agency. Adonis doesn't want to hunt, and, rather than being a figure abandoned, it is Venus who tells her lover to leave so that she can commune with her household. Adonis hardly appears in the production, as the majority of the masque involves Venus teaching her graces and Cupid how best to emulate her.

Unlike the records which survive for *Calisto*, we know nothing of the process of the production of *Venus and Adonis*, and the only certain performance record is from a girls' school in Chelsea in 1684. However, again unlike *Calisto*, we do have the full score. The music was written by John Blow, a rising star at the Stuart court, but for centuries the identity of the writer remained a mystery. Now, however, there is good reason to believe that it was Anne Kingsmill, Maria's new maid of honour. Images that occur in the script for *Venus and Adonis* recur again and again in her oeuvre, and the ideas she was playing with as a maid at Maria's court continued to be developed throughout her writing career. And the two plays that she subsequently wrote, at the end of the 1680s and beginning of the early 1690s, are also courtly erotic pastoral works, and though they are not full operas they do make use of music and have arrangements for dances.

To add to this, an early work which we know was written when Kingsmill was at court was preserved in manuscript (now held at the Northamptonshire Record Office) under the title 'The Grove. Written when I was a Maid of Honour'. The very image of 'The Grove' as a place of retirement is one Kingsmill would revisit throughout her career, but it is striking that it makes an appearance in both the opera and the poem as a place of refuge. Scholars have seen numerous stylistic links with Kingsmill's later poetry, and in one poem, dedicated to her husband on his birthday, Adonis appears in 'the groves' followed by Venus and their 'wandering loves', a clear echo of this earlier work.

But perhaps Anne Kingsmill did not work alone. The libretto contains images and rhymes that Anne Killigrew used in her poetry as well, though her oeuvre is so much smaller that it is harder to trace recurrent language in the same way. But whether or not they worked together on the script, the project was certainly collaborative, as Killigrew created accompanying paintings. Indeed, *Venus Attired by the Graces* itself may stem from this production. In the opera, Venus orders Cupid, 'Call, call the Graces'; he responds by saying, 'Come, all ye Graces! 'Tis your duty / To keep the Magazine of Beauty'. It is the role – the 'duty' – of the Graces to dress their goddess, and to adorn her in precious jewels, just as we see in Killigrew's painting, and just as Anne Killigrew and Anne Kingsmill will have done for their mistress on countless occasions.

But another role of the Graces, and of maids of honour, was to dance and to adorn, and in the opera this becomes their priority as they hand over their role of attiring their goddess to the putti: the stage directions say, 'While the Graces dance, the Cupids dress Venus, one combing her head, another ties a bracelet of pearls round her waist etc'. Perhaps in the opera the Graces were to be played by Maria's maids. The dance begins *l'istesso tempo* (at the same speed), so that it blends in with the music played for the singing which has preceded it, but it is to be composed of three parts: it soon turns to *allegro* for a 'Gavatt', or a gavotte, a French folk dance popular in ballets at the court of Louis XIV, and then to *lento* for a Saraband, and then *maestoso* (stately) for what is described as 'A Ground', a dance which would mimic a kind of procession or march, to end. The Graces of Maria's court would have ample opportunity here to show their talents. And maybe this was the aim; perhaps Maria commissioned this masque, as she had commissioned *The Masque of Calisto* a decade earlier. But here she was able to demonstrate far greater creative abilities in the women around her.

Two other of Anne Killigrew's paintings for the series – *Satyr Playing the Pipe* and *Venus and Adonis* – are now lost, though the latter is known from a mezzotint copy made by Bernard Lens some years later. From this we can see that the painting follows a fairly traditional treatment of the subject and seems to correspond with the postures of Venus and Adonis as found, for example, in Titian or van Dyck. Anne Killigrew very likely had access to either an original or a copy of the Titian; the painting was popular, and several were produced in his studio, and other artists made copies of the great work. At least one such work (perhaps original, perhaps a copy) was owned by Lord and Lady Sunderland, and Lady Sunderland (Anne Digby Spencer) was a lady-in-waiting to Maria, so Anne Killigrew might have seen this work at any time. Anne Digby was also close to Sarah Churchill, much to the chagrin of Princess Anne, who called Digby 'the greatest jade that ever lived!'[22]

However, though Killigrew's painting has close links to the Titian, hers has a twist. The posture is far more risqué than even that of Titian, as we see Venus's naked body from the front. As a woman, Killigrew was not allowed to learn to draw from life, and even for men the chances of painting a naked woman from life were slim. But this does not put her off the attempt to recreate the female form, and she uses this as a chance to show her abilities; indeed, the unity of proportion is impressive. As well as showing off her skill, Killigrew subtly shifts the power dynamic between the title characters in a way that is far more in line with what we find in the masque: Venus does not cling to Adonis, as she traditionally does both in Ovid's narrative and in the Renaissance image, but she is turning away from him. It is as though she has just embraced him and is now letting go, and she seems to be gesturing off canvas, to the forest where Adonis will go to hunt. Within the opera Venus does not beg Adonis to stay, but encourages him to go, asserting an independence she had never been afforded before. Where Titian's piece is full of portent, Killigrew's is calm; where Ovid is all about the tragedy of Adonis's demise, the Kingsmill/Killigrew collaboration is all about Venus spending her time with Cupid and her Graces. She is given agency.

Another of Anne Killigrew's extant paintings may also have been made as part of this series. A closer look at what is thought to be a self-portrait presents Venus after the death of her lover, sitting at the foot of his tomb. As she leans on the monument, her expression is melancholy. That this is the tomb of Adonis is suggested by the stone behind her, which is engraved with martial symbols, a helmet, a sword, a shield. And looking to the ground we can just see a few red anemones around her feet: according to the myth, as Adonis died his blood spilled onto the ground and anemones grew where it had fallen. Unfortunately, the painting was at some point trimmed, so we cannot see the full composition.[23]

Whether or not this portrait belonged to the series, it shows how courtly life and courtly entertainments, and the collaborative atmosphere fostered by Maria in the production of these entertainments, influenced women's artistic production. Vulnerable and revealing, this painting was a vehicle for Anne Killigrew's self-expression. The psychological depth goes beyond anything found in other late seventeenth-century English paintings.

We do not know how Anne Killigrew learned to paint. For how, indeed, could a woman in the seventeenth century learn to paint in a country like England, which had little in the way of home-grown artistic production? Killigrew had no family connections to painting, and lived in a society which was far less open to the idea of a woman painting than a country like Italy, where there had been women painters for at least a century. When a man trained as a painter in the seventeenth century, he would join the studio of an older, more established artist, and work for him as an apprentice. In his training he would study the human form from life, and in the studio he would have a ready supply of materials and the space to learn his craft. As an artist he would have joined a guild or academy, which would offer him protection and status. None of this was readily available to a woman. It is no surprise that the women who successfully became artists in the sixteenth and seventeenth centuries were almost always the children of artists: Lavinia Fontana, daughter of Prospero; Artemisia Gentileschi, daughter of Orazio; Elisabetta Sirani, daughter of Giovanni – each trained in their father's studio.

The young Anne Killigrew would have found little precedent. But, luckily for her, the first two English women who had forged successful careers as artists – Joan Carlile and Mary Beale – were both still living at the time that she would have been discovering her own ambitions and it is likely that she came into contact with both of them while she was a young girl, in and around the court. In the 1670s, both Carlile and Beale were living around Pall Mall, not far from where Anne Killigrew will have grown up, and she may even have taken lessons from one of them. There certainly is a similarity between her work and that of Joan Carlile, who, like Killigrew, was pioneering in her interest in landscapes. And there is another clue. Some years after her death, the art historian and antiquary George Vertue wrote that 'Mrs Carlile taught a Lady to draw & paint'. He recalls, too, that she 'drew her own picture ... with a book of drawings in her lap & this Lady Standing behind her'.[24] This painting is now lost, but was this 'lady', described by Vertue, our Anne Killigrew?

If these women did work together, it is most likely that they were introduced by their mutual acquaintance, Peter Lely. In fact, Lely is also a candidate as her tutor; in a painting thought to be a portrait of Anne Killigrew he shows us a young woman, facing out of the canvas with a faint, slightly inscrutable smile on her lips. She is dressed as a courtier, in yellow silk and pearls. Behind her hangs a velvet curtain, drawn to show a classical column. A window looks out to a beautiful sunset. It is a classic portrait of a noble young woman. But look more closely at what lies on a table before her. It is a sketch of a young woman, a self-portrait, and in her hand she holds a porte-crayon (a brass instrument split at the ends to hold chalk or crayon). She is ready to continue her work. Maybe her rather arch look suggests that she is scrutinising the portraitist as he paints? Or perhaps she is just keen to get back to her own art, rather than sitting for someone else's.

For women to be taught painting and to 'work' as amateur painters was far more common at that time than we tend to assume, and these women's talents did not go unrecognised or unpraised by the men around them. John Evelyn's wife, Mary, was an amateur painter, and their youngest daughter Susanna seems also to have undertaken some artistic 'training'. John Evelyn wrote in 1661 of a miniature of the Madonna that Mary had copied from a Raphael, which she 'presented to his Majesty, who was infinitely pleased with it and caused it to be placed in his cabinet among his best paintings'.[25] Of Susanna he wrote that 'she has a peculiar talent in design, as painting in oil and miniature, and an extraordinary genius for whatever hands can do with a needle.'[26]

Anna Scott, Duchess of Monmouth, was one of several women (including Elizabeth Pepys, wife of Samuel) to be taught painting by the portraitist Alexander Browne, who even dedicated his *Ars Pictoria* to Scott in 1675. And in Holland Princess Mary took almost daily lessons, specialising in miniatures, from her great favourite, Richard Gibson, though she was reported to have had little talent.

As many of the great poets of the seventeenth century were courtiers and not 'professional' in the sense of making a living by their art, it was possible for an amateur artist still to be hugely ambitious of their talent and potential. Anne Killigrew certainly falls into this category. Given her position at court, and her illustrious relations – her father as almonist to the Duke of York, her uncle the Master of the Revels, her cousin as Lord Chamberlain – it would have been inconceivable for Anne to aim for a public career as a painter akin to Joan Carlile or Mary Beale. But this should not undermine her ambitions to be known as a painter and as a poet. Indeed, in her surviving oeuvre (small though it is) we find some of the most experimental and ambitious work to have been produced in England at that time by man or woman, of any age.

Much of her painting focuses more on landscape than people. In *Venus Attired by the Graces*, the figures make up very little of the canvas, the majority of which is given over to the russet-coloured trees, the rolling hills receding into the background and the layers of cloud, all bathed in autumnal light. Killigrew understood how landscape could be used to set a mood. Indeed, nature is integral to the atmosphere produced in her works. In *Venus Attired by the Graces*, the dusky hues, the setting sun, the stillness of the leaves on the trees all contribute to a sense of peace and calm as these women commune in the woods. It is also quite a large painting (112 x 95 cm). If we picture Killigrew painting this, we cannot see a modest young lady sitting daintily painting at a little easel; this required real physicality. More likely we must imagine her standing, with paint on her hands, reaching up, moving around, on a work which will have taken time to produce. This was clearly more than a hobby.

But Killigrew's ambitions went beyond ingenuity. We know from her paintings and her poetry that she was well versed in ancient Greek and Roman literature; in her reading of Horace's *Ars Poetica*, she will have come across his motto '*ut pictura poesis*': 'as in painting so in poetry'.[27] Perhaps more than any of her peers, she took this motto for her own. Throughout tracts on poetry and painting from antiquity and the Renaissance the central theme of discussions between the two subjects was one of contest between the arts: poetry can never successfully imitate the visual work it seeks to describe, as it can never recreate what is seen; but poetic ekphrasis can nevertheless do things that painting cannot – it allows us to grasp qualities in objects that are not apparent to visual inspection, it offers extra psychological depth or narrative movement, and thereby facilitates a superior 'sight' of the object, rather than being a diminished version of reality. Whatever psychological depth she gestures to in her paintings, it will never capture what she is able to explore as a poet. But for Killigrew, ultimately, this was not a competition, but a marriage of forms. The poems and the paintings were designed to exist alongside each other. Sadly, none of these companion works survives, but Dryden's assertion that this 'Accomplished Young Lady' was 'Excellent in the two sister-arts of Poesie and Painting' lives on.

14

Courtships and Scandals

Maria's court in 1683 was full of creativity and intellectual promise – and the masque of *Venus and Adonis* was in many ways the apotheosis of her creative ambitions. But it was also the scene of romance. A young courtier named Heneage Finch had been appointed Groom of the Bedchamber to James in 1683, and it was not long before he first saw and fell in love with Anne Kingsmill.

Heneage Finch was born in 1657, to Heneage Finch, 3rd Earl of Winchelsea, and Mary Seymour, the daughter of William Seymour, Duke of Somerset, and Frances Devereux (the daughter of Elizabeth I's great favourite, the Earl of Essex). The Finches had been ennobled in the previous century but could trace their lineage back to the Norman conquest. They were part of the Herbert family from which the Earls of Pembroke are descended. The Seymours were descended from royalty and counted Henry VIII as an ancestor. Heneage Finch, then, grew up in a family of ancient noble stock, but he was the third child of five, and the second son, so for most of his life he seemed unlikely to inherit either land or title. Nonetheless, he was of aristocratic blood and was raised as such.

Heneage had been well educated and had shown a particular aptitude for and interest in history and antiquarian studies, which was encouraged by his father's gifts, sent home from the Ottoman Empire where he was serving as an ambassador. He was raised to be a courtier, and his family had high hopes for him there. He was good-looking, intelligent and personable, all the attributes required for public life. He joined the army and rose through the ranks. By the age of twenty-five he was already captain of the elite Coldstream Guards. He cut a dashing and impressive figure.

Anne and Heneage probably first met at court in the apartments of Maria or James, and they will have found themselves together often. But Anne was not interested in marriage, though she admired him. She was wary of marrying, and much of her early poetry is concerned with the loss of freedom which would inevitably follow should she agree to do so. She saw matrimony as a trap, and love as a snare. Indeed, she may even have been nursing a broken heart. In 'The Grove', which dates from this period, we can see signs of this. Looking at the manuscript, it is apparent that the page has been heavily excised (though whether by Anne or by a later hand, we cannot know), but from what we can make out we can see that the poem looks forward to her later poetry of retirement. Even in her happy state at court she is thinking of pastoral refuge. Here the speaker seeks a sanctuary where they will be free from the pains of love and betrayal. If the poem is autobiographical, we must assume that early in her life at court Anne had her heart broken. She speaks of 'his Soft Deluding wayes, / With hopes and flatr'ngs he betrayes'. All this works within conventional lines of love poetry, and there would perhaps be no reason to think of it as expressing any personal experience of Anne, but for the lines which speak of 'shun[ning] . . . / Publick Assemblies, and the Court'. Though there are lines missing here, it reads as if it is Anne speaking, saying that she feared to go out in public, that everyone knew she had had her heart broken, that she was humiliated and wanted to seek the sanctuary of the pastoral grove. Whether the speaker is Anne herself, an invented character or another member of the court she observed receiving this treatment, it was written at a time when Anne may well have considered her heart to be in danger.

In May 1683, the ducal court took a trip to Oxford. The group included, among others, James and Maria, Princess Anne, John and Sarah Churchill, Anne Kingsmill, Heneage Finch and probably also

Anne Killigrew. The university awarded honorary Doctor of Civil Law degrees to James and some of the most promising members of his household, including John Churchill (though he was called away on official business so was unable to accept it) and Heneage Finch. To be singled out for such an honour was a testament to the young man's abilities and to the potential of a promising future, and this will not have been lost on Anne Kingsmill as she watched him receive his doctorate.

At the beginning of 1684 Anne Kingsmill received some devastating news: her brother had killed their cousin, William Haslewood, in a duel and was in prison. It must have been devastating for Anne; the Kingsmills had grown up with their cousins as if they were siblings, and the boys had been inseparable. What happened that night is shrouded in mystery, though her brother (also called William) always claimed it was self-defence, that his cousin insulted him and drew his sword on him. William was pardoned for the crime while the Haslewood sisters demanded revenge. It was not long after this that Heneage again proposed to Anne, and this time he was accepted. They married on 15 May 1684.

Once they were married, the Finches continued to live around court, taking up residence at Westminster Palace, and Anne continued to spend her time at Maria's court, though she had to resign her post as maid of honour. She also continued to write. Heneage was proud of his wife's talents and one poem which can tentatively be dated from these early years was later copied out by Heneage, who called it 'The Bargain, a Song between Bachus & Cupid, made at my request by Ardelia'. Like Anne Killigrew, Anne Finch was clearly inspired by the legacy of Katherine Philips's Society of Friendship, and Ardelia was her pastoral name. Perhaps she adopted it when part of the society of friendship she found in Maria's circle.

Anne was also translating French works by Montaigne and most likely began work on her translation of Tasso's *Aminta*, a project close to Maria's heart. When the original had been staged in Ferrara, Maria's ancestors Leonora d'Este and Lucrezia d'Este had played two of the leading roles. There were English translations readily available in London, indeed the text had been printed as recently as 1681, but a note on the manuscript in Heneage's hand tells us that Anne was translating from the Italian in parts and was using a French translation for others. Anne's decision to adapt this work into English was as much an intellectual exercise in translation as in poetic expression.

The marriage was a happy one, and within the first year she wrote a poem to Heneage when he was away from home on some court business. Looking at the original manuscripts it is probable that this was the first time she gave him his pastoral name, Daphnis. First was written Mr Finch, then this was crossed out and Daphnis added. In mythology Daphnis was sometimes the pipe-playing follower of Artemis who was found under a laurel tree, a fitting image for the husband of a great poet. But it is more likely that Anne took the name from a Greek pastoral by the poet Longus called *Daphnis and Chloe*, which tells of two lovers who spend the narrative overcoming obstacles, but who marry in the end and live out a bucolic life together. This poem was no doubt in Anne's mind, as it was the inspiration behind Tasso's *Aminta*, which she was translating when she wrote this poem. It is a beautiful display of love, of joy, and also of a shared creative endeavour. It opens:

This, to the Crown, and blessing of my life,
The much lov'd husband, of a happy wife.
To him, whose constant passion, found the art
To win a stubborn, and ungratefull heart;
And to the world, by tend'rest proof discovers
They err, who say that husbands can't be lovers.
With such return of passion, as is due,
Daphnis I love, Daphnis my thoughts persue,
Daphnis, my hopes, my joys, are bounded all in you.

The following line, 'You know who writes; and I who 'tis that reads', suggests that he was always her first reader, even of other unrequested poems.[1]

But all was not plain sailing. Anne Kingsmill suffered from depression throughout her life, and in her poem 'The Spleen' she writes with brutal honesty about what she is going through. She draws on the medical language of the day, which had it that the body was ruled by different humours, and that both mental and physical illness occurred when they were out of balance. The spleen was associated with melancholy, and Anne addresses the poem to her 'spleen', which is gradually taking over her life. She describes how she feels when 'Trembling sometimes thou dost appear' and she 'Dissolved into a panic fear'. She cannot sleep and her mental state becomes completely debilitating. She writes, 'I feel thy force, whilst I against thee rail; / I feel my verse decay, and my cramped numbers fail'. But while her condition makes it hard to write, at the same time she clearly uses writing poetry as a means through which she copes:

> Through thy black jaundice I all objects see,
> As dark and terrible as thee,
> My lines decried, and my employment thought
> An useless folly, or presumptuous fault:
> . . .
> My hand delights to trace unusual things,
> And deviates from the known and common way.

Though Heneage was always a support, we can see in one poem from August 1685 that Anne's depression initially put something of a strain on their marriage. She wrote from Tunbridge Wells where she had gone to take the waters. The poem is a letter in response to what we must assume were pleas from him asking her to go home to him:

> Daphnis no more your wish repeate
> For my returne nor mourn my Stay
> Least my wise Purpose you defeat
> And urg'd by love I come away.

She tells him that she misses him, too – 'My own desires I scarce Resist / But blindly yield if you persist' – but that she needs to be apart from him in order to be 'Restor'd to health'.

Anne Kingsmill was not the only person who was being wooed at court in 1683; there were some concerns about Princess Anne who, it was discovered, was secretly being courted by John Sheffield, Earl of Mulgrave. Sheffield was a once-dashing thirty-five-year-old with a terrible reputation, who had been sending the princess amorous letters. He was a known philanderer and seductor, who had led several maids at court to ruin. When James and Charles found out about the liaison they were horrified and banished him from court. But there were rumours that they were too late, and the affair had gone beyond improper letters. Court gossips put about that Princess Anne had been seduced, and a scurrilous poem was soon doing the rounds: 'That with nauseous Courtship durst defile / The Sweetest Choicest beauty of our Isle.'[2] Ralph Verney wrote to his brother that 'the town has given [him] the nickname of King John' as he had 'gone so far as to spoil her for marrying any-one else'.[3] To add to this, some rather risqué poems by Sheffield's hand seemed extra proof. In these poems he imagines her naked in his arms:

Ready to throw me at the feet
Of that fair nymph whom I adore,
Impatient those delights to meet
Which I enjoy'd the night before.
...
There my Celia's snowy arms,
Breasts and other parts more dear,
Exposing new and unknown charms,
To my transported soul appear.[4]

If this poem was indeed about Anne, her father and uncle were right to be concerned. She had already been rejected as a wife for George of Hanover, on the grounds that her mother had been a commoner. This stain of having a mother who was not royal or noble was carried by the princesses all their lives; even William of Orange had considered his right to the English throne greater than that of his wife, since his parents had both been blue-bloods. Anne could not afford to compromise her honour and was unlikely to have fallen for his charms. She had seen enough young women lose their reputations to risk losing hers, and she will have remembered Mary Kirk, Maria's maid of honour, who was ruined by her association with both him and with Anne's father, James.

Not all satires on the topic were scurrilous: Aphra Behn wrote a mock-heroic epistle called 'Ovid to Julia' in which Mulgrave takes on the pathetic role of an injured lover who raised his sights too high and was rejected. But whatever the truth, there was a whiff of scandal in the air and Sheffield's discretion could not be relied upon. Princess Mary wrote to Frances Apsley:

> I believe my sister very innocent however I am so nice upon the point of reputation that it makes me mad she should be exposed to such reports, and now what will not this insolent man say being provoked.[5]

So, Sheffield was sent away and Anne was to be married, as quickly as possible. That she had not been married sooner is curious; royal women were almost always married around the ages of fifteen or sixteen, as Mary and Maria both had been. Anne was now eighteen.

The chosen prince was George of Denmark, and John Churchill was sent to escort him to London to begin negotiations. As Anne waited for her prospective husband to arrive, she spent many evenings dreaming with her bosom friend, Sarah Churchill, about the kind of man John was bringing back to her. Churchill's brother, Charles, was in the household of George of Denmark, so John was perhaps the most rational choice of convoy. But the fact that he was sent on this expedition is also a reflection of James's esteem for him – who could he trust more with his daughter's suitor? – and also of Anne's close relationship with Sarah, who expected some advancement in reward for her friendship when Anne was married.

George of Denmark, a handsome and passive man, seemed not to mind about her commoner roots, and had almost certainly heard nothing of her apparent 'loss of honour'. In fact, he did not seem to mind about anything at all: he was widely reported to be good-natured and extremely dull. Charles II said of him, 'I have tried him drunk, and I have tried him sober, but there is nothing in him.'[6] But Anne was no intellectual and she was happy enough with George's quiet banality. Sarah Churchill acted as chaperone during their early meetings, and the wedding took place just ten days after George's arrival in London. It would prove to be an enduringly happy union.

Once she was married, Anne's household was expanded; she was now to have her own maids of honour and Women of the Bedchamber. She immediately went to her father and Maria and requested that Sarah Churchill be given the highest post of First Lady of the Bedchamber. Though Sarah was no longer formally attached to Maria's court since she married in 1677, they continued to spend time together and she was often at court to see Anne and to be with John, who remained in James's household. James agreed to Sarah being made Anne's Second Lady of the Bedchamber, rather than First. His ear was bent by his brother-in-law, Laurence Hyde, who wanted to place his own people in this new establishment. Flower Backhouse Hyde was made First Lady of the Bedchamber. Flower was Anne's aunt by marriage (to Henry Hyde, Laurence's brother), and it was perhaps natural that the Clarendon family should be recognised. But Sarah was piqued, and she did all she could to turn Anne against 'the madwoman', as she called her.[7]

Though it was not the top job, it was a great honour, and Maria must have been delighted to see such advancement for the woman who had been such a favourite of hers. She would not have imagined the consequences of the friendship she was sanctioning. James's consent appears to have been given a little more reluctantly, and he worried about the effect of Sarah's company on Anne. Anne was obsessively devoted to Sarah in a way he thought unhealthy; it was called 'a passion without measure' by those who looked on from the outside.[8] It was around this time that Sarah and Anne began to use their nicknames for each other, Mrs Morley and Mrs Freeman.

After the marriage Anne, Sarah and Maria continued to spend much time together as a group, and in September it was reported that they had taken up hare hunting, which 'mightily pleased them' and they were often to be seen out with a pack of beagles. That winter was a particularly cold one, but they will have entertained themselves at the carnival that was set up on the frozen Thames. But though she laughed outwardly, Maria was suffering terribly. Catherine Sedley, though no longer a maid of honour, was back on the scene. And, what was worse, she was heavily pregnant with James's child. Maria suffered another miscarriage in October; Catherine gave birth to a son. It was a brutal blow. And when Maria miscarried again in May 1684, she became extremely ill and went to Tunbridge Wells with Princess Anne to convalesce. Anne, too, was in need of recuperation, having given birth to a stillborn child the same month. This was the first of many tragedies for Anne, who would have seventeen pregnancies, but not a single child who would survive to adulthood.

❖

In the winter of 1684 there was some excitement when Hortense Mancini had visitors from France. Among them was her seventeen-year-old nephew, Philippe de Soissons. Philippe had visited once before, in 1680, and his fiery temperament was well known. But this time, he fell madly in love with Hortense. At the time, Hortense was involved in an affair with a Swedish count, Gustav Banér, and Philippe became wildly jealous. He challenged Banér to a duel and, remarkably, fatally wounded the Swede. Hortense was devastated. She took to her rooms (which she covered in black cloths and hangings) and refused to leave them. Philippe, on the other hand, fled immediately.

Saint-Évremond, alarmed by Hortense once again professing that she would enter a nunnery, teased her in her grief, saying, 'there is nothing extraordinary in this adventure except your grief. Lovers are mortal like other men. Your lover is now no more than a sad empty shell formed by your imagination.' Hortense decided against the convent, but it was said that she had lost some of her zest for life.

A painting that dates from around this time, however, tells a different story. It is by Benedetto Gennari and presents Hortense as Diana, from the story of Diana and Actaeon. In the story, as told in Ovid's *Metamorphoses*, the goddess Diana is bathing with her nymphs when the hunter Actaeon accidentally stumbles upon her. So enraged is she that a mere mortal would dare to see her naked that she transforms him into a stag, and he is savaged to death by his own hounds. After this, she takes ownership of the dogs. The story was frequently depicted in paintings, perhaps most famously by Titian, and it was fashionable for women at the time to be presented in portraits as the virgin goddess, but Hortense's portrait offers something quite different. It is a huge work, measuring 1.8 x 2.3 m. Hortense is surrounded not by her female nymphs, but by her male slaves, each of whom wear silver collars, bearing her seal.[9] Her favourite, Mustapha, stands aloof from the others who are playing, looking at his mistress from beside the fountain. The colour of their skins contrasts with hers, which, combined with the darkness of the twilight around her, makes her seem almost luminously pale.

Hortense wears blue, white and red robes, asserting her French identity. One of her breasts is exposed, associating her with the female Amazons, who reportedly only had one breast, having cut the other off to make it easier to fire their arrows. She was described as such by her friend, Saint-Évremond: 'Madame Mazarin had the air, habit, equipage of a Queen of the Amazons; she appeared equally equipped to charm and fight.' Every aspect of this image is deliberate, as she presents herself as a force to be reckoned with, and this idea of her as both queenlike and Amazonian in power and charm was how she presented herself. Perhaps Saint-Évremond playfully called her an Amazon queen and she liked it. Perhaps this painting was conceived based on the way she knew she was seen and talked about. It is partly play, partly serious.

Actaeon is nowhere to be seen. His quiver and bow lie at her feet, and with her right hand she languidly gestures towards his dogs, who are being ridden by her slaves and are clearly already entirely hers. Perhaps Actaeon has already been conquered; if not, he soon will be. She gazes out at the viewer: is it they who must stand in for Actaeon, soon to fall under her power? Or maybe Actaeon is an allusion to her dead lover: the largest of the dogs has the name 'Prince Philippe' emblazoned on its collar. It is almost as though her nephew has become her tame and loyal dog, who has defended his mistress.

Not long after these tragic events – the duel, and the death of Banér – Hortense performed in another of the salon's entertainments; *Parodie d'une scene de l'opéra de Roland* was adapted from a cutting-edge opera written by Jean-Baptiste Lully the same year (1685) in Paris. That the salon was able to get the score so quickly shows how in touch they were with all the latest artistic trends. Saint-Évremond wrote the lyrics, and the members of the salon took part. Hortense's singing voice was much admired, and she performed alongside Henrietta Hyde, who had been governess to the princesses before their marriages.

The salon had gone from strength to strength after the threats of the Popish Plot subsided, and Charles was one of its frequent visitors. John Evelyn reported – rather disapprovingly, it must be said – seeing his king there in February 1685. He said: 'I can never forget the inexpressible luxury and profaneness, gaming, and all dissoluteness, and as it were total forgetfulness of God (it being Sunday evening), which ... I was witness of.' What seems to have most distressed him was the sight of the king himself, who was 'sitting and toying with his concubines, Portsmouth, Cleveland, and Mazarin ... while about twenty of the great courtiers and other dissolute persons were at Basset round a large table, a bank of at least 2,000 in gold before them'. He ends the account with a more sombre note: 'Six days after, was all in the dust.'[10]

15

A New Era

12 FEBRUARY 1685
THE KING'S BEDCHAMBER, WHITEHALL PALACE, LONDON

Charles had begun 2 February as any other day, though he had been 'pale as ashes', and had trouble speaking, appearing to see someone who wasn't there. He had risen at 7.30, his barber had arrived at 8.00, he had sat in his chair. Behind him, chattering away, were the previous night's chamber fellows, Harry Killigrew and Lord Bruce. The barber had leaned over to fasten the shaving smock around his neck, but when he looked into the face of his king, he saw an expression of horror: Charles stared fixedly at him, trying desperately to speak. Finally, he cried out, 'Oh God!' and fell back against the chair as though dead.[1] He was 'black and insensible like a corpse'.[2] All around sprang up in alarm. Bruce ran to fetch James and sent someone to find Caterina.

Maria was called soon after and when she entered the room she was greeted by the sight of Charles seated in a chair with a hot iron clamped to his head, his mouth forcibly held open. She remembered this moment for the rest of her life and wrote of it later as 'a fearful sight'.[3] It soon became too much for Caterina, who had to be carried from the room, prostrate with grief. For James the tension was terrible, though his sombre look could not prevent him from appearing rather ridiculous: he had been called to his brother's room while dressing and was sporting one shoe and one slipper. When he looked up and saw Maria they passed a look of recognition. If Charles were to die, James would be king, and what would become of them then?

After two hours sitting paralysed in the chair, Charles was moved to his bed. By this time word had got around the court and everyone came to gawp at their monarch. For four days he lay thus. It was clear that he was gravely ill, but some of his old spirit remained. At one point he apologised for taking 'such an unconscionable amount of time a' dying'.[4] The doctor told him to rest, not to speak. He responded with his usual barbed wit: 'That order would kill Harry Killigrew.'[5]

Caterina, a little recovered, found a moment to draw near to Maria and leaned to whisper in her ear. She said that the king would need a Catholic priest, that Charles had told her that, when his time came, he would wish to receive the Catholic sacrament and to be absolved. They were running out of time: over at a table by the bed Charles's Anglican ministers were setting up for him to take the sacrament. The Archbishop of Canterbury leaned forward and asked his king if he were ready. Charles replied ambivalently that there was time enough yet: he was stalling. Maria said that she would tell James, that Caterina was not to worry, between them they would see it done. Caterina smiled, thanked her and left the room. She was still overwhelmed with grief and went to be attended by her doctor in her rooms.

For hours Maria watched her brother-in-law slowly fading away, and tried to think of how such an impossible task could be achieved. There were so many people in the room. How could they ever get a Catholic priest in? She managed to catch her husband's eye and beckoned him over. She told him what Caterina had said. He replied that he knew of his brother's wishes, that it was all he could think about, but he could not see how it could be managed either.

Later in the day Louise de Kéroualle (who was banished from the bedchamber for propriety's sake) appealed to ambassador Barillon as he passed by, telling him, too, that Charles was a closet Catholic, and he wanted to die as a Catholic. Barillon found James and they agreed that they needed to act now, or risk missing their chance. James went to his brother's side and knelt down. He took his hand and leaned close to his face. 'Brother, you have refused the sacrament of the Protestant church, will you receive those of the Catholic?'[6] Charles sighed with relief and said that he would give anything in the world to have a priest but that he feared the consequences for James. James looked into his brother's eyes and promised that he would find one 'though it were to cost me my life'.[7]

Finding said priest was the next challenge. Such a man could not be anyone known or conspicuous: he could not be from James and Maria's household. Then James remembered a Benedictine named Father John Huddlestone who had been allowed to remain at court because of the great service he had done Charles many years before, when he had saved his life in the Civil War by hiding him after the Battle of Worcester. James ordered everyone out of the room, except for Caterina, Maria and two trusted courtiers, the earls of Bath and Feversham. Huddlestone entered through a secret door (through which many a mistress had passed before). He was disguised in an Anglican cassock and wore a wig. James said to Charles, 'Sir, I bring you a man who once saved your life; he now comes to save your soul.'[8] Charles replied, 'He is welcome.'[9] He then took the sacrament and made his confession. He recommended his children to James's care (though he omitted to mention Monmouth). He asked his brother to protect Louise de Kéroualle and uttered the famous words 'don't let dear Nellie starve'.[10] He spoke of Maria's 'incomparable virtues and marvellous talents'.[11] He hoped that James would listen to her and share the burden of monarchy with her. Some years earlier he had remarked that if he were to die, he did not think that James would last two years more as king. Perhaps he reflected on this prophecy now, as he felt death approaching.

On the morning of 6 February, Charles asked what time it was. He was told it was 6 a.m. He then said, 'Draw up the curtains and open the window that I may behold the light of the sun for the last time.'[12] He died at midday. In the bedchamber a voice rang out, 'The King is dead. Long live the King.' All around James his courtiers fell to their knees to bow before their new sovereign. James was pronounced King James II throughout the streets of London.

In Holland, Monmouth was attending a banquet at William and Mary's court. He was in good spirits. A few months before he had secretly visited his father in England, and Charles had told him that he planned to recall him to court. Monmouth even had hopes that his uncle would be sent back into exile. He may even have thought that he would be declared a legitimate prince. Few people knew of his hopes, but he had confided in his cousin William. When a servant holding a letter for him entered the room, Monmouth's heart must have leapt; here, he thought, was the summons. He was going home. But when he opened the letter and read its words, all hope left him. The king, his father, was dead.

❖

Maria found no joy in her new position as queen. She had loved Charles deeply and grieved equally profoundly at his death. James, too, could hardly bear the loss. Just before Charles died, he had kissed James's hand and called him 'the best of friends and brothers'.[13] The feeling was mutual, and James was bereft without his brother. He was the last one left: his father and mother were dead, and now he had outlived all his siblings, too. John Evelyn went to offer his condolences and found James lying on his bed in a state of undress, hardly able to rise to acknowledge visitors. But rise he did. He was the King of England now, and his grief would have to be hidden away. Dryden described him thus: 'Mute and magnificent, without a tear.'[14]

Maria found it too difficult to hide her sadness. She took to her bed and stayed there. She later said that she was afraid of being in public and of being thought false in her grief: 'I was so greatly afflicted by the death of King Charles that I dared not show how much, lest I be suspected of hypocrisy.'[15] At court everyone had so many ulterior motives that they assumed everything was done for personal gain.

Maria wrote to her brother a few days later, telling him how the death of the king 'has left us all so deeply affected'.[16] She tells him that she has been so ill with grief that she has been in bed ever since, but that 'this evening I am just well enough to write these two lines to you'.[17] When she was finally able to leave her rooms, she went straight to see Caterina who, still grief-stricken, had not left her bed. Maria's condolences were said to have been 'made more in sobs than in words'.[18] As the two women wept together, they must also have reflected on their exchange of roles: Caterina would now step back and Maria would take her place. She held her first meetings with ambassadors and courtiers under a large mourning canopy, draped in black cloth above and underfoot. As she sat upright on her throne, dressed in mourning, she cast a powerful figure. It was remarked that she emanated grace and dignity. She was Queen of England now.

Evelyn described the scene, on 5 March 1685: 'There came over divers envoys and great persons to condole the death of the late King, who were received by the Queen-Dowager on a bed of mourning, the whole chamber, ceiling and floor, hung with black, and tapers were lighted, so as nothing could be more lugubrious and solemn. The Queen-Consort sat under a state on a black foot-cloth, to entertain the circle (as the Queen used to do), and that very decently.'[19] In Evelyn's account we can also detect early hints of trouble. In the same entry he said that 'to my grief, I saw the new pulpit set up in the Popish Oratory at Whitehall for the Lent preaching, mass being publicly said, and the Romanists swarming at Court with greater confidence than had ever been seen in England since the Reformation.'[20] He reported that 'everybody grew jealous [worried] as to what this would tend'.[21] It was unwise of James to move so quickly and openly begin to practise his faith.

❖

James's rule started well, and peacefully, which was unexpected considering the tempestuous decade which had led up to it. He had called parliament immediately, had spoken softly of his hopes that they would work together and that he had no desire to impose on the Church of England. This had all been met with positivity, and with relief. Indeed, parliament were so relieved that they settled an enormous annuity on him of £400,000 (around £48,000,000 in today's money), far more than they had ever given Charles.

Preparations for the coronation soon followed. The official herald, Francis Sandford, was employed to make a detailed account of the entire process. As a result, for James and Maria's coronation we have the most thorough accounts of any coronation up to that point. On 19 February the first meetings took place. Over the course of many meetings, which were full of courtiers, the ceremonies of the previous coronation of Charles II were pored over in minute detail. But, of course, when Charles had been crowned, he had not been married. The ceremony would need to be adapted. There was little in the way of precedent for a joint coronation; when Charles I had been crowned, Henrietta Maria had refused to take part in the service, since it was Anglican. James I and Anne of Denmark was one example, but theirs had been a low-key affair, taking place as it did amid an outbreak of plague. Prior to this Elizabeth I, Mary I and Edward VI were unmarried at the time of their coronations, and Henry VIII's six wives did not perhaps offer the most ideal examples.

For a start, an entirely new set of crown jewels would have to be made for Maria. After the execution of Charles I and the establishment of the Protectorate the crown jewels had been melted down, and the gems were sold. When Charles II was crowned, a new crown was made, but Caterina never had a coronation, so no crown had been made for the Queen Consort. It was agreed that 'the Queens Crown be an Imperial Crown with Arches, but lighter than the Kings', on 28 February, but a good deal more discussion went into 'Whether the Queen is to have a Throne distinct from His Majesty'. The jewels that were finally commissioned were as follows:

> A Circle or Coronet of Gold, adorned with Precious Stones, which the Queen was to wear from Westminster-Hall to the Abbey-Church, and till the time of Her Anointing.
> A Rich Crown, wherewith Her Majesty was to be Crowned.

A Lesser Crown, which Her Majesty was to wear in Her Return from the Abbey.
A Scepter of Gold with a Cross.
An Ivory Rod with a Dove.
A Rich Ring.[22]

There seem to have been meetings twice a week, not all of which were useful. The meeting notes from 6 March, for example, provide some relatable content: they spent most of the meeting discussing what would be discussed in the next meeting. Alongside the official regulations of form and precedence, of titles, of who can wear what, we have a touching personal hint. James was in these meetings, too, and when the order of the procession was discussed he interceded. It had been decided 'that for the greater Splendor of the Solemnity, the whole Proceeding should march Four a-breast' but we are told that 'His Majesty was desirous that the QUEEN should go even with Him'.[23] In other words, he wanted them to walk side by side under their canopies of state. Unfortunately, even though he was the king, James had no jurisdiction here. There was not space for them to go together so, upon 'humble Application', he 'declared His Pleasure, That if the Narrowness of the Passage in some Places would not admit thereof, then that the Queen should immediately precede Him'.[24] This says something about the way James was approaching his rule; they would be side by side. Indeed, surviving coins from their reign tell a similar story. Medals and coins were cast to celebrate the event, some of which depict just Maria, some only James, but in both cases they wear the same laurel crown and are presented as equals. In another design we see them together. James is in the forefront, but they are represented as a pair.

The difficulties of organising a double ceremony were initially compounded by concerns around the fact that the couple were Catholic and the service Anglican. There was no precedent for this either. But James did not want much to change; he simply said that they would not take communion, and the procession from the Tower to the Abbey should also be cut (as a means of saving money), but all else was to be as it had been for his brother. Saving money does not appear to have been a high priority: Maria's clothing alone cost over £100,000 (around £12,000,000 in today's money).

The date of 23 April was decided on. It was the same day on which Charles II had been crowned and offered an important sense of continuity. On the morning of the great day, London's streets were lined with people. The air was filled with excitement and energy, children ran around with ribbons in their hair and the scent of roasting meat and of wine filled the air from the many stalls selling food and drink. By the riverbank a crowd had gathered to see the large ornate barge pulling up into dock. The cry 'Vivat Rex! Vivat Maria Regina!' resounded across the Thames as James and Maria stepped off the boat towards the cheering crowds.

Inside the Abbey, the lords waited to be summoned, in a room adorned with tapestries portraying England's defeat of the Spanish Armada in 1588. Such an image must have been profoundly perplexing, depicting as it did the successful saving of the nation from a Catholic invader, Philip II of Spain, on a day when they were crowning the first Catholic monarch since Mary I (who had been married to Philip).

As well as recording the meetings and the order of service, James had commissioned Francis Sandford to create a series of drawings to commemorate the day. All these records were assembled in a book which was published and sold, and extant copies survive in several museum collections. The book is a veritable treasure trove, telling us who was there and what position they were given, and indicates something of the extraordinary spectacle it must have been to those who witnessed it. As per James's instructions, Maria proceeded first with her large retinue. The post of flower woman was revived, and we see her with six young maids, distributing posies. As well as being St George's Day, 23 April is Shakespeare's birth date, and the flowers selected were those collected by Perdita in *The Winter's Tale*: carnations, daffodils, lilies, violets, lavender, marigolds. There are also nods to the favours Maria and James bestowed on their friends and loyal supporters: Heneage Finch is one of those who holds Maria's canopy of state.

They walked to the Abbey under canopies of gold, which will only have detracted slightly from their glittering clothes. Maria's dress was white with silver brocade, covered with embroidered pearls, and over this was 'a Surcoat or Kirtle of Purple Velvet, the Sleeves turned up Furred and Powdered with Ermine'.[25] Over this she wore a 'Mantle of Purple Velvet with a long Train' six metres in length, which was lined with white silk, with a gold lace and ermine border.[26] It was carried by Lady Peterborough, the first woman Maria met when she arrived in England twelve years before, who had gone into exile with her, and who now was made First Lady of the Bedchamber. On her head she wore a gold diadem covered in diamonds and pearls. James was wearing 'A Surcoat of Crimson Velvet, a large Mantle of Crimson Velvet, with a Hood suitable, Furred with Ermine, and bordered with Rich Gold Lace. A Cap of State of Crimson Velvet, turn'd up with Ermine.'[27]

As James entered the Abbey, Purcell's 'I Was Glad', with words taken from Psalm 122, heralded his arrival. This was one of two pieces of music that Purcell was commissioned to write to celebrate the occasion, along with another piece, 'My Heart Is Inditing' (adapted from Psalm 45 and sections of the Book of Isaiah for the words). It is striking that it should have been Purcell who was commissioned, rather than the Master of the King's Musick, Nicholas Staggins. Though Staggins was widely considered to have no musical talent, the position existed for such moments as these, as it still does today.[28] Henry Purcell, at twenty-nine, was a promising young composer and musician who had been associated with the court since childhood, having been a chorister in the Chapel Royal until his voice broke. He came from a musical family, all of whom had performed or composed for the crown, and his brother had even sung at Charles II's coronation some twenty-five years before. Purcell was precociously talented and had begun composing from at least the age of eleven, when he had written an ode to Charles II to celebrate his birthday. Maria and James were incredibly knowledgeable about music and were dedicated to patronising talented musicians. Their chapels over the next few years would house extraordinary singers, and Purcell would increasingly find himself doing Staggins's job for him. As well as Purcell, John Blow was commissioned to create several new works to be played throughout the service. But their patronage on this great occasion was not just for the British composer; Giovanni Battista Vitali, a Bolognese musician and composer working for Maria's brother in Modena, wrote 'Per l'Accademia della Coronatione delle Regina d'Inghilterra' at her request. This work is a joyful celebration of the raising of an Este princess to the role of Queen of England and looks optimistically at the future promised by a Catholic king and queen.

Maria entered the Abbey to 'My Heart Is Inditing', and when the music ended, and both Maria and James had made their way to the choir stalls, they were greeted with 'VIVAT REGINA MARIA' and 'VIVAT JACOBUS REX', though the accompanying music for this is not known. They took their places on their thrones (Maria's having been custom-made) in the middle of the choir stalls. In one panel of Sandford's visual account we can see where everyone will have sat to witness the crowning of their monarchs: in the gallery labelled 'P' would have been Anne Killigrew and the other maids of honour, and probably also Anne Finch and Sarah Churchill. John Churchill and Heneage Finch will have been in 'O', on the ground level, as Gentlemen of the King. Hanging from the walls of the Abbey were tapestries depicting 'The Stories of Abraham', which had been commissioned by Henry VIII and had been used in every coronation since Elizabeth I's (though Charles II had inexplicably bought inferior replicas to hang instead of these originals or the copies that had been made for his father at the royal tapestry workshop at Mortlake).

While the use of the Abraham tapestries at the coronation was a nod to the importance of continuity, they were also a potentially incendiary choice for James. Henry VIII had commissioned them after he broke from Rome and appointed himself Head of the Church of England. They celebrated his divine right to rule, chosen by God to receive God's word directly, superseding the Pope. But James, though he maintained his divine right to rule, was not claiming a personal relationship with God (he left that for the Pope), and he sat uneasily as a Catholic Head of the Church of England.

In Sandford's visual account, we can make out the topics of two panels used, one of which is 'The Circumcision of Isaac'. This was an appropriate story to display for a coronation. In Genesis, this is the manifestation of the covenant between God and Abraham, and Isaac as his hereditary heir. Just as James inherited from Charles, and both from their father before them.

In another image from the perspective of the other end of the hall, we see 'The Meeting of Abraham and Melchizedek'. This panel will have been directly facing James and Maria and seems a particularly contentious choice. It is the fourth in the set and depicts the moment in Genesis in which Abraham has just saved his brother, an act that promotes Abraham as a leader in times of war and also a broker of peace.[29] This panel focuses on the peace, not the war, and for James this could show that he will forgive those who have been his enemies, and that his reign will be one of peace even though he has essentially been at war with parliament up to this point. But, in the tapestry, the peace is celebrated with the bringing of bread and wine for Abraham and Melchizedek to share. When the tapestries were made, after the break with Rome, Henry initially maintained the veracity of transubstantiation, that the wine became the blood and the bread the flesh of Christ, but by 1685 this was very far from the Church of England's position. It was a Catholic belief. And, in fact, the taking of the sacrament was the only part of the service which was changed; James and Maria took Catholic communion the day before in their private chapel, and the communion was left out of the official service.

As James faced this tapestry and looked at its symbolism, he must have had a strong sense of the tension between his role as king and head of the Protestant Church of England, and his private self as a Catholic. But to observers of the ceremony this did not seem to hang heavily on the King's mind. While Maria's composure and regal bearing drew remarks – she intoned the prayers and oaths with solemnity and closed her eyes in earnest piety – James was reportedly constantly distracted, looking around him, muttering his replies and looking bored.

Just after the anointing, when the sounds of a new piece of music by John Blow, 'Behold, O God our defender', had finished reverberating around the Abbey, it was time to crown James as King of England. For this 'The King shall rejoice' was chosen. As the archbishop raised the crown, the choir sang out:

> The King shall rejoice in thy strength, O Lord.
> Exceeding glad shall he be of thy salvation.
> Glory and great worship hast thou laid upon him.
> Thou hast prevented him with the blessings of goodness
> and hast set a crown of pure gold upon his head.

And in great prophetic style, this mighty 'crown of pure gold' would not stay 'upon his head'. There were gasps all around. And this was not the only bad omen of the day: when the flag was raised at the Tower of London, to mark the crowning of the new king the wind swept up and tore it clean away. James and Maria made their way back to Westminster Hall for a sumptuous banquet – prepared by England's finest chef, a man called Patrick Lamb – of almost 1,500 dishes: lobsters, artichokes, puffins, and delights, too, from Emilia-Romagna in the form of bottarga, Bolognese sausages, parmesan and olives.[30] But as they walked to this feast, the golden canopy James walked under tore.

Once inside, the banquet seemed to go smoothly, but then James discovered that he had suffered a more personal tragedy: his son by Catherine Sedley had died earlier that day. Despite all that went wrong there was a air of celebration; bonfires lit up the streets and there was music and dancing all night long, as wine flowed from the fountains all over London. But it was little wonder that the great display of fireworks was delayed until the next day. James and Maria pleaded fatigue and returned to their rooms at 7 p.m.

❖

No sooner had the coronation been celebrated than word spread of a planned uprising. This had perhaps been expected. When James was declared king, some old friends of Monmouth, along with Rye House plotters who had escaped to the Continent, approached him in Holland. They renewed their addresses to him as the rightful heir to the throne, they told him that his uncle was a tyrant, that it was his duty to save England from the clutches of Catholicism. It was a hard sell. Monmouth was living peacefully and contentedly in Holland with Henrietta Wentworth. He said he was finished with plots, and with England; he wanted a quiet life. But by June he had been convinced to invade England and topple his uncle from the throne. He always claimed to have acted under duress, and maintained that he had not intended to take the crown but that once he had landed and began to make his way through the West Country, he found that he had no option but to proclaim himself king, and he led a rebellion to depose his uncle. These proclamations were made in a more personal manner as well, as we see in a letter which survives in the British Library. It is addressed simply 'Madam' and is dated 27 June 1685. Monmouth writes to his addressee that he knows her to be a good Protestant who would not want to see her country in the hands of 'a popish and wicked usurper'. He requests that she and her husband help by sending £500 'to our camp tomorrow without fail', promising that it will be paid back with interest when the campaign is successful. Monmouth signs the letter 'Your loving friend, James R' – James Rex.[31] It was one of several letters sent out to raise funds and men, but Monmouth misjudged. Though he was much beloved by the nation, and many of the working people came out and joined his army, the gentry and aristocracy did not join him. There was no appetite for another civil war and both they and parliament chose to side with the King James they had just crowned, rather than acknowledge this new one. James had, after all, spoken well of protecting their rights, of maintaining the status quo.

Monmouth's army had decent numbers but these men who joined had no weapons and were not trained soldiers. When they came up against the royal army – some of which was led by John Churchill – it was clear that they were no match for them. Monmouth will have known this all too well; he was a seasoned soldier who had trained and fought with the very army he now found himself opposing. The rebellion was put down, and, as the rebels were rounded up, the search went out for the defeated duke. After a few days he was found hiding in a cornfield. He had swapped clothes with a local man and was disguised as a common labourer. He was arrested and taken straight to London to await his fate. He begged to see his uncle, to see Caterina, or Maria. When he was first captured, he wrote a desperate letter to Caterina, sensing that she might have some grain of compassion, and that he might be forgiven as he had been by his father so many times before. He wrote:

> Madam,
>
> Being in this unfortunate condition and having none left but your Majesty that I think may have some compassion of me, and that for the last King's sake makes me take the boldness to beg of you to intercede for me. I would not desire your Majesty to do it if I were not from the bottom of my heart convinced how I have been deceived in to it, and how angry God Almighty is with me for it: but I hope, madam, your intersession will give me life to repent of it, and to show the King how really and truly I will serve him hereafter. And I hope madam, your Majesty will be convinced that the life you save shall ever be devoted to your service; for I have been and ever shall be,
>
> Your Majesty's most dutiful and obedient servant,
>
> Monmouth[32]

He thought that if he could at least see James face to face, he would have a chance of convincing him to have mercy. Perhaps Caterina felt a twinge of compassion for her handsome stepson; perhaps it was she who convinced James, against much advice, to see his nephew. In such a case as this there was no need for a trial and a jury, and Monmouth had already been sentenced to a traitor's death. It was thought that to see Monmouth would be to admit that he would grant clemency. As Monmouth was escorted by armed soldiers through the palace to meet with his uncle, those who saw him would always remember the sight of his handsome face, 'lean and pale and with a disconsolate physiognomy'.[33]

No one knows what was said between uncle and nephew in that room in Whitehall Palace; not even a servant was present. But the sentence was upheld, though it was commuted to execution by beheading instead of the grisly hanging, drawing and quartering that the sentence for treason carried. As he lay in his cell awaiting his execution, his wife Anna came to see him. She, too, had been locked in the Tower, not because anyone imagined she had anything to do with the rebellion, but so that the Monmouth children could not be used as figureheads for another uprising. Anna went to see him in his cell. She was furious. He hardly spoke to her but said that he had hopes of reprieve. She told him that this was never going to happen and told him to stop with his 'imaginary expectations of life'. She insisted he publicly state that she and her children were innocent of his crimes, that they knew nothing of it. They parted from this meeting coldly. When the chaplain came to take Monmouth's confession and give him absolution, he confessed to his many sins in plotting against his father and uncle, and in many of his affairs, but he refused to make confession of sin regarding his affair with Henrietta Wentworth. How, he said, could it have been a sin to have loved another person so much as he loved her. Consequently, he was not given the sacrament. He did not mind. He said his conscience was clear, that God would not see sin where there was none.

It would be easy to look back on the Duke of Monmouth as feckless, vain and foolish, but his love affair with Henrietta Wentworth portrays him in quite a different light. There have been many marriages of convenience, of politics, of power in this narrative, and his marriage to Anna Scott was no different. He said that he had been married when he was a child, without a choice. He said that he had never felt for her 'that perfect love and affection' that she had deserved. He said that Henrietta was the woman he would have chosen to marry if he could have made the choice for himself, that she had cured him of his philandering ways and brought him happiness. He said that he 'doubted not that it was pleasing to God and that this was a marriage'. Anna, too, could say that she had been married as a child, but she never had the freedom to choose another life. Instead, she had had to suffer his affairs, had had to live with the humiliation of his many brushes with treason. But Charles, James and Maria had always been kind to her, and with them she had found a family.

Before Monmouth was taken to the scaffold, James gave him permission to say a final farewell to Anna and to his two sons and daughter. He seemed to be at peace. But Anna found her usual restraint crumbling. Their marriage had not been a success, but she had cared for him. He told her that he knew she had tried to save him, to help him to be reconciled with his family, that she had been a dutiful wife. He asked her to forgive him for having been such a terrible husband to her and entrusted their children to her. Anna fell to the ground, overcome with tears. She threw her arms around his legs and, between sobs, asked him to forgive her, too. It was described as 'the mourningest scene in the world'.[34]

When Monmouth was taken out to Tower Hill on the morning of 14 July 1685, hundreds had gathered to watch, but there was not the usual tone of public executions. They were not there to jeer and taunt but stood in mournful silence. When he reached the scaffold, he said that of all his deeds his wife and children were wholly innocent. He did not speak of his crimes, just that he was there to die as a Protestant according to God's will. He added, 'I have had a scandal raised about me about a woman, a lady of virtue and honour. I will name her the Lady Henrietta Wentworth. I declare that she is a very virtuous and Godly woman. I have committed no sin with her; and that which had passed betwixt us was very Honest and Innocent in the sight of God.' He forgave his enemies and said, 'I never was a man that delighted in Blood; I was very far from it … I am sorry for invading the Kingdom and for the blood that has been shed and for the souls which may have been lost by my means, I am sorry it ever happened.' At this point his voice began to break. He was asked to acknowledge his crimes, but he stayed silent. He asked that James not punish his children but refused to state his loyalty to him. And when those around him said 'God Save the King', he looked to the ground and did not repeat the sentiment. The bishops asked him to say something on the importance of remaining loyal to the king. He said he was not there to make speeches: 'I come to die.'

According to John Evelyn, Monmouth knelt before the block, which James had ordered to be draped in black to respect Monmouth's position as a member of the royal family, and he turned to the executioner, Jack Ketch, and begged him 'to do his office better than to the late Lord Russell and gave him gold'.[35] Ketch replied, 'I hope I shall.' Monmouth laid his body down flat on the ground and put his head on the low block. But he changed his mind and, rising, he asked to feel the axe. As his fingers stroked the metal, he said it was blunt. But there was nothing to be done now. It was with 'all the calmness of temper and composure of mind that ever hath been observed in any that mounted that fatal scaffold before' that he again placed his head on the block. The bishops began to chant Psalm 51, 'Have mercy upon me, O God …', as Ketch swung the axe and heaved it down. He missed, and missed again, hacking away as he went. All the while Monmouth lived, writhed and gasped. Ketch threw the axe down saying, 'God damn me, I can do no more, my heart fails me.' The crowd screamed and shouted in fury, and the sheriffs commanded him to continue. All the while Monmouth lay there, still alive. Ketch tried two more swings which failed again. He took out a knife to sever the head finally from the body. When he held up Monmouth's head many in the crowd were in tears. The official record of the Tower states that it took five blows, though witnesses put it at eight. Evelyn reported that the crowd were 'so incensed … that had he [Ketch] not been guarded and got away, they would have torn him to pieces'.[36]

Evelyn went on to eulogise the hapless Duke of Monmouth:

> Thus ended this quondam Duke, darling of his father and the ladies, being extremely handsome and adroit, an excellent soldier and dancer, a favorite of the people, of an easy nature, debauched by lust, seduced by crafty knaves, who would have set him up only to make a property, and taken the opportunity of the King being of another religion, to gather a party of discontented men. He failed and perished.
>
> He was a lovely person, had a virtuous and excellent lady that brought him great riches, and a second dukedom in Scotland. He was Master of the Horse, General of the King his father's army, Gentleman of the Bedchamber, Knight of the Garter, Chancellor of Cambridge, in a word, had accumulations without end. See what ambition and want of principles brought him to![37]

Henrietta Wentworth had stayed in Holland for the rebellion and returned to England a month later. But she would not live long; she died in April the following year at just twenty-five years old, it is said of a broken heart.

When in Holland Mary heard of Monmouth's death, she was devastated and swore that she would never forgive her father for condemning Monmouth to death. She commissioned his friend, a physician named James Welwood, to write his history. She would have his story told from his perspective; she would not have him remembered as a traitor. Welwood wrote that all Monmouth had done was 'chiefly aimed at the good of his country'.[38] In striking contrast, in England, a medal was released depicting his gruesome end.

Anna Scott went back to her life at court, an intimate friend of James and Maria, but her heart was heavy. Evelyn reported seeing her on 6 February 1686: 'the Duchess of Monmouth, being in the same seat with me at church, appeared with a very sad and afflicted countenance.'[39]

We cannot know for certain how much Mary and William knew about the uprising. Both they and Monmouth always swore that Monmouth had acted without their knowledge. That Henrietta knew is certain: Monmouth had pawned her jewellery to help pay for the army. There certainly was little for William or Mary to gain by the invasion: if Monmouth had been successful then Mary's claim to the throne disappeared. Monmouth, after all, had two healthy sons – an heir and a spare. If they had banked on Monmouth losing (which is possible considering how many informants William had in London, who could have reported the positive mood around James's succession) then they will have been rid of a potential rival to the throne when it came to be Mary's turn. But this was surely unlikely considering the bond and love between them.

❖

When, in 1684, Aphra Behn anonymously published her novel *Love-Letters Between a Nobleman and His Sister* (a thinly veiled account of the recent scandalous affair of Lady Henrietta Berkeley and her brother-in-law, Ford Grey), she placed within its pages the character Cesario.[40] Cesario is the illegitimate son of the King of France who leads an uprising which would see him crowned king. He spends the play with his mistress, Hermione, in various political schemes and plots, but he eventually loses and is executed. The parallels with the late Duke of Monmouth were obvious. Behn was a great supporter of James and Maria, and the Jacobite cause, and would remain true to it for the rest of her life (though she would die just five years later), but she can't help showing some sympathy for the beautiful son of Charles II. The parallels with his death and Cesario's death scene in the novel are so accurate we might wonder if she was there to witness it, though Cesario's execution offers a cleaner escape than that suffered by Monmouth.

> While he remained in the *Bastille*, he was visited by several of the ministers of State, and cardinals, and men of the Church, who urged him to some discoveries, but could not prevail with him: he spoke, he thought, he dreamed of nothing but *Hermione*; and when they talked of heaven, he ran on some discourse of that beauty, something of her praise; and so continued to his last moment, even on the scaffold, where, when he was urged to excuse, as a good Christian ought, his invasion, his bloodshed, and his unnatural war, he set himself to justify his passion to *Hermione*, endeavouring to render the life he had led with her, innocent and blameless in the sight of heaven; and all the churchmen could persuade could make him speak of very little else … laying himself down, [he] suffered the justice of the law, and died more pitied than lamented; so that it became a proverb, 'If I have an enemy, I wish he may live like—, and die like *Cesario*': so ended the race of this glorious youth, who was in his time the greatest man of a subject in the world, and the greatest favourite of his prince, happy indeed above a monarch, if ambition and the inspiration of knaves and fools, had not led him to destruction, and from a glorious life, brought him to a shameful death.

And as Henrietta died not long after, Behn writes of the death of Hermione who,

> when she heard her *hero* was dead, (and with him all her dearer greatness gone) she betook herself to her bed, and made a vow she would never rise nor eat more; and she was as good as her word, she lay in that melancholy estate about ten days, making the most piteous moan for her dead lover that ever was heard, drowning her pillow in tears, and sighing out her soul. She called on him in vain as long as she could speak; at last she fell into a lethargy, and

> dreamed of him, till she could dream no more; an everlasting sleep closed her fair eyes, and the last word she sighed was *Cesario*. [41]

The novel may have been ostensibly about the scandalous affair of Grey and Berkeley, but it ends with the deaths of Cesario and Hermione. With the remark that he was 'more pitied than lamented' in death, Behn tells her reader where her true sympathies lay.

It seemed that James's reign was secure. For now, at least. But James was not a man who believed in mercy. Though he had won against his popular nephew, he made sure that the punishments would be remembered. The Bloody Assizes followed. Hundreds of men were executed and their bodies displayed in town squares. Some 800 more were sent into slavery to the colonies. It is estimated that around 1,400 were punished, either by execution or transportation, in total. This was James's first real mistake. The bloodiness was considered gratuitous, and many were appalled by the brutality of what they saw. James's inability to forgive or show mercy was a testament to how he would continue as king.

16

MEMENTO MORI

Upon his accession to the throne, James II conferred several titles and favours to those he esteemed at court. His daughter, Anne, had her settlement raised to £30,000, an income which exceeded the richest nobles in the land; in Holland, Mary was furious. Much to the chagrin of Maria, James's mistress, Catherine Sedley, became Viscountess Dorchester. And she did not hide her feelings: Evelyn wrote in January 1686,

> Passed the Privy Seal, among others, the creation of Mrs. Sedley (concubine to ——) Countess of Dorchester, which the Queen took very grievously, so as for two dinners, standing near her, I observed she hardly ate one morsel, nor spoke one word to the King, or to any about her, though at other times she used to be extremely pleasant, full of discourse and good humor.[1]

But two recipients of royal favours which she will have wholeheartedly supported were Sarah and John Churchill. Sarah was finally promoted to the coveted position of First Lady of the Bedchamber to Anne, and John was thanked for his years of service – not least in the putting down of the Monmouth Rebellion – with the post of High Steward of St Albans and the title Baron Churchill of Sandridge. These honours were extended to the wider family when John's father, Winston, was made Deputy Lord Lieutenant of Dorsetshire. It was not simply a question of new titles; John was given the lucrative role of head of the Hudson's Bay Company, a colonial enterprise in Canada. The company had been founded in 1660, and Prince Rupert had been the first governor. James was made governor upon his death, and when James relinquished it, he gave it to John Churchill. This was an opportunity to build real wealth.

Other favours were to be granted, too. While she truly grieved the death of the king, for Maria, becoming queen was an opportunity for a new kind of patronage and she used it as an opportunity for artistic commemoration. She commissioned the court carver, Grinling Gibbons, to create a magnificent panel – a large work measuring 12 x 17.5 m – which she sent to Francesco back in Modena.

Francesco was a particular patron of music, and the Galleria Estense in Modena today is full of extraordinary instruments that he had commissioned to be played at his court. Maria's carved gift was primarily a memento mori: at this moment, when she is ascending to the throne, she commissions a work that reminds her and her brother that death will come even to the most powerful of mortals. But it is also an extraordinary work of decorative art and a demonstration of the knowledge available in the English court, containing surrounding images of game, shells and various kinds of botanicals. Characteristic of Gibbons's work, we see pea pods: rumour has it that Gibbons carved the pods closed and once he had been paid for the work, he would carve over them and open the pods. If the pods remained closed, then he had not been paid. Both Maria and James were known for their prompt and fair payments to staff and craftsmen, and here we see this confirmed in the open pod.

One of the most interesting parts, however, is the centre, which contains not only the memento mori skull, but a pendant self-portrait of the artist (with GIBBONS INVENTOR ET SCULPIST LONDINA carved around the edge) and beside it a musical score by a composer called Edward Coleman (not to be confused with Maria's late secretary), from a play by James Shirley that he had set to music. It is a funeral dirge and reads:

THE GLORIES of our blood and state
Are shadows, not substantial things;
There is no armour against fate;
Death lays his icy hand on kings:
Sceptre and crown
Must tumble down,
And in the dust be equal made
With the poor crooked scythe and spade.

There are coins above the head of the skull, representing previous kings and princes who have fallen. It is a fascinating gift to have sent at such a time. Maria was fond of Charles and genuinely grieved for him, but the panel is essentially a celebration of English artistic and musical court culture, sent to a prince of the Este dynasty who was particularly interested in music and in cultivating music at his court.

It was not long before the royal couple started on significant commissions. John Evelyn reported in October that they were undertaking huge building works, that 'range from east to west by the court and garden to the street, and making a new chapel for the Queen, whose lodgings were to be in this new building, as also a new Council chamber and offices next the south end of the banqueting house'. When he saw the results in January 1687, he reported: 'I saw the Queen's new apartment at Whitehall, with her new bed, the embroidery of which cost £3,000. The carving about the chimney piece, by Gibbons, is incomparable.'[2]

The coronation gave the opportunity for poets and painters to gain the patronage of the king and queen by honouring their new monarchs with celebratory verses and portraits. George Greville, who had written so graciously celebrating Maria's arrival in England when he was only eight, and again aged twelve when she visited Cambridge in 1677, took up his pen in earnest. Three poems to James reflect on his great martial prowess. And to Maria he wrote a succinct sestet:

WHEN we reflect upon our charming Queen,
Her Wit, her Beauty, her Imperial Mein;
Majestick *Juno* in her Air we find,
The Form of *Venus*, with *Minerva*'s Mind:
Who was so grac'd, she, she was fit alone
With Royal *James* to fill the *British* Throne.

Precedents for Maria being compared to Venus are plentiful. As we have seen, Dryden wrote of her as 'The Queen of Beauty, and the Court of Love' (in 'Prologue to the Duchess') who 'Brings every Grace triumphant in her Train', and the masque and paintings made by Anne Finch and Anne Killigrew are presented as homages to their Venus. But around the time of the coronation the associations between Maria and the goddess of love became even more plentiful. A striking example is found in a coronation poem written by Aphra Behn – 'A Pindarick Poem on the Happy Coronation of His Most Sacred Majesty James II and his Illustrious Consort Queen Mary' – which suggests that Behn knew the work of Maria's coterie. All through the poem Maria is likened to Venus, but there is one line which suggests a link with Killigrew's painting, and which also references Finch's opera: 'Behold Her now by *Loves* and *Graces* drest! / Like the Great Wife of Jove in Venus Cest'. Behn is explicitly making the link that Finch and Killigrew implied. Had Behn seen the opera, in which the Graces give the little cupids the role of adorning their goddess? Had she seen the painting, in which they dress her themselves? Another possibility, since the coronation came so soon after the opera was performed, is that the painting was in fact made at the same time as Behn composed her ode, either in homage or in collaboration.

Anne Killigrew may also have made a poetic offering. 'To the Queen' is thought to have been addressed to Queen Caterina, but considering Anne's relationship with Maria it is just as likely to have been a poem addressed to her. In fact, the poem makes more sense as a paean to Maria: it celebrates the queen as one who brings peace and stability to a nation in chaos, reflecting the years that James and Maria spent away in exile. It suggests that through the queen's beauty, grace and virtue, all strife will end:

> How dares bold Vice unmasked walk,
> And like a Giant proudly stalk?
> When Vertue's so exalted seen,
> Arm'd and Triumphant in the Queen?
> How dares its Ulcerous Face appear,
> When Heavenly Beauty is so near?[3]

Anne Killigrew was also commissioned to make portraits of her king and queen to celebrate the coronations, though the one made of Maria is now lost. Aged about twenty-four or twenty-five, Killigrew became the first recorded English female artist to paint their monarch from life: an extraordinary achievement. Paintings of Charles II, and of Maria, by Mary Beale survive, but these are copies of works by Peter Lely or Willem Wissing. By contrast, Anne Killigrew's coronation work of James II is entirely her own. It is in many ways the most assured of her paintings that survives: see, for instance, the dexterity of the shading of leaves behind him, or the precision of the statues and friezes on the staircase beside him. It was certainly considered a major work by Anne's peers: the poet laureate, John Dryden, admired its depiction of the 'martial king' standing 'with bold erected look … His warlike mind, his soul devoid of fear.'[4]

In this painting we can also see an intimacy between Killigrew and her king and queen. Look again at James's exquisite robe of rich red and orange brocade, the shimmer of the silk undertone, the weight of the velvet patterning. It is strangely familiar. Look again at the garment that Venus sits on in *Venus Attired by the Graces*. They are one and the same. It is unlikely that this was the companion portrait made of Maria, but it does suggest that the paintings were done at a similar time. Moreover, it harks back to that earlier work of

Maria, from 1675, by Verelst, in which Maria wore James's suit (or a replica of it) in a touching demonstration of the couple's intimacy and bond. Here it is the coronation suit that is shared, perhaps as a symbol of the shared responsibility of rule, or a wry joke between friends, that Venus has captured the King's heart.

These were the last works that Anne Killigrew would undertake. Just one month after the coronation, she contracted smallpox. She died on 16 June at the age of just twenty-five. Maria must have been devastated by the death of her friend, and the terrible waste of such a prodigious talent which was just beginning to bloom would not have been lost on her. Anne may have known she was dying when she wrote the following lines: 'When I am Dead, few Friends attend my Hearse, / And for a Monument, I leave my *VERSE*.'[5] The reality, however, is that she is remembered far more for someone else's verse: the remarkable elegy John Dryden wrote, called 'To The Pious Memory of the Accomplished Young Lady Mrs. Anne Killigrew'.

Anne Killigrew was buried beside her mother, Judith, at the Savoy Chapel, where her father held the title of Master of the Savoy. Though the chapel no longer stands as it did, and her tomb is lost, the epitaph written on it was recorded in the collection of her poems published after her death. It is a beautiful account from a proud family of a brilliant young woman, who died long before her time. And it seeks to remember her and have her remembered by others in the way she wished: as a great poet and painter. The epitaph praises her 'beauty, wit, virtue' and recalls her as someone 'in whom all those Graces did combine' and says that there are no words or images that can be made of her that would not be inferior to what she could have produced.

Who her, *so Great*, can paint beside,
The Pencil her own Hand did guide?
What Verse can celebrate her Fame,
But such as She herself did frame?

Anne Killigrew was known in life as both a writer and a painter. Though history would neglect her, her posthumous reputation as a poet was to some extent assured by a collection of her poems which was printed by her family. After her death there was an outpouring of grief, and several of the greatest poets of the day eulogised her untimely passing. But it is what these poets wrote about her that has shaped the way we view her. When we read her own words, we see that 'her wit was more than man', but do not necessarily detect the 'Innocence [of] a Child' found in Dryden, or the 'Sweet Mayd' created by E.E. (thought to be Edmond Elys).[6] The collection we have was edited by Anne's father; at the beginning he asserts that he only included choice works. We therefore do not have an exhaustive collection of her work and have no idea of the other things she was producing, or indeed even how much she produced. All our knowledge of her has been curated for us. The frustration that comes with this must, however, be mitigated by remembering that she could have been almost entirely forgotten had this effort not been made. She could simply have been assigned to posterity as a mysterious name in a poem by Dryden. It is sobering to think of how many women like Killigrew may have produced artistic work and have been entirely lost. In the collection of Killigrew's poems there are also anonymous works, perhaps written by other women in her circle.

So many women have been lost from history entirely. What survives in the historical record and what doesn't is often a question of luck, depending on what was thought worth keeping. Much of women's artistic work was discarded after their deaths. Even much of Anne Finch's work has come down to us piecemeal. There is at times a randomness as to what survives and what does not.

Anne Killigrew was not the only victim of 1685, and nor was she the only woman whose legacy was first fashioned and then forgotten after her death. Smallpox was rife at the court. Another casualty was John Evelyn's daughter Mary, who was only nineteen years old. She had been a fiercely intelligent and educated woman, the pride of her parents. She, too, had had literary ambitions, and, as we have seen, may have been part of the circle of friends that included Anne Kingsmill, Anne Killigrew and Isabella Bennet.

After Mary Evelyn died, her father went through her papers and made a list of what he found there. He reported how

> On looking into her closet, it is incredible what a number of collections she had made from historians, poets, travellers, etc., but, above all, devotions, contemplations, and resolutions on these contemplations, found under her hand in a book most methodically disposed, prayers, meditations, and devotions on particular occasions, with many pretty letters to her confidants.[7]

Perhaps these 'confidants' were women we have met in this story; she may even have been part of Maria's coterie. Certainly, there are poems found in her archive the authors of which are still unknown.

The literary world of women was to lose another talent that year of 1685 when, in June, Anne Wharton (née Lee), who had grown up with the princesses in the nursery, and had since penned several poems and plays while enduring an unhappy marriage, was seized by extreme pains in her stomach. Her end was slow and agonising, and when she finally died on 29 October it was amid rumours that her husband had already married – or was soon to marry – his mistress on the assumption that his wife would not live much longer. But unlike her husband, her fellow poets mourned the loss of Anne Wharton. The poet Robert Gould, who had been at her bedside, wrote a long lament in which he uses Wharton's pastoral name, Urania, the muse of celestial poetry. This was the pseudonym she had used when publishing her lament on the death of her uncle, the Earl of Rochester, a work highly praised by both Aphra Behn and Edmund Waller. The poem is intended to provide a lasting record of the woman Gould and Behn knew, a woman who could proudly call herself a poet.

These women died so young, it is hard to predict what they might have gone on to be or to produce had they lived through to artistic and intellectual maturity. But in each case their legacies were taken out of their hands. Works by each of them were published posthumously, without their consent, and writers of the day passed judgements on their characters in ways that have shaped their reputations through to the present day. These judgements may reflect the values and actions of those women, but they may have been projections by the men who made them; they may also have been complete fabrications. Once they were dead they lost their voice.

Anne Wharton suffered most from this. By the beginning of 1686, unauthorised copies of her work were being sold in London as a collection, *A play called Love's martyr, or Witt about Crownes, and other poems written by the Honnorable Mrs Wharton*. We do not know who was responsible, but it is most likely that one or some of her friends decided to print her writing to keep her reputation alive. There is no attempt to hide her name: it is there for all to see, without anybody trying to take credit for her talent. But her husband, Thomas Wharton, was having none of this. He wanted all traces of his first wife to be erased. The Stationers' Company were ordered to suppress the printing and selling of the work of Anne Wharton.

At the same time as her husband wanted her memory eradicated, her brother-in-law, Goodwin Wharton, was busy dragging her name through the mud. In February 1686 he started to write his autobiography. In it he claimed that Anne was a lewd woman who had multiple affairs, including with him, but, most scandalously of all, with her uncle John Wilmot. Though this was not published in his lifetime, and there is no evidence that it even circulated in manuscript, this account of Goodwin Wharton has been taken as fact ever since its discovery, even by feminist scholars who were rediscovering and republishing Anne's work. As a result, it framed her reputation not only in the eighteenth century, but also in the late twentieth century. We cannot say for certain that this account is inaccurate, but here are some of the other things that Goodwin claimed were true: he believed that he heard the voice of God and that God was telling him to seduce almost every woman he came into contact with; he believed that Maria of Modena was in love with him (though they never even met), and that it was his calling to impregnate her with a Protestant saviour; he believed that he communed with fairies. Is this really the account of a man whose word can be trusted?

It is perhaps not surprising that when John Evelyn published his daughter's great work, a satire called *Mundus Muliebris*, in 1690, he did so anonymously. After all, a woman's reputation was never entirely safe – even, or especially, after her death. Yet, even when he tries to celebrate her achievements, a patronising tone creeps in. In his first diary entry detailing her death, he begins by describing how well-read she was in 'history, and all the best poets, even Terence, Plautus, Homer, Virgil, Horace, Ovid; all the best romancers and modern poems'. When he talks of her writing, he belittles it, almost despite himself, claiming that she exhibited the 'ornaments belonging to [her] sex'.[8] That he published her satire anonymously suggests that, while he was prepared for her work to be publicly disseminated, he was not willing for the world to know who had written it.

The agency these women had gained during their short lives was lost in their deaths. Their reputations were in the hands of others, and so they disappeared from history, just as they had started to contribute to it.

❖

Within a matter of months, Maria became queen, but lost many of her closest friends and protégées. And she still had to contend with James's infidelity. Catherine Sedley had for a time been sent away; James thought it proper that a good Catholic king should not have mistresses, but her hold over him was such that he could not be without her for long. He began to meet her in the rooms of his Page of the Backstairs, William Chaffinch, and Maria soon found out. It was said that Maria 'loves her husband in all sincerity' but that 'she is an Italian, and very proud'. She decided she would not put up with it, like every queen had done before her. She told James to choose: his mistress or his wife. If he continued his affair, she would leave England and never return. She cried at him, 'Give her my dower, make her Queen of England, but let me see her no more!' If James was surprised by the force of her sentiments, he would soon be more so when, upon her request to visit her rooms, he found her surrounded by her priests, all on their knees, begging him to live free of sin, to send his mistress away. Overwhelmed, he agreed, and sent Catherine a note telling her that she was ordered to leave the country; he did not trust himself to see her again. Catherine sailed for Dublin, licking her wounds, but already planning how she might return. And, six months later, return she did, both to England and to the King's bed.

Maria's patronage took a devotional turn. All the grief she felt at the death of Charles, of her friends, of her many children, she threw into her devotion to God. And now that they were free to openly worship as Catholics, she turned her attention to her chapels, where she intended to set an example of piety. Evelyn wrote of going to Whitehall at the end of December 1686,

> I went to hear the music of the Italians in the new chapel, now first opened publicly at Whitehall for the Popish Service. Nothing can be finer than the magnificent marble work and architecture at the end, where are four statues, representing St. John, St. Peter, St. Paul, and the Church, in white marble, the work of Mr. Gibbons, with all the carving and pillars of exquisite art and great cost. The altar piece is the Salutation; the volto in fresco, the Assumption of the blessed Virgin, according to their tradition, with our blessed Savior, and a world of figures painted by Verrio. The throne where the King and Queen sit is very glorious, in a closet above, just opposite to the altar.[9]

The music at these services were widely remarked upon, and people flocked to hear the new singer who arrived at the court in 1687, a castrato called Giovanni Francesco Grossi, known as Siface. Evelyn wrote after hearing him that 'it was indeed very rare, and with great skill. He came over from Rome, esteemed one of the best voices in Italy. Much crowding – little devotion.'[10] It is curious that Evelyn said he was there from Rome; the Tuscan singer had been working for Maria's brother Francesco in Modena since 1679, having previously found success in Venice and Naples. Maria wrote to her brother in the middle of January 1687 to tell him that the great singer had arrived:

> the poor man is tired from his journey and I have hardly heard him sing, but I have heard him enough to judge that he has a beautiful voice and I see that he is a great man in his profession, and I assure you that I will take care of him, and I will send him back to you, whenever you wish.[11]

But Siface did not stay in England for long, and for the same reason that so many other Italian artists had given: the weather. By June of that year, he had left London and returned to the Este court in Modena: the musical world of the court lamented the departure of this great operatic talent, so much so that Purcell composed a piece of music called 'Sefauchi's Farewell': this was a work for the harpsichord, unsung, so the loss of his opulent singing voice was made more apparent. In a letter to her brother dated 16 June 1687, Maria said:

> I send you this letter by Siffface, who is returning to your service, as this country and the countryside are so little suited to his genius and health that he cannot remain here for much longer. But he goes with my good permission, as I am more than satisfied with him, whom I consider to be the best musician in the world. Keep him dear to you and remember that if you send him to me some time later, I shall be obliged to you.[12]

There is a reserve in this letter that we did not find in her earlier correspondence, and we can see Maria's temperament shifting slightly after she became queen. Princess Anne described it as a haughtiness, but a note in Evelyn's diary tells us more about her state of mind: 'standing by the Queen at basset [cards], I observed that she was exceedingly concerned for the loss of £80; her outward affability much changed to stateliness, since she has been exalted'.[13] As time passed Maria began to feel more and more the weight of her position. And as James became increasingly estranged from government, and she did not know who she could trust, it is not surprising that she began to close off a little from those around her – in sending her brother's musician back to him in Modena, she will have felt increasingly cut off from her family in Italy. By this point she had lost hope of seeing her brother again. Over the years she had implored him to visit, but to leave Modena unattended would be to welcome trouble, and he never came. Her life as Duchess of York had been continually plagued by loss: the loss of leaving her home, the deaths of her children, the loss of her friendship with Sarah, the deaths of the king and Anne Killigrew. She must have wondered what her life as queen would hold, and how many more losses she would have to suffer.

17

The Queen's Body

ALL HAIL, –
O Sacred *VESSEL*, fraught with *England's STORE*;
(A *PRIZE* more valu'd, *ATLAS* never bore)
Guard safe our *TREASURE* to the wish'd for *Shore*.
— Aphra Behn, 'A Congratulatory Poem to Her Most Sacred Majesty'

AUGUST 1687
THE CROSS BATH, BATH

The air is thick with the smell of sulphur emanating from the thermal waters. Music flows from an orchestra playing near the pool in the centre of the large stone room. The chamber is open to the elements above, and all around the top runs a gallery in which the citizens of Bath bustle to get a good view. In the baths below, a young woman enters and slowly walks across the room, followed by her closest maids and ladies-in-waiting. She tentatively puts a foot into the warm water. Her billowing yellow robes hide her body from prying eyes. Her body, which had been the object of scrutiny for so many years, is painfully thin; she is grieving for her mother and fearful for her future. Her doctors in London fear for her health, and there are rumours circulating that she will not live for long. She is slowly languishing. But she walks with steady steps, aware that all eyes are on her.

Maria's last two pregnancies had ended in miscarriages, the last of which had been three years ago, and she had no living children. Though at twenty-nine she was still a young woman, there were whispers that she was past it and would never fall pregnant again. Maria's mother, Laura, had died just a month earlier. One of the last things she had done before she had been taken ill was to visit the shrine at Loreto to pray that her daughter would conceive an heir. As Maria lay in the warm sulphuric waters, looking up at the sun shining down, seeing out of the corner of her eye her subjects gawping at her, she was grieving for her mother, grieving for all her lost children, worrying about the chasm opening between her husband and his parliament, wondering what would happen next.

During her time as Duchess of York, Maria had built an intellectual life of patronage and of friendship, but when she became queen all this was suddenly very far away. She could never forget that first and foremost it was her duty to produce children, as the Pope had told her all those years ago when she was little more than a child living in Modena. He had said that through her marriage 'an end might come to the persecution still smouldering in that kingdom'. During many periods of her life in England that smouldering persecution of Catholics had ignited, and it was looking to gather momentum again. An heir was surely what was needed: a true Catholic heir to ensure the future of the Stuart dynasty, and the future of all Catholics in the three kingdoms. James, too, was praying for a miracle. He had gone to St Winifrede's Well in the north of Wales and had immersed himself in its holy waters.

Maria stayed for several months in Bath. Her mornings were spent taking the waters, and in the afternoons she would ride around the countryside in her carriage. She would often hold public audiences, and locals would flock to catch a glimpse of the famously beautiful queen. Maria was always gracious, and over the course of her time in Somerset she became deeply loved by the local people, to the extent that this area remained as loyalist as possible during the Glorious Revolution.

When James visited Maria on his way from his site of pilgrimage to London, they held such audiences together, and James performed the ritual of touching for the king's evil, though he made a far less favourable impression on those who saw him. By this time, the king had become increasingly supercilious with his people; he felt that, as absolute monarch, he should automatically command their respect rather than have to earn it. He had learned all the wrong lessons from the execution of his father, and from the years he had spent in exile as his brother tiptoed on the precipice. He did not see the reality of the world in which he lived.

The time they spent together in Bath was brief, but effective, and on Christmas Eve 1687 there was a royal announcement. The queen was pregnant. A day of thanksgiving was ordered at the beginning of 1688 and clergy were told to read out the following prayer at their church services:

> That the Queen might become the joyful mother of children; that God would command His holy angels to watch over her and defend her from all dangers or evil accidents: that the King might behold his children's children ... that his gracious consort, Queen Mary, might be as a fruitful vine upon the walls of his house, and his children like the olive branches about his table.[1]

It was a slightly tortured image, but in the end this did not matter; Lord Clarendon reported that when he went to hear the thanksgiving day service, 'there were not two or three in the church who brought the form of prayer with them'. He said that it was 'as if scarce anybody believed it to be true'.[2]

James had already written ahead to William and Mary in Holland to inform them of the wonderful news. Letters of congratulation were sent back, but William was far from pleased at this development. In London the news was not greeted with joy by James's other daughter; the Tuscan ambassador reported 'words cannot express the fury of the Princess of Denmark at the Queen's condition'.[3] By this point, relations between Anne and her father and stepmother had entirely disintegrated, though James and Maria probably did not yet know the extent of it. Anne's anti-Catholicism had steadily increased to the point of obsession, and the idea that she and Mary might be supplanted in the line of succession by a Catholic brother was more than she could bear.

Anne took up her pen and wrote to her sister, beginning a diatribe against her stepmother which would continue throughout the pregnancy. She wrote on 14 March:

> I can't help thinking it is a little suspicious. It is true indeed she is very big, but she looks better than ever she did, which is not usual: for people when they are so far gone, for the most part look very ill. Besides it is very odd that the Bath, that all the best doctors thought would do her a great deal of harm, should have so very good an effect so soon, as that she should prove with child from the first minute she and Mansell met, after her coming from Bath. Her being so positive it will be a son, and the principles of that religion being such that they will stick at nothing, be it never so wicked, if it will promote their interest, give some cause to fear there may be foul play intended.[4]

Anne had already begun to use code names for her father and stepmother, knowing that the things the sisters would exchange might border on treason. She chose 'Mansell', though the change of name could hardly hide the identities of the people she referred to; Anne had never had the sharpest mind. She promises her sister to 'do all I can to find it out, if it be so: and if I should make any discovery, you shall be sure to have an account of it'.[5]

Mary did not share Anne's fervent hatred of James and Maria, but she was certainly more emotionally detached than she had been when they had last met. She was angry about Monmouth, and her years at the Calvinist court in Holland had influenced her; she, too, feared the consequences of Maria having a son. The letters between the sisters were often about religion, and they were both convinced that James would try to force Anne to convert to Catholicism. Though Mary did not consider herself in danger of being influenced, she did not think the same could be said of Anne. In a letter from April 1686,

Anne wrote to Mary, 'I hope you don't doubt but that I will be ever firm to my religion whatever happens … I abhor the principles of the Church of Rome as much as it is possible for any to do.' She calls Catholicism 'wicked and dangerous' and thanks God that 'we were not bred up in that communion'. She tells Mary that 'nobody has yet said anything to me about religion'. The princesses clearly fed and stoked up each other's fears about James's desire to convert them. In August, Anne wrote,

> because you think in my last I seemed too much at ease, I must justify myself and tell you that I don't think that I am all the more secure for the kindness the King has showed me lately. For I am of your opinion, that it is more likely he will use fair means rather than force; and I am in as great expectation of being tormented if he had not some hopes that in time he may gain either you or me. Therefore you may assure yourself that I will always be on my guard.

Anne's mention of the king's kindness is a reference to his frequently paying her enormous gambling debts. Every letter between them contains some allusion to the fact that James has not yet tried to convert Anne, but she asserted that '[I] expect every minute to be spoken to about my religion, and wonder very much I have heard nothing of it yet'. This was in May 1687.

As Maria's pregnancy progressed the scrutiny of her body increased. Her maids were asked if they had seen signs on her shift of her breasts leaking milk – one of her bedchamber women was so obliging as to tell Anne that she 'has seen it upon her smock, and that it began to run at the same time it used to do of her other children'.[6] To add to this there were constant comments of how large or small her breasts appeared. Anne wrote again to Mary:

> Whenever one talks of her being with child, she looks as if she was afraid one should touch her. And whenever I have happened to be in the room as she has been undressing, she has always gone

> into the next room to put on her smock. These things give me so much just cause of suspicion, that I believe, when she is brought to bed nobody will be convinced 'tis her child, except it prove a daughter. For my part, I declare I shall not, except I see the child and she parted.[7]

She told Mary after the birth: 'I never heard anybody say they felt the child stir; but I am told Lady Sunderland and Madam Mazarin say they felt it at the beginning. Mrs Dawson tells me she has seen it stir but never felt it.'[8] Later in life, Maria attested that 'she had asked Princess Anne to put her hand on her stomach and feel how the child was moving, but she had not wanted to do so'. We do not know for certain which is true – it is one word against another – but Anne seems so poisoned against her stepmother and future sibling that it is more likely that Maria's account is favourable. Perhaps Maria offered once, and Anne declined, but is it not surprising that Maria might shy away from being looked at and being touched in this way? Especially when she knew that these people did not wish her well. This is one of the many examples of the tension Maria had to face every day. She was both a queen and a human being. Her royal body was of public interest, and the child she carried might be the future monarch, but she was also a young woman being stared at and prodded throughout her pregnancy. One case was used against her by Anne, who reported some hearsay to her sister: 'once in discourse, Mrs. Bromley [Maria's bedchamber woman] told Mrs. Robarts, one day Roger's daughter came into the room, when Mrs. Mansell was putting off her clouts, and she was very angry at it, because she did not care to be seen when she was shifting.'[9]

In this same letter, which is dated 20 March 1688, we can see Anne already paving the way for William's invasion. She opens the letter to her sister with the request: 'I hope you will instruct Bentley what you would have your friends to do if any alteration should come, as it is to be feared there will, especially if Mansell has a son, which I conclude he will, there being so much reason to believe it is a false belly.'[10] Though the rumour may have originated with Anne, she was far from the only one who circulated it; whispers flew around the court, all saying that Maria wasn't pregnant at all. These were given fuel when on two occasions Maria seemed close to miscarrying, one of which was after some correspondence from Italy which informed her (wrongly) that her brother had died. People said, 'her Majesty's condition is a fiction' and that 'she wears a cushion'. Lord Clarendon, the uncle of Princesses Mary and Anne, and a supporter of James, reported 'scarce anybody believed it to be true. Good God, help us!'[11]

Alongside the rumours that the pregnancy was fake were those that said the child was not James's. Scurrilous pamphlets began circulating on the streets of London, saying that James was a cuckold. Some wrote that the father was actually the papal nuncio, Count d'Ada, others that it was James's hated adviser, Father Petre, which is ironic since Maria herself despised him.

That Maria knew these rumours existed outside of the court is clear from a letter that Francesco Terriesi (a Florentine diplomat and close friend of James) wrote to the Grand Duke of Tuscany, who wished for regular updates of Maria's health since, after hearing she had been so ill, he was already hatching a plan to marry his daughter to James. 'The Queen's condition continues to make good progress. Her majesty is however greatly afflicted at hearing of the satires (which are already being published) against her.'[12] Terriesi defends Maria against these slanders by writing that she is 'most innocent in all her actions, she has never given cause to any one save to worship her'.[13] Though she knew what was said about her, whether or not she knew that Anne was one of those circulating the rumours we do not know, but she was increasingly aware that her stepdaughter was no longer a friend to her.

That the birth might be contested seems to have been considered quite early on. The Earl of Danby wrote a pointed letter to William of Orange, saying:

> Because it is fit that her majesty should always have the greatest persons near her in this condition, I hope that the Princess Anne will be always within call to see (when the time is near) that the midwife discharges her duty with that care which ought to be had in a case of so great concern.[14]

Anne wrote to Mary saying:

> If the King should desire you and the Prince of Orange to come over and make him a visit, I think it will be better (if you can make any handsome excuse) not to do it.[15]

When the time came, Anne was not there. She had recently miscarried, and her doctors suggested she might go and take the waters to recover. Rather than going to Tunbridge Wells, as was her custom (and which was far closer to London), she chose to go to Bath. When Maria was told of her plans, she responded by saying that surely Anne would not travel so far so close to Maria's due date. Anne looked at her stepmother coolly, and replied, 'I do not think Madam that you will have the child before I return.'[16] It was almost a challenge. Anne was perhaps hoping that exactly this would happen, that she wouldn't have to be called upon as a witness at the same time as she fuelled rumours that the birth was a hoax, that she could say how convenient it was that the baby came early while she was away. Maria and James were counting on having Anne there, and though the birth was not expected for another two weeks, to have such an important witness leave now was far from ideal.

Maria had initially hoped to give birth at Whitehall, but the offices beside the royal apartments there were being rebuilt, and there was so much dust and noise that it soon became apparent that this was impossible. The household at St James's was notified to get ready for the royal couple to move there in one week. But they took some time to get the place ready, and Maria became increasingly fretful. She went to St James's to hurry things along, assuring those preparing the apartments, 'I mean to lie in at St. James tonight if I lie on the boards!'[17] That evening she ate a light supper, played a game of basset, and at 11 p.m. was carried to her apartments in St James's Palace in a sedan chair, her ladies-in-waiting walking alongside her.

18

A ROYAL PRINCE

Birds, feed on *Birds*, *Beasts*, on each other prey,
But Savage *Man* alone, does *Man* betray
— John Wilmot, *Satire on Mankind*

10 JUNE 1688
THE QUEEN'S BEDCHAMBER, ST JAMES'S PALACE, LONDON

Maria rose from her bed at 8 a. m. and began her levee, as usual. But soon she felt a familiar swell of pain. She called out to her ladies in the room, 'Send for the King!' James had only himself risen a quarter of an hour before, having spent the night with her in her rooms – unusually for royal couples, they often shared a bed – and he was starting to prepare for the day ahead. But he was soon back in her rooms. He had sent for Caterina, for his council and for a substantial number of members of the court. It was soon all over St James's and Whitehall: the queen was in labour.

As the room began to fill, Maria's ladies helped her back into her bed. It was a cold morning, so a serving woman placed a bedpan full of hot coals under the blankets. As the minutes ticked by, the room began to fill with people. As she lay there, Maria was entirely exposed; there was no screen to separate her from the gaping crowd: the curtains of the bed were drawn open. James sat beside her, the midwife on a chair at the foot of the bed. Behind her stood her Woman of the Bedchamber Margaret Dawson. When Caterina arrived, she went first to her side to offer her support before taking her place a little to one side, next to the clock.

Maria's labour progressed quickly but the pain was excruciating, and she cried out, 'I die! Oh! You kill me! You kill me!'[1] Her cries were thought so terrible that many of the men present reported that they could hardly bear to listen. But James called to his chancellor and members of the council to come nearer. To look more closely. The Lord President, Lord Privy Seal, the two Chamberlains, Lord Middleton, Lord Craven, Lord Huntingdon, Lord Powis, Lord Dover, Lord Peterborough, Lord Melfort, Lord Dartmouth, Sir John Ernley, Lord Preston, Sir Nicholas Butler, the Duke of Beaufort, Lord Berkeley, Lord Moray, Lord Castlemaine, all stood at the very foot of the bed, with the Lord Chancellor on a step beside them. Only slightly removed were Lord Feversham, Lord Arran, Sir Stephen Fox and Mr Griffin, the Pages of the Backstairs, Maria's priests, Lady Peterborough, Lady Belasyse, Lady Arran, Lady Tyrconnell (Frances Jennings as was), Lady Roscommon, Lady Sophia Buckley, Lady Fingall, Madam Mazarin, Madam Bouillon, Lady Powis, Lady Strickland, Lady Ceary, Mrs Crane, two of Caterina's ladies, Mrs Bromley, Mrs Waldegrave, Mrs Wentworth and Pelegrina Turini.

On seeing all these faces so close to her as she was giving birth, Maria became overwhelmed and asked James to hide her face with his head and periwig, saying that she could not give birth and have so many men look on her. But while she could cover her face, the rest of her was on full display. At nearly 10 a.m. it was over. The child had been born. A boy. He was named James Francis Edward Stuart, and he was the new heir to the throne of England, Scotland and Ireland. In the *London Gazette* that evening, the citizens of the capital read the news: 'This day between nine and ten in the morning the Queen was safely delivered of a PRINCE.'[2]

This was not the joyful occasion that it might have been. John Evelyn wrote in his diary, 'A YOUNG PRINCE born, which will cause disputes. About two o'clock, we heard the Tower ordnance discharged, and the bells ring for the birth of a Prince of Wales. This was very surprising, it having been universally given out that her Majesty did not look till the next month.'[3] Though the pregnancy had been witnessed by nearly seventy members of the court, many of whom were trustworthy Protestants, the events that took place this day would be reported on and twisted for decades to come. It would become known as the baby in the bedpan scandal. Only a decade after Oates had wreaked havoc with his Popish Plot, another anti-Catholic conspiracy was set in motion which would tear apart the lives of James and Maria, and all who supported them.

James immediately sent a letter to Princess Anne in Bath. She would have been the most important witness to the birth, and he knew that her absence might be a monumental problem. The man sent to give her the letter, Colonel Ogledorp, was instructed not only to give her the letter but to give her an eyewitness account of the birth. We can infer from this that Colonel Ogledorp was one of the sixty-seven people present at the birth. The damage of Anne's absence was done, but he would do what he could now to get her on side. He wrote, too, to Mary and William in Holland. William sent over his loyal friend Count Zuylestein with a letter of congratulations to James and Maria. Zuylestein stayed in London for a month, monitoring the political situation and sounding out likely turncoats, one of whom was John Churchill. Churchill was already part of what was known as the Association of Protestant Officers, an organisation which sought to resist the employment of Catholic officers in the army.

When Anne returned, she went to see her new baby brother in the royal nursery. By now rumours were beginning to spiral out of control. They said that the child had not been born at all but had been smuggled into the chamber in a bedpan. Maria could not believe that people could think this. She exclaimed to Anne, how could 'such ridiculous falsities gain the least credit?' Anne paused a moment before replying, but her answer confirmed what Maria had long suspected: that she was no longer a friend to her father and stepmother. She looked coldly at Maria and said that it was 'not so much to be wondered at, since such persons were not present as ought to have been there'.[4]

If Anne had planned this herself she was perhaps possessed of more intellect than she has been given credit for: to spread rumours that the pregnancy is fake, to then be away for the birth, and stoke the flames of doubt once the child was born a boy. It is more likely that the clever Sarah Churchill suggested these things to her, which she acted on. It was, after all, Sarah's idea that she go to Bath. Sarah knew that, with the hold she had over Anne, she and John could rise higher at her court. If Maria's son was pronounced a fraud, Anne was second in line to the throne. And Mary in Holland, it was by now clear, was not going to have any children. She was also to some extent protecting Anne; by being absent, she could not be called on for testimony. If she had then she would either have had to lie or to admit that the child was real, both of which would have been painful to her and to the Protestant cause which wanted to see Mary and William on the throne of England.

Mary was furious that Anne had absented herself from such an important event. She had been reading Anne's conspiracy theories for months and had done so in good faith. She needed to know what had happened. Anne wrote back with contrition and promised to get an account of the birth from a reliable witness. She went to Margaret Dawson, one of Maria's Women of the Bedchamber. Margaret had held this post at the court of Anne Hyde and had therefore been present at all six of Hyde's births, including Princess Anne's, and she had also seen all of Maria's. She was a loyal servant of the crown and a good Protestant. This was the first of many accounts which would be gathered over the next few months, and those who were called on to testify in 1688 would continue to be asked for decades to come. Even at the beginning of the eighteenth century, Margaret Dawson was still being asked to recount her tale. It is because of this that we have such detailed accounts of what took place that day, accounts which offer an unparalleled insight into the conditions in which royal women were expected to give birth, with dozens of witnesses. In these moments they were treated as little more than cattle. The account that Anne sent is long; it begins with Maria's pregnancy and goes all the way through to the days after the birth. She reports the birth in granular detail, with the information we have already seen, but there are some moments that are worth considering further. The account is presented in the form of a list, and it is picked up here from point number 12:

> 12. As soon as the child was born, the midwife cut the navel-string, because the after-burthen did not follow quickly; and then she gave it to Mrs. Labaudie [Maria's seamstress], who, as she was going by the bedside, cross the step, to carry it into the little bed-chamber, the King stopped her, and said to the privy councillors, that they were witnesses there was a child born, and bid them follow it into the next room and see what it was, which they all did; for till after they came out again, it was not declared what it was; but the midwife had only given a sign that it was a son, which is what had been done before.[5]

That James knew what people were saying, and predicted what they might say, is crystal clear here. As soon as the baby is born, he calls on all those many people present and points out that they could never say the child had not been born, they had all witnessed it. As Anne goes on with her account, she begins to throw in suggestions of foul play:

> 15. Her labour never used to be so long.
> 16. As for seeing it dressed or undressed, they avoid it as much as they can. By all I have seen and heard, sometimes they refuse almost anybody to see it; that is, when they say it is not well; and methinks there is always a mystery in it, for one does not know whether it be really sick, and they fear one should know it, or whether it is well, and they would have one think it is sick, as other children used to be. In short, it is not very clear anything they do; and for the servants, from the highest to the lowest, they are all Papists.

> 17. The Queen forbid Lady Powis to bring the child to her before any company; but that, they say, she used to do with her other children. I dined there the other day, when it was said it had been very ill of a looseness, and it really looked so; yet when she came from prayers she went to dinner without seeing it, and after that played at comet, and did not go to it till she was put out of the pool.[6]

But despite these facts, there was clearly not enough room for scandal in this account of the faithful Mrs Dawson, for Anne ends her letter with some desperate attempts to cast a shadow over it: 'All that she says seems very clear; but one does not know what to think; for methinks it is wonderful if there is no cheat.'[7] Her last line offers a titbit from which a rumour might flow: 'One thing I had forgot, which is, that the last time she was brought to bed, the reason of her being delivered in the great bed was because she was catched; and this time, Mrs. Dawson says, though the pallet was up, the Queen would not go into it because the quilts were not aired.'[8] This 'great bed' still exists, and can be seen at Kensington Palace.

Anne declared that she would go to Tunbridge Wells almost immediately, but that 'Lady Churchill does not go with me at first, and as long as she stays here I am sure she will do all in her power to give you and I an account of anything that happens that is worth knowing.'[9] Poor Maria: little did she know how her stepdaughter and one of her oldest friends were conspiring against her. When she saw Sarah in the drawing room, or passed her in the corridor, could she have had any idea of how closely she was being scrutinised, or of what was going through her old favourite's mind?

Meanwhile, rumours were circulating through London like wildfire. Surely, people said, at twenty-nine she was far too old to have had a baby, or to have been pregnant at all. Some said the pregnancy was a hoax, others that she had miscarried and pretended she hadn't, or that the child had been a girl and replaced with a boy. What they could all agree on, though, was that the child who was now called the Prince of Wales had been smuggled into the room in a bedpan.

This despite the fact that at least two Protestant witnesses had testified that they saw the bedpan full of hot coals at the beginning of the labour.

The stories were wild; one was of a Catholic woman desperately trying to buy babies in London for eyewatering amounts of money in the lead-up to the birth. Others told of pregnant women being smuggled into St James's Palace in the dead of night. James and Maria responded by trying to act as though all was well, and they asked the court painter Godfrey Kneller to paint the child. But they went beyond this; the painting was made into a print, which was widely circulated in England and abroad (particularly in Holland) with an inscription saying it was painted from life. Indeed, when Kneller heard the rumours that the child was an imposter he replied:

> What devils! The prince of Wales the son of a bric a brac woman? It is a lie! His father and mother have sat for me about 36 times a piece and I know every line of their face! I say the child is so like both that there is not a feature in his face but what belongs to either father or mother.

The Dutch printing press also got to work, issuing propaganda in many languages, given titles such as 'on the success of making and inventing the prince of Wales'. And there were accompanying images, too. On one we see Maria rocking her child to sleep in his orate crib, while a lascivious man, who represents the much hated Father Petre, approaches from behind her chair and reaches his hand around to her breast. The image has captions below, which speak of conflicting claims. On the one hand it says, 'Here is Father Peters, with the royal queen and son, here in front of everyone, Father Peters, shrewd and cleverly deceiving, knows how to lull prince, queen, and people, to sleep deeply' (in other words, James has been cuckolded by his priest, and the prince is not his son at all.) But it also says, 'The Prince of Wales nods, the windmill wood stands, grinds king, queen, and child from England', which invokes another piece of propaganda, which claimed that the child was not Maria's either – that it had actually been born of a miller and his wife and was not royal at all.

Amid all these rumours about his parentage, few noticed that the boy was not doing well. And no wonder: his doctors prescribed a milk-free diet of water gruel, barley, oatmeal sugar, currants and canary wine. To add to this, a running sore was kept open on his arm to release any bad humours. When he started to ail he was piled with medicines which, when a drop was spilt, burned through the tablecloth. At one point a visitor counted thirty bottles of potions on the table. The outlook was bleak, and the child seemed likely to die. Maria, unable to cope with the thought of losing yet another child, took matters into her own hands and sent for a wet nurse. She forbade the doctors from treating the child, and gradually, the prince recovered. When we consider how this baby was treated, the horrifying infant mortality rates do not seem quite so surprising. Though Maria and James breathed a sigh of relief, the illness of the prince, the banning of the doctors and the baby's recovery only led to more conspiracy theories, this time saying that the child had died and been replaced.

That such propaganda – both verbal and visual – was circulating in Holland shows just how much William was already preparing to rise against his uncle. But how much Mary knew of what William was planning is not clear. She wrote in her memoirs of 'the melanckolly prospect' of seeing 'my husband and father so far engaged against each other', but we cannot be sure whether she was writing from the heart rather than simply setting down for posterity the way she wanted to be perceived.[10] In reality, William had already said (to a man called Edward Russell) in April, two months before the child was born, that he was willing to set sail to England, that by the end of September he could be ready, but that he required a formal invitation to do it. This arrived in July, when Admiral Herbert left England for Holland, disguised as an ordinary sailor. He carried with him a letter signed by seven members of the aristocracy: Henry Sidney, Earl of Romney; Edward Russell; Charles Talbot, Earl of Shrewsbury; William Cavendish, Earl of Devonshire; Thomas Osborne, Earl of Danby; Richard Lumley, Viscount Lumley; and Henry Compton, Bishop of London. They became known as the 'Immortal Seven'.

William began preparations in earnest, awaiting the perfect moment. In August Henry Sidney journeyed to Holland to offer support for an invasion and to join the invading army. He was appointed major general. Sidney also carried a personal note to William from John Churchill. It read: 'Mr Sidney will let you know how I intend to behave myself; I think it is what I owe to God and to my country.'

James knew something of these plots, and he knew that his nephew was making preparations to set sail with his army. As early as the beginning of August, Evelyn had heard the rumour of 'the Prince of Orange intending to come over', and James had his own spies in The Hague to report the news sooner. He began to build up his own army, ready to fight for his throne if needs be. September and October in Evelyn's diary give us a blow-by-blow account of what it felt like to be adjacent to the court at that time.

> 18th September 1688. I went to London, where I found the Court in the utmost consternation on report of the Prince of Orange's landing, which put Whitehall into so panic a fear, that I could hardly believe it possible to find such a change.
>
> 30th September 1688. The Court in so extraordinary a consternation, on assurance of the Prince of Orange's intention to land, that the writs sent forth for a Parliament were recalled.
>
> 7th October, 1688. Hourly expectation of the Prince of Orange's invasion.
>
> 14th October, 1688. The King's birthday. No guns from the Tower as usual. The sun eclipsed at its rising ... The wind, which had been hitherto west, was east all this day. Wonderful expectation of the Dutch fleet. Public prayers ordered to be read in the churches against invasion.

> 29th October, 1688. Lady Sunderland acquainted me with his Majesty's taking away the Seals from Lord Sunderland, and of her being with the Queen to intercede for him … The Queen Dowager, and all the ladies and lords who were present at the Queen Consort's labor, were to give their testimony upon oath of the Prince of Wales's birth, recorded both at the Council Board and at the Chancery a day or two after.
>
> 2nd November, 1688. It was now certainly reported by some who saw the fleet, and the Prince embark, that they sailed from the Brill on Wednesday morning, and that the Princess of Orange was there to take leave of her husband.[11]

William landed in Torbay on 5 November 1688 with an army of 20,000 men. He had made sure to land on the 5th. On a day when the people of Britain ritually burn effigies of Catholic conspirators, the arrival of the Protestant hero (even a Calvinist one) would be sure to stoke up support and anti-Catholic sentiment in equal measure. As soon as he arrived he began distributing a document titled his *Declaration of The Hague* as he went. This detailed 'the Reasons inducing him to appear in Arms in the Kingdom of *England*, for preserving of the Protestant Religion, and for restoring the Laws and Liberties of *England, Scotland, Ireland*'. William met with no resistance and began to make his way through the country to London.

❖

James was in Salisbury with an army, ready to fight for his crown. But things did not go to plan. He began to have chronic nosebleeds and instead of going to survey his troops, to give rallying speeches to them, he was consigned to bed. On 24 November, after having a cordial supper together, George of Denmark and John Churchill deserted James on the battlefield, taking their regiments with them. The husband of Isabella Bennet, Henry Fitzroy, Earl of Grafton, and nephew of James, deserted with them. On the 26th, James was told Anne had fled Whitehall Palace in the night to join William, with Sarah Churchill at her side. When James was told the news he cried out: 'God help me, my own children have forsaken me!' It was reported that he was so grief-stricken that he almost lost his reason for a time. His protégé, John Churchill, uncle to two of his illegitimate children, was gone. His son-in-law, George, was also gone. His wife's protégée, Sarah Churchill, had absconded with his daughter in the night. All had left him to join his nephew, the husband of his favourite daughter, who had just invaded to take his crown.

When Maria learned that Anne had absconded with Sarah, she knew that it was her old favourite's idea; it was said at the time that she had 'tutto il potero imaginabile sopra lo spirito della principessa' – 'all the power imaginable over the spirit of the princess'. She also found that Anne had left her a letter. In it she says that she is simply being a dutiful wife, and that she is sure that William is only trying to help. When taken alongside all that came before, this letter reeks of insincerity. But Maria and James saw how it might be used, and they had it published and circulated.

MADAM,

I Beg your pardon if I am so deeply affected with the surprising News of the Prince's being gone, as not to be able to see You, but to leave this Paper to Express my humble Duty to the King and your Self; and to let You know that I am gone to absent my self to avoid the Kings displeasure, which I am not able to bear either against the Prince or my self: and I shall stay at so great a distance, as not to return before I hear the happy News of a Reconcilement: And as I am confident the Prince did not leave the King with any other design than to use all possible means for his Preservation; so I hope You will do me the Justice to believe that I am uncapable of following him for any other end. Never was any one in such an unhappy Condition, so divided between Duty and Affection to a Father, and a Husband and therefore I know not what to do but to follow one to preserve the other. I see the general falling off of the Nobility and Gentry, who avow to have no other end than to prevail with the King to secure their Religion, which they saw so much in danger by the Violent Counsels of the Priests; who to promote their own Religion, did not care to what dangers they exposed the King: I am fully perswaded that the Prince of Orange designs the Kings safety and preservation, and hope all things may be composed without more bloodshed, by the Calling a Parliament: God grant a happy end to these Troubles, that the Kings Reign may be prosperous, and that I may shortly meet You in perfect peace and safety; till when let me beg You to continue the same favourable Opinion that you have hitherto had of,

Your most Obedient Daughter and Servant, ANNE.

Morale at the camp was low after the Churchill/Denmark exodus, and the troops really needed to see their king to boost their spirits. He needed to be an emblem for them to follow. But in a state of stress and shock, James had another attack of chronic nosebleeds and was forced to take to his bed. Soldiers continued to drift away, either to William, or just back home. It was not long before James was on his way back to London. He needed to get Maria and the baby out of England. He may not have realised it yet, but the battle was lost before it had even begun. The only blood spilled in the 1688 coup came from the nose of the king.

19

Farewell to England

In October 1688 Maria had celebrated her thirtieth birthday. She had been in England for almost fifteen years, nearly half her life, and in this time she had had four miscarriages, had seen three daughters and a son die, and had one living baby. She had been twice in exile. At times she was adored and celebrated, at others she had been the object of scandalous rumours and insults. Lord Peterborough had said when he first saw her that she existed for no purpose other than to bring princes into the world. Now she was Queen of England and had fulfilled that purpose, as the Pope had instructed her all those years ago: to bring England back to the Catholic faith by breeding Catholic heirs. But here she was, on her thirtieth birthday, unbeknownst to her, on the brink of her final exile. And this great event that had been her main ambition was to be her downfall.

James summoned Maria's Surveyor of the Robes, an Italian named Francesco Riva (brother-in-law to her painter, Benedetto Gennari), to Maria's rooms. There were few people they could trust, but Riva was a devoted servant, and James and Maria decided they would put their lives in his hands. We have a detailed account of what followed from Riva, who reported the events to his family in August 1689. He said, 'I was called on Sunday evening, 11 December, by order of the King by one of his valets, who told me that [the King] was in the Queen's flat, and when I went in I found him alone, and as soon as he saw me he told me that he had a secret to tell me ... I bowed my head humbly in obedient resignation to his supreme commands.' James told him that the following Tuesday he wanted Maria and the baby to travel by sea to France from Portsmouth and instructed Riva to secretly make the arrangements. The child was already there, with Lady Powis.

But on Monday they found that Portsmouth was not possible, as part of the fleet was in harbour there; it was too risky. They would not be sailing the following day. They also learned that one of the captains of the fleet at Portsmouth had been instructed to find the child and to hand him over to William. James sent word to Lady Powis to get the child with all haste back to London, by any means possible. For a full day they had no news of the whereabouts of their son, but then, as if by some miracle, Lady Powis arrived in London. The new plan was for Maria to take the child to Anne and Heneage Finch, in Eastwell, and then they would travel to France from Margate at a later date. But by the following Sunday, Riva reports that 'riots began to be heard throughout the kingdom ... people were in such a frenzy', and it was considered too dangerous. They decided to go through Dover; a boat called the *Isabella* (named to celebrate the birth of their daughter who had died a decade earlier) awaited them there. But this, too, became impossible when they received news that Dover was taken by William, and the town was in chaos.

The country was on the brink of revolution, and possible civil war, and the atmosphere was febrile. With the memory of James's father, Charles I, at the forefront of their minds, they knew that they had to get their son out of the country quickly. James decided they would be safer if they travelled separately, an idea that Maria could hardly bear. She said they would send away the child, but she would stay with James, as she always had. But in the end, she was persuaded to go, too. On the chosen day, they dined in public, as though everything were normal, and then retired to bed at 10 p.m., where they made their final preparations. Riva reported:

> It was an hour after half-past midnight when I dressed myself in Barcaruolo's clothes and left behind all my furniture and other

> belongings (which were later stolen from Withall's new apartment) I promptly took up my weapons and went by a secret staircase to the King's Chamber where, having found their majesties and passed them the disguise that I had provided for the Queen, I said that everything was in order. I told Queen's Majesty that everything was ready to leave, and afterwards I withdrew to another chamber ... until the Queen was in order.[1]

When Maria stepped outside her rooms and saw James and Riva standing there, she threw her arms around her husband and begged him to let her stay with him, to send the child on with their trusted servants. She was terrified of leaving him and never seeing him again. James promised that he would follow her the next day.

> By now it was two hours after midnight, we descended by another staircase corresponding to the Royal Cabinet ... where the Prince had been taken in hiding some time before, and there the people who were to serve the Queen and the Prince were assembled, who were the following: the Count of Lauzun, the two wet nurses and myself. First of all we passed through the middle of the long gallery and then through the private garden, at the door of which was a carriage taken by me from Mr Teriesi, the Florentine Ambassador, and my very dear and particular friend.

Maria, dressed as a laundry maid, crossed a small stone courtyard to where the child and the wet nurses were waiting and got into a carriage. Riva sat by the coachman to keep an eye on the road ahead. They went to the river where a small hunting boat waited for them. They were to cross over to Lambeth. The rain began to bucket down and Riva wrote that 'no one could see each other in the great darkness of the night in the midst of unspeakable distress'. Miraculously, the baby remained asleep. Maria was reported to have cried the whole way, constantly looking back to try to catch a glimpse of the palace where she had left James behind. When they disembarked, the Count de Lauzun (a Frenchman who had fought with James in his youth) was there to meet them, with a carriage to take them to Gravesend, where fifteen years earlier Maria had first met Charles II and the Duke of Monmouth on the river. They were now to take to the river again, as entering the town was too risky. When they arrived, the carriage could not drive down to the bank since the rain had made the track impassable. They got out of the boat and trudged through the boggy marshes to the shore where they were met by Donna Vittoria and Pellegrina Turini, disguised as washerwomen. They were waiting in a packet boat they had hired.

The royal party stayed down in the hold for the entire voyage. As the freezing wind buffeted the boat across the Channel, they were all terribly sick. The wet nurses were so ill that they could not feed the child. They reached Calais at 9 a.m. The captain of the boat had been handsomely paid to ask no questions about who he carried to France, but at the end of the journey he turned to Maria and said, 'Madam, I shall be hanged on my return, but had it cost me my life I would have done my duty.'

Just fifteen years after Maria had left the shores of Calais, she stood again on the same shore. Across the Channel was England, the country she had learned to call home, but which she would now never see again. In her arms was the longed-for prince, the fulfilment of the destiny the Pope had envisaged for her all those years ago. He would grow up at the French court, an exile, like his father had before him, but he would never sit on the throne of England.

Maria's arrival in France was completely unexpected, but she was taken to, and put up at, the home of the Governor. Maria attended mass at a Franciscan convent nearby. She prayed God to guide her, to protect her husband and her son, to show her what she should do. When she left the chapel, she sat down to write to her brother:

Boulogne 27 October 1688

Caro fratello,

You will be quite astonished to hear that I am in this country and the manner in which I came here, having escaped at night with my son, and having had a very great, but favourable wind in little more than twenty-four hours from London to Cales, from where I came to this place and I find myself in an unspeakable uneasiness for not having any news of the King after my departure, which is just eight days ago. He told me that he would leave the day after me, but all the seaports are stopped, and I can neither see him nor know any news about him, for they do not let letters pass. You can believe in what state I find myself; I am sure that if you saw me you would pity me, my only consolation is to see that my son is well, and that he is getting fat despite his sufferings. He alone is happy. He does not know his misfortunes, nor does he know in what state he is reduced and to what he has reduced his parents. Pray to God for me, dear brother, that he may give me gratitude and resignation, because without the help of God, I believe that I will go mad. Everyone tells me to go to Paris and to speak to the King of France, from whom I receive a thousand graces, but I do not know how to resolve to leave the sea, and until I have some news from my King, I do not know how to think of anything else. I am here with very few people, and I have no one in my confidence, except Donna Vittoria, whom alone with Pellegrina I have brought with me. Mr. Ragnoni and Abbot Rizzini must have been taken away from the sea, otherwise I am sure that they would be here, and I have no news of M. Cattaneo, but I hope that he is in Paris, and I thank you for the thousand times that you have sent him to me. What a relief it would be for me to have you with me in this new place, but I have longed for it so much, without being able to keep it, that I have stopped hoping for it, nor do I know how to hope for it now. Dear brother, pity me, advise me, and with your affection lift up your poor afflicted sister, who, in whatever state she may be, will always love you from the heart, and will be with all sincerity and affection all yours. MR[2]

Maria was terrified when she wrote this letter. She had no way of finding out if James was on his way, or if he had been captured. If the latter, she, of course, knew exactly what had happened to James's father, Charles I. She knew that she might never see James again. The man she had so desperately hoped she would never meet was now the only person she wanted to see.

After spending two days almost exclusively in the convent – according to Madame de Sévigné, 'weeping without intermission because she neither sees nor can hear any certain news of her husband, whom she loves passionately' – she received news. James was alive but was being held prisoner.[3] Her instinct was to return to England, but she was persuaded to go to Louis. He would help to bring James to France. And so Maria continued to reverse her steps of fifteen years earlier. She wrote to Louis:

Monsieur,

A poor fugitive queen, bathed in tears, has gladly risked the perils of the sea, in order to seek comfort and shelter with the greatest and most generous monarch on Earth. Owing to her particular regard for him, she wishes to entrust to him her most precious treasure, in the person of the Prince of Wales, her son; he is as yet too young to share the gratitude which fills my heart, and in the midst of all my enemies I rejoice to live under your protection. I am, Monsieur, with deep feeling, your very affectionate servant and sister,

The Queen of England.[4]

Back in England, James had indeed been discovered. After Maria had gone, he had first called a council in which he said the queen and prince were gone, but that he would make a stand. It was a bluff. He began to make his own preparations to leave. He summoned Lord Ailsbury and told him he was going. Ailsbury recorded in his memoirs that James said: 'If I should go, who can wonder after the treatment I have found? My daughter hath deserted me, my army also, and him that I raised from nothing the same, on whom I heaped all favours; and if such betrays me, what can I expect from those I have done so little for.'[5] Ailsbury tried to convince James to stay, that all was not lost, that he might still be able to 'treat honourably with the Prince of Orange'. But James would not take the risk. On 21 December, at around one in the morning, James left Whitehall Palace via a secret passage. A coach was waiting with a trusted friend, Sir Edward Halles. They made their way to Maidstone where another trusted friend, Ralph Sheldon, waited with horses. They rode fast and reached Sheerness at ten o'clock the next day, where a boat was waiting to take them to France.

But the winds were blowing fiercely and kept the boat in harbour. They finally left twelve hours later, and they had made little progress before their boat was stopped and searched by three rowing boats nearby. James carried with him an ornate cross, and they were arrested in the belief that they were Catholic priests fleeing the country, James being mistaken for Father Petre. They were taken to Faversham to be questioned by the mayor, a lawyer called Mr Napleton. James was made to go on foot through the muddy roads. They reached an inn called the Arms of England, and there James was recognised by a man loyal to the crown who fell on his knees before his king. Crowds began to gather and James pushed his way to an upstairs room. He wrote to Heneage Finch's father, who was Lord Lieutenant in those parts, and who arrived quickly and arranged for him to stay at the mayor's home. As they walked from the inn to the house they were closely guarded, and the crowds pressed in around them, shouting and calling. Some were loyal, some were not. James began to fear that he would not leave Kent alive. The mayor was not a loyalist; he stood beneath James's window and read out William's declaration. The rooms that James was given were closely guarded by a group of seamen. They took up their watch to keep him safe, but it meant he could not leave undetected. Sheldon had got away, but he found he could not get near his king to help him escape, and he fled to France. The mayor went to William's trusted friend Bentinck, who was garrisoned nearby; expecting to be thanked for his actions, he was not. Bentinck asked why he did not let him go; the last thing they needed was the king on their hands.

But James had smuggled out a letter via an old sailor who had remained loyal, and who took this letter to London where it was read aloud in the council chamber. Its request for help was met with an embarrassed silence. After half an hour, Lord Ailsbury proposed that they send an escort to James begging him to return. Ailsbury himself led the escort. He wrote that he found James 'sitting in a great chair, his hat on, and his beard being much grown'. He reported that James 'rose up to meet me' but 'with an air of displeasure' led him to the window. James said accusingly: 'You were all Kings when I left London.'[6] But by the end of the meeting, he thanked Ailsbury for coming. He knew he had risked much in doing so.

James returned to London as king, and crowds came out to celebrate. He still had supporters who were relieved to see that their monarch had not abandoned them to a Calvinist invasion, as they feared. But James did not stay long; William and his army were fast approaching, and he knew he could not stand against them. His armies had already shown that they would not fight for him in great enough numbers, and William's troops were extensive and well trained. James left again, in the dead of night. As he made his way in a boat down the Thames, he dropped the Royal Seal in the river. He hoped that, without the seal, William would be unable to govern, but it was interpreted as a sign of abdication. New seals were made when William was crowned King of England in April the following year. He gave his monogrammed ring, which held a lock of his hair, to Sir Peter Halkett, a loyal Royalist who had helped him. When James left England, for the last time, William of Orange would have breathed a sigh of relief. It was far better for him not to have to execute James for treason, forty years after James's father, Charles I, had been sent to the scaffold.

In France, Louis sent Maria clothes to change into on her journey, but she refused them. She wanted to 'continue to wear the simple black silk gown in which she left London'. Her composure was remarked upon; though she wept, she held herself like a queen and had not for one moment succumbed to hysteria. But when she was stopping at Beauvais, she received a note saying that James had landed at Ambleteuse: he was in France. Maria collapsed and had to be carried to her bedroom where she spent several hours with pains in her body, prostrate with weeping. The relief that James was alive was mixed with the knowledge that, if he was in France, then England was lost.

Louis met Maria on the road. The carriages stopped; the royal party emerged. Louis took the baby James in his arms and kissed his forehead. Then he kissed Maria and promised that she and her son would be safe in France. Louis remembered this beautiful young Este princess from when she had stopped there on the way to England all those years earlier, but he must have been struck by the change in her. She was remarkably thin, and she wore her cares on her face. But she stood tall as she bowed to the King of France and thanked him for giving them a refuge.

When James arrived at Saint-Germain, he was met by Louis. They kissed each other on the cheek, wept and promised friendship. Then Louis took James to Maria's rooms, where she was lying on her bed. The stress of the past few months – indeed years – had taken their toll. Louis said: 'Madame, I bring you a man whom you will be very glad to see.'[7] There were several courtiers in the room, and others soon arrived to observe the meeting of the exiled monarchs. But James and Maria had been through too much to stand on ceremony. He swept across the room, took her in his arms and kissed her. She clung to him, and they wept in each other's arms for some time. Their behaviour was scandalously titillating to the French courtiers, for whom life at court was bound by strict codes of behaviour and ceremony. After they had comforted each other, they proceeded to the royal nursery to see their son. He lay in a huge, ornate cot, in a room richly decorated with bright blue plastering, and little fleur-de-lis in white and gold. The prince was doing well. He was the healthy boy that they had so longed for.

❖

Back in England, medals were minted. They read almost like newspaper headlines. On the obverse, the face of James II, without a crown, the words JACOBUS II BRITAN REX FUGITIV (James II King of Britain fled). On the reverse the image shows a broken oak tree next to a fruitful orange tree. The wording reads POST FUGUM REGIS DELATA REGNI ADMINISTRATIO PRINCIPI AURIA (After the flight of the king, the administration of the kingdom was brought to the ear of the prince). It is framed as an abdication and says that William was offered the 'administratio' of the country, without mentioning the crown. The symbolism was clear: the royal oak of the Stuarts had fallen, and the reign of the House of Orange had begun. But that word 'administratio' is key. William and Mary were not divine rulers, who imposed their rule on the nation. They were to be administrators. The divine right of kings was over.

EPILOGUE

The Final Exile

Since man, by swift returns of good and ill,
In all the course of life's uncertain still;
By fortune favour'd now, and now opresst,
And not 'till death, secure of Fame or rest.
— Anne Finch, *Aristomenes, or, the Royal Shepherd, a Tragedy*

After the revolution of 1688, Maria was in France, the other women in our story were scattered across England, and their loyalties were divided. It must have been a fearful time as each considered who they would follow and what they would do. As in the Civil War less than fifty years before, when brother fought brother, families found themselves again on opposing sides. 'La belle Jennings', now Frances, Lady Tyrconnell, went into exile with James and Maria, while her sister, Sarah Churchill, had joined William and Mary. And John Churchill found himself against his nephews: Arabella Churchill's sons by James – Henry and James FitzJames – fought for their father and went with him into exile.

The judgement the Churchills made, even before the revolution began, ensured their long-term success. But even their alignment with the new regime was not so straightforward. Sarah chose her side, and she stuck to it. But John kept his options more open. He began to write to James in exile. He even promised support if James were to invade. He did not tell Sarah. William knew that this back-channel communication was going on and, though he and Mary never fully trusted John and Sarah, he let him carry on. He understood all too well that playing a dual game was a necessity of political life. John was briefly imprisoned in the Tower, but his life was never in serious danger. He ultimately stayed true to the Williamite cause, though he continued his correspondence until after the death of Queen Anne in 1714, when parliament put through a law that no Catholic would ever again sit on the throne of England. The next fifty-two people with claims to the crown were all Catholics, and they were all passed over for the Protestant George of Hanover, the man who had, some thirty years before, scoffed at the idea of marrying the semi-commoner Princess Anne.

When Anne died and George became king, who should have been there to welcome this George I to the throne? James's mistress, Catherine Sedley, had stayed at court through the reigns of William and Mary, and Anne, too. And she remained much as she ever had been. When, after the 1688 revolution, she met Louise de Kéroualle and Elizabeth Hamilton (William III's mistress), at court, she exclaimed, 'God! Who would have thought that we three whores should meet here!' And at George I's coronation, when all courtiers were asked to swear their allegiance, Catherine took note of a large military presence, and remarked with her usual caustic wit: 'Does the old fool think that anyone will say No?' At the age of thirty-nine she married David Colyear, Earl of Portmore, who had led a regiment of William III's army when they landed on the shores of Dorset in 1688. She died in 1717, when taking the waters in Bath.

Some of the defectors to William's side are perhaps more of a surprise. Like Sarah Churchill, Isabella Bennet chose the winning side. Mary and Isabella had grown up together and she was at home at William and Mary's court. She was also independent for the first time in her life: her feckless husband, Henry Fitzroy, died in 1690, fighting in Ireland on the side of William against his uncle. She was still only twenty-two, and she was rich, clever and beautiful. Isabella had a son from her marriage to Fitzroy, Charles, who she raised to be an educated and erudite man. He became a leading politician under George I and was a founding member of the Kit-Kat Club[1]. Isabella married a second time in 1698, to Sir Thomas Hamner, an intelligent and successful politician, who flourished under the constitutional reforms of 1690 as Speaker of the House of Commons and also edited the works of William Shakespeare. Isabella died in 1723.

Anna Scott, Duchess of Monmouth, also chose to stay in England. Her childhood friendship with Mary was renewed, and she remarried in 1688. Her husband, Charles Cornwallis, was made an admiral in William's army. Their three children all took her name rather than their father's. She died in 1723 at the age of eighty.

With her deranged husband in France still desperate to claim her back, exile at the court in Saint-Germain was not an option for Hortense Mancini, so she too stayed in England. But she was never welcomed into the fold. She ended her life in poverty. Her salon had reached its apogee under James and Maria, who had given her a generous pension. But when they fled to France, William and Mary had no interest in helping the cousin of the deposed queen. Hortense became an alcoholic and committed suicide in 1699, at the age of fifty-three. Her body was sent back to her husband, whose obsession with her had not abated. He carted her corpse around with him as he travelled through France, before he finally buried her with her uncle, Cardinal Mazarin, in Paris.

We know that James and Maria never returned to England, that their son was never crowned king, that his son, Bonnie Prince Charlie, never gained the throne. But in 1688 it was hard to see what the future would hold, and it must have seemed an impossible task to pick your side. Take, for example, Dorothy Ogle, Anne Finch's sister. At the end of 1688, Heneage Finch was in James's army, and Anne received word that Dorothy was stranded alone in London. She had joined the court of Princess Anne as a maid of honour at the beginning of 1687, but when the princess and Sarah Churchill left London to join William and Mary, Dorothy was left behind.

What must have gone through Dorothy's mind at this moment in November 1688? On the one side there was the mistress she served and a promising future at her court. On the other, there was the deposed monarch who her family had always supported. When she had gained one of the coveted positions of maid of honour to Princess Anne at the beginning of 1687, she could never have imagined that less than two years later this family would have torn itself apart.

If she, or others like her, were thinking strategically, there was more on offer to her at the new court of William and Mary: she could keep her position as maid of honour to Anne and live comfortably at the court, where the opportunities for marriage were certainly greater given that her dowry would be paid by the monarch. But how could she know if this court would prevail? Who was to say that the exiled James wouldn't return to reclaim his crown? How would he treat those who had deserted him? And what of her conscience? Her family had long been loyal to the Stuarts: they had supported James's father, Charles I, and remained true to the exiled princes during the Protectorate. Would she now desert them? Or did she, too, fear the effects of a Catholic monarch on the English throne? She had to decide with so little time to choose, and with so little idea of what the consequences would be.

We do not know for certain what she did, but by 1691 she was no longer attached to the court. In a letter from Sarah Churchill, we see her described as 'a very worthy but unhappy woman who had no prospect of marrying having been long at court and not handsome'. Sarah goes on to say that Dorothy had no money beyond 'a thousand pound I had begged for her just to give her bread when she retired'.[2] Whether this retirement was in 1688 or later, Sarah leaves unclear, but the fact that she went out of her way to help Dorothy suggests at least some sentimental attachment still to the Finch family.

Little is known of Dorothy Ogle, but she must have been a woman of some nerve. Women at this time, both within and outside the court, did not enjoy a great deal of political agency. But it was precisely people like Dorothy Ogle who, in the end, could have had an impact on the outcome of this bloodless battle. To successfully oust the monarch and replace him, to alter the line of succession, William and Mary needed support. If many of Anne's maids had deserted her and chosen James's side, it would have been terrible for the new monarchs. Dorothy Ogle is just one example of what many people faced at this moment in 1688.

For someone like Harry Killigrew – Anne's brother, and friend and confidant of Charles II – who was in the navy, the opportunities offered by William, the overseer of the greatest fleet in the world, were far more tempting than going into exile.

As the next year arrived it became clear that there was little hope for the Jacobite cause. William and Mary were offered the crown in February 1689, and the new monarchs required everyone attached to the court and to politics to take an oath of allegiance, something that Heneage Finch could not bring himself to do. Anne and Heneage returned to Heneage's nephew Thomas's estate of Eastwell Park in Kent, and Anne's poetry from this time shows a strong political bent. She writes of the glory of those who fight against the new regime and who are suffering as Jacobites. One poem from this time, 'On the Earl of Dundee', proudly attests that posterity will remember those who suffered and who stood firm:

Fame, shall the gloomy Tyrant disposess,
And bear you, on her golden wings,
You, that have borne the cause of Kings
To the most distant parts, of the wide universe.[3]

Another poem has a more personal note of anger. It is called 'Caesar and Brutus', a story apposite for the betrayal James must have felt from his nephew and favourite daughter. It is short but succinct:

Though Caesar falling, shew'd no sign of fear,
Yett Brutus, when thou did'st appear,
When thy false hand, against him came,
He vail'd his face, to hide that shame,
Which did on the mistake attend
Of having own'd thee, for his Freind [sic].

Anne included a variation of this poem in her 1713 anthology, *Miscellany Poems, on Several Occasions*. The version above, written at the moment of the fall of James, is full of anger; the one below, written years later, has little of that anger, but, rather, a kind of quiet sadness. Perhaps after all those years Anne decided to depoliticise her poem, or at least to tone down her allegiance to the old regime.

> WHEN *Caesar* fell, he brav'd each killing wound,
> And awfull lay Dictator on the ground:
> But when a Friend, or something nearer thought,
> Impos'd a stab, who should relief have brought;
> The dying hero hid his gen'rous face,
> Where blushes rose in scorn of human race.[4]

With Heneage's career over, and their home in Westminster gone, the Finches had two options: to live in exile in England, or to join the exiled court in France. Heneage could fight in the army, they could do their bit for their monarchs. They chose to be reunited with James and Maria. In April 1690, under cover of darkness, Heneage and five unknown companions made for the coastal town of Hythe, on the edge of Romney Marsh. They travelled separately and met on the shore. A small boat was ready to take them to France. But just before they boarded, they were discovered. The group took to their horses and fled. As they rode hard, Heneage's horse reared and he was thrown. He was arrested and taken to London. There are no records of the charges against Heneage, which says something of the gravity of his position. During times of crisis, a warrant might be issued directly to save time, and therefore not enter the annals. In trying to leave England for France, Heneage had committed treason.

He was held in prison in London for seven months, while he awaited and stood trial. This was relatively short in comparison to many; court cases could drag on for years while the accused languished in jail. But these months must have seemed long to Anne, who waited powerlessly in Kent to discover her husband's fate. By this time she was living in a house called Godmersham, a large priory near her family in Eastwell, though we do not know who she was living there with. The endless days spent sitting around were torturous to her. She needed an outlet, and she took up her pen. We know that she had been writing for some years at this point, but the years immediately following the revolution appear to have been prolific. She may not have been able to change what was happening, or to go out into the world and express her views, but she could create alternative literary worlds. The two plays she is known to have penned probably date from this time: *The Triumph of Love and Innocence*, and *Aristomenes, or, The Royal Shepherd*. When these were published in 1713, she wrote in a preface of how they had become a means to distract herself:

> I know not what effect they will have upon others, but I must acknowledge, that the giving some interruption to those melancholy thoughts, which posesst me, not only for my own, but much more for the misfortunes of those, to whom I owe all immaginable duty, and gratitude, was so great a benefitt, that I have reason to be satisfy'd with the undertaking, be the performance never so inconsiderable. And indeed, an absolute Solitude, (which often was my lott) under such dejection of mind, cou'd not have been supported, had I indulg'd my self, (as was too natural to me) only in the contemplation of present, and real afflictions.[5]

In the epilogue to *Aristomenes*, she even goes further, writing,

> For her own sake, the Author thought itt fitt
> To lett the Audience know when this was writt,
> 'Twas not for praise, or with pretence to witt:
> But lonely Godmersham th'attempt excuses,
> Not sure to be endur'd, without the Muses;[6]

Both plays show Anne processing what is happening in the world around her. In *Triumph*, the Queen of Cyprus takes refuge in Rhodes, and in *Aristomenes*, the title character is captured by his enemy and imprisoned. These plays were never intended for performance; they are closet dramas, designed for circulation or to be read aloud in a small group. But the majority of her works are poems. She writes of her struggles with depression, which pervaded her life; her poems offered some release from her predicament, a kind of consolation.

The case against Heneage did not stand up in court. There was too little evidence and he refused to talk. He joined Anne in Eastwell where the couple prepared to settle down to rural life. The companionship they had always enjoyed, and his support of her literary talents, would see them through this difficult time. They worked collaboratively on her work, as he acted as her scribe and editor, though it is always clear from his annotations that she was in charge. His role as transcriber was practical as well as supportive: her handwriting was often nearly illegible. These poems were often sent out to friends in manuscript and Anne began to establish the kind of coterie of women that Maria had encouraged at her court. It was modelled on Katherine Philips's Society of Friendship, with the members taking pastoral names: Laura, Ephelia, Valeria, Lamira, and even Arminda, taken from Tasso. These names appear throughout her work though we do not know who they all refer to. This community was Anne Finch emulating that world of friendship she had found at Maria's court, where Urania – the muse of celestial poetry – reigned over her Graces.

When Princess Mary arrived in England in 1689, twelve years after she had left for Holland, she was met by William at Greenwich. He told her that she needed to maintain at least an outward show of good cheer. Whether or not she felt it, we cannot know, but Sarah Churchill observed acidly that she 'wanted bowels'; in other words, her merriment bordered on heartlessness. John Evelyn described the scene at Whitehall, in February 1689:

> I saw the new Queen and King proclaimed the very next day after her coming to Whitehall, Wednesday, 13th February, with

> great acclamation and general good reception. Bonfires, bells, guns, etc. It was believed that both, especially the Princess, would have shown some (seeming) reluctance at least, of assuming her father's crown, and made some apology, testifying by her regret that he should by his mismanagement necessitate the nation to so extraordinary a proceeding, which would have shown very handsomely to the world, and according to the character given of her piety; consonant also to her husband's first declaration, that there was no intention of deposing the King, but of succoring the nation; but nothing of all this appeared; she came into Whitehall laughing and jolly, as to a wedding, so as to seem quite transported. She rose early the next morning, and in her undress, as it was reported, before her women were up, went about from room to room to see the convenience of Whitehall; lay in the same bed and apartment where the late Queen lay, and within a night or two sat down to play at basset, as the Queen, her predecessor used to do. She smiled upon and talked to everybody, so that no change seemed to have taken place at Court since her last going away, save that infinite crowds of people thronged to see her, and that she went to our prayers. This carriage was censured by many.[7]

The coronation was set for 11 April. When James heard, he wrote to his daughter:

> I have been willing to overlook what has been done, and thought your obedience to your husband and compliance to the nation might have prevailed. But your being crowned is in your own power; if you do it while I and the Prince of Wales are living, the curses of an angry father will fall on you, as well as those of a God who commands obedience to parents.[8]

Mary may never have seen this letter. It was William who answered for her that all they had done they had done together, and the coronation went ahead. They were crowned as joint monarchs, and

Mary had new crowns made to reflect this. They were larger and more ornate than that which Maria had worn four years earlier. Mary's was exceedingly heavy, and Anne was reported to have whispered cattily 'I pity your fatigue madame', to which Mary replied, 'a crown is not so heavy as it seems'.

The medal struck to celebrate the coronation of William and Mary illustrates how propaganda operated during the revolution. On one side we see William and Mary, positioned just as James and Maria had been, with their laurel crowns. But on the other side is Andromeda being saved by Perseus from the evil sea monster. The inscription reads PRETIUMUS ET CAUSA LABORIS (The value and reason for labour). The symbolism is clear: William and Mary are Perseus, rescuing Andromeda (England) from the evil monster (James and Catholicism).

The coronation ceremony had one key difference from previous ones: rather than swearing to uphold the laws according to their birthright, William and Mary swore to uphold 'the statutes in Parliament agreed upon and the laws and customs of the same'. This shift was the first step towards the kind of democracy that we live under today.

William and Mary took a very different approach to the monarchy from those which had come before, and particularly to the hedonistic court under Charles II. But they found a balance between the austerity of Holland and theatre- and music-loving London, and the court poets and musicians found that they would do well enough under the new regime, though their new patrons were far less knowledgeable or appreciative of their offerings. Purcell, for example, wrote his greatest works for these monarchs: *Dido and Aeneas* was written to celebrate their coronation, and *The Faerie Queen* to mark their fifteenth wedding anniversary. But on the whole, commissions were for particular occasions rather than for general court entertainments. Writers and painters found that they would not suffer for having been prominent at James's court; though Dryden, who had converted to Catholicism upon James's accession, was removed from the role of poet laureate when he refused to take the Oaths of Allegiance to William and Mary.

Mary set the tone for how she expected the women of her court to behave by commissioning a set of paintings from Sir Godfrey Kneller. These were known as the Hampton Court Beauties, and are in direct contrast to the set her mother had commissioned from Peter Lely some thirty years before – the Windsor Beauties. Lely's works had portrayed the women in languorous postures, with loose-fitting clothes, plunging necklines and seductive expressions, and many of them were mistresses of the king. Pride of place had been given to Barbara Villiers, who was painted as the goddess Minerva. When Pepys wrote in his diary in 1668 of having been to see them, he wryly remarked that they were 'good, but not like'.[9] Lely had been famous for flattering his sitters, and these paintings were very much of his style.

Kneller's paintings, on the other hand – which Daniel Defoe (who became close to William and worked for him as a spy) described as 'of the principal Ladies attending upon her Majesty, or who were frequently in her Retinue' – portray eight of Mary's closest companions standing tall, aloof and distinctly covered up. They stare down at us imperiously from where they now hang on the walls of William and Mary's Private Dining Room at Hampton Court Palace. Some are familiar faces: the portrait of Isabella Bennet was the first that Kneller began work on, and it is a testament to how successfully she had navigated the transition from one court to the next. Unlike the other beauties, she looks over her right shoulder, eluding the viewer's gaze. Her husband, Henry Fitzroy, son of Charles II, had died in battle fighting for William against James's army the year that this was painted. Perhaps her evasive gaze suggests some grief.

And what of Maria, the 'Phoenix Queen'? She did not rise from the ashes but lived in France, at the Palace of Saint-Germain, for the rest of her life. This would seem to mark the end of Maria's story in Britain. But the events as they played out were not so neat as that, and the reality was that life in exile was one of constant expectation of return. The initial military events failed, but there was still the possibility of being asked back. The baby in the bedpan myth was a convenient one for the new monarchs, but when in 1692 Maria fell pregnant again, James saw an opportunity. He invited prominent members of the court and parliament, including Mary and William themselves, to go to France to witness the birth. No chances would be taken this time. When it came to it, however, the invitations were declined, and the child was a girl. They called her Louise-Marie, and for the nineteen years that she lived she was a light in her parents' darkness. James nicknamed her 'La Consolatrice': their consolation in their exile. He doted on her, perhaps even more so because of what his other daughters had done. And this time, Maria had full control over the education of her children, and both her son and daughter were taught English, French, Italian and Latin.

Throughout James and Maria's life in France, they continued to keep up appearances – they were often painted as monarchs, with their heirs. Take, for example, the family portrait by Pierre Mignard from 1695: they sit in their royal regalia, and to the side of Maria stands her son. He is only a child of seven, but he stands like a royal prince. Both he and Maria point down to a crown that rests on the floor. The statement is clear: he is the heir to the throne of England. This painting was made as a gift to Maria's family in Modena, though today it is part of the British Royal Collection.

In fact, in exile, Maria's patronage of artists increased hugely. Now she had an image to create and to project, and paintings were made and sent to courts across Europe.

In 1694, Mary in England died of smallpox. It is not clear how James and Maria felt when they heard the news, but they refused to go into mourning for her. This was thought strange at the French court, where formality and ceremony reigned almost as supremely as Louis XIV himself. Perhaps it was from anger, or perhaps they had simply drawn a veil over their daughters in England and refused to lift it. Mary's death did not change their position, as it might have done. William continued to rule as king. When he began to ail it was said that he hated the thought of Anne becoming queen – living in close proximity for the last fourteen years had bred a mutual loathing – and, of course, he would not countenance James returning. But in secret he offered the exiles a deal: their son, James Francis, could return as king after William's death, provided he convert to Protestantism. The offer was, unsurprisingly, refused. Maria said that dear as her son was to her, she would rather see him dead than to disgrace himself by converting and supplanting his father in that way.

Anne succeeded William as monarch. And so James and Maria continued with their splendid but precarious lives as exiles. But in August 1700, they received a surprising letter. Princess Anne had written to them in secret in a moment of great distress. Her son had just died of scarlet fever. If we think of what Maria had suffered with miscarriages and the deaths of her children, it was nothing in comparison to what poor Anne had been through. By the time she wrote this letter she had had seven miscarriages (one of which had been twins), five stillborn children, three daughters and two sons, all of whom had died. Other than the child she wrote of, William, who had lived to eleven, none had reached the age of two. She told her father that she feared that God was punishing her for having betrayed him and said that she would hold the throne in trust for her brother, who was the natural heir to the crown. But there was a catch: he had to convert to Protestantism. When the offer was placed before James Francis himself, when Anne was dying, he refused, saying, 'I have chosen my own course, therefore it is for others to change their sentiments.'

Though the exiled Stuarts continued to fight for their throne – the Battle of Culloden in 1746, led by Maria's grandson, Bonnie Prince Charlie, was the last lost chance – they never regained it. But freed from the obligations of queenship, Maria became the patron of a convent of the Visitation, the same order that she had wanted to join as a child. This was in Chaillot and had been founded by her mother-in-law, Henrietta Maria, when she, too, had lived in exile during the Civil War. In some ways Maria's life had come full circle and she dedicated the rest of her life to her devotion in God. Maria died in 1718, at the age of fifty-nine, and her body was interred at the convent in Chaillot. In England, her former maid of honour Anne Finch wrote an elegy, 'On the Death of the Queen'. She remembers her time at court when she 'in Her Domestick train hadst stood' when 'ebon locks o'erspread / My youthfull neck my cheeks a bashfull red' and 'When early joys my glowing bosom warm'd / When trifles pleas'd & every pleasure charm'd'. She speaks of Maria's perfections in form, spirit, mind and voice, and recalls how,

> Bless't were the hours when thro' attendance due
> Her numerous charms were present to my view
> When lowly to her radiant eyes I bowed
> Suns to my sight but Suns without a cloud
> Towards me their beneficial aspect turn'd.

And she laments that such a queen should be cast out from England's shores. By this time, Anne Finch was a celebrated poet who had, after much persuasion, embraced the printing press and had published work under her name titled *Miscellany Poems, on Several Occasions*, Written by the Right Honourable Anne, Countess of Winchelsea.[10]

When James was on his deathbed in 1701, he called his daughter, Louise Marie, to his side. He took her hand and said that the best way she could live would be to try to emulate her mother who, he said, 'has been overwhelmed with calumnies. But time, the mother of Truth, will I hope, at last make her virtues shine as bright as the sun.'

So how do we remember Maria of Modena, England's last Catholic queen? Perhaps as the mother of the child who brought down a monarch. As the young girl plucked from a convent. As a woman who, like so many around her, before her and after her, was used as a pawn in the political games of men. How *should* we remember Maria of Modena? As a patron of painters, musicians and writers. As a nurturer of talented women. As a woman who might have achieved all manner of things if she had only had the time and freedom to do so. The same might be said for every one of the women in this story, for all the Graces.

DRAMATIS PERSONAE

ITALY

The Estes

Alfonso IV b. 1634 Modena, d. 1662 Modena, m. Laura Martinozzi 1655, Duke of Modena 1658–62, father of Maria Beatrice d'Este and Francesco II d'Este.

Lucrezia Barberini b. 1628 Rome, d. 1699, known as 'Madama', third wife and widow of Francesco I d'Este (m. 1654), mother of Rinaldo d'Este, grandmother of Maria Beatrice d'Este and Francesco II d'Este.

Francesco I b. 1610 Modena, d. 1658 Savoy, Duke of Modena 1629–58, father to Alfonso IV d'Este and Rinaldo d'Este, grandfather of Maria Beatrice d'Este and Francesco II d'Este.

Francesco II d'Este b. 1660, d. 1694, Duke of Modena 1662–94, brother to Maria Beatrice d'Este, son of Alfonso IV d'Este and Laura d'Este Martinozzi. Francesco never married so the dukedom passed to his uncle, Rinaldo, on his death.

Laura d'Este née Martinozzi b. 1639 Fano, d. 1687 Rome, niece of Cardinal Mazarin, one of the *Mazarinettes*, Duchess and Regent of Modena, m. Alfonso IV d'Este 1655, mother of Maria Beatrice d'Este and Francesco II d'Este.

Leonora d'Este b. 1643 Mantua, d. 1722 Modena, daughter of Francesco I d'Este and his first wife Maria Farnese (1615–46), cousin of Maria Beatrice d'Este. Leonora became a nun in 1674 and took the name Maria Francesca dello Spirito Santo, before founding a convent in Reggio Emilia in 1689. She became a spiritual director to many noblewomen there before she died, allegedly with the 'odour of sanctity'.

Maria Beatrice d'Este b. 1658 Modena, d. 1718 Paris, Duchess of York, Queen of England, m. James, Duke of York in 1673.

Rinaldo d'Este b. 1655 Modena, d. 1737 Modena, only son of Francesco I d'Este and Lucrezia Barberini. After much assistance from his niece, Maria Beatrice (for years she wrote letters to the Pope requesting his Cardinal hat), he was made a Cardinal in 1686 though he had to resign this role in 1694 to become Duke of Modena when Francesco II died without an heir; m. Princess Charlotte Felicitas of Brunswick-Lüneburg in 1696. The children from this marriage secured the Este dynasty until 1796 when a French invasion saw the end of the Duchy of Modena.

The Este Court

Matilde Beatrice Bentivoglio Lady-in-waiting to Maria Farnese (first wife of Francesco I, mother of Alfonso IV), and then confessor to Duchess Laura, she acted as governess to Maria and Francesco. She founded two Carmelite convents, one in Modena, the other in Sassuolo. It was the convent in Sassuolo that Princess Leonora d'Este joined in 1674. Her biography was written by Father Giovanni Taddeo, a monk in a Carmelite monastery in Milan, in 1722; it bore the title *Account of the Life and Exemplary Virtues of the Most Excellent Lady Donna Matilde Beatrice Bentivoglio, First Lady of Honour to the Three Most Serene Duchesses of Modena, and Founder of the Monastery of Saints Joseph and Teresa of the same City*. The Bentivoglio family were an important dynasty who were the de facto rulers of Bologna in the fifteenth century.

Donna Vittoria Davia Montecuccoli b. 1655, d. 1703, Italian noblewoman and lady-in-waiting to Duchess Laura until her marriage to Virgilio Giuseppe Davia (a Modenese statesman) in 1672, she joined Maria in exile in both Brussels and Edinburgh. When Maria became queen in 1685, Vittoria moved to England to join the court, and she went into exile with them in 1688. James and Maria gave her the title of Duchess of Almond in 1689 in gratitude for her loyalty. She remained close to James and Maria and was present at James's death. When she died in 1703, Maria was devastated and went into a long period of mourning.

Lucrezia Vezzani Pratoneri Italian noblewoman, travelled to England with Maria and became her Lady of the Bedchamber.

Francesco Riva a painter apprenticed in Guercino's studio in Bologna, sometimes referred to as cousin and sometimes as brother-in-law to Benedetto Gennari, Master of the Robes to Maria. He helped facilitate Maria's escape to France with the baby prince. In 1689 he wrote a detailed account of the escape in a letter to his family.

Pelegrina Turini Italian noblewoman, travelled to England with Maria and became her Woman of the Bedchamber. She was one of the women asked to give testimony as a witness to the birth of James Francis Stuart in 1688.

ENGLAND

Royalty

Anne Hyde b. 1637, d. 1671, first Duchess of York, m. James, Duke of York in 1660, mother of Princesses Mary and Anne.

Princess Anne b. 1665 d. 1714, daughter of James, Duke of York and Anne Hyde, m. George of Denmark in 1683, became Queen Anne in 1702.

Caterina de Braganza b. 1638, d. 1705, Princess of Portugal, m. Charles II in 1662, Queen of England until his death in 1685. After the revolution she initially stayed in London at the court of William and Mary but by 1692 relations between them had broken down and she returned to Portugal where she acted as Regent.

Charles II b. 1630, d. 1685, King of England, brother of James, Duke of York.

George of Denmark b. 1653, d. 1708, second son of Frederick III of Denmark and Sophie Amalie of Brunswick-Calenberg, m. Princess Anne in 1683.

James Stuart b. 1633, d. 1701, Duke of York, future James II, brother of King Charles II, husband of Maria Beatrice.

Princess Mary b. 1662, d. 1694, daughter of James, Duke of York and Anne Hyde, married William of Orange in 1677, became Queen Mary II and ruled jointly with her husband from 1689.

William of Orange b. 1650, d. 1702, nephew of Charles II and James II, m. Princess Mary in 1677, led an invasion of England in 1688 which became the Glorious Revolution, after which he and Mary ruled as Mary II and William III of England.

Courtiers

Frances Apsley b. 1653, d. 1702, maid of honour and close friend to both Princesses Mary and Anne, m. Sir Benjamin Bathurst.

Anthony Ashley Cooper First Earl of Shaftesbury, b. 1621, d. 1683; an important politician under Charles II, he was instrumental in the birth of the Whigs and the two-party system.

Susan Bellasyse Baroness Bellasyse of Osgodby, d. 1713, mistress of James II when Duke of York, Lady of the Bedchamber and close friend of Maria.

Gilbert Burnet b. 1643, d. 1715, Scottish philosopher, historian, cleric and man of letters, he was a staunch supporter of the Whigs and became a close friend and supporter of William III, who made him Bishop of Salisbury and Chancellor of the Order of the Garter in 1689. His works *Bishop Burnet's History* *of His Own Time* and *History of the Reformation* are fascinating contemporary accounts of the politics of the sixteenth and seventeenth centuries in England.

Arabella Churchill b. 1648, d. 1730, sister of John Churchill, Lady of the Bedchamber to Anne Hyde, mistress of James II.

John Churchill b. 1650, d. 1722, close friend and Gentleman of the Bedchamber to James (both as Duke of York and as king), m. Sarah Jennings in 1678, was instrumental in the success of William III and the Glorious Revolution, gained particular favour under Queen Anne, who made him Duke of Marlborough. Sarah and John Churchill amassed enormous power and wealth and were the founders of a great dynasty.

Sarah Churchill née Jennings, b. 1660, d. 1744, maid of honour to Maria when she arrived in 1673, m. John Churchill 1678, a close confidante of Princess Anne under whom she gained great favour, wealth and power.

Edward Coleman b. 1636, d. 1678, Catholic secretary to Maria, he had close ties to the French court which ultimately led to his downfall when he was falsely accused of conspiring against Charles II in the Popish Plot. Executed as a traitor in 1678, in 1929 he was beatified by Pope Pius XI.

Margaret Dawson dates unknown, Lady of the Bedchamber first to Anne Hyde and then to Maria, she was one of those asked to give testimony as to the birth of Prince James Francis in 1688. For the rest of her life she was asked to continue to testify as to what she saw, sometimes officially, sometimes unofficially; in her old age the young poet Alexander Pope visited her to ask about what she saw that day.

John Evelyn b. 1620, d. 1706, writer, courtier, founding member of the Royal Society; the meticulous diaries he kept throughout his life are some of the most significant contemporary accounts of late seventeenth-century London.

Mary Evelyn b. 1665, d. 1685, daughter of John Evelyn, writer and intellectual, she was highly educated and her work

Mundus Muliebris: or, The Ladies Dressing Room Unlock'd (published posthumously in 1690) is a brilliant satirical study of the seventeenth-century marriage market. Among her papers were several poems by Anne Wharton and Anne Killigrew, as well as others by unnamed authors.

Anne Finch née Kingsmill, b. 1661, d. 1720, daughter of the amateur poet Sir William Kingsmill, maid of honour and close friend to Maria from the early 1680s, m. Heneage Finch in 1684. Finch is now considered one of the most significant poets of the later seventeenth and early eighteenth centuries. After the revolution she and Heneage lived in exile in the country where she established a 'circle of friendship'.

Heneage Finch b. 1657, d. 1726, Groom of the Bedchamber to James II, m. Anne Finch in 1684, after the revolution he was caught trying to escape to France; he lived the rest of his life in exile in the country. He acted as scribe and editor for Anne's writing and after her death continued to edit and publish her work, keeping her legacy alive.

Isabella Fitzroy née Bennet, b. 1668, d. 1723, daughter of Henry Bennet and Elisabeth of Nassau. Through her mother she was a distant relative of William of Orange; she was a friend of Anne Killigrew who wrote poetry to her using the pastoral name Alinda; m. Henry Fitzroy (illegitimate son of Charles II and Barbara Villiers); after his death in 1690 she married Sir Thomas Hanmer (Speaker of the House of Commons). She was one of the Hampton Court Beauties painted for Mary II and was one of those who carried the train at Queen Anne's coronation.

Nell Gwyn b. 1650, d. 1687, actress and mistress of Charles II; some of his last words were famously about her: 'don't let dear Nellie starve'. James gave her an annual pension of £1,500 (equivalent to around £170,000 today). She died of apoplexy most probably brought on by syphilis, after suffering a stroke which left her paralysed on one side. She had two sons by Charles II, James and Charles. James died as a child, but the descendants of Charles's family are the current Dukes of St Albans.

Louise de Kéroualle Duchess of Portsmouth, b. 1649, d. 1734, Lady of the Bedchamber to Charles II's sister, Minette. When Minette died Charles appointed her Lady of the Bedchamber to Queen Caterina; she became Charles's mistress soon after. She left for France after his death in 1685, though she was present at the coronation of George I.

Anne Killigrew b. 1660, d. 1685, part of the Cornish Killigrew piratical family who became courtiers under James I, daughter of Henry (James II's almoner), niece to the writer Thomas Killigrew. She became maid of honour to Maria in the 1680s, and was a gifted writer and painter.

Charlotte Lee née Fitzroy Countess of Lichfield, b. 1664, d. 1718, daughter of Barbara Villiers and Charles II, m. Edward Lee in 1677. Charlotte was one of those asked to give testimony about the birth of James Francis Stuart in 1688. She unequivocally stated that while she had not been present at the birth, she had been constantly with Maria, had seen her without her clothes, had seen milk run from her breasts and had felt the child in her belly. She testified that she was certain that the pregnancy was real.

Hortense Mancini Duchess of Mazarin, b. 1646, d. 1699, *salonnière*, one of the *Mazarinettes*, niece of Cardinal Mazarin, cousin of Duchess Laura, m. Armand Charles de La Porte de La Meilleraye in 1661; after fleeing from her tyrannical husband she lived at the court in London from 1675; she remained in London during the reign of William and Mary though in reduced circumstances. She committed suicide in 1699.

Henry Mordaunt Earl of Peterborough, b. 1621, d. 1697, Governor of Tangier for six disastrous months in 1662; Groom of the Stole and Gentleman of the Bedchamber to

James, he was made Ambassador Extraordinary in 1673 to negotiate James's second marriage.

Penelope Mordaunt née O'Brien, Countess of Peterborough, b. 1622, d. 1702, m. Henry Mordaunt in 1644; she was made Lady of the Bedchamber to Maria in 1673 and First Lady of the Bedchamber in 1685, a role she held until the 1688 revolution.

Barbara Palmer née Villiers, Lady Castlemaine, Duchess of Cleveland, b. 1640, d. 1709, mistress of Charles II, with whom she had five children; Lady of the Bedchamber to Queen Caterina; mistress of John Churchill, with whom she allegedly had a daughter, Barbara, though he never recognised the child and Charles gave her the name Fitzroy. When her husband died in 1705 she married a fortune-hunter named Robert Fielding, who she then discovered was a bigamist. She died of dropsy a few years later.

Father Edward Petrè b. 1631, d. 1699, English Jesuit, chaplain and close adviser to James II, member of the Privy Council; he was much hated and became the target of scurrilous rumours surrounding the birth of the prince in 1688. He initially went into exile with James in 1688 before becoming the head of the College at Saint-Omer where he had studied in his youth.

James Scott Duke of Monmouth, b. 1649, d. 1685, eldest illegitimate child of Charles II; his mother was Lucy Walter. Rumours which circulated throughout his life that his parents had secretly been married led to his becoming a figurehead in opposition to his uncle, James; m. Anna Scott in 1663; he was involved in several plots against his uncle, and his father, too, and was executed for treason in 1685.

Anna Scott Duchess of Monmouth, b. 1651, d. 1732, daughter of the Earl of Buccleuch; when her two elder sisters died she became the sole heiress of a large fortune as well as the heir to her father's titles (unusual for a woman). She was an amateur painter; m. James Scott, Duke of Monmouth, in 1663;

the couple were close friends of Maria, and Anna remained a much-loved part of the York household after Monmouth's execution. She stayed in England after the revolution and married Charles Cornwallis in 1688.

Catherine Sedley b. 1657, d. 1717, the only legitimate child of Charles Sedley (a notorious court wit and poet); her mother was Lady Catherine Savage, who was sent away to a psychiatric institution in Ghent when Sedley was in her early teens. For a time, Catherine was banished from her father's house when he brought home a 'common-law wife', a woman named Anne Ayscough. She became a maid of honour to Maria, and long-term mistress to James II. She did not find a welcome at the court of William and Mary, but she remained on the periphery of court life.

Frances Talbot née Jennings, b. 1649, d. 1731, known as 'la belle Jennings', sister of Sarah Churchill, married first to George Hamilton, and then to Richard Talbot, Earl of Tyrconnell, went into exile with the Jacobite court in 1688 and was a Lady of the Bedchamber to Maria at Saint-Germain-en-Laye.

Henrietta Wentworth b. 1660, d. 1686, daughter of Thomas Wentworth and Philadelphia Carey, she became the mistress and de facto wife of James, Duke of Monmouth. She died a few months after his execution, reportedly of a broken heart.

Writers, Artists, Actors

Mary Beale née Cradock, b. 1633, d. 1699, one of England's first professional female artists, she was the primary breadwinner of her family from the 1670s and ran a studio from her house in Pall Mall. Her husband, Charles Beale, acted as her agent, accountant and studio manager. She was a friend of the court artist Sir Peter Lely, who acted as her mentor. She was also a writer and penned the manual *Observations* in 1663 and the polemical essay *Discourse on Friendship* in 1666.

Aphra Behn b. 1640, d. 1689. Little is certain of her roots, but Behn was employed initially as a spy for Charles II, who sent her to Antwerp. She was one of the first women to make a living as a professional writer and is primarily known as a playwright, though she also wrote poetry and prose. She was a close friend of several who appear in this book, for example Thomas Killigrew and John Wilmot. She wrote under the pastoral name Astrea, which had also been her code name as a spy.

Joan Carlile b. 1606 d. 1679, England's first professional female artist, m. Lodowick Carlile (Gentleman of the Bows and Keeper of Richmond Park to Charles I) in 1626. We do not know how she learned to paint but her earliest works show she had access to the Royal Collection. She was a friend of Van Dyck, who became her mentor. Charles I was much pleased with her work: he gave her and Van Dyck a joint gift of the coveted pigment ultramarine, worth an enormous £500 at the time (some £60,000 in today's money).

Delarivier Manley d. 1724, writer of plays and satires including *The Secret History of Queen Zarah and the Zarahians* (1705), which was based on Sarah Churchill. Her book *New Atalantis* (1709) was so scandalous that she was arrested for libel; she later collaborated with Jonathan Swift on pro-Tory pamphlets and worked as an editor on his newspaper, the *Examiner*. Manley claimed that she was to have become maid of honour to Maria in 1688 but was prevented by the Glorious Revolution.

Anne Wharton née Lee, b. 1659, d. 1685, niece of John Wilmot, Earl of Rochester, friend and correspondent of Aphra Behn, she grew up with Princesses Mary and Anne in the royal nursery before marrying Thomas Wharton in 1673. She wrote poetry and at least one play, called *Love's Martyr; or, Witt above Crowns*. She wrote under the pastoral name Urania.

Children of Maria and James

Princess Catherine Laura b. January 1675, d. October 1675.
Princess Isabella b. August 1676, d. March 1681.
Prince Charles, Duke of Cambridge b. November 1677, d. December 1677.
Princess Charlotte b. August 1682, d. October 1682.
Prince James Francis Edward b. June 1688, d. January 1766, the longed-for son whose birth sparked the Glorious Revolution. Later styled James III and also the Old Pretender, he led several failed campaigns to regain his crown, m. Maria Clementina Sobieska of Poland in 1717, father to Charles Edward Stuart (also known as Bonnie Prince Charlie or the Young Pretender).
Princess Louise Marie b. June 1692, d. August 1712, known as 'La Consolatrice'.

ACKNOWLEDGEMENTS

While this book has benefitted immeasurably from the guidance and advice of so many, any errors which remain are my own.

The book grew out of a review of the exhibition *Bright Souls*, at the Lyon & Turnbull Gallery in London. So it feels fitting to start by thanking its curators, Bendor Grosvenor and Rohan McCulloch, firstly for creating such an inspiring exhibition, but subsequently for their generosity with conversations, advice and expertise during the years I spent researching and writing *The Graces*.

I was fortunate to study in the School of English and Drama at Queen Mary, University of London: an extraordinary intellectual community, and especially so for scholarship on early modern literature and culture. Among the academics past and present, I owe a particular debt of gratitude to Warren Boucher, Jerry Brotton, Claire Preston and Kirsty Rolfe; while the solidarity and friendship of Abbie, Cathie, Danny, Denise, Di, Joel, Julie, Katie, Katy, Lauren and Sophie made it easier to confront the vicissitudes of doctoral research. I am particularly grateful to Jade, for reading drafts, listening to me whinge and bringing endless good cheer.

This book has also benefitted from the insights and practical assistance (everything from reading drafts to talking through ideas to visiting archives I couldn't get to) of Elizabeth Ashby, Federica Collorafi, Ophelia Field, Elena Fumagalli, Scarlett Hirst, Katherine Hunt, Hester Lees-Jeffries, Giacomo Mariani, Josh Owens, John-Mark 'Latin Master' Philo, Keiron Pim, Linda Porter, Loris Rabiti, Irene Romano, Gaby

Schwartz, Steven Veerapen, and particularly Annalisa Nicholson, who so generously shared her groundbreaking research on Hortense Mancini.

I was able to access manuscript materials at the Archivio di Stato di Modena, the Archivio Storico Diocesano di Modena-Nonantola, the Archives Nationales de France, the Heinz Gallery at the National Portrait Gallery, the Northamptonshire Records Office, the Bodleian Library and the British Library (a particular thank you to Carlos in Manuscripts for bringing levity and gravitas in equal measure to my many visits). Thank you to the Paul Mellon Centre for British Art for awarding me a Research Support Grant that enabled me to undertake the early research for the project.

While writing, whenever I encountered a problem or drew a blank (which was often) I would take myself, with pen and paper, to Kofra on Upper St Giles in Norwich. The smiles and chats, as well as the best coffee I've ever tasted, always managed to get me back on track. I would like to thank Jose and Mariana, and the Kofra baristas: Bonnie, Cara, Charlie, Diego, Hannah, Kate, Matt, Nadia, Richard and Stella.

Thank you to everyone at Bloomsbury who supported and loved this book from the beginning, particularly Carmen, for designing such a beautiful cover, Elisabeth, Gurdip, Helen, Jasmine and Thea; Catherine, my proofreader; David, for the index; Phil, for his care with the plate section; and Richard, my brilliant copyeditor. Thank you too to Cora, Margaret, Patrick and everyone at PEW Literary Agency.

My mum, Stephanie, instilled in me a deep love of history and reading virtually from the womb; my father, Patrick, always encouraged my ambitions; while my sister, Fern, was (I believe) the first person to buy this book on pre-order. I am grateful to them all.

It is a great sorrow to me that my mother-in-law, Rosalind Delmar, passed away before this book was published, as our shared interest in the women intellectuals of the late seventeenth century was a source of great pleasure to us both. I hope she would think that the book 'reads well'.

To David, thank you for the conversations, wisdom, counsel, patience, relentless optimism - making everything and anything feel possible and exciting. This book would not have been written without your encouragement and support.

Perhaps most of all, my thanks go to Rebecca Sandell, my forever agent and dear friend, without whom this book would never have existed, and without whose support, dedication and – frankly – courage over the last three years, it would have been a shadow of what it became.

And finally, thank you to Maria Beatrice d'Este and to all the Graces.

SELECT BIBLIOGRAPHY

Carol Barash, *English Women's Poetry, 1649-1714: Politics, Community, and Linguistic Authority*, Oxford University Press, Oxford, 1999.
Ben Bathurst, *Letters of Two Queens*, R. Holden & Co, London, 1925.
Elena Bianchini Braglia, *O Regina O Santa: L'unica Italiana sul trono d'Inghilterra*, I Fari, Modena, 2005.
Eleonore Boswell, *The Restoration Court Stage*, Harvard University Press, Cambridge, Mass., 1932.
John Callow, *The Making of King James II: The Formative Years of a Fallen King*, Sutton, Stroud, 2000.
Sarah Churchill, *Letters of Sarah, Duchess of Marlborough*, John Murray, London, 1875.
---- *Memoirs*, ed. W. King, Routledge, London, 1930.
Luciano Chiappini, *Gli Estensi a Ferrara e Modena*, Editalia, Rome, 1994.
Patrick Dillon, *The Last Revolution: 1688 and the Creation of the Modern World*, Jonathan Cape, London, 2006.
Memoirs of Mary, queen of England, (1689-1693) together with her letters and those of kings James II and William III to the electress, Sophia of Hanover, R. Doebner (ed.), Verlag Von Weit & Co, Leipzig, 1885.
Ophelia Field, *The Favourite*, Weidenfeld & Nicholson, London, 2002.
Antonia Fraser, *The Weaker Vessel: Woman's Lot in Seventeenth Century England*, Weidenfeld & Nicholson, London, 1984.
Elizabeth C. Goldsmith, *The Kings' Mistresses: The Liberated Lives of Marie Mancini, Princess Colonna, and Her Sister Hortense, Duchess Mazarin*, Public Affairs, New York, 2012.
Edward Gregg, *Queen Anne*, Yale University Press, London, 1980.
Bendor Grosvenor, *Bright Souls: The Forgotten Story of Britain's First Female Artists*, Lyon & Turnbull, London, 2019, Exhibition Catalogue, 24th June – 6th July 2019.

Martin Haile, *Queen Mary of Modena: Her Life and Letters*, J.M. Dent & Co, London, 1905.

Frances Harris, *A Passion For Government: The Life of Sarah Duchess of Marlborough*, Oxford University Press, Oxford, 1991.

Tim Harris, *London Crowds in the Reign of Charles II: Propaganda and Politics from the Restoration Until the Exclusion Crisis*, Cambridge University Press, Cambridge, 1987.

Christopher Hibbert, *The Marlboroughs: John and Sarah Churchill, 1650-1714*, Viking, London, 2001.

Lisa Hilton, *The Scandal of the Century*, Penguin Books, London, 2024.

Mary Hopkirk, *Queen Over the Water*, John Murray, London, 1953.

Penelope Hunting, *My Dearest Heart: The Artist Mary Beale*, Unicorn, London, 2019.

Claire Jackson, *Devil Land: England Under Siege, 1588-1688*, Penguin Books, London, 2022.

Anna Keay, *The Last Royal Rebel*, Bloomsbury, London, 2016.

Mark Kishlansky, *A Monarchy Transformed: Britain 1603-1714*, Penguin Books, London, 1996.

John Miller, *Popery and Politics in England 1660–1688*, Cambridge University Press, Cambridge, 1973.

---- *James II*, Yale University Press, London, 2008.

Annalisa Nicholson, *The Mazarin Salon: French Exiles in Seventeenth- Century London*, PhD Thesis at the University of Cambridge, 2021.

---- *Hortense Mancini Letters: A Bilingual Edition*, Iter Press, New York, 2025.

Carola Oman, *Mary of Modena*, Hodder & Stoughton, London, 1962.

Steven Pincus, *1688: The First Modern Revolution*, Yale University Press, London, 2009.

Linda Porter, *Mistresses: Sex and Scandal at the Court of Charles II*, Picador, London, 2020.

Kevin Sharpe, *Rebranding Rule: The Restoration and Revolution of Monarchy: 1660–1714*, Yale University Press, London, 2013.

Simon Thurley, *Palaces of Revolution*, William Collins, London, 2021.

Janet Todd, *The Secret Life of Aphra Behn*, Pandora, London, 2000.

Jenny Uglow, *A Gambling Man: Charles II and the Restoration*, Faber and Faber, London, 2009.

Andrew R. Walkling, *Masque and Opera in England, 1656-1688*, Taylor and Francis, London, 2016.

James Winn, *Queen Anne: Patroness of Arts*, Oxford University Press, Oxford, 2014.

John Harold Wilson, *Court Satires of the Restoration*, Ohio State University Press, Columbus, 1976.

Barbara and Henri Zan der Zee, *1688: Revolution in the Family*, Penguin, London, 1988.

IMAGE CREDITS

PAGE 1

Anne Killigrew, *Venus Attired by the Graces*, c.1685 (© Falmouth Art Gallery)

PAGES 2–3

Willem Van de Velde the Elder, *Mary of Modena landing at Dover* (Fitzwilliam Museum University of Cambridge, UK © Fitzwilliam Museum Bridgeman Images)

PAGE 4

Peter Lely, *Princess Mary*, c.1672 (Danvis Collection / Alamy Stock Photo)

French School, *Queen Anne when a Princess*, c.1670 (Royal Collection Trust / © His Majesty King Charles III, 2025/ Bridgeman Images)

PAGE 5

Simon Verelst, *Mary of Modena*, c.1675 (Jimlop collection / Alamy Stock Photo)

PAGE 6

Henri Gascar, *James, Duke of York*, c.1673 (Niday Picture Library / Alamy Stock Photo)

Godfrey Kneller, *Catherine Sedley*, c. 1684 (World History Archive / Alamy Stock Photo)

PAGE 7

Unknown Artist, Sarah Jennings (later Churchill), c. 1678 (courtesy of Brave Fine Art)

Unknown Artist, John Churchill, 1st Duke of Marlborough (The History Collection / Alamy Stock Photo)

PAGE 8

Benedetto Gennari, *Hortense Mancini*, c.1685 (painting and photography copyright are owned by The Ramsbury Manor Foundation. Photograph © A J Photographics of the Ramsbury Manor Foundation)

PAGE 9

Simon Verelst, *Mary of Modena*, c.1680 (Yale Center for British Art, Paul Mellon Fund)

Peter Lely, *Princess Isabella, c.1677* (courtesy of Lawrence Steigrad Fine Arts)

PAGE 10

Popish Plot playing cards (Private Collection: Look and Learn / Peter Jackson Collection/Bridgeman Images)

PAGE 11

Jacob Huysmans, *James Duke of Monmouth, as St John the Baptist*, c.1662–5 (Bowhill House, Scottish Borders: The Buccleuch Collections/Bridgeman Images)

Medal commemorating the death of the Duke of Monmouth, 1685 (© The Trustees of the British Museum)

PAGE 12

Peter Lely, *Anne Killigrew*, 1670s (Album / Alamy Stock Photo)

Peter Lely, *Aphra Behn*, (Yale Center for British Art, Paul Mellon Fund)

Peter Cross, *Anne Finch*, (Zoom Historical / Alamy Stock Photo)

PAGE 13

Anne Killigrew, *Self-Portrait as Venus*, c.1682-5 (courtesy of Bendor and Isabel Grosvenor)

PAGE 14

Anne Killigrew, *James II*, 1685 (© Royal Collection Enterprises Limited 2025 | Royal Collection Trust)

William Wissing, *Mary of Modena,* c.1685, (Yale Center for British Art, Paul Mellon Fund)

PAGE 15

Unknown Artist, *Cartoon on Mary of Modena and Father Petre*, c.1689 (BTEU/RKMLGE / Alamy Stock Photo)

John Smith, *Mezzotint of James Francis Stuart after a portrait by Godfrey Kneller*, c.1689 (Sepia Times / Contributor / Getty)

PAGE 16

Pierre Mignard, *James II and Family*, c.1694 (Royal Collection Trust / © His Majesty King Charles III, 2025/Bridgeman Images)

ABBREVIATIONS

ASMo	Archivio di Stato Modena, ASE, Cancelleria, Carteggi con principi esteri – Inghilterra, b. 1609/2
CSP Ven	Calendar of State Papers, Venetian, ed. Allen B. Hinds (London, 1947)
CTB	Calendar of Treasury Books, ed. William A. Shaw (London, 1911)
BL	British Library, London
BLO	Bodleian Library, Oxford
PL	Portland Literary Collection, University of Nottingham
RCT	Royal Collection Trust
SP	State Papers, The National Archives, London

NOTES

PROLOGUE

1 Bendor Grosvenor, *Bright Souls: The Forgotten Story of Britain's First Female Artists*, Lyon and Turnbull, London, 2019, Exhibition Catalogue, 24th June – 6th July 2019.

1 PRINCESS OF MODENA

1 Martin Haile, *Queen Mary of Modena: Her Life and Letters*, J. M. Dent & Co., London, 1905, p. 21.
2 Ibid.
3 Ibid.
4 Ibid.
5 Carola Oman, *Mary of Modena*, Hodder & Stoughton, London, 1962, p. 15.
6 Gilbert Burnet, *Bishop Burnet's History of his Own Time*, vol. 1, A. Rhames, London, 1753, p. 493.
7 Ibid., p. 235.
8 Robert Halstead, *Succinct genealogies of the noble and ancient houses of Alno or de Alneto, Broc of Stephale, Latimer of Duntish, Drayton of Drayton, Mauduit of Westminster, Green of Drayton, Vere of Addington, Fitz-Lewes of Westhornedon, Howard of Effingham and Mordaunt of Turvey justified by publick records, ancient and extant charters, histories and other authentick proofs, and enriched with divers sculptures of tombs, images, seals, and other curiosities*, London, 1685, p. 418.
9 Ibid., p. 423.
10 Ibid.
11 Haile, *Queen Mary of Modena: Her Life and Letters*, p. 15.
12 Ibid.
13 Mary Hopkirk, *Queen Over the Water*, John Murray, London, 1953, p. 11.

14 Ibid., p. 10.
15 Ibid., p. 12.
16 Haile, *Queen Mary of Modena*, p. 14.
17 Halstead, *Succinct genealogies*, p. 426.
18 Ibid., p. 427.
19 Ibid.
20 Ibid.
21 Ibid.
22 Ibid.
23 Ibid.
24 Ibid., p. 428.
25 Ibid.
26 Ibid., p. 429.
27 Rachel Wriothesley, Lady Russell, *Letters of Rachel Lady Russell*, vol. 1, Parry & Macmillan, Philadelphia, 1854, p. 22.
28 Ibid.

2 CROSSING THE WATER

1 Haile, *Queen Mary of Modena*, p. 38.
2 'T. Derham to J. Williamson, 5 November 1673', in *Letters Addressed from London to Sir Joseph Williamson While Plenipotentiary at the Congress of Cologne in the Years 1673 and 1674*, vol. II, Camden Society, London, 1874, p. 63.
3 Haile, *Queen Mary of Modena*, p. 33.
4 Ibid., p. 34.
5 Ibid.
6 Halstead, *Succinct genealogies*, p. 431.
7 RCT, *Family note book of James, Duke of York (later James II) giving details of his children born between 1662 and 1677*, c. 1677–8.
8 Oman, *Mary of Modena*, p. 35.
9 For further reading see Simon Thurley, *Palaces of Revolution*, HarperCollins, London, 2022.
10 Hopkirk, *Queen Over the Water*, p. 23; Agnes Strickland, *The Lives of the Queens of England*, vol. 9, Henry Colburn, London, 1846, p. 208.
11 Haile, *Queen Mary of Modena*, p. 42.
12 CSP Ven, 1673–1675, vol. 38, n. 256.
13 BL Stowe MS 203, fol. 209.
14 Haile, *Queen Mary of Modena*, p. 44.
15 SP 29/360, fol. 291.
16 ASMo, 23 August 1674, fasc. 1, n. 11.

3 DUCHESS OF YORK

1 Haile, *Queen Mary of Modena*, p. 54.

2 BLO MS Rawl., A.269 fol. 7a.

3 5 January 1674, *The Diary of John Evelyn*, ed. William Bray, M. W. Dunne, London, 1901, vol. 2, p. 95.

4 16 March 1673, ibid., p. 87.

5 21 August 1674, ibid., p. 97.

6 Anon., 'Advice to a Painter to Draw the Duke By', l. 41; l. 54, in *Poems on Affairs of State Augustan Satirical Verse, 1660–1714*, vol. 1, ed. George DeForest, Yale University Press, New Haven, Conn., and London, 1963, pp. 216–17.

7 Anon, 'Signor Dildo', in John Harold Wilson, *Courtly Satires of the Restoration*, Ohio State University Press, Columbus, 1976, ll. 1–8, p. 15.

8 Edmund Waller, 'To the Duchess', in *The Poetical Works of Edmund Waller*, ed. Robert Bell, John W. Parker, London, 1854, p. 197.

9 Ibid., 'These Verses were writ in the Tasso of her Royal Highness', p. 198.

10 Dryden was the first poet to officially hold the title of poet laureate, though the role was notionally created when Ben Jonson was given a pension as court poet by Charles I. Dryden continued in the role until 1689, when he was forced to resign by William III. Thomas Shadwell replaced him.

11 *Paradise Lost* was first published in 1667, but it had been reissued in 1674 with some revisions.

12 John Milton, *Paradise Lost*, ed. Alastair Fowler, Longman, London, 1997, I:63, p. 64.

13 4 December 1676, *The Diary of John Evelyn*, vol. 2, p. 113.

14 Kevin Sharpe, *Rebranding Rule: The Restoration and Revolution of Monarchy: 1660–1714*, Yale University Press, London, 2013, p. 119.

15 Thomas Betterton, *The history of the English stage, from the restauration to the present time. Including the lives, characters and amours, of the most eminent actors and actresses. With instructions for public speaking*, E. Currl, London, 1741, p. 17.

4 A STEPMOTHER TO PRINCESSES

1 Margaret Cavendish, *Sociable Letters*, ed. James Fitzmaurice, Routledge, London, 2012, Letter 26, pp. 36–7.

2 20 June 1668, Samuel Pepys, *The Diary of Samuel Pepys*, vol. 9, ed. Robert Latham and William Matthews, HarperCollins, London, 1995, p. 247.

3 Henry Bennet was no friend to James, or indeed to Maria. When, in 1673, he learned of the marriage and that Maria was on her way, he advised the king that it would be better for her to go straight back to Italy, and not to set foot on English soil. And only a few years later he would support the bill that sought to exclude James from the line of succession.

4 For more information see Ophelia Field, *The Favourite*, Weidenfeld & Nicolson, London, 2002.

5 Hopkirk, *Queen Over the Water*, p. 31.

6 Princess Anne gave her a large pension in thanks once she became queen.

7 John Crowne, *Dramatists of the Restoration: The Dramatic Works of John Crowne*, vol. 1, H. Sotheran & Co., London, 1873, p. 236.

8 This may be the same panel which, now lost, was valued in the Commonwealth Sale inventory at £420. It is labelled as '1 tapestry, Diana and Callisto, a piece of naked women, 6.86 high'.

9 Crowne, p. 237.

10 Eleanore Boswell, *The Restoration Court Stage*, Harvard University Press, Cambridge, MA, 1932, p. 205.

11 Ibid., p. 204.

5 *THE MASQUE OF CALISTO*

1 *The Dramatic Works of John Crowne*, p. 242.

2 'Lady Chaworth to Lord Roos, 23 November 1676', in *The Manuscripts of His Grace the Duke of Rutland Preserved at Belvoir Castle: Letters and Papers, 1440–1797*, ed. Sir H. C. Maxwell Lyte, vol. 3, p. 32.

3 Crowne, p. 265.

4 Ibid., p. 275.

5 Though we can see many parallels, it is also important not to take them too seriously; they were playful jokes aimed at an openly licentious court. Maria and Crowne may well have been exposing things they disapproved of, but they weren't out to get into trouble.

6 Richard Bulstrode, 'Thursday 19th August, 1675', in *The Collection of Autograph Letters and Historical Documents formed by Alfred Morrison: The Bulstrode Papers*, vol. 1, Printed for Private Circulation, 1897, n. 284, p. 311.

7 Hopkirk, *Queen Over the Water*, p. 31.

8 Oman, *Mary of Modena*, p. 48.

9 ASMo, Maria to Francesco, 1 March 1675, n. 13.

10 Ibid., 6 June 1675, n. 15.

11 Ibid., 15 August 1675, n. 17.

12 Ibid., 30 October 1675, n. 22.

13 Ibid., 17 December 1675, n. 31.
14 Ibid., 18 December 1675, n. 30.

6 THE DUCHESS OF MAZARIN

1 Hortense Mancini and Maria Mancini, *Memoirs*, ed. and trans. Sarah Nelson, University of Chicago Press, Chicago, 2008, p. 68.
2 Ibid.
3 His father, César, had been the illegitimate child of Henri and his mistress Gabrielle d'Estrées, whom Henri had relied on as an adviser and confidante. The Mercœur title came from his mother, Françoise of Lorraine.
4 These rituals were at this time less convoluted than they would become as Louis XIV grew older.
5 Elizabeth C. Goldsmith, *The Kings' Mistresses: The Liberated Lives of Marie Mancini, Princess Colonna, and Her Sister Hortense, Duchess Mazarin*, Public Affairs, New York, 2012, p. 27.
6 Molière had been introduced to the king by Armand de Conti, with whom he had been a student at Le Collège de Clermont.
7 Denis Bingham, *The Marriages of the Bourbons*, Chapman & Hall, London, 1890, vol. I, p. 463.
8 Marie-Catherine de Villedieu, 'À Madame la Duchesse Mazarin', *Recueil de poésies de Mademoiselle Desjardins*, Claude Barbin, Paris, 1662.
9 Hortense Mancini and Maria Mancini, *Memoirs*, p. 41.
10 Ibid., p. 43.
11 A peruke was a kind of man's wig which was very popular at this time. It was made of long curls which were often fastened at the back of the neck.
12 Elizabeth C. Goldsmith, *Publishing Women's Life Stories in France, 1647–1720: From voice to print*, Ashgate, Aldershot, 2001, p. 107.
13 Julia Marciari Alexander and Catharine MacLeod (eds), *Politics, Transgression, and Representation at the Court of Charles II*, Yale University Press, New Haven, Conn., and London, 2007, p. 169.
14 SP Dom, 1660–1685, 29/376, fol. 34.
15 Hortense Mancini, in Hortense Mancini and Marie Mancini, *Mémoires d'Hortense et de Marie Mancini*, ed. Gérard Doscot, Mercure de France, Paris, 1965; 1987, p. 36.
16 *Letters from the Marchioness de Sévigné to Her Daughter the Countess de Grignan*, Longman, London, 1801, vol. 4, p. 48.
17 Haile, *Queen Mary of Modena*, p. 52.
18 Denys Potts, 'The Duchess of Mazarin and Saint Évremond, The Final Journey', in *'The Wandering Life I Led': Essays on Hortense Mancini, Duchess Mazarin and Early Modern Women's Border Crossings*, ed. Susan

Shifrin, Cambridge Scholars Publishing, Newcastle upon Tyne, 2009, p. 164.

19 Bryan Bevan, *Charles II's French Mistress*, Robert Hale, London, 1972, p. 84.

20 ASMo, 5 February 1676, no. 33.

21 Ibid., no. 38.

22 A. Nicholson, 'Introduction', in Hortense Mancini, *Letters: A Bilingual Edition*, ed. and trans. Annalisa Nicholson, Iter Press, New York, 2025.

23 'Rochester's Farewell', in *Poems on Affairs of State*, vol. 1, Printed for Thomas Tebb and Theoph. Sanders, London, 1697–1716, p. 168.

24 Ibid.

7 THE SALON

1 10 December 1660, *The Diary of Samuel Pepys*, vol. 1, p. 315.

2 Goldsmith, *The Kings' Mistresses*, p. 148; Toivo David Rosvall, *The Mazarine Legacy*, Viking Press, New York, 1969, p. 189.

3 Saint-Évremond to the Comte d'Olonne, *Charles de Saint-Évremond, The Letters of Saint Evremond*, ed. John Hayward, Routledge, London, 1930, p. 152.

4 Quentin Hope, *Saint-Evremond and His Friends*, Librairie Droz, Genève, 1999, p. 387.

5 Ibid.

6 Ibid.

8 A TEMPESTUOUS COURTSHIP

1 Frances Harris, *A Passion For Government: The Life of Sarah Duchess of Marlborough*, Oxford University Press, Oxford, 1991, p. 20.

2 Delarivier Manley, *Secret Memoirs and Manners of Several Persons of Quality of Both Sexes From the New Atalantis, an Island in the Mediterranean in Four Volumes, Written Originally in Italian*, London, 1736, vol. 1, p. 186. Sarah Churchill owned a copy of this book in later life; it was catalogued as part of an extensive collection (BL Additional MS 75402).

3 Harris, *A Passion For Government*, p. 14.

4 BL Additional MS 61435, fols 76–99.

5 BL Additional MS 61421, fols 75V–76.

6 BL Additional MS 61474, fol. 5.

7 Ibid., fols 1–4.

8 Ibid., fol. 1.

9 A perspective means a telescope, and it tells us much about the prevalence for such objects at the court that she then writes that was 'such a one as you never saw in your life'.
10 I keep the original spelling of St James's in order to retain a sense of the time. I encountered this spelling many times in documents and letters from the period, and therefore think it important to retain.
11 Anthony Hamilton, *Memoirs of Count Grammont*, trans. Horace Walpole, Grebbie & Co., Philadelphia, 1888, p. 312.
12 Ibid.
13 Thomas Babington Macaulay, *The History of England from the Accession of James II*, vol. 1, Harper and Brothers, New York, 1852, p. 347.
14 Hugh Montgomery Massingberd, *Blenheim Revisited*, Beaufort Books, New York, 1985, p. 24.
15 Field, *The Favourite*, p. 17; Hamilton, *The Duke of Gramont's Memoirs*, p. 407.
16 Bryan Bevan, *Marlborough the Man: A Biography of John Churchill First Duke of Marlborough*, Robert Hale, London, 1975, p. 39.
17 Harris, *A Passion For Government*, p. 17.
18 'Letter 2', in Ben Bathurst, *Letters of Two Queens*, R. Holden & Co., London, 1925, p. 37.
19 Ibid.
20 Ibid.
21 Ibid, 'Letter 3', p. 38.
22 Ibid.; Eleanor Needham had further children by the Duke of Monmouth in the 1680s, so the affair continued. It is not known what her position was at this point, though she does not appear on the list of Maria's household after 1676, so it seems likely that she was dismissed as her maid of honour. Anna Keay, in *The Last Royal Rebel*, Bloomsbury, London, 2016, p. 164, posits that Monmouth installed her in a house in Russell Square, Bloomsbury.
23 Bathurst, *Letters of Two Queens*, p. 35.
24 It is thought she was hiding from debt collectors, but this is not known for certain. She was certainly involved in unpleasant financial disputes after the death of her husband, so it is possible.
25 In letter from 1675, Sarah wrote to her sister Frances, 'I will constrain myself as much as is possible but sometimes she would provoke a saint.' BL Additional MS 61453, fol. 40.
26 These two maids must be a reference to Sarah's fellow maids of honour.
27 Keay, *The Last Royal Rebel*, pp. 161–2.
28 Hopkirk, *Queen Over the Water*, p. 33.

29 Bathurst, *Letters of Two Queens*, p. 41.
30 Harris, *A Passion For Government*, p. 16.
31 BL Additional MS 61446, fol. 17. This comes from a letter to her grandson, who wished to marry the niece of Mary Trevor. Sarah's letter is a strong attempt to dissuade him, and she tells him that she has drawn up a new will that would disinherit him, which she is ready to sign if he disobeys her wishes. She writes, 'You may depend upon it that the whole world will blame you.' He responds saying that he doesn't want her money, and he will marry the woman he chooses, which he did. Further documents in the manuscript show that she did all she could to cut him out of the entail.
32 Sarah Churchill, *Letters of Sarah, Duchess of Marlborough*, John Murray, London, 1875, p. 152.
33 'John Churchill to Sarah Jennings' (undated), BL Additional MS 61427, fol. 1; fol. 5.
34 Ibid., fol. 11.
35 Ibid., fol. 4; fol. 10.
36 Field, *The Favourite*, p. 23.
37 Courtin to Louvois, 27 November 1676, in Forneron, *Louise de Kéroualle*, E. Plon Nourrit, Paris, 1886, p. 131. The ball was hosted by Maria and took place in her rooms on 7 December 1676. Or perhaps on the 4th, as Evelyn's diary noted. 'I saw the great ball danced by all the gallants and ladies at the Duchess of York's' (4 December 1676, *The Diary of John Evelyn*, vol. 2, p. 113).
38 Samuel Pepys recorded one instance in his diary, reporting how Sedley, on the balcony of an Oxford tavern, 'showed his nakedness – and abusing of scripture and as it were from thence preaching a mountebank sermon from the pulpit, saying that there he had to sell such a pouder as should make all the cunts in town run after him, 1000 people standing underneath to see and hear him, and that being done he took a glass of wine and washed his prick in it and then drank it off, and then took another and drank the Kings health. The crowd which had gathered around the tavern rioted in horror at the scene, and Sedley found himself in the courts, where the Lord Chief Justice scorned him, saying that it was because of men like him '"that God's anger and judgement hang over us"', 1 July 1663, Samuel Pepys, *The Diary of Samuel Pepys*, vol. 4, p. 209.
39 13 June 1673, *The Diary of John Evelyn*, vol. 2, p. 89.
40 Forneron, *Louise de Kéroualle*, p. 131.
41 Ibid.

42 Ibid.
43 Ibid.
44 BL Additional MS 61427, fol. 12.
45 Harris, *A Passion For Government*, p. 17.
46 Ibid.
47 BL Additional MS 61427, fol. 21.
48 Ibid., fol. 25.
49 Ibid.
50 Ibid., fol. 35.
51 Ibid.
52 Ibid., fol. 36.
53 Ibid.
54 Ibid.
55 Ibid.
56 Ibid., fol. 38.
57 Ibid., fol. 45.
58 Ibid., fol. 33.
59 Ibid., fol. 10.
60 Ibid., fol. 57.
61 Ibid., fol. 62; fol. 19.
62 Ibid., fol. 8; fol. 55.
63 17 June 1683, *The Diary of John Evelyn*, vol. 2, p. 178.
64 John and Lady Castlemaine were finished with at this point so there seems little reason to assume that she would have helped him.
65 BL Additional MS 18958, fol. 3.
66 Ibid., fol. 13.
67 Garnet Wolseley, *The life of John Churchill, Duke of Marlborough, to the accession of Queen Anne*, Richard Bentley & Son, London, 1894, pp. 202–3.
68 CTB, 26 October 1677, vol. 5, *1676–1679*, pp. 754–69.

9 THE PRINCE OF ORANGE

1 Haile, *Queen Mary of Modena*, p. 63.
2 Hopkirk, *Queen Over the Water*, p. 37.
3 Gilbert Burnet, *Bishop Burnet's History of His Own Time*, vol. 2, Clarendon Press, Oxford, 1897, n. 1, p. 129. This unusual phrase is described as Charles's 'usual oath'.
4 John Bancks, *The History of the Life of William III*, Charles Marsh and Thomas Davies, London, 1744, p. 62.
5 Gilbert Burnet, *Bishop Burnet's History of His Own Time*, vol. 1, p. 122.

6 Edward Lake, October 21st, 1677, in *The Diary of Edward Lake*, ed. George Elliot, The Camden Society, London, 1846, p. 5.
7 ASMo, 11 November 1677, n. 76.
8 Lake, *The Diary of Edward Lake*, October 21st, 1677, p. 5.
9 Bryan Bevan, *James, Duke of Monmouth*, Robert Hale, London, 1973, p. 88.
10 Lake, *The Diary of Edward Lake*, November 4th, 1677, p. 6.
11 Ibid., November 7th, 1677
12 Ibid., November 16th, 1677, p. 9.
13 ASMo, 23 December 1677, n. 78.
14 Waller, 'Upon Our Late Loss of the Duke of Cambridge', p. 156.

10 'THE POPISH PLOT'

1 Frances Williams Wynn, *Diaries of a Lady of Quality from 1797 to 1844*, Longman & Co., London, 1864, p. 26.
2 Jane Lane, *Titus Oates*, Andrew Dakers, London, 1949, p. 23.
3 ASMo, 6 October 1678, n. 111.
4 Ibid., 3 November 1678, n. 114.
5 Ibid., 14 January 1681, n. 188.
6 Ibid., 8 December 1678, n. 121.
7 Ibid., 16 December 1678, n. 123.
8 Goldsmith, *The Kings' Mistresses*, p. 157.
9 Ibid.
10 ASMo, 26 January 1679, n. 131.
11 Bryan Bevan, *I Was James II's Queen*, Heinemann, London, 1963, p. 43.
12 ASMo, 15 April 1679, n. 135.
13 BL Additional MS 24901, fol. 5.
14 John Miller, *James II*, Yale University Press, London, 2008, p. 98.
15 Further reading: Tim Harris, *London Crowds in the Reign of Charles II: Propaganda and Politics from the Restoration Until the Exclusion Crisis*, Cambridge University Press, Cambridge, 1987; Tim Harris, *The Final Crisis of the Stuart Monarchy: The Revolutions of 1688–91 in Their British, Atlantic and European Contexts*, Boydell Press, Woodbridge, 2013; John Miller, *Popery and Politics in England 1660–1688*, Cambridge University Press, Cambridge, 1973.
16 Richard Bulstrode, *Memoirs and Reflections Upon the Reign and Government of King Charles*, Charles Rivington, London, 1721, p. 425.
17 Hopkirk, *Queen Over the Water*, pp. 53–4.
18 Wolseley, *The life of John Churchill*, p. 219.
19 Hopkirk, *Queen Over the Water*, p. 54.

20 Strickland, *The Lives of the Queens of England*, p. 92.
21 6 November 1697, *The Diary of John Evelyn*, vol. 2, p. 138.
22 Ibid.
23 For more information see Steven Veerapen, *Witches: A King's Obsession*, Birlinn, Edinburgh, 2025, p. 231, and Maurice Lee, Jr, 'The Buccleuch Marriage Contract: An Unknown Episode in Scottish Politics', in *Albion: A Quarterly Journal Concerned with British Studies*, vol. 25, no. 3 (Autumn, 1993): 395–418.
24 Hopkirk, *Queen Over the Water*, p. 60.
25 ASMo, 8 May 1680, n. 176.
26 Wolseley, *The life of John Churchill*, p. 231.
27 Burnet, *Bishop Burnet's History of His Own Time*, vol. 1, p. 583.
28 Ibid., vol. 1, p. 524.
29 Charlotte was an illegitimate daughter of Charles II and Barbara Villiers. She was married to Edward Lee when she was thirteen and he was fourteen. We know little of Charlotte's life or personality, and little of the marriage, though we must suppose it was reasonably happy since it resulted in some eighteen children. She was a much-loved daughter of Charles: a letter from father to daughter in 1682 says, 'I must tell you I am glad to hear you are with child, and I hope to see you here before it be long, that I may have the satisfaction myself of telling you how much I love you, and how truly I am your kind father, Charles Rex.'
30 ASMo, 28 January 1681, n. 188.
31 Andrew R. Walkling, *Masque and Opera in England, 1656–1688*, Taylor & Francis, London, 2016, p. 127.
32 Since there is no record of the play at the public theatres, it is most reasonable to assume that this performance she 'grace[d] him with' was a court entertainment.
33 BL Additional MS 75402, fol. 6.
34 ASMo, 3 December 1680, n. 184.
35 BL Additional MS 75356, n.p.

11 GOING HOME

1 Henry Duff Traill, *Shaftesbury: The First Earl*, Longmans, Green, London, 1886, p. 182.
2 Ibid.
3 BL, Sloane MS 1008, fol. 305.
4 ASMo, 27 January 1682, n. 190.
5 Ibid., 21 April 1682, n. 192.

12 'THE RYE HOUSE PLOT'

1 John Dryden, 'Prologue to the Duchess on her return from Scotland', in *The Poems of John Dryden*, vol. 2, ed. Paul Hammond, Taylor & Francis, London, 2014, p. 35, ll. 1–6.
2 Ibid., l. 16; p. 36, l. 13.
3 Ibid., p. 36, l. 18.
4 Ibid., p. 37, l. 41.
5 Hopkirk, *Queen Over the Water*, p. 71.
6 Haile, *Queen Mary of Modena*, p. 109.
7 Ibid.
8 Ibid.
9 Hopkirk, *Queen Over the Water*, p. 71.
10 D. P. Hogan and D. I. Kertzer, 'The social bases of declining infant mortality: lessons from a nineteenth-century Italian town', *European Journal of Population: Revue européenne de démographie*, vol. 2, 3–4 (1987): 361–85; Hannah Newton, 'The Dying Child in Seventeenth Century England', *Pediatrics*, vol. 136.2 (2015): 218–20.
11 Hopkirk, *Queen Over the Water*, p. 71.
12 ASMo, 23 June 1683, n. 202.
13 Haile, *Queen Mary of Modena*, p. 111.
14 James Scott, Duke of Monmoth, 'Song', in *The Roxburgh Ballads: Illustrating the Last Years of the Stuarts*, ed. J Woodfall Ebsworth, The Ballad Society, Hertford, 1885, vol. 7, p. 394.
15 ASMo, London, 22 November 1683, n. 204.
16 *Memoirs of Mary, queen of England (1689–1693) together with her letters and those of kings James II and William III to the electress, Sophia of Hanover*, ed. Dr R. Doebner, Verlag Von Weit & Co., Leipzig, 1885, p. 4.
17 Hopkirk, *Queen Over the Water*, p. 51.

13 THE COTERIE

1 Anthony à Wood, *Athenæ Oxonienses: An Exact History of All the Writers and Bishops who Have Had Their Education in the University of Oxford*, ed. Philip Bliss, F. C. & J. Rivington, London, 1820, p. 263.
2 To read more about the development of St James's for the aristocracy see Simon Thurley et al., *St James's Palace: From Leper Hospital to Royal Court*, Yale University Press, New Haven, Conn., and London, 2022.
3 Anne Killigrew, 'Upon the saying that my Verses were made by another', in *'My Rare Wit Killing Sin': Poems of a Restoration Courtier*, ed. Margaret Ezell, Iter Press, Toronto, 2013, pp. 70–2, p. 71, ll. 31–4.

4 A coterie was a select group of people, which varied in size, who would circulate work between them. In the case of Maria's coterie, the evidence I have found suggests a small group: Anne Killigrew, Mary Evelyn, Isabella Bennet, Anne Kingsmill, and possibly Anne Wharton and a woman called Anne Chamberlayne (daughter of the chronicler). There are also several poems in Mary Evelyn's archive at the British Library which are anonymous, suggesting potential others who we cannot identify.

5 Ibid., ll. 35–8.

6 Ibid., l. 39.

7 Ibid, ll. 41–2.

8 Ibid., l. 54.

9 Ibid., l. 40.

10 Ibid., l. 21.

11 Ibid., ll. 23–4.

12 Ibid., l. 56.

13 Ibid., l. 54; l.60.

14 Ibid., l. 64; l. 65.

15 Ibid., l. 32.

16 Ibid, l. 1, l. 49.

17 Anne Killigrew, 'Alexandreis', in *'My Rare Wit Killing Sin'*, pp. 43–6, p. 43, l. 1; Virgil, *The Aeneid*, trans. John Dryden, Penguin Books, London, 1997, book 1, p. 3, l. 1.

18 Killigrew, 'Alexandreis', ll.13–14.

19 Anne Finch, 'The Preface', in 'Miscellany Poems with Two Plays by Ardelia', *The Cambridge Edition of Works of Anne Finch, Countess of Winchilsea*, eds Jennifer Keith and Claudia Thomas Kairoff, Cambridge University Press, Cambridge, 2019, vol. 1, p. 27.

20 Anne Finch, 'On the Death of the Queen', in 'Miscellany Poems with Two Plays by Ardelia', vol. 2.

21 Killigrew, 'The Discontent', in *'My Rare Wit Killing Sin'*, pp. 75–8, p. 78, ll. 96–8.

22 Georgina Battiscombe, *The Spencers of Althorp*, Constable, London, 1984, p. 51.

23 My thanks to Bendor Grosvenor for alerting me to this.

24 M. Toynbee, 'Some friends of Sir Thomas Browne', *Norfolk Archaeology*, xxxi (1955–7): 377–94, 393.

25 11 May 1661, *The Diary of John Evelyn*, vol. 1, p. 337.

26 27 April 1693, *The Diary of John Evelyn*, vol. 2, p. 320.

27 Horace, *Satires, Epistles and Ars Poetica*, trans. H. Rushton Fairclough, Loeb Classical Library, Cambridge, MA, 1945, p. 361.

14 COURTSHIPS AND SCANDALS

1 Anne Finch, 'A Letter to Dafnis April: 2d: 1685', in 'Miscellany Poems with Two Plays by Ardelia', vol. 1, pp. 21–110, p. 37.
2 PL, Anon, 'The Parallel', Pw V 45.3.
3 John Harold Wilson, *Court Satires of the Restoration*, p. 270.
4 John Holroyd, Earl of Sheffield, 'The Dream', in *The Poetical Works of the Most Noble John Sheffield, Duke of Buckingham With the Life of the Author*, London, 1780, p. 35.
5 Bathurst, *Letters of Two Queens*, Letter 61, p. 154.
6 Edward Gregg, *Queen Anne*, Yale University Press, London, 1980, p. 35.
7 Ibid., p. 38.
8 Ibid., p. 50.
9 It was not unusual for domestic slaves to wear ornate silver or gold collars, often depicting the family crests or names of their owners. It is hard to make out what these collars say, but the collar on the boy at the front of the painting would seem to have some design. For more information on this painting, and particularly the collars, see Annalisa Nicholson, *The Mazarin Salon: French Exiles in Seventeenth-Century London*, PhD Thesis, University of Cambridge, 2021; Susan Shifrin and Andrew R. Walkling, ' "Idylle en Musique": Performative Hybridity and the Duchess Mazarin as Visual, Textual, and Musical Icon', in *'The Wandering Life I Led': Essays on Hortense Mancini, Duchess Mazarin and Early Modern Women's Border Crossings*, ed. Susan Shifrin, pp. 48–101.
10 4 February 1685, *The Diary of John Evelyn*, vol. 2, p. 210.

15 A NEW ERA

1 Hopkirk, *Queen Over the Water*, p. 77.
2 Ibid.
3 Ibid., p. 78.
4 Oman, *Mary of Modena*, p. 80.
5 Ibid.
6 Ibid.
7 Ibid.
8 Ibid.
9 Ibid.
10 Ibid., p. 81.
11 Ibid., p. 82.
12 Ibid., p. 81.
13 Ibid.

14 John Dryden, 'Threnodia Augustalis: A Funeral Pindaric Poem, Sacred To The Happy Memory Of King Charles II', in *The Poems of John Dryden*, vol. 2, ed. Paul Hammond, Taylor & Francis, London, 2014, p. 390, l. 51.
15 Oman, *Mary of Modena*, p. 82.
16 ASMo, 22 February 1685, n. 217.
17 Ibid.
18 Haile, *Queen Mary of Modena*, p. 118.
19 5 March 1685, *The Diary of John Evelyn*, vol. 1, p. 212.
20 Ibid.
21 Ibid.
22 Francis Sandford, *The history of the coronation of James II and of his Royal Consort Queen Mary*, Thomas Newcomb, London, 1687, p. 21.
23 Ibid, p. 28.
24 Ibid.
25 Ibid, p. 21.
26 Ibid.
27 Ibid, p. 22.
28 When Charles III was crowned in 2023, Judith Weir (who held that title) wrote a coronation overture, *Brighter Visions Shine Afar*.
29 Thomas P. Campbell, *Henry VIII and the Art of Majesty*, Yale University Press, London, 2007, p. 286.
30 Sandford, p. 108.
31 BL Additional MS 38175, fol. 121.
32 BL Lansdowne MS 1236, fol. 229. It has been suggested that this letter was written to Maria, but I think it more likely that it was to Caterina, due to the phrase 'for the last King's sake'. Maria is less likely to have been moved by a reference to Charles II than Caterina, since Maria's loyalty must be to her husband as Caterina's was to hers.
33 Thomas Ailsbury, *Memoirs of Thomas, Earl of Ailesbury*, vol. 1, The Roxburgh Club, London, 1890, p. 119.
34 Keay, *The Last Royal Rebel*, p. 371.
35 15 July 1685, *The Diary of John Evelyn*, vol. 1, p. 227.
36 Ibid., p. 228.
37 Ibid.
38 James Welwood, *Memoirs of the most material transactions in England, for the last hundred years, preceding the Revolution in 1688*, Tim Goodwin, London, 1718, p. 148.
39 6 February 1686, *The Diary of John Evelyn*, vol. 2, p. 342.

40 For more information on this scandal and Behn's drama, see Lisa Hilton, *The Scandal of the Century*, Penguin Books, London, 2024.

41 Aphra Behn, *Love-Letters Between a Nobleman and His Sister*, London, printed for D. Brown, J. Tonson, J. Nicholson, B. Tooke and G. Strahan, 1712, p. 504, p. 505.

16 MEMENTO MORI

1 19 January 1686, *The Diary of John Evelyn*, vol. 2, p. 247.

2 24 January 1687, ibid., p. 259.

3 Anne Killigrew, 'To the Queen', in *'My Rare Wit Killing Sin'*, p. 49, ll. 63–8.

4 John Dryden, 'To the Pious Memory Of the Accomplisht Young Lady, Mrs. Anne Killigrew, Excellent in the two Sister-Arts of Poesie and Painting. An Ode', in *The Poems of John Dryden*, p. 101, l. 131.

5 Anne Killigrew, 'An Epitaph on Herself', in *'My Rare Wit Killing Sin'* p. 94, ll. 1–2.

6 John Dryden, 'To the Pious Memory Of the Accomplisht Young Lady, Mrs. Anne Killigrew, Excellent in the two Sister-Arts of Poesie and Painting. An Ode', p. 99, l. 70; E.E., 'On the Death of the Truly Virtuous Mrs Anne Killigrew, who was related to my (Deceased) Wife', in Anne Killigrew, *'My Rare Wit Killing Sin'*, p. 110, l. 1.

7 16 March 1685, *The Diary of John Evelyn*, vol. 2, p. 218.

8 Ibid.

9 29 December 1686, *The Diary of John Evelyn*, vol. 2, p. 258.

10 Ibid., 30 January 1687, p. 259.

11 ASMo, 17 January 1687, n. 248.

12 Ibid., 16 June 1687, n. 100.

13 13 July 1686, *The Diary of John Evelyn*, vol. 2, p. 254.

17 THE QUEEN'S BODY

1 Hopkirk, *Queen Over the Water*, p. 118.

2 Ibid.

3 Bryan Bevan, *King William III: Prince of Orange, the First European*, London, Rubicon Press, 1997, p. 95.

4 Princess Anne to Mary of Orange, The Cockpit, 14 March 1688, in *The Letters and Diplomatic Instructions of Queen Anne*, ed. Beatrice Curtis Brown, Funk & Wagnalls, New York, 1968, p. 34.

5 Ibid.

6 'Princess Anne to Mary of Orange, The Cockpit, July 24th, 1688', in *Letters of Queen Anne*, p. 39.
7 Princess Anne to Mary of Orange, The Cockpit, March 20th, 1688', in ibid., p. 35.
8 'Princess Anne to Mary of Orange, The Cockpit, July 24th, 1688', in ibid., p. 39.
9 Ibid., p. 40.
10 'Princess Anne to Mary of Orange, The Cockpit, March 20th, 1688', in ibid., p. 35.
11 Hopkirk, *Queen Over the Water*, p. 124; p. 118.
12 Haile, *Queen Mary of Modena*, p. 174.
13 Ibid.
14 Hopkirk, *Queen Over the Water*, p. 120.
15 'Princess Anne to Mary of Orange, The Cockpit, March 13th, 1687', in *Letters of Queen Anne*, p. 27.
16 Strickland, *The Lives of the Queens of England*, p. 162.
17 Hopkirk, *Queen Over the Water*, p. 125.

18 A ROYAL PRINCE

1 Hopkirk, *Queen Over the Water*, p. 126.
2 Barbara and Henri Van der Zee, *1688: Revolution in the Family*, Penguin Books, London, 1988, p. 75.
3 10 June 1688, *The Diary of John Evelyn*, vol. 2, p. 273.
4 Strickland, *The Lives of the Queens of England*, p. 186.
5 'Princess Anne to Mary of Orange, The Cockpit, July 24th, 1688', in *Letters of Queen Anne*, p. 40.
6 Ibid.
7 Ibid., p. 42.
8 Ibid., p. 43.
9 Ibid.
10 Doebner (ed.), *Memoirs of Mary, queen of England*, p. 3.
11 29 October 1688, *The Diary of John Evelyn*, vol. 2, p. 280; ibid., 2 November 1688, p. 281.

19 FAREWELL TO ENGLAND

1 Private collection, Bologna. A copy of this letter is also found in the British Library, BL Egerton MS 1677, fols 18–35.
2 ASMo, 27 October 1688, n. 256.
3 Strickland, *The Lives of the Queens of England*, p. 205.

4 Hopkirk, *Queen Over the Water*, p. 155.
5 Ailsbury, *Memoirs of Thomas, Earl of Ailesbury*, p. 195.
6 Ibid., p. 209.
7 Strickland, *The Lives of the Queens of England*, p. 286.

EPILOGUE

1 The Kit-Kat Club was a political and literary club for Whigs established at the end of the seventeenth century. For further reading see Ophelia Field, *The Kit-Kat Club*, HarperCollins, London, 2008.
2 The Final Exile, BL Additional MS 61414, fols 116r–118v.
3 Anne Finch, 'On the Earl of Dundee', in 'Miscellany Poems with Two Plays by Ardelia', vol. 1, p. 57.
4 Anne Finch, 'The Fall of Caesar', in 'Additional Poems', *The Cambridge Edition of Works of Anne Finch, Countess of Winchilsea*, eds Jennifer Keith and Claudia Thomas Kairoff, Cambridge, Cambridge University Press, 2021, vol. 2, p. 223.
5 Anne Finch, 'The Preface', in 'Miscellany Poems with Two Plays by Ardelia', vol. 1, p. 32.
6 Anne Finch, 'Epilogue to Aristomenes or the Royal Shepheard s Tragedy', in *The Cambridge Edition of Works of Anne Finch, Countess of Winchilsea*, vol. 1, pp. 193–286, p. 285.
7 21 February 1689, *The Diary of John Evelyn*, vol. 2, pp. 289–90.
8 Gilbert Burnet, *Bishop Burnet's History of his Own Time*, vol. IV, quoted in John van der Kriste, *William and Mary: Heroes of the Glorious Revolution*, The History Press, Stroud, 2011, p. 115.
9 21 August 1668, Samuel Pepys, *The Diary of Samuel Pepys*, vol. 9, p. 284.
10 Anne Finch, *Miscellany Poems, on Several Occasions*, Written by the Right Honourable Anne, Countess of Winchelsea, J. B., London, 1713.

INDEX

Abraham tapestries 210–11
absolutist monarchy 5–6, 239
Aesop's fables 173
Ailsbury, Lord 265–6
Alexander the Great 175
Altieri, Cardinal 19
Anna of Austria 77
Anna of Denmark, Queen 35, 206
Anne, Queen (Princess Anne)
  and Anne Digby 183
  contracts smallpox 127–8
  death 270
  and Dorothy Ogle 271–3
  early life 55–60, 63, 65, 71–2
  friendship with Sarah Churchill 60, 118, 129, 140, 149–50, 172, 195–7, 257
  gambling debts 241
  income 223
  joins William and Mary 256–8, 271
  and Maria's pregnancy 239–44, 249–50, 252
  her marriage 194–7
  and Mary's coronation 278
  and *Mithridates* 58–9, 149–50
  her mother's death 15
  pregnancies 197, 244, 281
  and Princess Mary 134–5
  succeeds as queen 280–1
  visits Holland 137, 140
Aphrodite 3, 95
Apsley, Allen 140
Apsley, Frances 40, 58–60, 106–7, 140, 149, 165, 195
Ariosto 51, 75
Arlington, Henry Bennet, Earl of 19, 59, 82, 90, 121–2
Arran, Lady 248
Arran, Lord 248
Arundel, Henry 135
Ashbury, Joseph 150
Association of Protestant Officers 249
Assumption of the Virgin 233
Aubrey, Mary 177

Bacon, Francis 169
ballet 44, 52, 77–8, 121–2, 182
Banér, Gustav 197, 199
Banks, John 53
Banqueting House, Whitehall 36
Barberini, Lucrezia 26
Barillon, ambassador 136, 139, 146, 160, 202
Barry, Elizabeth 53
basset 93, 152, 199, 236, 245
Bath, Earl of 203
Beale, Mary 2, 95, 184–6, 227
Beaufort, Duke of 248
Beaumont, Francis 53
Behn, Aphra 5, 53, 93, 173, 195, 230
  Love-Letters 219–21
  'A Pindarick Poem' 226
  Romulus and Hersilia 164
Bellasyse, John 135

Bellasyse, Lady Susan 16, 40, 135, 138, 145, 150, 248
Bennet, Henry 172
Bennet, Isabella 59, 68, 121–3, 142–4, 172, 177, 230, 256, 270–1, 279
Bentinck, Lord 266
Bentivoglio, Matilde 14
Berkeley, Lady Henrietta 219–21
Berkeley, Lord 248
Berkley, Mrs 117
Berry, Sir John 157
Betterton, Mary 59–60
Betterton, Thomas 53
Bill of Rights 6
Blagge, Margaret 65
Blenheim Palace 4, 116–17
Bloody Assizes 221
Blow, John 181, 210, 212
Bombay 66–7, 79
Bouillon, Madame 248
Boulanger, Jean 20
Bourbon, Louis de 76
Boyle, Robert 170
Boynton, Isabella 40, 106, 150
British Empire 6
Bromley, Elizabeth 40, 89, 242, 248
Brooke, Miss 150
Browne, Alexander 186
Browne, Thomas 170
Brownley, Mrs 117
Bruce, Lord 201
Buccleuch, Anna Scott, Countess of 45
Buckingham, George Villiers, Duke of 25, 82
Buckley, Lady Sophia 248
Burgundy, Duke of 147
Burnet, Gilbert 147
Butler, Sir Nicholas 248

Caravaggio 77
Carlile, Joan 2, 184–6
Carracci, Annibale 77
Carteret, Sir Edward 154
Castlemaine, Lord 142, 248
Caterina de Braganza, Queen 4, 11, 16, 37–40, 46, 57, 69, 73, 86, 126, 131, 136, 149, 161, 206, 226, 247
  and Charles II's death 201–3, 205
  her dowry 66–7, 79
  introduces tea drinking 147
  and Monmouth's rebellion 214–15
Cavendish, Margaret 57, 92
Ceary, Lady 248
Cervantes, Miguel de 94
Chaffinch, William 232
Chamberlayne (chronicler) 150
Charles I, King 25, 33, 38, 50, 52, 139, 144, 206, 260, 272
  his art collection 21–2, 46, 77
  execution 21, 77, 206, 239, 267
  and masques 61, 66
Charles II, King 3–5, 15–17
  and Anna Scott 216
  and anti-Catholic plots 131–2, 136–8
  his art collection 22
  birthday celebrations 121–2
  birthday ode 210
  coronation 206, 209
  death as a Catholic 201–4
  depicted as Hercules 162
  dislike of Scotland 144
  dissolution of parliament 153–5, 179
  friendship with Maria 35–6, 44, 142, 204
  and Hortense Mancini 78–9, 82, 86–8, 90, 94–5, 199
  illness 140–1
  and John Churchill 104–5, 119
  and Maria's arrival at Gravesend 35, 262
  and Maria's marriage 30, 34–7
  and masques 61–4, 66, 68–70
  portraits 227
  and Princess Anne's marriage 194, 196
  and Princess Mary's marriage 123–6

relationship with Louis XIV 47, 125
and Royal Society 67, 92
and Rye House Plot 161–5
and slavery 118
and theatre 52–3
Charles, Duke of Cambridge 15, 127–8
Chaworth, Lady 86, 109–10
Church of England 126, 205, 211–12
Churchill, Arabella 43, 103, 269
Churchill, Charles 195
Churchill, Frances 106
Churchill, Harriot 145–6
Churchill, Henrietta 148
Churchill, John 103–19, 126, 139–42, 145–6, 148, 190–1, 210
and Barbara Villiers 104–106, 118
and Sarah Churchill 103, 105, 110–119, 139–40, 190, 223
Churchill family motto 103
joins William and Mary 249, 255–8, 269–70
and Monmouth's rebellion 214, 223
and Princess Anne's marriage 195–6
royal favours 223–4
Churchill, Ralph 118
Churchill, Sarah (née Jennings) 4–5, 40, 56, 65, 68, 72, 94, 190, 210
and Anne Digby 183
and Barbara Villiers 135
and birth of Prince of Wales 250, 252
courtship 103–19
friendship with Maria 99, 105–10, 117–19, 129, 139–40, 148–9, 196–7, 235
friendship with Princess Anne 60, 118, 129, 140, 149–50, 172, 195–7, 257
and Hortense Mancini 97–9
joins William and Mary 257–8, 269–71
and King Charles Spaniels 116–17
her letters 8
and Mary Fortrey 99–102
and *Mithridates* 149–50
pregnancies 140, 145–6, 148
and Queen Mary's arrival in England 276
Churchill, Sir Winston 103, 223
Clarendon, Edward Hyde, Lord 15, 239, 243
Clarke, Mary 150
Clement X, Pope 11–13, 24–5, 41, 43, 129, 238
Cleveland, Barbara Villiers, Duchess of 32, 40, 69, 88, 93–4, 104–6, 113, 118, 122, 147, 199
Cleyn, Francis 62
Clifford, Elizabeth 151
Codebò, Guglielmo 27, 34–5, 37
coffee houses 91–2
Coldstream Guards 190
Coleman, Edward (composer) 224
Coleman, Edward (secretary) 106, 136
Colonna, Prince of 81
Colston, Edward 67
commedia dell'arte 52, 94
Commonwealth Sale 22, 77
Compton, Henry 126, 255
Conti, Armand de 77
Convent of the Visitation in Modena 77–8
Conway, Lord 39
Cornwallis, Catherine 40
Cornwallis, Charles 271
Cornwallis, Mary 60
Courcelles, Sidonia, Marquise de 83–4
Courtin, Honoré 97–9, 102, 112–13
Crane, Mrs 248
Craven, Lord 248
Cromwell, Oliver 4, 50
crown jewels 206–7
Crowne, John 62–3, 69–70
Culloden, Battle of 281

d'Ada, Count 243
Danby, Thomas Osborne, Earl of 132–4, 244, 255
dancing masters 57–8, 63

Dangeau, Marquis de 36
Dartmouth, Lord 248
D'Avaux, ambassador 166
Davenant, William 53
Davis, Moll 66, 93
Dawson, Margaret 40, 137, 242, 247, 250, 252
de La Porte de La Meilleraye, Armand Charles 79–81, 87
de la Porte, Charles 79
Declaration of The Hague 256
Defoe, Daniel 279
democracy 6, 278
d'Este, Alfonso II 14, 77
d'Este, Cesare 14
d'Este, Francesco I 14, 20, 26
d'Este, Francesco II 13–14, 27, 41, 70–2, 87, 123, 125, 128, 134–8, 146, 148, 150–1, 157, 161, 164, 204, 210, 243, 262–4
  as patron of music 224–5, 234–5
d'Este, Isabella 46, 92
d'Este, Leonora 18–20, 23, 26, 191
d'Este, Lucrezia 26, 191
d'Este, Rinaldo 24, 36, 39, 49
Devereux, Frances 189
Devonshire, William Cavendish, Earl of 255
divine right of kings 211, 268
Dorset Garden Theatre 62
Dover, Lord 248
Dryden, John 50–1, 59, 61–2, 133, 187, 204, 227–9, 278
  Aurungzebe 145, 151
  'Prologue to the Duchess' 159–60, 178, 226
Duke of York's Theatre 52–3

East India Company 67
Edward II, King 138
Edward VI, King 206
Edwards, Daniel 91
Elizabeth I, Queen 53, 156, 206, 210
Elliott, Catherine 40
Elys, Edmond 229
Ernley, Sir John 248
Essex, Earl of 162
Este Palazzo Ducale 21, 36
Etherege, George, *The Man of Mode* 150–1
Evelyn, John 44, 52, 113, 118, 122, 143, 178, 185–6, 199, 204–5, 217–18, 223, 225, 232–4, 248, 255, 276
  and his daughter's death 229–30
Evelyn, Mary 5, 143, 185, 229–30
  Mundus Mulieribus 232
Evelyn, Susanna 185–6
Exclusion Crisis 139, 144, 148, 151, 153, 155

Falmouth, Lady 39
Felicitas, Claudia 16
Feversham, Lord 204, 248
Finch, Anne (née Kingsmill) 4–5, 167, 169–70, 172–3, 176, 178, 180–3, 189–94, 210, 226, 229–30, 260
  Aristomenes 269, 275–6
  life under William and Mary 271, 273–6, 282
  marriage 189–92
  'On the death of the Queen' 282
  The Triumph of Love and Innocence 275
Finch, Heneage, 3rd Earl of Winchelsea 189, 265
Finch, Heneage 189–92, 209–10, 260, 271, 273–4, 276
Fingall, Lady 248
FitzJames, Henry 269
FitzJames, James 269
Fitzroy, Charles 270
Fitzroy, Henry (Earl of Grafton) 59, 122, 142–4, 177, 256, 270, 279
Fletcher, John 53, 177
Fontana, Lavinia 184
Fontenelle, Bernard Le Bovier de 75
Fortrey, Mary 99–102, 150

Fox, Sir Stephen 248
French Revolution 7

Gennari, Benedetto 52, 95, 198, 259
Gentileschi, Artemisia 184
George I, King (George of Hanover) 4, 194–5, 271
George of Denmark 195–6, 256, 258
Gibbons, Grinling 157, 224–5, 233
Gibson, Richard 58, 186
Giorgione 77
Glorious Revolution 6, 8, 238
Goa 66–7
Gohory, Monsieur 57–8
Gonzaga collection 46
Gould, Robert 230
Grammont, Count 68
Great Fire of London 36, 133
Greville, George 225
Grey, Ford 219–21
Griffin, Colonel 158, 248
Grignon, Madame de 83
Guercino 11, 20, 52
Gunpowder Plot 156
Guy Fawkes Night 30
Gwyn, Nell 88, 93, 203

Halkett, Sir Peter 266
Halles, Sir Edward 265
Hamilton, Anthony 68
Hamilton, Elizabeth 270
Hamilton, Lady Frances 97–8, 112
Hamilton, George 98
Hamner, Sir Thomas 271
Hampden, John 162
Hampton Court Beauties 279
Hampton Court Palace 4, 279
Harvey, Lady Elizabeth 84
Haslewood, William 191
Heneage, Thomas 273
Henri IV, King of France 76
Henrietta Maria, Queen 15, 33, 38, 66, 206, 281
Henry VII, King 57
Henry VIII, King 37, 189, 206, 210–11
Herbert, Admiral 254
Herbert, William 135
Hobart, Mrs 68, 88
Holyrood Palace 144–5, 152
Homer 232
Horace 187, 232
Hôtel de Bassigny 138
Hôtel de Conti 17
Hôtel des Hornes 139
Howard, Willliam 135
Huddlestone, Father John 203
Hudson's Bay Company 224
Hunt, Arabella 65
Huntingdon, Lord 248
Hutchinson, Lucy 175–6
Hyde, Anne 15–16, 28, 40, 55–7, 98, 103, 106, 250
Hyde, Flower Backhouse 196
Hyde, Henrietta 199
Hyde, Henry 196
Hyde, James 157–8
Hyde, Laurence 196
Hyde, Mrs 89

'Immortal Seven' 255
infant mortality 160–1
Isham, Justinian 169
Isham, Zaccheus 155

James I, King 144, 206
James II, King (James, Duke of York)
  and anti-Catholic plots 131, 134–5, 137–9, 142, 146, 156, 161–2
  appointed Lord High Admiral 104
  awarded law degree 191
  and birth of Prince of Wales 247–54
  and Charles II's death 201–5
  and his children 55–6, 97, 126–7
  conversion to Catholicism 43, 57
  coronation 206–13
  death in exile 282

his diaries 7
exile in France 279–80
exile in Scotland 141–2, 144–52, 156–8, 178, 227
flight from England 259–68
and *Gloucester* shipwreck 157–8
granted annuity 206
and Hortense Mancini 86–7, 94
imprisoned during civil war 38
and Isabella's death 148–9
and John and Sarah Churchill 103–4, 110, 117, 119
and king's illness 140–1
and Maria's arrival in England 29–30, 32, 34–5
and Maria's pregnancies 70–1
and Maria's waiting women 40
marriage 12–13, 15–28
and masques 65, 70
his mistresses 16–17, 40, 43, 68, 98, 113, 135, 138, 150, 161, 195, 197, 212, 223, 232–3
and Monmouth's rebellion 213–19
pilgrimage to Wales 238
portraits 227
and Princess Anne's marriage 194–7
and Princess Mary's marriage 123–6, 128
return to England 157–60
and Royal Society 67, 92
only surviving letter to Maria 29
and Siege of Maastricht 45
and 'Signor Dildo' 47, 89
and slavery 118
and theatre 52–3
visits Holland 137–40
and William III's invasion 256–8
James II, King of Scotland 146
Jennings, Frances (Lady Tyrconnell) 56, 116, 140, 248, 269
Jennings, Mrs 68, 108, 110
Jennings, Sarah, *see* Churchill, Sarah
Jermyn, Henry 94, 172
Jesuits 132–3
John of Austria, Don 134
Jones, Inigo 36
Justel, Henri 93

Keeling, Joseph 162
Ken, Dr 166
Kéroualle, Louise de 93, 105, 140
Ketch, Jack 217–18
Killigrew, Anne 1–5, 7, 9, 66, 167, 169–78, 181–6, 191, 210, 226–30, 235
early life 66, 169–172, 184–185
at Maria's court 172–187, 190–191, 210, 226–228
death 228–230
Venus Attired by the Graces 1–4, 182, 186–7, 227
Killigrew, Elizabeth 170
Killigrew, Harry 171, 201–2, 273
Killigrew, Henry 170, 229
Killigrew, Judith 228
Killigrew, Thomas 53, 170–1
King Charles Spaniels 116–17
Touching for the King's Evil 238
King's Theatre 52–3, 170
Kingsmill, Anne, *see* Finch, Anne
Kingsmill, Sir William (father) 169
Kingsmill, William (brother) 191
Kirk, Mary 40, 97, 106, 110, 195
Kirkby, Christopher 132
Kit-Kat Club 270
Kneller, Sir Godfrey 95, 253
Königsmark, Count Karl Johann 108

La Fontaine, Jean de 94, 99
La Roche-Guilhen, Anne de
Rare-en-Tout 121–2
Labaudie, Mrs 251
Lake, Dr Edward 125
Lamb, Patrick 212
Lauzun, Count de 262
Lee, Nathaniel, *Mithridates* 59, 149–51
Lely, Sir Peter 51, 93, 95, 185, 227, 279

Leonardo da Vinci 46, 77
Leti, Gregorio 93
Levant Company 91
Lichfield, Charlotte Lee, Countess of 147, 152
Ligne, Prince of 138
Locke, Matthew 44
London Gazette 248
Longus, *Daphnis and Chloe* 192
Louis XIV, King of France 17–19, 38, 47, 76–7, 81–2, 87, 125, 146, 160, 182, 264, 267, 280
Louvre Palace 77
Lowestoft, Battle of 157
Lully, Jean-Baptiste 199
Lumley, Richard, Viscount 255

Maastricht, Siege of 45, 106
Mancini, Hortense 5, 73, 75–90, 136, 197–9
  death by suicide 271
  her salon 92–5, 99, 121, 199
Mancini, Laure-Victoire 76
Mancini, Lorenzo 75
Mancini, Marianne 75, 78, 122
Mancini, Marie 75, 77–8, 81, 136
Mancini, Olympe 75
Mancini, Philippe 81
Manley, Delarivier 98
Mantegna, Andrea 46, 77
Maria of Modena 3–5, 7–8
  and anti-Catholic plots 135–7, 142, 146, 156, 161–2, 164
  arrival at court 35–41
  arrival in England 29–35
  and arrival of Hortense Mancini 79, 81, 84–9
  and the arts 44–53
  bedpan scandal 5, 247, 249, 252–3, 279
  birth of Prince of Wales 247–54
  her chapel 38–9
  and Charles II's death 201–5, 224–5, 233, 235
  coronation 206–13
  dancing lessons 58
  death at Chaillot 281–2
  early life 11–15
  education 13–14
  and embroidery 151
  exile in France 279–80
  exile in Scotland 141–2, 144–52, 156–8, 178, 227
  first impression of William of III 123
  flight from England 259–68
  friendship with Charles II 35–6, 44, 142, 204
  friendship with Sarah Churchill 99, 105–10, 117–19, 129, 139–40, 148–9, 196–7, 235
  and *Gloucester* shipwreck 158
  and Isabella's death 148–9, 151, 158
  likened to Venus 226
  marriage 12–13, 15–28
  and masques 61–70
  and Monmouth's rebellion 214, 216, 219
  new apartment at Whitehall 225
  patronage 224–6, 233–4, 238
  portraits 51–2, 227–8
  pregnancies 41, 70–2, 87, 126–8, 152, 158, 160–1, 197, 237–45, 247–54, 280
  and Princess Mary 125, 128, 134, 138–40
  return from Scotland 159–60, 178
  riding accident 151–2
  and 'Rochester's farewell' 89
  and Shrove Tuesday festivities 178–80
  and 'Signor Dildo' 47, 89
  and her stepdaughters 55, 60–1, 71–2
  ultimatum to James 232–3
  visits Holland 137–40
Marlborough, Dukes of 103
Martinozzi, Anne Marie 17, 75, 77

Martinozzi, Laura 13–14, 18–24, 26, 36, 38–9, 44, 75, 77, 81, 140–1, 160, 238
Mary I, Queen 206, 208
Mary II, Queen (Princess Mary),
  and anti-Catholic plots 139
  offered the crown 268
  arrival in England 276–8
  coronation 277–8
  death from smallpox 280
  early life 28, 55–60, 63, 65, 68, 71–2
  friendship with Monmouth 166–7
  and James II's accession 223
  and Maria 107, 125, 128, 134, 138–41
  and Maria's pregnancy 239–42, 249–50, 254
  marriage 123–8, 165–6
  and Monmouth's rebellion 218–19, 240
  and mother's death 15
  and painting 186
  pregnancies 134, 138
  and Princess Anne's marriage 195
Mary Queen of Scots 147
Mary, Sister (Mother Superior) 12, 30–1, 40, 162
Masham, Abigail 60
masques 50, 58, 226
  Calisto 61–70, 106, 112, 122, 163, 181–2
  Venus and Adonis 178, 180–4, 189
Massinger, Philip. 59
Mazarin, Cardinal 17, 75–80, 87, 93, 271
Mazarin, Duke of 87
Mazarin, Madam 242, 248
Mazarinettes 75–6
Mazzarini, Girolama 75
Medici, Maria de' 35
Melfort, Lord 248
Middleton, Lord 248
Mignard, Pierre 280
Milton, John 50, 176
Modena (city) 11–14
Molière 78
Molza, Count Ugo 21
Monaco, Prince 90
Monck, General George 33
Monck 33
Monmouth, Anna Scott, Duchess of 70–1, 134, 142, 163, 165, 186, 271
  and Monmouth's rebellion 215–16, 219
Monmouth, James Scott, Duke of 44–5, 65, 71, 89, 94, 97, 105–7, 109, 262
  and anti-Catholic plots 131–2, 139, 153, 155, 161–5
  and Charles II's death 203–4
  exile in Holland 166–7
  and king's illness 140–1
  and Maria's arrival at Gravesend 35
  rebellion and execution 213–21
  and Rye House Plot 161–5
Mons Meg 146–7
Montagu, Ralph 81–2, 84, 86, 90, 95
Montaigne, Michel de 94, 191
Montecuccoli, ambassador 44
Montecuccoli, Donna Vittoria 262–3
Monteverdi, Claudio 44
Moray, Lord 248
Mowdie, Mrs 117
Mulgrave, John Sheffield, Earl of 194–5
Mumper (James's dog) 157–8
Musgrave, Earl of 97
Mustapha 83–4, 94, 198

Napleton, Mr 265
Nardi, Paolo Antonio 18, 23–4
Needham, Eleanor 40, 106–7, 110, 163
New Academy of Compliments, The 69
Nonconformists 147, 155
Nottingham, Heneage Finch, Earl of 154

Oates, Titus 133–4, 136, 156, 249
Oaths of Allegiance 278
O'Brien, Lord 158
Ogle, Dorothy 271–3
Ogle, Elizabeth Percy, Countess of 108

Ogledorp, Colonel 249
ombre 70, 93
opera 44, 121–2, 181–3, 199, 226
Order of the Visitation 14, 26, 30, 281
Orrery, Robert Boyle, Earl of 53
Ottoman Empire 91–2, 189
Ovid 62–3, 183, 232
Owen, Anne 177

Paisible, Jacques 121
Parker, Martin 144
Parry, William 156
Pepys, Elizabeth 186
Pepys, Samuel 45, 59, 91
Peterborough, Lady 31, 40, 140, 158, 209, 248
Peterborough, Henry Mordaunt, Lord 16–27, 30, 34, 140–2, 248, 259
Petre, William 135, 243, 253, 265
Philip II, King of Spain 208
Philips, Katherine (Orinda) 58, 173–4, 177, 191, 276
  Society of Friendship 58, 177, 191, 276
  pirates 170–1
Plautus 232
Plutarch 78, 94
Po Valley 11, 14
Popish Plot 139–40, 146, 155–6, 199, 249
Portmore, David Colyear, Earl of 270
Portsmouth, Louise de Kéroualle, Duchess of 82, 86, 88, 199, 202–3, 270
Powis, Lady 142, 248, 252, 260
Powis, Lord 248
Pratoneri, Contessa Lucrezia Vezzani 40, 60, 85, 137
Preston, Lord 248
propaganda
  coins/medals 162, 218, 278
  Dutch printing press 253
  playing cards 156
  prints 253–4
Purcell, Henry 209–10, 234, 278

Racine, Jean 94
Raphael 46, 77, 185
Reformation 6, 205
Restoration 33, 46, 50, 78, 169, 173
Restoration court, sexual politics 3–6
Richard II, King 139
Richelieu, Cardinal 79
Richmond Palace 56
Riva, Francesco 259–61
Rizzini, Abbé Gaspar 18, 20, 160–1, 263
Robarts, Mrs 242
Rochester, Anne Wilmot, Countess of 56
Rochester, John Wilmot, Earl of 47, 56, 62, 70, 89, 230–1, 247
'Rochester's Farewell' 89
Roncagli, Dom Andrea 25
Roos, Lord 86
Roscommon, Wentworth Dillon, 4th Earl of 106
Roscommon, Lady 137, 248
Rosée, Pasqua 91
Rottenhammer, Johann 62
Royal Africa Company 67
Royal Exchange 91
Royal Navy 157
royal palaces 21–2
Royal Seal 266
Royal Society 67, 92, 132, 169
Rumbold, Richard 162
Rupert, Prince 224
Russell, Edward 254–5
Russell, Lucy 92
Russell, Rachel, Lady 28
Russell, Lord William 162, 217
Ruvigny, Marquis of 87
Rye House Plot 161–5, 167, 213

Sackville, Charles 69
St André, Monsieur 63
Saint-Évremond, Charles de 88, 94–5, 121, 136, 198–9
St Germain, Père 71
St Winifrede's Well 238

Sandford, Francis 206, 208, 210–11
Sassuolo 11, 20
Savoy, Duchess of 81
Savoy, Charles Emmanuel II, Duke of 81–3
Savoy Chapel 228
Scottish bishops 147
Sedley, Catherine 112–16, 119, 150, 197, 212, 223, 232–3, 270
Sedley, Charles 69, 112
Seneca 78
Sévigné, Madame de 85, 264
Seymour, Mary 189
Shadwell, Thomas 44
Shaftesbury, Anthony Ashley Cooper, Earl of 135, 139, 154–5, 161–2
Shakespeare, William 53, 171, 180, 208, 271
  The Winter's Tale 208
Sheldon, Father 29
Sheldon, Ralph 265–6
ships
  The Catherine 11, 32
  The Cleveland 32
  The Gloucester 157–8
  The Happy Return 158
  The Isabella, 260
  The Mary 33
Shirley, James 224
Shrewsbury, Charles Talbot, Earl of 255
Shrove Tuesday entertainments 178–9
Sidney, Algernon 162
Sidney, Henry 166, 255
Sidney, Mary 92
Siface (Giovanni Francesco Grossi) 233–4
Sirani, Elisabetta 184
slave trade 67, 118
smallpox 34, 47, 127–8, 146, 228–9, 280
Smock Alley Players 150
Soissons, Philippe de 197, 199
Sole Bay, Battle of 157
Somerset, William Seymour, Duke of 189
Somerset House 37–8, 64, 66
Spanish Armada 156, 208
Spencer family letters 8
Staggins, Nicholas 209–10
Stationers' Company 231
Streeter, Robert 64
Strickland, Lady 248
Stuart, Catherine Laura 71–2
Stuart, Charles Edward (Bonnie Prince Charlie) 271, 281
Stuart, Charlotte 160
Stuart, Henriette 82
Stuart, Isabella 97, 127, 137, 140, 142, 148–9, 158
Stuart, James Francis Edward 247–54, 281
Stuart, Louise-Marie ('La Consolatrice') 280, 282
Sunderland, Lady 183, 242, 256
Sunderland, Lord 183, 256
Sussex, Anne Fitzroy, Countess of 69, 88, 97

Tangiers 79
Tasso, Torquato 48–51, 75, 176
  Aminta 191–2
tea drinking, introduction of 147
Terence 232
Terriesi, Francesco 243
Test Act 32
Thanet, Earl of 163
Thynne, Thomas 107–8, 110
Tintoretto 21
Titian 20, 46, 62, 77, 182–3, 198
Tongue, Israel 132–3
Trevor, Mary 97, 99, 106–8, 110
Turenne, Marshal 105
Turini, Pelegrina 40, 137, 248, 262–3
Tyrconnell, Lord 39

van de Velde, Willem, the Elder 31–3, 35–6
van Dyck, Sir Anthony 182
Verelst, Simon 70, 228
Verney, Ralph 194

Veronese 20
Vertue, George 185
Villedieu, Marie-Catherine de 80, 84
Villiers, Anne 134
Villiers, Barbara 99, 134–5
Villiers, Elizabeth 134, 166
Villiers, Frances 56, 127
Villiers, Katherine 134
Virgil 175, 232
Vitali, Giovanni Battista 210
Vivonne, Catherine de, Marquise de Rambouillet 92
Vossius, Isaac 93

Waldegrave, Mrs 248
Waller, Edmund 48–50, 93, 128–9, 230
Walter, Lucy 45, 131
Welwood, James 218
Wentworth, Lady Henrietta 68, 106, 163, 165, 167
  and Monmouth's rebellion 213, 215–19
Wentworth, Mrs 248
Wentworth, Philadelphia Carey 163, 165
Westminster Abbey 206–10, 212
Wharton, Anne (née Lee) 5, 56, 178, 230–1
Wharton, Goodwin 231–2
Wharton, Thomas 56
William III, King (William of Orange) 71, 119, 135, 141, 146, 204
  offered the crown 268
  claim to throne 129, 160, 195
  coronation 277–8
  death 280–1
  friendship with Monmouth 166–7
  invasion of England 242, 254–8
  and James II's flight 259–68
  and Maria's pregnancy 239, 244, 249–50, 254
  marriage 123–8, 165–6
  and Monmouth's rebellion 219
Windsor, Lord 86
Windsor Beauties 4, 279
Wise, Lucy 40
Wissing, Willem 227
Wood, Anthony à 91, 171
Worcester, Battle of 203
Wren, Christopher 64

Zuylestein, Count 249

A NOTE ON THE AUTHOR

BREEZE BARRINGTON is a historian specialising in the artistic cultures of the seventeenth century, with particular focus on women's history and female artists. She holds a PhD on the literary and artistic cultures of the early Stuart court and has written for outlets including the *Financial Times* and the *TLS*. She has also worked as a consultant for Working Title and Monumental Pictures. Barrington has taught at several universities, including the University of Cambridge, and is an Associate Fellow of the Royal Historical Society.

A NOTE ON THE TYPE

The text of this book is set in Fournier. Fournier is derived from the romain du roi, which was created towards the end of the seventeenth century from designs made by a committee of the Académie of Sciences for the exclusive use of the Imprimerie Royale. The original Fournier types were cut by the famous Paris founder Pierre Simon Fournier in about 1742. These types were some of the most influential designs of the eight and are counted among the earliest examples of the 'transitional' style of typeface. This Monotype version dates from 1924. Fournier is a light, clear face whose distinctive features are capital letters that are quite tall and bold in relation to the lower-case letters, and *decorative italics, which show the influence of the calligraphy of Fournier's time.*

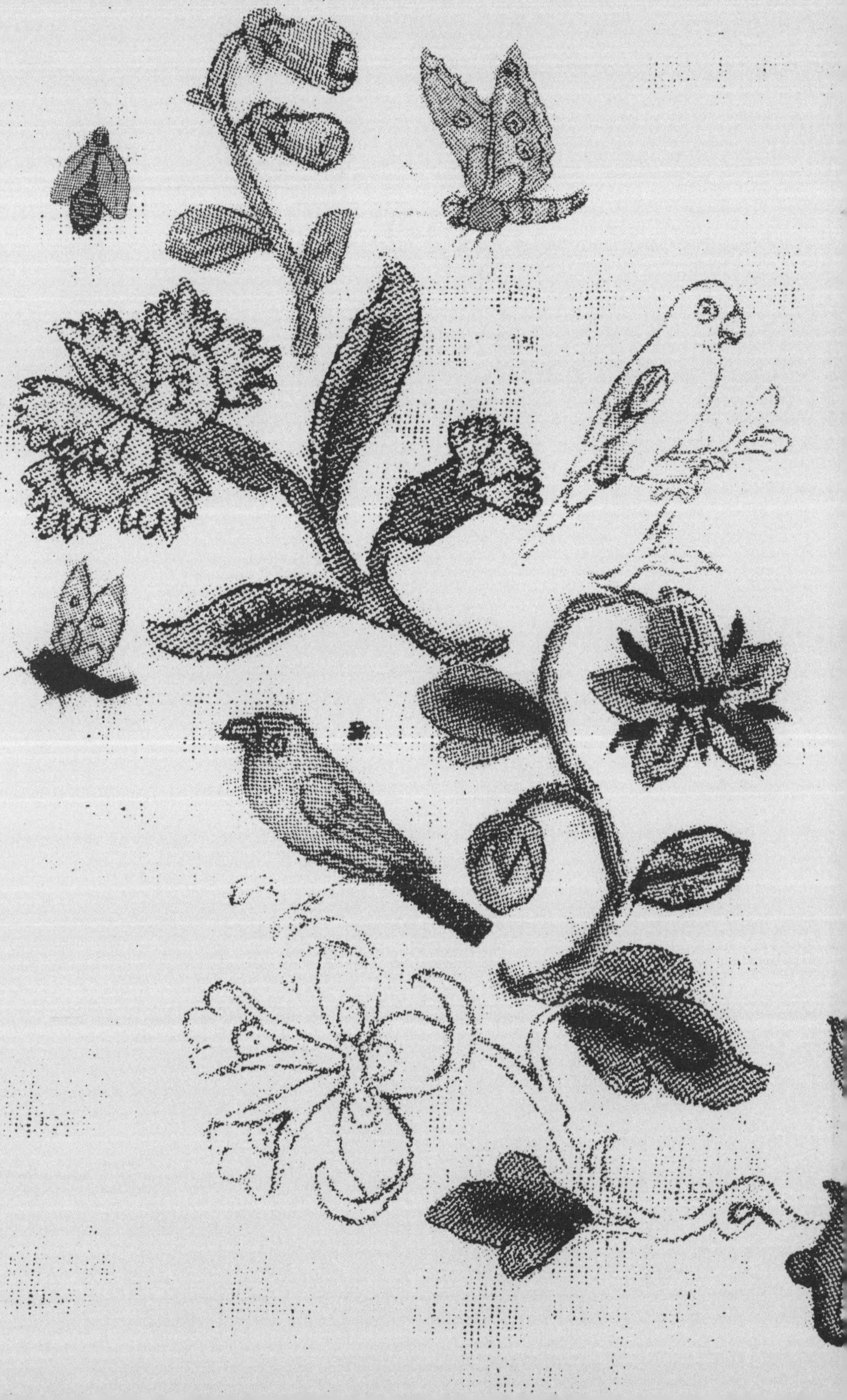